# CONVERSIONS AND CITIZENRY

*Xavier Centre of Historical Research (XCHR) Studies Series*

No. 1 : João de Barros: Portuguese Humanist and Historian of Asia by *C.R. Boxer*

No. 2 : Coastal Western India: Studies from the Portuguese Records by *M.N. Pearson*

No. 3 : Black Legend of Portuguese India (The): Diogo do Couto, His Contemporaries and the Soldado Prático-A Contribution to the Study of Political Corruption in the Empires of Early Modern Europe by *George Davison Winius*

No. 4 : Health and Hygiene in Colonial Goa (1510-1961) by *Fátima da Silva Gracias*

No. 5 : Trade and Finance in Portuguese India: A Study of the Portuguese Country-Trade, 1770-1840 by *Celsa Pinto*

No. 6 : Goa and the Revolt of 1787 by *Charles J. Borges* (ed.)

No. 7 : Goa and Portugal: Their Cultural Links by *Charles J. Borges* and *Helmut Feldmann* (eds.)

No. 8 : Goa-Kanara Portuguese Relations 1498-1763 by *B.S. Shastry* and *Charles J. Borges* (ed).

No. 9 : Goa's Foremost Nationalist: José Inácio Candido de Loyola : The Man and His Writings by *Charles J. Borges* (ed).

No. 10 : Goa and Portugal: History and Development by *Charles J. Borges*, *Óscar G. Pereira* and *Hannes Stubbe* (eds).

No. 11 : Conversion and Citizenry : Goa Under Portugal 1510-1610 by *Délio de Mendonça.*

---

**About the Author**

**Vitor Délio Jacinto de Mendonça** (*b.* 1958) is Director, Xavier Centre of Historical Research, Alto Porvorim, Goa. After completing his schooling in Beira (Mozambique), he entered the Society of Jesus in Goa in 1979. He did his M.A. and Ph.D. in History and M.A. in Portuguese Literature. He lectured in the Department of Portuguese at Goa University.

*XCHR Studies Series No. 11*

# CONVERSIONS AND CITIZENRY

## Goa under Portugal 1510 – 1610

**Délio de Mendonça**

CONCEPT PUBLISHING COMPANY, NEW DELHI - 110 059

ISBN 81-7022-960-X

First Published 2002



*Published and Printed by*

Ashok Kumar Mittal
**Concept Publishing Company**
A/15-16, Commercial Block, Mohan Garden
New Delhi-110059 (India)

*Phones:* 5648039, 5649024
*Fax:* 091-(11)-5648053
*E-mail:* publishing@conceptpub.com

# PREFACE

This is about a perennial debate in the history of Goa. The subject of conversions in Goa in the sixteenth century is controversial and sensitive. This topic never goes out of fashion. For these and other reasons it has become, at the same time, very interesting and basically necessary to understand the behaviour and culture of the Goans. *Conversions and Citizenry* discusses, among other things, historiographical difficulties that one encounters in re-writing the history of conversions and the perspectives that have resulted thence. It also considers the strategies used to make that citizenry that was expected to sustain the political, social and economic system that the Portuguese wanted to create in their eastern empire. Moreover, it delves into the ideology and theology that justified and supported the secular and missionary activities respectively, and most importantly the reception / rejection of conversion by target groups and their overt / covert reactions to it. Reactions and profitability compelled the Portuguese to devise overlapping discourses in the *Estado da India* — one official and another more pragmatic.

This is not a missionary history, much less a reactionary or apologetic historical narrative. Re-writing history about a period so distant from us requires that we reconstruct carefully the circumstances that, in the mind of the policy-makers of the time, justified or explained the conversion policy as an exigency of the *Estado.* The changing socio-cultural reality of, and demands made on, the local people are other constituents of our analytical framework. In other words, an analysis of mentalities and practices, to enable us to understand conversions on the spot, the 'whys' and 'hows' of conversion and their relationships have been taken into account here. Unfortunately, situations of violence, conflicts, strong reactions by the locals and what embarassed the Portuguese themselves were not recorded extensively, on purpose of course. I call it 'Historiography of Silence'. Nevertheless, I have also focused our attention on this dimension in *Conversions and Citizenry*.

Further, it is equally important to understand the complex factors and forces operating in a society that was changing rapidly. Important events and the apparently not so important ones, as shown by the historical sources, have been recalled in this study to show social and religious continuity / change in the life of the Goans, as a consequence of accepting / rejecting conversion. This work has also tried to emphasize the existence of conflicts and compromises between *cristandade* (Christendom) and *gentilidade* (Heathenism/ Hinduism). The Portuguese power believed that in the pluralistic context of Goa, the new order and political allegiance to itself would not be possible without conversion of their native vassals but ironically conversion created weak and useless vassals.

The official Portuguese ideology prompting and underpinning the efforts to convert their vassals in order to better expand and sustain the empire as well as the Christian space (Christendom) forms the broad framework of my discussion. The Portuguese kings frequently invoked the defence and propagation of the Catholic faith as the main reason for conquests and territorial expansion and for conflicts and wars with others. Curiously, the Portuguese official statements of that period read that political and economic considerations of the state were not dominant factors in their affair of conversion. However, as has been mentioned, there were two concurrent discourses — one official / religious (Christian discourse) and another economic (spice discourse). Although official statements need to be considered carefully vis-à-vis their praxis too, the important task consists in tracing emphatic continuity and change in the idea / praxis of conversion. Both, continuity and change, were necessities that can be easily recognized.

Works on conversion in Goa do exist indeed, nevertheless a more objective and provocative study had to be undertaken. Many of the existing works beg the question, and many more do not address themselves to pertinent questions. Why, in spite of the economic decadence of the *Estado da India*, did they continue to make, and stress on the need of, conversions as well as to maintain religious intolerance? Why is it that, in spite of religious intolerance, relations between the locals and the Portuguese seemed to be cordial most of the time? It is hard to explain why in spite of the decrees and privileges in favour of Christendom and strict vigilance to maintain the supremacy of Christendom, the majority refused to be converted and the converts continued to adhere to many 'Gentile' customs and practices and to mix freely with the Hindus. What about historiographical problems and gaps that prevent us from answering these and other questions in a convincing manner? Nevertheless, such questions demand answers, and I must say that this book proposes a point of view for each of these and other issues.

This study is essentially a factual account based on original sources. It is an interpretation of the affair of conversion not just because it has been viewed in relation to the social, political and historical demands of the Portuguese empire; the official ideology that prompted proselytization, the royal and missionary attitudes that justified it and the foreign influences on the locals have been examined in detail in this book too. It is a narrative because the events placed in a chronological order enable the reader to gain with objectivity some insights into the Goan life in the sixteenth century and today. It has tried to avoid all kinds of biases so that facts may help to form opinions and re-create historical events. This work may have answered some questions or solved some long-standing problems, but it may have also created a few more. This, of course, was not intentional, but very much in keeping with the nature of this subject as something perennially alive.

I can claim to have re-written a history of conversions in an unbiased manner after taking into consideration the distant factors, but directly related to our issue and to the Goan context. It is not enough to be just over-critical. It is still worse to be only apologetic. Even a synthesis of both mentalities or approaches would offer us only 'one or two' sides of history. But my aim has been also to retrieve the 'third side' of the issue of conversion, i. e. to make an impartial assessment without taking sides (rather taking all sides into account). This has been an attempt to write a more 'provocative', not a 'dogmatic' or 'diplomatic' history of conversions in Goa. This has also been an effort to challenge any reductionist approach and the legends that vested interests have created about conversions. There is some known material in this work, but both the new and the known material have been used interpretatively to re-create the origins and affair of conversion in Goa. Obviously, it is far from being comprehensive. There are lacunae that need to be filled.

Délio de Mendonça

# ACKNOWLEDGEMENTS

I wish to express my gratitude to Prof. Dr. A.R. Kulkarni, to Dr. Luís Filipe F. R. Thomaz and to Dr. William R. de Silva for their invaluable insights to me. I am grateful to Dr. Teotónio R. de Souza and to Prof. Dr. Hira Adyantaya too. To Mrs. Lília Maria D'Souza, librarian at the Xavier Centre of Historical Research, Goa, who showed me the relevant material available there, my sincere thanks. I also thank my Jesuit collegues at the Xavier Centre of Historical Research: Fr. Dr. Cajetan Coelho, Fr. Moreno de Souza and Fr. António Pereira. The Jesuits at Rua da Lapa, Lisbon: Fr. António Reis, Fr. José Azeredo, Br. José Oliveira and the others in the community. The Jesuit community at Braga, particularly Fr. Manuel Morujão and the late Fr. Dr. José P. Bacelar e Oliveira. The Jesuit community of Brotéria, Lisbon, and Fr. Dr. Nuno da Silva Gonçalves. I also wish to thank the Jesuits at the House of Writers and Archivum Romanum Societatis Iesu both in Rome, in particular Fr. Dr. Silas Laszló and Fr. Dr. Francisco Zurbano. I thank my Jesuit friends Fr. Ignacio Arregui for making my stay at Rome a very memorable and historical one, and Fr. Richard Schniertshauer for his companionship. Thanks to the encouragement and support of my friends, Dr. José Miguel Ribeiro Lume and Dr. José Victor Adragão, I could finish this work faster than I expected.

I thank Frs. Gregory Naik, Gerald Rodrigues, Joseph Ubelmesser and Patrick de Melo. I cannot forget the Jesuit Community at the Jesuit House, Panaji, Goa, for their understanding and co-operation during my stay there.

I wish to show my gratitude to Dr. Maria Farinha, Dr. Maria Emilia Fressinet, Dr. Maria de Deus Beites and Dr. Maria do Céu Barreto.

I am very thankful to Fr. Ronnie D' Souza, Mr. Bonfilio de Cruz and Prof. Ms. Anne Menezes for going patiently and carefully through my manuscript and for offering many suggestions for improvement.

I wish to record my gratitude to my father Isaías de Mendonça, my mother Antónia Gonçalves, my sister Blanche de Mendonça and my brother Victor de Mendonça.

I also want to express my gratitude to Dr. Sérgio Mascarenhas de Almeida, Delegate of Orient Foundation in India, for showing interest in my work and for his assistance.

I am unable to register here the names of all the persons who have supported me but I wish to thank them as well as the institutions and libraries that helped me promptly.

My special thanks go to Dr. José Blanco, Trustee, and Dr. João Pedro Garcia, Director (Serviço Internacional) of the Calouste Gulbenkian Foundation at Lisbon. I must say that this work was made possible by its generous grants to me in 1994 and 1996 that allowed me to consult several archives in Europe.

# CONTENTS

# GLOSSARY

Adilshah — title of the Muslim rulers of the kingdom of Bijapur.
*Ariqueira** — sacred tree for the Hindus.
*Bailadeira** — nautch-girl, temple dancer.
*Batismo Geral** — group baptism
*Botto* — Hindu priest
*Bramane** — Brahman
*Canarim** — native of Goa.
*Casado** — Portuguese married settler in Goa.
*Castiço** — Portuguese of pure breed residing in Goa.
Catechumen — Christian to be under religious instruction.
Catechumenate — period of Christian faith formation before baptism.
*Concílio Provincial** — council convoked by the church of Goa.
*Confraria** — pious confraternity
*Cristandade** — Christendom
*Cruzado** — ancient Portuguese gold coin.
*Cujo regio, Illius religio* — the religion of the king is the religion of the people.
*Estado da India** — Portuguese territories in the East.
*Faraz* — outcaste person.
*Fidalgo** — person of social standing, gentleman.
Firm land — (*terra firme*) Hindu and Muslim territories bordering Goa. Firm land of Goa refers to the districts of Bardez and Salcete in Goa.
*Foral** — short letter with local rights, or rights given by a feudal lord or a civil authority but frequently signed by the king.
*Gaunkar* — original inhabitant of Goa, cultivator in Goa.

*Gaunkaria** — agricultural community, assembly of local Goans that discussed and settled village issues.

*Gentilidade** , *Gentilismo** — Gentilism

*Gentio** — Gentile

*Honrrado** — noble person

*Jogue** *(Jogi)* — a Hindu ascetic or a mendicant and penitent Hindu who went about scantily dressed. Normally, his body would be covered with ashes and he would keep long hair.

*Kolvont* — temple dancing-girl

*Lascarim* — Indian soldier

*Língua** — official local interpreter for the Portuguese.

Lusitanian — The Portuguese people are a result of a long process of fusion of peoples and cultures. The earliest inhabitants that history could register in Portugal were the *celtas* (Celts) and the *iberos* (Iberians). The fusion of these two groups resulted in one of the biggest Iberian tribes, the *lusitanos* (Lusitanians). Hence, the term Lusitanian has been applied to the Portuguese people.

*Mafamede** — Muslim, Islam

*Mar clausum* — closed sea

*Mazania* — local cultic association

*Mestiço** — Eurasian, half-caste or of mixed blood.

*Mouro** — Moor, Muslim.

*Neiqebary* — village administrator, captain of local troops.

Neophite — person recently converted to Christianity.

*Novas Conquistas** — New Conquests

*Padroado Real** — Crown Patronage

*Pagão** — pagan

*Pagode** — Hindu temple, feast, statue, coin.

*Pardau** — gold or silver coin in Portuguese India.

*Pay dos Christãos** — Father of the Christians

*Propaganda Fide* — Propagation of Faith

Provincial Council — Ecclesiastical Council

*Rendeiro** — tax-collector

*Regedor** — chief magistrate

*Regimento** — standing order, instruction.

*Reinól** — Portuguese born in Portugal.
*Sati* — widow burning
*Solteira** — spinster
*Terra Firme** — Hindu and Muslim territories bordering Goa.
*Terra Firm de Goa** — the districts of Bardez and Salcete in Goa.
*Thanadar* — captain of a military fort, village judge, tax-collector of a village or custom house.
*Vedor da Fazenda** — chief revenue superintendent.
*Velhas Conquistas** — Old Conquests
*Xenddi* — hair-tuft
*Zagor* — Hindu festival

* Portuguese word.

# ABBREVIATIONS

| | |
|---|---|
| AHU | Arquivo Historico Ultramarino, Lisbon |
| AN/TT | Arquivos Nacionais / Torre do Tombo, Lisbon |
| *APO* | *Archivo Portuguez-Oriental* by J. H. da Cunha Rivara |
| ARSI | Archivum Romanum Societatis Iesu, Rome |
| *BFUP* | *Boletim da Filmoteca Ultramarina Portuguesa*, Lisbon |
| BNL | Biblioteca Nacional de Lisboa, Lisbon |
| *Bullarium* | *Bullarium Patronatus Portugalliae Regum in Ecclesiis Africae, Asiae atque Oceaniae* by Paiva Manso, (ed.) |
| CC | Corpo Cronológico, Lisbon |
| CEHU | Centro de Estudos Históricos Ultramarinos, Lisbon |
| *CEO* | *Conquista Espiritual do Oriente* by Paulo da Trindade |
| *DI* | *Documenta Indica* by Josef Wicki, (ed.) |
| *Doc* | *Documentação para a História das Missões do Padroado Português do Oriente* by Antonio da Silva Rego, (ed.) |
| *LFC* | *Leis a Favor da Cristandade*, Goa |
| *LPC* | *O Livro do "Pai dos Cristãos"* by Josef Wicki, (ed.) |
| *MR* | *Monções do Reino*, Goa |
| *OCJC* | *Oriente Conquistado a Jesus Cristo pelos Padres da Companhia de Jesus da Provincia de Goa* by Francisco de Sousa |
| *Registo de cartas* | *Registo de cartas, provisões etc. para a India par os viso reis e mais autoridades,* Lisbon |

## Map of Goa

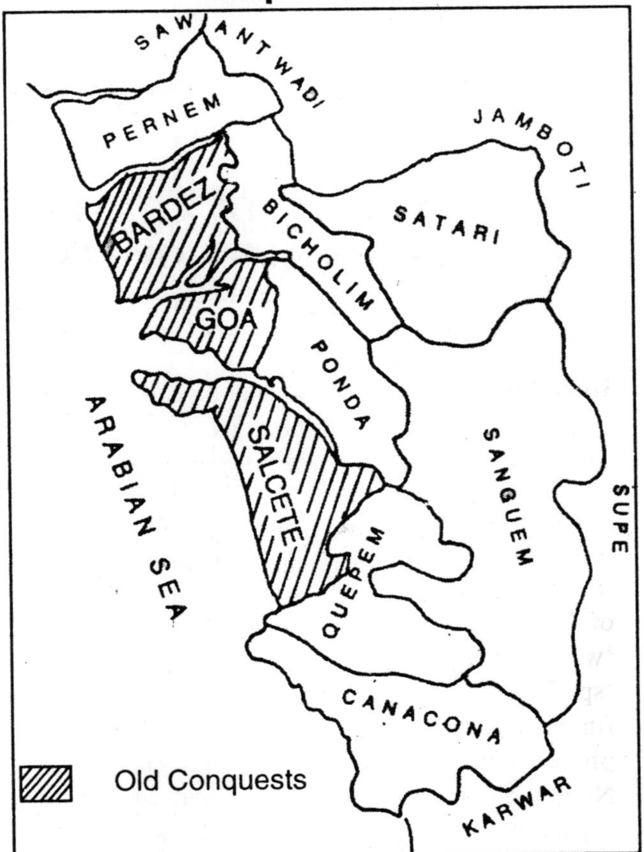
SAWANTWADI
PERNEM
JAMBOTI
BARDEZ
BICHOLIM
SATARI
GOA
PONDA
ARABIAN SEA
SALCETE
SANGUEM
SUPE
QUEPEM
CANACONA
Old Conquests
KARWAR

Bombay
Goa

# 1

# AGENTS OF CONVERSION AND HISTORIOGRAPHY OF CONVERSIONS

## Introduction

The subject of conversions has always attracted the curiosity of scholars. The conversion of Hindus and Muslims during the Portuguese rule in Goa in the sixteenth century is, at the same time, polemic and interesting. Indo-Portuguese historiography reveals that the 'spice business' absorbed more than ninety percent of the official attention during the sixteenth century.[1] However, the 'work of conversion' continued flourishing much longer than the 'spice business', even when the *Estado da India* was in dire financial straits. This can be attested by the statistics of the phenomenal number of conversions in Goa at that time. Nevertheless, spiritual conquest and commerce were only two aspects of one single and powerful project that contributed to each other's successes or failures.

Conversions had to be 'marketed' just as spices had to be. The means and approaches used by the agents of conversion 'to market' Christendom differed considerably not only in time and space but also in function, from the political and economic interests of the seaborne empire, a fact often not sufficiently emphasized by historical research on this topic. A statement or generalization that an association with Christendom brought material rewards to the converts has to be interpreted with due care. Truly the Portuguese needed more citizens or converts to sustain their scattered sixteenth century empire and Christendom, but these convert-citizens were not necessarily the most privileged, since they did not possess in most cases the expertise and the capital required for the empire.

It is fundamental to pay attention to the process of conversions throughout the sixteenth century to understand the history of Goa. It is not sufficient to know only 'what' happened and 'how', but it is pertinent as also necessary to examine carefully 'why' and 'when' these events took place, in order to re-create a broad historical framework to understand the facts of conversion and their effects. Chapter three will deal with the 'Idea and Practice of Conversion', as it was understood during the sixteenth century, an essential element in our historical framework.

The question of conversions will be treated in all its implications and complexities in the present book. Conversion, as it is understood here, takes into account the transformation or results in the life of Hindus, Muslims and new converts, who were either favoured or made to suffer directly or indirectly, due to the rigorous methods and pressure of several decrees issued by the Portuguese authority to change their local religion and customs. It deals with the Portuguese mechanisms and institutions of control to discipline and change the locals into loyal vassals for the empire. It also deals with the Goan cultural impact on the life of the Portuguese settlers here.

If the history of conversions in Goa in the sixteenth century has already been written, we need to ask who wrote it, how and with what purpose. If this history does exist, would it then preclude further investigation? Has that historiography taken into consideration all possible issues and questions? Has it tried to understand events within a larger context, without ignoring their complexities and historiographical difficulties that we encounter today? It seems to me that facts have been presented and conclusions arrived at, but most studies do not respond satisfactorily to all the possible arguments and polemics related to this complex and sensitive issue of conversions. Some studies are devoid of any conceptual or theoretical framework. Most of them stress on the methods of conversion, namely, on the use of force or freedom of choice; and they are generally either a harsh critique of the methods of conversion or an apology for, or denial of them. Now I am thinking of, and referring to two books with antithetical views: *The Goa Inquisition* by A. K. Priolkar although written in 1961, it continues to represent the hardliners of today and the *Christianisation of the Goa Islands: 1510 - 1567* by Anthony D'Costa (1964) which offers a reprieve to the apologists. In any case, I believe that the issue of conversions in Goa needs to be written in a new and wider framework. Therefore, this work has tried to go beyond the 'missionary successes' and 'providential' approach to conversion, or it has attempted to question the two extreme positions, which have just been pointed out, that have dominated the debate on conversions. It is obvious that conversions were not meant simply to make citizens for the celestial city. This book is an attempt to challenge any simplistic criticism of the issue of conversions.

A historian needs to pay special attention to the social responses or reactions of the local people on encountering with a new and different political, religious and economic group, and to the persistence of 'idolatry' and syncretic elements in the life of the neo-converts. A study from this historical perpective will answer more questions and make clear certain positions taken here. Re-writing history is precisely the endless process of inquiring into the old facts from new positions and an attempt has been made in this direction in this book.

Continuity rather than obvious change characterized the sixteenth century Goa: continuity of the same mentality, of the same religious zeal and of the same kind of decrees on conversions. Changes, however, did occur in praxis and even more in legislation. Striking discontinuities between decrees and practice, and between official ideology and local pragmatism are easily seen. Nevertheless it is undeniable that the aims and responses to conversions did vary, although not so drastically, even during the century in question. But the significant hiatuses deserve our attention. This fact revealed three distinct phases of conversion, which in no way periodized the history of conversions in Goa during this century.

These different phases indicate conspicuous discontinuity

or significant changes resulting either from the Portuguese action or from the reaction of the locals. We find continuity and changes not only during the sixteenth century but also during the following century. The new Portuguese pragmatism did change its old ideological and religious approach without eliminating them totally. During the second phase of conversions (1540-1580) the new pragmatism and proselytizing attitudes tended to impose themselves more radically either by denying the previous tolerant phase (1510-1540), or by justifying it as temporarily necessary. Generally, the local Christians or Hindus responded with silent opposition to any denial of their religious freedom and social customs: with syncretic forms of religion in the case of neo-converts or by migrations to the Muslim territory (land bordering Goa), or with continuing their practices in hiding, in the case of Hindus. The old cultural forms continued to exist side by side with new historical and political demands. No matter how firm the decrees and vigilance, cultural and religious syncretism were never radically eliminated. During the third phase (1580-1610) the missionaries appeared more preoccupied with instructing the neo-converts than with simply converting the Hindus. By then it was not easy to convert them either.

Conversions in Goa had raised many questions already during the sixteenth century, not only owing to the methods used to convert the Hindus, but also to the large number of conversions effected in a short period of time. Fortunately, while quantitative information cannot be easily produced, Goa has perhaps left more records of numbers than any other Portuguese-controlled territory. Numbers may have been inflated to show the 'hand of God' in conversions. The last chapter has been another attempt to present, in broad outlines, some statistics on conversions.

At this point, we could ask ourselves whether the sixteenth century conversion drive, including its methods, was in any way different from that in the following centuries. A complete study on conversions would be necessary to answer this question, which, obviously, goes far beyond the scope of this book. Nevertheless, we know that during the seventeenth century the religious orders had been accused of showing less zeal for the cause of conversion and of adopting a life of comfort. Their critics also remarked that they were more preoccupied with temporal or personal interests than with commitment to God. They spent more time quarreling among themselves than with the work of conversion; and intolerance among the various religious orders grew,[2] although, the religious did try to show themselves as a united group, naturally, following the 'edifying principle'.[3] It may be argued that what characterized the seventeenth century were the difficulties faced in the field of conversion, namely, the local reactions, the decadence of 'Golden Goa' in particular and of the *Estado da India* in general, the lack of funds together with a new mentality then emerging, not of less religious zeal but of more intolerance.[4] During the seventeenth century the missionaries still believed that sooner or later all the Hindus would embrace Christianity. Militant proselytizing tendencies had not disappeared. In 1647 the Portuguese continued to destroy the idols of the Hindus in order to prevent them from performing religious ceremonies.[5] It is interesting to compare the 'Old Conquests' with the 'New Conquests' too.[6] When the 'New Conquests' were annexed to Goa (in the last quarter of the eighteenth century), the Portuguese had assured the locals residing in the newly acquired territories of their freedom of religion and customs, just as they had assured the people in the 'Old Conquests' after its conquest in 1510. Despite this assurance in 1510, the missionaries began interfering with their religious and social freedom in the 'Old Conquests' to which the locals objected.[7] However, the same sort of interference did not occur in the 'New Conquests'. Therefore, after taking into account the political and social factors that led the Portuguese to disfavour any aggressive policy of conversions from the seventeenth century onwards, and the defects of the religious orders, need not the historiography that accused the missionaries of relaxing their zeal for conversions after the sixteenth century be re-considered?

A discussion on conversions in the sixteenth century certainly raises some problems and it is more complex than it may appear. A problem arises first from the very terms used then, such as the 'service to God' versus 'service to demons', terms found often in our documents;[8] or terms like 'pagans', 'idolaters',[9] 'Gentiles', 'infidels' or 'good examples' of the high caste converts that were supposed to motivate others to be converted. Other problems are the questionable methods used by the missionaries, the decrees in favour of conversion, etc. The sixteenth century European mentality vis-à-vis the 'natives' makes the whole issue of conversions a sensitive topic to deal with. But the historian has also the duty to present facts as they happened, the 'questionable' and 'sensitive' terms, the racial and religious prejudices — these plain facts can tell us the story better than any present-day modified discourse.

The complexity of the matter arises from the need to do more than simply evaluate the good and worthy goals and intentions, criticize the excesses or accept the silence of the documents as the normal local response to religious and cultural changes affecting the Goan society. Further, the difficulties that a historian encounters if he/she wishes to understand continuities-discontinuities from legislation to execution or praxis, the existing power conflicts and relationships among the competing social interests and groups, both at the local level and others, make this issue even more complex. In spite of efforts to promote the 'laws and privileges in favour of conversion' or Christendom the locals continued to adhere to their ancestral religion and customs for a long time, and this fact may escape an unattentive reader.

A treatise on conversions in the Goan society from available historiography, but devoid of an analytical framework would only eliminate internal or local societal contradictions, power relationships and unjust mechanisms of control. Without such a framework one could be led to interpret the Portuguese colonial presence as if it were a scapegoat for our undesirable and unresolved problems, which have entirely their roots in our own past or present-day history and traditions. Goa was not religiously and socially an empty space, a *tabula rasa*, of no local caste conflicts.[10] This reality adds a new dimension to the already highly sensitive and complex narrative about conversion.

## The Exigency of Conversions

Religion played a very decisive role in the life of the people in Goa and Portugal. The function of religion was similar to that of the government authority. The former was even a superior means of exercising control over the society and conduct of its individuals or communities. It could create and maintain an intended social order more efficiently by proposing lasting rewards and punishments. A particular brand of religion propagates or sustains a certain type of social and economic order, but religion need not be used consciously as a strategy of social and political control over the individual or society to achieve programmed goals. Therefore, religion, as reminder of supernatural sanctions or sanctification, could be far more effective than government law and its enforcing agents.[11]

Religion acted as a factor of social and political control and cohesion in Goa before and after the arrival of the Portuguese. The new rulers did not take long to understand that in the Goan society, government decrees as compared to religion proved relatively inadequate to secure conformity of the local behaviour with the new regime, to create new political duties and extract services from the locals. This sort of mentality and the prevailing social and political order tended necessarily to conversion of others. Church architecture and elaborate church ceremonies were just some of the means to impress target groups with the rulers' competence, glory and magnificence. These things were also supposed to favour conversions to a religion that claimed to be the only one capable of offering sanctification and awarding punishment.[12]

The Portuguese brought overseas an institutional religion which was controlled by missionaries, who boasted of their militant and Counter-Reformation mentality. In Goa each village community had one or several deities as its own exclusive gods or goddesses, with the Brahman caste profiting the most from this traditional religious arrangement. What impact or pressure could the new religion exert on the life of a people with a long-established traditional religion? Religious deities of an agrarian society meant more than simply bringing eternal salvation to its adherents.[13] Moreover, it was certainly not easy to make a transition from a multiplicity of deities to only One, who was not presented as being directly concerned with the agrarian or village community character.

The colonial policy of the Portuguese and Spanish, unlike that of the Dutch and British, lent state support, in terms of money and laws, to the conversion drive in their overseas territories. The Portuguese have been taken for 'religious fanatics', because, unlike any other colonial power, they interfered ordinarily and aggressively with the local religious practices and social customs.[14] The British and the Dutch have not been associated with fanatics or proselytizers, since they appeared unconcerned with religion. However, it is sufficiently known that the Bristish wanted to change local religious and social practices by means of civil legislation and a sort of western education devoid of any idea of freedom, equality and independence, in order to make a few locals good civil servants for the British empire. However, the reality was that the Portuguese layman worried less about social and religious impurities than the British. For this reason the former's social behaviour became more syncretic than that of any other European group overseas. And we can state that more syncretism was practised and even permitted in the Portuguese empire than what is attested by their own discriminatory civil and religious legislation.

Religion in the Lusitanian[15] empire had its patron and agents to carry out the activity of conversion. To sponsor missionaries or agents of conversion and to convert the inhabitants in the newly acquired territories were urgent for the survival of the Portuguese state overseas.[16] Christendom could prosper only if these agents obeyed their patron. However, we often find these agents working against each other and above the patron, obviously, harming the work of conversion considerably.

## Agents of Conversion

### (a) *Kings — Patrons of Conversions*

The kings of Portugal claimed that conversions were their most important duty.[17] They also proclaimed themselves to be the supreme spiritual and temporal head of Portuguese India. This included the royal right to present bishops and other prelates for the *Padroado* lands, a right often stressed and demanded. The pope acknowledged and confirmed these titles and other 'spiritual' demands by the crown. The decrees on conversions were ratified by the kings. Further, they took a personal interest in the affairs of conversions as well as in the welfare of converts.[18] The missionaries and priests were paid by the kings.[19] Personnel for the main posts in the institutions such as the *Pay dos Christãos* (Father of the Christians), the Inquisition or top appointments in *Padroado* lands had to have the approval of the kings. Several royal decrees in favour of conversions and a sizeable royal revenue alloted to the work of conversion were some other features of this patronage. I think this is what distinguished the sixteenth century model of conversions from the previous models: the state and the crown, in collaboration with the church, made the spread of the religion of the state their main and urgent duty.

The Renaissance popes preoccupied with European politics, the rising tide of Protestantism and the Turkish threat to the Holy Roman Empire and to Italy, did not concern themselves closely with the evangelization of the 'new worlds' 'discovered' by the Portuguese and the Spanish. Those popes saw no harm in letting the two Iberian crowns bear the expenses of building chapels and churches, maintaining a colonial religious hierarchy and sending missionaries to convert the heathens. In exchange, the popes granted these two crowns extensive privileges by way of allowing them to present bishops to vacant sees in the mission lands, the collecting of tithes and the administering of ecclesiastical taxation in the lands attributed to them by the Treaty of Tordesillas. In 1452 pope Nicholas V through his bull, *Dum diversas*, granted to the kings of Portugal the rights over the temporal matters in all their conquests. Moreover, the bull granted plenary indulgences to all those who went to these conquests to help Christendom.[20]

In 1454 the same pope sent to D. Afonso V, king of Portugal, the bull *Romanus Pontifex*. It praised the outstanding services Portugal rendered in spreading the Christian faith and its bravery. For more than twenty-five years Portugal had been sending annually its caravels to the south in order to discover the route to the Indies where, it was believed, the Christians lived and who could serve as their allies in the war against the Turks. The pope, therefore, to prevent other European rival nations from disturbing Portugal's duties and rights in these new regions, granted to the Portuguese king and his successors the monopoly for subduing, trading with, and converting all the lands that he had hitherto conquered and those still to be conquered from Cape Bojador to Guinea and beyond. A year later in 1455 pope Callistus III confirmed this monopoly through his bull *Inter cetera*.[21] The pope issued many other bulls or licences for Portugal to operate unopposed.

The papal acknowledgement of the king of Portugal, and the ratification of the same, as the patron of converts in his empire, encouraged the Portuguese monarch to take his *Padroado* duties and rights very seriously. No papal brief, bull or document emanating from Rome, was regarded as valid in the Portuguese colonial empire until it had been endorsed and registered in the respective chancery at Lisbon. The crown controlled the movement of all missionaries and ecclesiastical personnel destined to, and in, its colonies. This union of the cross and the crown came to be known as the *Padroado Real* or Royal Patronage. This was a combination of rights, privileges and duties of Portugal, in areas alloted permanently to them, since the end of the fifteenth century, by the Treaty of Tordesillas.[22] The exclusiveness given by this Treaty and the content of the papal bulls established convictions and a programme for spiritual and economic conquest. The Treaty, concluded between Portugal and Spain in a small Spanish town of Tordesillas in June 1494, marked the beginning of modern Christendom and European colonialism. The Treaty restricted the movement and interests of other European powers. The interests of those who were going to be subdued were ignored. The same Treaty permitted the Portuguese to open the doors of Goa with arms, so necessary for God to give them successes and victories to preach 'Christendom'.[23] The Europeans thought that peoples like the Red Indians, the Africans and the Hindus could be easily brought under their control, since they had neither civilization nor religious beliefs.[24] Ignorance of Christianity implied the absence of culture. For this reason, the Hindu, the Muslim and the African were considered much inferior to the Christian.[25]

During the sixteenth century the concept of *cuius regio, eius religio*, namely, that the vassals had to follow the religion of the king, was a rule in Europe, Africa and Asia.[26] It was the duty of the king of Portugal to convert his vassals to his religion, so much so, that even when the state had hardly any funds to support itself, the 'royal duty' or conversion activity remained alive.[27]

By a decree, D. Sebastião, king of Portugal, ordered all the missionaries to pass through Portugal and India (Goa) on their way to any land of the *Padroado* in the East. This measure was taken to prevent the non-Portuguese or foreign missionaries, especially Spanish missionaries, who collaborated with their own merchant countrymen, from going directly from the Spanish possessions to the Portuguese ones. This condition was meant to be a check on the Spanish merchants, who might follow the Spanish missionaries to the Portuguese lands, thus resulting in serious economic reverses to the crown of Portugal and to its colonies in the East.[28]

Conversion of Hindus was in continuity with the reconquest and re-conversion of Portugal's own inhabitants, so long under the Arab and Muslim influence. The spirit of crusades, not in its original version or linked to the liberation of the holy places but a modified version reaching out to the entire Muslim world, emerged anew at the beginning of the sixteenth century.[29] Now, it was at the service of an expansionist political programme of the state or Christendom. The old idea of crusades against the enemies of God, the Muslims, changed. The Canon Law (law of the church) condemned the wars of religion. The new idea was that the Portuguese believed that faith could be preached to, and alliances could be established with, the conquered people.[30]

Earlier, the fourth century was the last peaceful period for Iberian Christian propaganda. First the disorder created by the barbarians in the Roman empire and then the Muslim tide that spread all over western Asia, northern Africa and the Iberian Peninsula, withheld any missionary drive for several centuries until the appearance of the crusades. The crusades were not missionary movements. They were rather motivated by economic gains, and by the liberation of the holy places from Muslim control. During the fifteenth century some missionary work had been done on the western coast of Africa. Finally, the voyage of Vasco da Gama to India opened new possibilities of reviving missionary activity and exalting the leadership and talents of the kings of Portugal. Now the missionaries with a new crusading mentality put greater demands on the patron to expand the Christian space.

It is probable that the papal bulls were not sent to the Portuguese crown by pontifical initiative, but they were rather requested from the popes in the wake of increasing competition and rivalries among the Catholic states. The pope possessed great authority over the Catholic princes which enabled him to play the role of an arbitrator regarding disputes of rights and duties among them in the newly discovered lands. The self-given titles of the kings of Portugal as "masters of conquest, navigation and commerce...", rather than reflecting an accomplished fact, served to influence European opinion and to express claims to exclusiveness of rights and privileges. They were public discourses. These titles or claims, as well as the papal bulls and the Treaty of Tordesillas, meant nothing to the 'discovered' peoples. No, in fact they meant much. It encouraged their holders and beneficiaries to conquer, rule, trade, convert and wage war in case of local resistance, thus setting a precedent. The patronage of the state to the church came to an end with the emergence of Portugal as a Republic in 1910. From this moment the patronage of the crown in conversions and the *cuius regio, eius religio* ceased officially in the overseas Portuguese territories too.[31]

### (b) *Governors and Government Officials*

The king of Portugal, as the head of *Padroado*, was the direct and the prime sponsor and patron of conversions, but the overseas administration was almost always, especially in post-manueline period (after 1521), in the hands of governors and nobles who served their own interests rather than that of their patron. The church administration and the *Padroado* came increasingly under

the control of the missionaries. Often the government officials and the clergy cooperated with each other, especially when this alliance benefited both the parties. The governors wanted to make the best of the three years of their tenure,[32] and they showed the least concern for solving social and economic problems that confronted the administration.[33]

Most governors left Lisbon with a personal *Regimento* or Instructions from the crown on how to govern India. However, the execution of this depended, to a very large extent, on the initiative and character of the local government and clergy. The *Regimento* to the governor, Afonso de Albuquerque, did not even suggest to him, for instance, to acquire Goa. Hence, its conquest and retention was questioned and debated in high political circles.[34] But the same *Regimento* explicitly recommended the conquest of Hormuz and Malacca. Every *Regimento*, however, contained an explicit or implicit instruction to take the work of conversion rather seriously.

Although no governor or nobleman would dare to oppose or react to the instructions of the king directly, in practice these meant little to them. Hence, the work of conversion depended more on the governors or viceroys and government officials than on the distant prime patron.[35] The local government authorities were constantly at loggerheads with the missionaries on certain conversion issues: the continual disagreement, for example, on the question of converting the Hindus, or of expelling them from Goa. (The civil authority alleged that the conversion or expulsion of Hindus harmed the rents of the crown.) It is not that the local authorities cared for the welfare of the Hindus or their religious well-being, or for that matter to serve the king and the empire; rather they were ever more interested in the high revenues brought by the Hindus. We recall that mass conversion diminished the income for the state that accrued from the taxes levied on the Hindus and Muslims, since the converts were exempted from paying them.

Undoutedly, the Portuguese laymen, although shaped by the crusading mentality, did not come here to do missionary work. The imperial policy permitted an outflow of dissatisfied nobility, who then used their bellicose spirit of crusades against the infidels in their colonies.[36] These could be the ones whom the missionaries often wrote against, for their scandalous and indisciplined behaviour.[37] These men came to India to make money, and their lifestyle became a serious impediment to the work of conversion.[38]

The missionaries continuously complained to the king about certain governors who disfavoured conversions. But the usual and vociferous complaint was that where there were many Portuguese, the least number of conversions were possible. The Portuguese captains protected and favoured the Hindus,[39] and they did not release the salaries to the missionaries.[40] We read in 1581, about the government officials keeping the rent of the temples for themselves, thus harming the work of conversion and the houses for catechumens.[41] Royal instructions to these officials in 1585 to pay the personnel who worked in the houses for catechumens, went unattended. The work of conversion was not carried out uniformly or steadily by its agents.

### (c) *Missionaries*

The church naturally played the main role in the conversion drive. Traditionally and commonly the church is referred to as the clerical, institutional and hierarchical organization that holds and controls the power of making decisions, and in the sixteenth century the church overseas was closely associated with the missionary agents and activity. Only more recently, the local Christians and native clergy have been incorporated into 'that' concept of church.[42] Unquestionably, the missionaries or the religious orders constituted the backbone of conversion work and policies, and they could be held responsible for much of that militant and proselytizing tendency and activity, witnessed during the sixteenth century. They also pressurized the local government and the king to issue stringent decrees in favour of conversions. The constant missionary meddling in government affairs that did not concern them was also very conspicuous. The sure way to obtain a great number of conversions was by winning the civil authority's support for the church.[43] Obviously, the government on its part also used the missionaries to further its own interests. The missionaries, who were the most permanent settlers overseas, knew the local language and situation better than the viceroys and other officials who came for a period of three years, after which the majority returned to Portugal, whilst the missionary was the permanent adviser to new officials.

Regarding conversions, the missionaries argued that the adult Hindus and infidels were like children and without knowledge whatsoever about God. Hence, force could be used to convert them. This argument emerged from the belief that the non-baptized would go to hell, and the missionaries had the sacred duty of preventing this from happening at any cost. Thus any means or methods of conversion were considered appropriate and legitimate.

Missionaries were closely associated with, and decided on the methods of conversion to be employed, as shown by their historiography. Often the common argument of today to explain and justify certain common conversion methods and missionary praxis used during the sixteenth century, is founded on the historical context in which those actions took place, and on the mentality of the times. The argument of defence simply affirms that the circumstances then were very different from ours. Then by the same logic, ought we not to evaluate that missionary 'heroism' and their 'feats' by the same context and mentality of that period too? If so, the 'sacrifices' and 'virtues' of those missionaries ought to be confined only to 'that' past context, an argument which would certainly be unacceptable to the apologetic school of thought. Minimizing and relativizing intolerance and prejudices of the past, may be a reasonable and pragmatic approach for today, but then we should also likewise speak of 'virtues' and 'feats' of the same intolerant or prejudiced group or epoch. The present work does not aim at minimizing, tolerating, judging or condemning anything or anybody; it is primarily a quest to understand historical changes, myths and reality — prejudices, intolerance, virtues, feats, resistance, etc. — in their complexities and relationships. This is how I have understood the question of conversions in Goa during the sixteenth century and I present my findings to you for your consideration and impartial evaluation.

How did these religious orders influence the life of the Goan people? Europe in the sixteenth century witnessed a historical phase that emphasized religious renewal and attitudes to proselytism. In many cases the secular power used the clergy, who best represented that zeal and religious fanaticism, to control and direct certain organized aspects of society. Often the various initiatives, religious and secular, appeared to diverge, but the necessity of complementarity for survival regulated ecclesiastical and civil contracts. The people knew that the viceroys came and went, but the religious members came to stay; and this meant that they could not escape the influence of the missionaries and that conversions were always something to be expected. The Hindus could either anticipate or postpone the moment of their conversion, or as a last resort they could migrate to the Muslim land to avoid it altogether.

Some months before the arrival of the ships from Portugal the Hindus used to go to the firm land to consult their sorcerers and astrologers to find out about the number of ships and the kind of new government that would follow.[44] Some *gaunkars* or local residents believed that their situation could change and improve with the arrival of another viceroy or governor, but others expressed strong views on the subject, namely, that the civil authority was not responsible for conversions, but the priests of the Society of Jesus or the Jesuits. The locals argued that this religious group and others would always remain among them. Therefore, sooner or later they would have to become Christians.[45] However, the religious orders were not always as powerful as they wished to be, or as the locals believed them to be. Each religious order had its moments of prosperity and decadence, and they functioned accordingly.

The Portuguese missionary activity was intense and extremely aggressive in the middle of the sixteenth century. The religious orders were engaged in competitive conversion activity, resulting in several conflicts among themselves, since the royal financial assistance to each religious order depended on the number of conversions they reported.[46] They were missionaries who were out to conquer everything and everybody for the militant church.

The Jesuits spoke often of missionaries with a 'vocation for India', meaning zealous persons with a proselytizing mentality, having great zeal and enthusiasm to instruct and convert Hindus.[47]

Intellectual talents were not demanded from them. But some missionaries overseas had complained that many religious men sent to India lacked learning.[48] Fr. Nicolao Lanciloto, a Jesuit, wrote in 1545 against sending ignorant missionaries to Goa, because there were already many here.[49] But it seems, he was referring to the lack of skilful administrators to govern the Society of Jesus, and not so much to the missionaries directly involved in the work of conversion, for in this field anybody would be useful. Nevertheless, a good number of missionaries sent to India were the best that Europe could provide.

Francis Xavier demanded from a candidate who claimed to have a 'vocation for India' the following profile: he should not be a young man but between 30 and 40 years of age possessing all virtues, but especially the virtue of chastity, since occasions to sin against it, presented themselves everywhere. The heat and the licentious life in Goa itself, offered sensual temptations not only to the European layman but to the religious person alike.[50] The climate of India being unfavourable to the observance of chastity imposed a heavy burden on the spirit. Therefore, it demanded candidates with a special 'vocation for India'.[51] This term 'vocation for India' appears often in Jesuit writings of the sixteenth century.[52] This requirement might have been strongly present in other religious orders too.

Some Franciscan missionaries turned up as soldiers and captains in time of war, and after the war several soldiers entered religious orders;[53] and strangely, even during peace time some missionaries went about the town exhibiting their weapons.[54] Five religious with the cross in one hand and a sword in the other accompanied the captain of Bardez;[55] some religious men went about with arms in Goa in 1557,[56] to the extent of making the Hindus remark that the *bottos* (Hindu priests) of the Portuguese made good soldiers.[57] No wonder, then that the monasteries needed to have a prison for their indisciplined clergy.[58] The Constitutions of the Archdiocese of Goa (1568) decided against priests carrying weapons, settling disputes by use of arms, and threatening or hurting anyone with such objects.[59] Some members of these religious orders said masses for six or seven years without being dutifully ordained priests.[60]

Soldiers who fought in wars offered themselves as canditates for religious life, despite the canonical impediment it involved. It is probable that they entered religious life not for the priesthood but rather for brotherhood, for which there was no canonical impediment. Francisco Rodrigues Silveira, a Portuguese soldier who lived in India from 1585 till 1598, wrote that the Portuguese soldiers fought like wild animals and without any sense of military discipline during the war.[61] When some of these soldiers had no other alternative but to join the religious ranks to keep themselves alive, we should realize that they carried with them the same sort of indiscipline for making conversions.

Surplus clergy in Portugal became a burden on its economy. Hence, it seemed good to send many of these undesirable persons to the colonies. At the beginning of the seventeenth century when even little conversion activity became difficult overseas, missionaries continued to come in great numbers. But the locals were not in any position to support them.[62] The Portuguese soldier understandably, considered the permission granted by the crown to build so many churches and monasteries in Goa, and the spending of so much money on the clergy, a great mistake. He argued that much of the money spent in the name of charity and Christian zeal, could have been channeled for more profitable military purposes, for example, for the defence of the Portuguese lands.[63]

We should not forget the work of the missionaries in the field of education, health care and diplomacy.[64] If missionaries were killed and imprisoned it was mainly for forcing people to receive baptism when they were least interested in it. I think that one of the greatest contributions made by the missionaries in their geographical expansion, was the possibility they created for an encounter or confrontation of two different societies or cultures: one caste-ridden and the other casteless society, although divided hierarchically. But this was not their main intent. The Portuguese authority and the missionaries doling out favours and privileges to those who were converted, might have encouraged directly or indirectly the peasants to question the traditional roles and the high-handedness of the higher castes, especially when these prevented conversions. At the same time, throughout the sixteenth century, there had been social and religious relapses in the life of the new converts, which constantly threatened to undo long years of missionary activity. The happy result of this was a cultural synthesis in the life of the convert Goan.

Disproportionate attention has been given to the missionaries and almost none to the local clergy and local Christians, as dedicated collaborators of the former in the conversion activity. Unfortunately, the latter did not escape the criticisms of the missionaries, who had almost nothing good to say about them. The missionaries' arguments that the locals possessed a weak morality and a non-rational character, were sufficient to exclude them from their religious orders and from other secular positions that mattered. Very few spoke about the 'virtues' and 'good examples' of the local Christians and local clergy, but much has been written about the unchristian behaviour or 'misconduct' of the Portuguese. Unfortunately but not surprisingly, even today one particular brand of mentality continues to repeat uncritically but consciously the same missionary discourse only to sing the 'heroic deeds' of these missionaries.

Evangelization in Goa was not an exclusive enterprise of the missionaries. When it was certain that the Portuguese diocesan priests were not easily forthcoming to the colonies and that the doors of religious orders had remained closed for the locals, only then the Goan secular clergy was created. High caste converts could become secular priests, but only in secondary roles and under the strict supervision and command of the missionaries. Despite missionary complaints and prejudices against the local clergy, to the point of discrediting the latter and taking all the merits of spreading the Christian religion for themselves, the locals continued to join the clerical life. The Franciscans received a few locals in the beginning to compensate for the lack of European missionaries, but just enough to be mere keepers of their beautiful church and house in Goa. The Jesuit policy on formation of local clergy is sufficiently known. Some locals joined the Augustinian order in Goa, but on the whole their recruitment practice could not have been very different from that of the other religious orders.[65]

The more we delve into the Indo-Portuguese historiography,

especially church history in Goa, we find that hardly any attention was given to the locals here. The opinions of the locals were a matter of very little importance, *de facto et de jure,* until the Vatican Council in 1964. The missionary church or its decision-making body without participation of the locals need not surprise us. We should not forget that the missionaries had local collaborators, recruited mostly from among the high caste converts, who constantly clamoured for a better status. The loss of their former social privileges created in them new social ambitions and demands. Some conflicts that existed between the local clergy and the Portuguese authority reflect antagonistic interests and social ambitions. The locals were not easily allowed to express and fulfil their social ambitions during the sixteenth century.

## The Making of a Citizenry for the Empire

The increase of citizens for Christendom depended on the alliance between the state (kings and government officials) and the church (religious orders and clergy). Christendom and the Portuguese empire became almost synonymous. But Christendom in the East turned out to be more a duty or task to be accomplished than an achievement or victory. This empire, supported by the *Padroado* or the permanent rights and duties of the Portuguese crown in the conquered lands, needed a citizenry to sustain the empire. (As seen earlier Christendom or the model of conversions in the sixteenth century, now supported by the *Padroado*, distinguished itself from the previous models.) This close cooperation between the state and the church did not exclude conflicts between them. The crown, the local government and the missionaries formed the three strata of power in the society, each one with its own vested interests to achieve and protect. The new citizens or converts formed a new stratum.

How were the new citizens made? It is alleged that conversions were effected violently rather than evangelically. It must be stressed that conversions were also effected with decrees, social and economic pressure that left, at times, little alternative or freedom of choice to the Hindus. Often migration became the only solution to those who refused to convert. Conversions were not made at the point of the sword but under its protection.

The early sixteenth century Europe had been characterized by a war of religious beliefs and conflicts to gain supremacy in the commercial sphere. This mentality and goal justified any method used in making citizens for the empire. However, the official doctrine of the state and of the church stood for the uplift of the Hindus by mild methods: by way of free conversion, a single language and miscegenation, in other words, the social and cultural integration of Hindus through one religion, one culture and mixture of races. Even if they were not one with the Portuguese by religion, language or ethnically, all the inhabitantes residing in the territories under the Portuguese control would continue to be associated with the Portuguese by their duty of political vassalage, suggested the Portuguese official policy.[66] By the middle of the sixteenth century the Hindus as well as the new converts were not yet total citizens of the empire, for they still adhered to their traditional customs and deities.[67] Suave methods had failed to produce results and the 'rigour of mercy' had to be introduced to expand Christendom.

Denial of extra-mild methods in conversions, just by quoting a few decrees of the Provincial Councils, the Canon Law or a few royal instructions that condemned the use of force, only distorts historical reality. An uncritical and simplistic jump from decrees to practices leads to false inferences and startings. One looks only for 'some facts' when one wants to defend personal interests and justify pre-conceived notions. Historical imagination devoid of prejudices is necessary to situate decrees and praxis in their proper perspective, relationships and contexts. When the context is re-created with historical imagination a lot of questions can be addressed differently and prejudices kept in check. Prudent historical inquiry cannot take place with loaded questions or with closed conclusions. A historian may be inclined to defend or criticize positions, to make compromises and judgemental remarks, but historical inquiry has to be kept in mind.

When the Portuguese arrived in India, peaceful methods of conversion had given way to more aggressive methods in Europe. Conquest of land had to precede conversions. Re-conversion of the peoples of the lands once in control of Christian Europe, like in parts of northern Africa in possession of Islam from the fourteenth century, could be effected only through the reconquest of these lands. It was necessary to bring these lands under their control before thinking about any work of re-converting their population. Christendom or military and political presence or (re)conquest of territories in the name of (re)conversion, preceded the preaching of the gospel.[68]

The Portuguese did not have pre-conceived ideas regarding the methods of conversion used overseas just as they did not have much foreknowledge about the peoples they met. Promotion of Christian communities, both in number and strength, to secure Portuguese rule was a late development. The garrisons, the naval bases and the narrow circuits of fortresses and factories of the Portuguese, formed the first nuclei from where the local citizens for the empire emerged. These nuclei also served as platforms from where the missionaries launched out to the lands of the *Padroado* spiritually unconquered yet. Churches were erected near these factories and within fortresses, chiefly for the spiritual care of the Portuguese — of their local wives and children, of the new converts and baptized slaves. These became the first citizens for the eastern Lusitanian empire.

The optimistic and ignorant Portuguese believed that the Hindus, unlike the Jews and the Muslims, would accept the gospel peacefully and spontaneously. But before this, they expected to find more Christians than Hindus and Muslims in India. It is a well-known fact that the Portuguese did not bring Christianity to India. But perhaps it is not so well known that the official policy of the Portuguese stated that all vassals of the king of Portugal — those who lived in his territories — should be turned into Christians, meaning that the act of conversion did not make anyone a vassal or political ally. They were already vassals of the king before their conversion.[69]

Life in Goa before 1540 was cosmopolitan with intense competitive commercial traffic. But at the same time it was the meeting point of the three main religions and cultures. This means that there was sufficient religious tolerance in Goa. The insufficient number of Portuguese in Goa and elsewhere prevented them from achieving the desired goals more easily and quickly.[70] The lack of immediate successes opened a new chapter in the history of conversions in Goa. Then, strong political and religious measures were devised to achieve rapid successes, particularly in the field of conversions. Although hard to understand, even until the middle of the eighteenth century, when success of any sort was almost impossible the crown ordered the demolition of temples, and continued to uphold the ban against the performance of Hindu rituals or functions in public.[71] This is to indicate that in spite of the orders during the sixteenth century to demolish all the temples, they continued either to exist or to be rebuilt; and it also confirms that Christianity was not accepted peacefully nor spontaneously.

Several steps were taken to convert the local vassal population and to prevent the relapses of the neo-converts: persuasion, economic and political favours, land gifts, tax concessions, jobs in public services, social emancipation of slaves, the 'rigour of mercy', the retention of caste or previous status, the expulsion of those who prevented conversion from the Portuguese territory, etc.[72] These measures resulted in a new social code which permitted continuation only of certain traditional customs; these steps worked as mechanisms of inclusion and exclusion so necessary to discipline the locals for a new socio-political order. Hence, a new code of behaviour emerged which defined what the local vassals of the Portuguese could retain of their own culture, and what they had to adopt.

A study on conversions in Goa cannot ignore references to the main institutions or pillars of Christendom: the *Pay dos Christãos*, the Santa Casa da Misericordia (House of Charity), hospitals, seminaries, the Tribunal of the Inquisition, confraternities and houses for catechumens. These institutions had ample government support. They 'marketed' conversions too.[73] But the houses of charity, hospitals, works of charity and the good example of their officials might have suggested alternatives to the locals living in a closed and caste-ridden society. These institutions will be treated in some detail in other chapters.

Other methods had to be created to integrate socially the

new citizens, who after their baptism lost their traditional communitarian place and privileges. How did this integration take place? The Jesuits initiated conversions *en masse* and the other religious orders, Franciscan, Dominican and Augustinian, followed this trend. This device permitted the individual convert to retain his/her traditional place or status within the local community. However, it seems obvious and inevitable that the converted group would be cut off from its mainstream, especially at the beginning when they were more supervised by the church, and made to lose Hindu traits. But did these new citizens or converts improve their economic situation, or did they acquire more social privileges under the Portuguese law? These questions will be dealt with later on especially in chapters five and eleven.

The noble or high castes would not willingly join Christianity unless they could be persuaded that it was a superior and purer religion than the one they followed. But no matter how far this persuasion went, many preferred exile than to suffer conversion. It is impossible to estimate the number of Hindus that left Goa, but there are reports lamenting that at times Goa remained uninhabited and its fields abandoned. Then, new decrees had to be issued, persuading or pressurizing them to return or to forfeit their property. Again our historical sources show us that the high castes resisted conversion much more than the low castes, and that religious elements and customs of a life-time found their own ways of surviving among the non-converts and neo-converts alike, even in the then very hostile political and religious environment of Goa.

From the middle of the sixteenth century Portugal turned its attention and interests to colonizing Brazil, to the development in Angola and to the commerce of sugar in São Tomé and Príncipe. The Cape route continued to be indispensable for the spice trade and precious metals between Portugal and the East. If, however, the Portuguese presence in the Cape route continued for political, economic and religious reasons, the Atlantic had become the arena where the Portuguese founded their overseas maritime power. The decadence of the *Estado da India* took place rapidly during the second half of the sixteenth century, and Goa was no exception. Portugal exhausted in its resources led many to think that India was a project without any future.[74] But intolerance and proselytizing attitudes of the missionaries had reached their peak. Ironically, it is during this period that many 'laws and privileges in favour of conversions' had been issued to increase the number of citizens for the empire.

## Historiography of Conversions

The way we re-create history depends considerably on how we interpret historiography. Several published informative documents and manuscripts on conversions in Goa during the sixteenth century can serve as basis to re-interpret history. However, it is pertinent to stress from the outset that Goa certainly occupied a privileged and central position in the Portuguese network in the East. The headquarters of all the religious orders and the main government offices established here influenced directly and to a very large extent, unlike in other places, the work of conversion, providing, thus, a different outlook to the city of Goa. No doubt, Goa appears to be just one more city, although the most celebrated of all, amidst the other Portuguese controlled cities, even from a first reading of the Indo-Portuguese historical sources. Besides, Goa was not an isolated historical and geographical space, and the acceptance of this can prevent us from making any exaggerated statement and taking an uncritical historical position.

We could divide that vast body of information useful to us into two broad categories: first, the accounts and letters written by the missionaries, and secondly, the information that includes the accounts of chroniclers and travellers, letters and reports written by, and to, the kings of Portugal, viceroys, governors and civil administrative officials. Probably, ninety percent of the historiographical material on conversions belongs to the first category. Reportings about conversions in the *Estado da India* were generally sent to Portugal in particular and to Europe in general, and replies or suggestions, encouragement or reprimands to the agents of conversion active in the mission, followed from their superiors or the kings, at times together with the opinion of the learned on some disputed issues.

*Aumento e conservação da cristandade* (increase and preservation of Christendom) and *fazer cristandade* (to make Christendom) are expressions used frequently in the sixteenth century documentation, and the preoccupation with it led the king, the secular and religious authorities to create a vast body of laws, instructions and orders in favour of conversions. As a result, we also have a large amount of material on legislative measures. Missionary practices and Portuguese interests differed considerably from decrees on conversions and royal instructions. Besides discrepancies between praxis of conversion and decrees on conversion, the disagreements or differences of opinion arising from personal ambitions and interests of the agents of conversion created adverse conditions for the work of conversion. The Hindus might have taken advantage of this chaotic situation to impede the activity of conversion.

We know that the government issued continuously several decrees: many were anti-Hindu and anti-Muslim, to favour conversions, others were to protect the converts, and not a few were anti-relapse decrees.[75] It has been suggested that the large number of decrees called 'laws and privileges in favour of Christendom' or conversion and their frequent repetition often with a slight change of details, raise doubts about their enforcement. If that is the case, it only goes to show that the Portuguese did not conform strictly to the written law or official orders.

The existence of conflicts at the civil and religious level on the one hand, together with several compromises at the state and personal interest level on the other hand, were unavoidable, not only among the Portuguese themselves but between the Portuguese and the locals as well. Nevertheless, compromises were indispensable to avoid any social and religious local unrest against the state, and collaboration was fundamental to fulfil economic ambitions at a more personal level. However privileges in favour of the converts were not easily granted. The constant ratification of decrees in favour of conversion had the objective of making public the 'royal duty' towards Christendom — the often alleged main reason for conquest and the moral justification for the Portuguese economic monopoly — but these ratifications also showed what the Portuguese had done and achieved in reality and what they intended to do and achieve in and outside the field of conversions. The non-enforcement of the decrees goes only to show that the Portuguese in their colonies were, by and large, guided by their 'personal interests' rather than by the 'royal duty', although the former hardly showed itself openly in conflict with the latter.

Often our historiographical sources do not record whether a particular law or decree had always been implemented or whether it had been translated into an acceptable practice. The impracticality of much of the legislation meant that the exceptions to it often far exceeded the rule. Decrees consistently enforced were sometimes reversed. So, it is difficult to ascertain links or discrepancies between decrees and praxis in several cases. Despite this difficulty we can appreciate the effects of these decrees. At times and not surprisingly, before legislation came into existence, execution had already taken place. As already stated we have also several instances of decrees being ratified but without achieving the desired results, and one of the reasons for this could be that the intentions of the law enforcing agents did not correspond with the intentions and demands of the law-makers. Besides, there were not enough willing agents to enforce the law and maintain vigilance. Nevertheless, the entire legislation, as a given historiographical evidence, can lead us to rich insights to understand the complexities involved in the work of conversions. But knowing that many of these decrees had been half-heartedly executed, one cannot certainly take them as a starting point or basis for one's assumptions and conclusions. Unfortunately, many recent works on history of conversions in Goa during the sixteenth century seem to make several categorical statements based simply on these decrees and royal orders, thus arriving at wrong conclusions.

We have also to take into account the manner in which the exchange of information took place. During the second half of the sixteenth century, some ships carrying the letters containing these decrees and recommendation from India to Portugal and vice-versa might have made a temporary halt in Brazil, and the correspondence between Goa and Lisbon would have been held up in those ships for a long time. This devious journey could take over eighteen months during which time problems could have been solved without waiting for replies, making thus, the incoming official instructions and decrees partly or totally irrelevant in the new context. Sometimes, for lack of information or delay in receiving further recommendations, perhaps no action would be taken. Even the exchange of letters sent by different routes would take rather long. All these considerations are very relevant to understand the problems of the administration in the empire.

### (a) *Missionary Historiography*

Missionary letters, obviously, constitute the bulk of material we have about conversions and much of that belongs to the Jesuits. Letters written by the missionaries to the kings or more frequently to their superiors, informing them of their progress in the work of conversion, were more reports about their status and achievements than about the people they converted. Besides, the purpose of reporting about their own life and status was to show their acts of heroism in the cause of Christendom and to persuade their superiors about the need to send good vocations to India and above all to arrange for financial assistance and royal favours. Reports on the heroism and suffering of the missionaries edified the Europeans. Hence, the edifying letters of the Jesuits. We cannot ignore the fact that many things were written to please an eager relative or group in Europe to the point of distorting the historical truth and creating new myths.[76] The kings normally responded to the needs of Christendom in India, through their viceroys and governors after hearing reports, and orders from above were not contested at least not in writing. The kings made specific suggestions at times, reminding their viceroys and governors to execute all decrees and recommendations in favour of conversions, for the 'welfare of the people and service to the king', another expression frequently used in the sixteenth century historiography.[77] On the other hand the missionaries reminded the kings of their duty of expanding Christendom, especially when the local authority refused to cooperate with them.[78]

The news sent by the Franciscans was very scarce indeed, and this negligence had cost them dearly by the turn of the century.[79] The Franciscans did not care to write or report about their accomplishments, as reporting about their conversion feats did not go well with their simplicity and spirituality, so they believed. At first, when their opponents accused them of neglecting their missionary work, perhaps the Franciscans did not preoccupy with historical evidence in their favour. When these accusations reached the ears of the king, he expressed his feelings of concern and displeasure to the Franciscans. It was only then that these religious members realized that they had very few arguments and concrete evidences to prove their enemies wrong. On the other hand, the edifying letters written by the Jesuits brought them and for their activities much dividend. Hence, it is only after the arrival of the Jesuits in 1542 that we have more historiographical material regarding the history of conversions in Goa, specifically, for the city of Goa, the islands of Divar and Chorão, and Salcete where the Jesuits laboured. For Bardez, the jurisdiction of the Franciscans, we have comparatively little documentation. Perhaps, we could conclude that elsewhere in Bardez things could not have been very different, but it is known that Christianity in Bardez in the seventeenth century was terribly victimized by the Inquisition for relapses into Hindu practices, whereas the inquisitors did not trouble the Jesuit-controlled areas with the same rigour.[80]

What was the missionary concept of history? The prevalent view of the Europeans then, was that man originally had one religion and one set of God-given values, but as they migrated to different continents with diverse environments, and as time passed, they tended to forget their common stock: one true religion and one culture. For the Europeans diversity represented degeneration, and Christendom the true original stock; hence the need to reform any custom that differed from the original.[81] We may recall that most missionaries working in Goa were of Portuguese origin, and many of them had a poor theological formation believed to be sufficient in the mission lands. Portugal had not been considerably influenced by the ideals of humanism in the sixteenth century and such ideas had scarcely entered the seminaries. Besides, the theological and religious formation of the time stressed cultural ethnocentrism.

The missionary writer was not writing history, he was writing religion. These writings acquire the character of historical evidence only posthumously in virtue of our own historical attitude towards them.[82] Every history (or theology) writer was thoroughly imbued with religious zeal, and the missionaries were equally proud of their nation's achievements. Every glorious feat as well as any defeat was divinely sanctioned, but the latter as punishment for their sins. Whether the story spoke about the feats or defeats, things mundane or spiritual, the cause and purpose was always the same : God and conversions respectively. But this sort of 'historiography' does not preclude useful historical evidence for reconstructing history and society.

The missionaries wrote a 'selective' and 'edifying' history, in which the theological truth had precedence over all others. Since the purpose was to edify religiously an eager European reading or listening public, or to fascinate them, the writers were forced to omit unpleasant facts. This historiography aimed, therefore, at recording the examples of virtues of the missionaries in planting Christendom among 'uncultured and barbarian peoples'; to give thanks to God, and to move with zeal all those who would come here later; and accounts were written not to forget several things 'they did' that could be useful some day. Things about the local customs and religion, like summary of Hindu scriptures, superstitions, etc., were written and sent to their superiors in Rome or Portugal to prepare the newcomers for the work of conversion. A sizeable information about the local customs and religion came to us, thanks to the missionary writings, coated thickly by their prejudices as we shall see in chapter eleven. However, an attentive reader will notice some of their sharp and lengthy analyses of the society, peoples and events, which also betray the missionaries' difficulties, and the frustrations they encountered while trying to convert the Hindus and prevent the neo-converts from relapsing.

Generally, conflicts and quarrels among religious orders or between them and the state, and difficulties they faced in the activity of conversion were minimized or eliminated from such writings. Nevertheless, secular historiography tells us that when the religious orders found themselves no longer able to draw large revenues from the *Estado da India*, they turned against the government under which they had accumulated large wealth, and acted in hostile opposition to it.[83] It is worth keeping in mind these conflicts in order to understand that the missionaries did not always behave like good vassals of the king of Portugal. Letters and reportings that have come down to us can prove some lack of cooperation between the secular and spiritual agents.

We find in missionary writings a clear distinction between 'conversion' and 'baptism', and these two realities differed from another much-stressed one, namely, Christian 'instruction'. Invariably, the missionary letters show us that a genuine conversion or change of religion passed consecutively through these three stages: first 'conversion', followed by 'religious instruction', or the catechumenate period, and finally 'baptism'. The constant missionary stress that every 'conversion' was the work of God alone aimed at impressing upon the reader that there was no human intervention or force in making conversions. Although the missionaries held that conversions were caused by the grace of God, they did not exclude the presence of material motives in, and importance of favours to, the converts or those to be converted. These elements, however, were considered just secondary and temporal causes, a bait used by Providence to attract them to the true faith.[84] Hence, they proved that humam freedom remained intact when they made either individual or group conversions.[85] For this reason all those mass conversions seemed extraordinary and humanly inexplicable to the missionaries.[86] The missionaries were firmly convinced that the state protection to Christianity was a new means God used to obtain numerous conversions.[87]

Although God was the cause of every conversion, some conversion accounts received more attention and were given more publicity. Many narrations about the conversion of the high castes have been dramatized, the conversion of the daughter of Meale, claimant to the throne of the Bijapur kingdom, being one such case.[88] Conversion of local nobles and village chiefs appear as something prodigious, whereas that of the commoners lacked detailed description. The missionaries held the high caste converts, who had braved initial difficulties and social resistance, in high esteem. Interestingly, the hindus who were inclined and ready to accept baptism were already considered as honourable people and with good understanding by the missionaries. And the exemplary life of the high caste converts drew many others to conversion, so believed the missionaries.[89]

Constant reporting back home about conversions among the high caste group was meant to convey not only that their work was being favoured and guided by God, but also that no élite Hindu would ever fall a prey to force or pressure. Reports had reached home that the missionaries resorted to unchristian or unlawful methods to convert, thus harming also the revenues of the state. The missionaries did not take great pains to narrate plain truths or those happenings that did not help to gain souls for God and vassals for the king of Portugal. They wrote on things that could console, edify and be profitable to conversions.[90] And conversions from among the local élite was by far the most profitable. The caste people could be turned into partners of the Portuguese ruling class who needed the expertise and capital of these locals.

Francis Xavier wrote some guidelines on the manner of reporting conversions to the Jesuits of his time: "They shall write a detailed account on the work of conversion and let it be on edifying matters, and care shall be taken not to write about matters which can be unedifying... Remember that many people will read these letters..."[91] The criterion of writing had to correspond always with the interests of the Society of Jesus which meant selective reporting. Conversions in the East were publicized from the pulpits in Europe and the king of Portugal ordered this to be done in his country.[92] But in spite of the great care they took to avoid unedifying things, this documentation informs us about the persistence of idolatry among the neo-converts, thus betraying a sort of missionary despair for not being able to effect genuine conversions. Good examples of this sort of frustration are the reportings regarding the people of Salcete, informing us about their stubborn behaviour to persist in their religion and customs and about their opposition — with great hostility and warlike attitude — to any conversion activity.[93]

Heroes and martyrs were those who fought and defeated

hostile local populations or those who destroyed temples, idolatry and converted a multitude of Hindus and infidels. Local converts were considered incapable of doing this. European historiography knows no local hero. We need to recall momentarily that those local Christians, killed together with the Jesuit missionaries in Salcete, Goa, could never be on par with these missionaries. The Jesuits were beatified as martyrs, not the local Christians who suffered the same fate. (This is in no way a claim for equality and for their beatification too). Decrees ordering the destruction of 'idols' and temples as 'deeds of a civilized culture and revealed religion' need a separate treatment.[94]

In short, most missionary historiography is a discourse about the expansion of Christendom, spiritual conquests, heroes of worship and heroic deeds of the missionaries, either straight forward or subtly, with little consideration of the people. We cannot expect more from this type of historiography, and any attempt to write a history with empathy for the locals, based on this information, is bound to be difficult and very limited.

(b) *Secular Historiography*

According to an anonymous report, the king D. Manuel sent to India four ships commanded by Vasco da Gama to look for 'spices' (this was probably the original Portuguese plan for India). However, when the Portuguese reached India (Calicut) and on being asked by the locals the purpose of their visit, they replied that they had come in search of 'Christians and spices'.[95] The precise and original objective of Vasco da Gama's expedition was the search for 'spices', according to the description of Álvaro Velho, the official reporter in the fleet. But when it arrived in Calicut its purpose had changed to 'Christians and spices', most probably, to give a spiritual tone to the real and sole material objective that had brought them there. When a little later Vasco da Gama himself met the Samorim, the ruler of Calicut, the former told the ruler that the intention of the king of Portugal was only "friendship and commerce, and that on meeting the other Gentile princes along the African coast, they only intended to instruct the latter in the faith of Christ".[96] João de Barros, the official chronicler of the king of Portugal, stated that the purpose of Vasco da Gama's discovery was to convert the Hindu princes,[97] but he went on saying that the Muslims on perceiving that the purpose of Vasco da Gama's voyage was the commerce of spices, they did not appreciate it. The arrival of the Portuguese could send the Muslims' commercial monopoly to its doom, and as if this was not enough, these Portuguese were Christians, the declared enemies of the Muslims.[98]

After the Christian kings cleansed Portugal of its infidels, the Arab people, they restored the Roman church in some areas beyond its frontiers, where it had lost its jurisdiction and went on planting the banner of Christ even in India which for long had been under the control of the prince of darkness, through his mosques and temples.[99] The plan of the Infante D. Henrique was to make war with the infidels.[100] The conquest of the islands of Madeira and of Guiné was in order to save the souls of their inhabitants, not for any other reason.[101] The aim of discoveries and conquests was conversion of peoples, we were told. Further, João de Barros informed us that the same Infante had reminded the Portuguese captains not to wage war against the inhabitants of the newly discovered lands, but rather to offer them faith, peace and friendship.[102] The principal justification for undertaking discoveries and conquest was 'service to God and his majesty'.[103] Portugal a small nation was, nevertheless, chosen to confound the great ones; the act of sustaining Christendom and the crown's possessions would bring forever glory to the Portuguese country.[104] A strong sense of spiritual duty accompanied by nationalist feelings marked the Portuguese historiography of conversions.[105]

Till 1500 the Portuguese had been under the impression that the majority of Indians were Christians. Vasco da Gama and his men after spending three months in India had not understood that they had met Hindus here, and not Christians. The Hindus were taken for Christians who had gone astray from the Roman Catholic church, and who needed only to be led back into orthodoxy, and the spiritual mission of Portugal was to help them.[106] The mistakes of taking the Goddess Kali for the Virgin Mary, and even praying to her, and of confusing the Hindu temples with churches were the result of this ignorance and misconception. The Portuguese were familiar with Islam and they knew the impossibility of converting its followers in Africa or elsewhere; but since the Indians were believed to be Christians, it is hard to think of a plan about conversions for India right from the beginning. Therefore, conversions in India could not be a decisive element in their expansion programme until the beginning of the sixteenth century. Evangelization or proselytism drive in the sixteenth century was more a consequence rather than the main cause of expansion.[107] The common view held by scholars in the field of Portuguese expansionism in present times, insists that propagation of faith could not be the main concern in the original Portuguese plan, although later several royal orders speak of the 'service to God' as the most natural reason for conquest and expansion.[108] Be that as it might, conversion duty justified conquest and geographical expansion and this idea is strongly present in the Portuguese writings of the sixteenth century. In brief, according to the Portuguese official policy to give faith and to teach morals and good social customs to their vassals had precedence over personal and royal economic gains.[109]

As mentioned earlier, from the Indo-Portuguese historiography we can infer that ninety percent of the secular attention and efforts was diverted and devoted to acquiring 'spices'. In principle, the aim of the Portuguese was to conduct war with the Muslims and trade with the heathens and Hindus.[110] The Genovese and Florentine mercantile community established at Lisbon together with the Portuguese merchants, desired to make the best of the new sea route to India to compete with Venice.[111] The other parties that supported the Portuguese commercial enterprise in the East had little interest in any conversion activity. Likewise, there were no religious barriers for the Portuguese merchants, when it came to commerce and trading with the Hindus and Muslims.[112]

The occupation of small territories by the Portuguese in their geographical expansion and the policy of mixed marriages was not meant to simply locally root Portuguese society. The aim was more pragmatic. It intended making the newly created Portuguese network a viable one, meaning, with safe ports for their fleet and protected zones for factories. In turn it would demand and force only some Portuguese to settle down here. These conditions were fundamental for their commercial activity.[113] The nature of geographical discontinuity of this empire, and the existence of factory-forts system along the coast, show us a network meant for navigation so essential for trade.[114] Despite this strange territorial presence of Portugal in the East, an empire without territory, and with a racially mixed Portuguese presence controlling the seas and their factories and forts, the Portuguese presence overseas continued to be justified on religious grounds. Neither the 'unoccupation' of land nor the 'occupation' and monopoly of the seas could ever make possible any plan of conversion. But 'Christendom' not 'spices' continued to be projected in royal or official historiography throughout the sixteenth century as the main reason for territorial conquest and occupation.[115] It is also necessary to look out for schemes and mentalities that shaped Indo-Portuguese historiography, as well as to detect historical reasons that may facilitate the construction of backdrops, to understand better the work of conversions.

Several humanists in the sixteenth century doubted the religious or spiritual character of the Portuguese conquests. They stated that conquests aimed at pure commercial activity.[116] Note that the Portuguese blockaded the Cape sea route to India to other nations, and sold at great profit the spices they took from here. The *Padroado* was an 'area' interdicted to any non-Portuguese or foreign missionary who wanted to come here directly or without the Portuguese permission. The doors to preach the gospel and to convert were closed to the foreign missionaries, in spite of the often alleged great need in the *Padroado* for more missionaries. The former's intentions and objectives were held with suspicion by the Portuguese authority. The official reason and argument for this exclusion was that the foreigners posed a great danger to the purity, increase and preservation of the faith.[117] Foreigners like the Venetians, Jews and Muslims were barred from entering the Portuguese territory in India because their bad examples and practices harmed the orthodox faith.[118] Further, the non-Portuguese or foreigners remained excluded for being potential meddlers in the work of conversion. However, later, from the beginning of the seventeenth century, the *Padroado* and the *Propaganda Fide* would continuously quarrel, not in the name of purity of the faith or increase of converts, but for the sake of their own privileges, rights and historical claims.

Portugal wanted to show the world that its sole concern was the spread of the Catholic faith.[119] However, it was a difficult task to prove to Europe in particular, and to the world in general, that after facing so many dangers at seas, fighting in wars and with hostile peoples, Portugal, a nation known for its Catholic values, had not settled down comfortably to an office so low as that of buying and selling. It was also not easy to convince anyone that weapons were used only for the defence of the Catholic faith. Likewise it was hard to show that Portugal did not use the local Christians against the Muslims to further their own political and economic interests.[120] Yet, the constant claim and formula that Portugal fought for the faith and that its successes came from God alone.[121]

The Portuguese policy of the *mare clausum* (patrolled or blockaded sea) for commercial monopoly was therefore justifiable, and the monopoly of spices was historically and juridically legitimate.[122] The money acquired from the sale of spices was destined to uphold the crusading spirit in the lands of infidels. Portugal also asserted that in discovering lands and propagating the faith here, it did a fine work for their peoples. Hence the advantages resulting from its monopolistic policies were but a compensation for much expenditure and incurred losses, for future works to be undertaken, and for the blood shed in the cause of the faith. In this way the great Portuguese humanist and chronicler, Damião de Góis, defended Portugal's claims, and further stated that the other European nations that merely sought political supremacy should also follow the example of that truly Christian nation.[123] The kings of Portugal intended to plant the holy faith or destroy radically the presence of idolatry and paganism; or to elevate thousands of souls living in superstition and to purify them with the healthy waters of baptism.[124] A great number of royal instructions urged the Portuguese to spread and defend the Catholic faith.

Can we find any striking difference between the Muslim and Portuguese schemes of converting the local populations in India? The Portuguese had no intentions of staying permanently in India or in any of their conquests. They wanted to control their empire with the help of just a few strategic land bases. Hence, unnecessary conquest of land was officially questioned. The viceroy, D. João de Castro, did not permit the Portuguese to move even a span further into the Indian territory.[125] It has been argued that the Muslims came to India to stay, and their conversion drive was rather religiously motivated than politically; whereas the Portuguese came essentially for 'spices' and not in big numbers to populate India.[126] But the fact that the Portuguese did use religion to make more citizens for the *Estado da India* or their empire, despite royal allegations to the contrary, is subtly present in the sixteenth century Portuguese historiography.[127] After all, political ends were not divorced from religious ones (even for the Muslims), and this is what characterized the official Portuguese policy, in spite of its stress on faith expansion. The difference between the old evangelization of the apostle St Thomas and modern conversion drive initiated by the Portuguese, with Francis Xavier as its best representative, lies in the fact that the former came as a simple apostle of Jesus Christ, whereas the latter came not only as a missionary, but also as an envoy sent by the king of Portugal and with papal authority.[128] This speaks eloquently for the Portuguese missionaries of the Vasco da Gama epoch.

The much discredited Fernão Mendes Pinto, a sixteenth century traveller in India and Asia and with a first hand experience, said that much that had been written till then about the Portuguese deeds in the East was completely from the Portuguese point of view or without any strong sense of self-examination; however, the Asians suspected the actions of the Portuguese.[129] This Portuguese traveller wrote that the Asians accused the Portuguese of coming to Asia disguised as merchants in order to spy on the land, and return here later only to conquer it.[130]

The discoveries and geographical expansion — the European historiography before this based itself on pure imagination the fantastic and phantasmagoric about Africa and Asia — produced a more realistic picture.[131] However, this reality turned out to be more shocking to them. Neither trade nor propagation of faith came as easy affairs. Perhaps, this historiographical framework and arguments could help us to look for insights concerning conversions in Goa.

### (c) *Native Historiography*

There is hardly any historiography by the locals. Generally the Portuguese historiography did not pay attention to the deeds or customs of the locals. However, at times we find interesting descriptions about them. The Portuguese took interest in the local customs and traditions of the land in so far as these things helped them to know with whom they were dealing. Otherwise, the history of the locals found very little place in missionary or secular historiogrphy.[132] Language and prejudices formed strong barriers to learn things local. Besides the missionaries had come here to teach and not to learn, to give and not to receive anything from the natives.[133] And the Portuguese layman came neither to teach nor to learn anything from the locals. 'Reforming of customs', 'victory over the infidels', 'conversion of infidels', etc., was the dominant narrative and not 'encounter and appreciation of cultures'.

The Portuguese found many differences, be they in law, in lifestyles and in customs, between the Muslims and the Hindus. They knew about the customs and manners of the Muslims as being the same everywhere. But the life of the Hindus, being unfamiliar to them, seemed somewhat strange. The latter fascinated the Portuguese as well. But the life of the high castes, especially of the Brahman, besides fascinating the foreigners, also annoyed them. The foreigners could not stand the 'superstitions' of the Brahmans, and they wrote that the Brahman caste was more prone to superstitions than the other castes. For this and other reasons the Brahmans were made to stand apart, as a social and religious group, from the rest of the local Hindu population, a fact attested by several writings.[134] The conversion of Brahmans had become highly instrumental in converting others, hence the former became greatly prized and esteemed. No wonder, therefore, the abundant information that reached us about the Brahman caste is much more than the information we have about any other caste group, or perhaps all groups put together.[135]

The conversion of a Brahman and that of a non-Brahman was not viewed in the same manner as already mentioned above; nor were they valued equally by the Portuguese. After conversion, previous social differences were deliberately maintained, accepted and respected by the Portuguese. But most probably the élite converts, collaborators of the Portuguese, had better and more social opportunities and privileges. It was natural and easier for the élite groups to identify themselves with the ruling group. Stories of conversions tell us that some newly converted Brahmans, who used to dress and behave in strict conformity with their caste norms just before their baptism, soon after their conversion, began going about on horseback, wearing boots with golden spurs and a retinue of slaves. And in this way they strolled in the city with the *fidalgos* and the Portuguese captains. These converts appeared so much like the Portuguese in their conduct to seem as if they had been brought up in this way itself.[136] Another Brahman after his conversion began going about in the city with five or six servants, as the *fidalgos* used to do.[137] The importance given to describe the conversion of the high caste people and the place given them in the Indo-Portuguese historiography also betrays the missionary mentality.

Conversion narratives about the village chiefs and about the nobles were certainly exaggerated accounts to serve as edifying examples, and to influence others. The missionaries understood well the importance of conversions from amongst the high castes, but while preferring the conversion of the Brahmans to all others, the missionaries found it extremely difficult to secure their conversion. Further, the baptism of the Brahmans or of the village chiefs demanded special and more expensive religious ceremonies and feasts.[138]

It is imperative to explain certain concepts at this point. Leaving the Brahmans aside, the 'Moors', the 'Gentiles' and the 'Negroes' generally speaking were grouped together. In fact these vocables did not have fixed semantics. Throughout the fifteenth and sixteenth centuries we see an oscillation in their meanings. A 'Moor' could be either any African in general or a Muslim in particular; a 'Gentile' could be any Indian as much as it could be any Chinese or Japanese.[139] 'Gentile' was a generic term used to signify a non-Christian, a non-Jew and a non-Muslim person. The term 'Gentile' was also often used as a synonym for 'pagan', another generic term used by the Europeans to designate all non-Christians and non-Muslims in their mission lands. Broadly speaking, Gentiles were all those who did not profess Christianity. The Hindus came within the ambit of 'Gentiles' and the Muslims into the category of 'infidel' and 'Moor', although the terms 'Gentile' and 'infidel' were very often used synonymously. Perhaps these terms had a pejorative connotation too, since the Christians considered themselves as a superior group. But they certainly also denote religious differences. Besides the question of semantics, the 'Gentiles' without religion and the 'Moor' with a false religion constituted the different other, the opposing other or the anti-Christian element.[140] In short, these groups were so rooted in their religions, nevertheless it was necessary to convert them.[141]

The Portuguese sociological and historical discourses appear excessively derogatory to us, but this formed part of their socio-religious mentality from which they perceived and judged the other and by which they shaped their historiography. We do not find terms such as 'Hindu' and 'Muslim' in the entire sixteenth century Indo-Portuguese historiography. We do not find the term 'Goan' either. Instead we come across the word *Canarim* very often, used by the Portuguese to designate an inhabitant of Goa.[142] The terms 'Hinduism' or 'Hindu' were terms made in West and brought to India much later.[143] We recall that the Portuguese had not come to India to look for the different other, rather they had come in 'search of Christians'. This book has consistently used the term Hindu for 'Gentile' and Muslim for 'Moor' without intending to soften down the European hardliners' mentality and stereotypes of the century in review. The present work has used 'conversion' and 'proselytism' synonymously too, but the latter term does not appear in the sixteenth century historical sources. Likewise, the words Christianity or Christianism do not appear, but the word 'Christendom' (*Cristandade*). I have used them synomymously.

### (d) *Historiography of Silence*

Historiography of silence seems to be a paradox. However, history is made of this silence too. Historiography of silence is the history of violence in the empire — by locals themselves and others — that was little reported. It is the history of the powerless as well. Unfortunately, this vast area in the history of Goa will remain obscure to us. The life of the women in Goa could speak volumes about violence. Hindu widows were forced to shave their heads by traditional society, but the Portuguese forbade this practice, since widowhood prevented their conversion and re-marriage.[144] The convert women, the first local citizens, were certainly used or misused for the expansion of the empire. Women, despite being more conservative, were also greater victims in a traditional society. Hence, under the missionary pressure and lured by economic and social gains, some women, probably, preferred to be converted. Whether conversion brought them personal freedom and gains is altogether another issue. We know very little about them and what they did after their conversion. Much of what we know about women came down to us from the chroniclers. The missionaries would not easily report about them. But it seems obvious that more pressure and violence was borne by the local convert women in the absence of women from Portugal. We should not forget the violence done to local women through historiographical statements. It is true that the 'best' (whatever it meant) local women were the favourites of the Portuguese, who then used them to satisfy their own libido. The nautch-girls or *bailadeiras* were persecuted by the Portuguese religious authority, but curiously they were much sought after and protected by the Portuguese soldiers and *fidalgos*. However, it would be absurd to think only of the anti-feminine aspects the chroniclers reported, although that is what we have galore. It would be historically dishonest to consider the issue of conversions in Goa without distinguishing or revealing the local feminine face of the empire, the portrait of the first Lusitanian citizens of the East. Hence, chapter ten dedicated a part of it to some considerations concerning the absence of Portuguese women here, and the life of local convert women in the context of expanding Christendom.

It is not surprising to hear that the absence of women on board the ships prevented offences to God. But in case Portuguese women travelled overseas, they had to be locked inside at night.[145] The Portuguese would certainly not have treated the local women with more respect. Further, the empire needed sailors. The helpless people sent to the galleys for an indefinite period of time is another facet in this historiography of silence that needs more attention.[146] Were the converts exempted from working in the ships? Although the task of unfolding the 'historiography of silence' is rather difficult, it is necessary to give voice to this silence and violence to the *Canarins* (Goan converts) and others.

## Re-evaluating the History of Conversions

It is with the help of this kind of historiography available to us that we have to re-write and re-interpret history. The issue of conversions in Goa has been studied or dealt with from various perspectives: political, social, ecclesiastical or missionary, apologetical, etc. But many of these studies and conclusions lack a theoretical framework, hence their failure to situate facts in their proper perspective as mentioned earlier. There are also many conversion myths that have gone unquestioned and survived for too long just because they serve some group interests.

The history of conversions in Goa is not synonymous with the history of missionary activity, and much less with the exploits of religious orders. Unfortunately, we have to rely heavily on missionary historiography and one may end up by being totally influenced by it. It is easy to tell the story of great people and of their heroic deeds, but of the small and voiceless, it is neither easy nor historically exciting. Will the views proposed in this book lead anyone to change or re-assess his/her opinions and questions on conversion activity in Goa during the sixteenth century? Maybe not. Perhaps it may only confirm what has been already said many times. However and above all, as mentioned earlier, I wish to present these views for your historical assessment.

A theoretical framework of mentalities, terms, intentions and definitions could help us to analyse historical documents and historiography of conversions better, to compare and contextualize facts and events, and to understand continuity and changes in concrete moments. Hence, besides presenting facts, I have attempted to construct an analytical framework to understand them. I have also tried to review the various issues of conversions with regard to their broader social aspects and power relationships, and conflicting interests. A particular social reality, to be properly understood, needs to be conceived in relation to the entire system and to its parts, obviously within that time frame. But I think that it is in the domain of interpretation of that reality that much work on conversions must be done. Further, it is essential to create a more complete picture surrounding the conversion events to denounce perspectives that serve the interests of those who want only one side of the story to be known.

We can go beyond sensitive issues and inquire into the role played by religion or conversions in a caste-ridden society, and the social transformation it effected. Even under political pressures kinship and kindred factors and the ancestral religion played a dominant role in the society, thus minimizing at times the significance of the religion of adoption. Syncretic practices and tendencies were always present. But if traditional kindred and kinship factors proved stronger than the new religion they adopted, to what extent did the neo-converts abandon the former and snap ties with their 'unconverted' family and relatives in Goa during the sixteenth century? Conversions certainly created new distance or social barriers between the Hindus and the converts, but there was far more social interaction among themselves than the documents reveal.

Further, the village communities in Goa during the period under review were guided by caste considerations or norms. Nevertheless, it is not an easy task to unfold the existence of these dividing social lines in daily interaction, especially among converts themselves, because missionary historiography tended to erase them, for being something to do with Gentile customs. Baptism did not eliminate the existing social and economic differences, or in other words the post-conversion life depended considerably on one's pre-conversion status.

There has been also undue stress on the methods of conversion. One of the greatest lacunae in several studies on conversions has been the uncritical tendency to consider all the converts as if they formed a homogeneous group. There has been a failure for not taking into serious account cultural and economic differences among the locals, caste ambitions and internal conflicts. As a result of this, other interesting and meaningful facets of conversions, as for instance cultural and religious syntheses or issues connected with questions asked below, have remained largely unanswered. What was the response by the different caste groups to conversion? What did conversions do about existing conflicts between landowners and peasants, the local élite and their subalterns? Was the new religion trying to change the traditional power relationships or to honour the local élite? Was it concerned about strengthening the position of the socially and religiously exploited, including that of women? Did the conversion of landlords or dominant groups take place in great numbers? Numbers are difficult to come by, but the Brahmans and the Hindu priests would not convert nor let conversions take place. Was their expulsion from Goa the only and certain way of making more conversions, or were material favours and state protection to the prospective converts equally necessary? Did the opponents of conversion soften down their stand when the Portuguese extended some privileges and honours to them? Did the conversion of Hindus differ from that of the Muslims? There was migration due to severe anti-Hindu decrees, but who migrated from Goa? Was there any social or symbolic protest at this time? How did the Hindu population perceive the new converts? Did they doubt about, or preoccupy with the intentions and motives of the converts? Were conversions something that integrated the Goan society or tore it apart? What sort of conflicts did conversions create within the traditional community? Perhaps the local chiefs did not take conversions seriously until they constituted a threat to the established social, economic and religious order. Even free conversions of the masses (*gente meuda*) made the Hindu élite react. There were also many conversions among the élite.[147] Despite the Portuguese apparent indifference to the system of castes, they dealt with the local converts according to their former social position. Nevertheless, a caste convert might have enjoyed more social freedom than their Hindu counterpart. The sixteenth century historiography can offer us rich insights into some of these questions.

It would be ingenious to engage in some sort of comparative study, for instance, regarding the Muslim influences on the Goan society, on their converts and on the Hindus alike, prior to the arrival of the Portuguese. The Muslims were in Goa for a short period of about thirty years, since 1482. The Portuguese rule during its first thirty years might have appeared religiously and culturally in continuity with the Muslim rule, since both governments did not interfere with the local religious freedom and social customs.

The Portuguese conversion project created many conflicts between two power groups, namely, the Portuguese and the local élite spearheaded by the Brahmans, who prevented the work of conversion on the existential and ideological level. But on the economic level they willingly collaborated with each other. In the economic sector there were less enemies but more competitors than in the religious and ideological sector. The Portuguese had sold many guns, spears and swords to the Muslims, the enemies of the Catholic faith, more than enough to wage a war against the Portuguese themselves.[148] Since going to the infidels to trade was against the Canon Law (law of the church), the Portuguese made the infidels come to them, which act did not violate any church law. When the economic situation of the Brahmans came under serious threat, they did not hesitate to keep the Muslims informed of what was happening in Goa.[149] But it was not only the Brahmans who resisted conversions as we shall see in the following chapters.[150]

The locals did not always receive the new religion as passive spectators. The issues mentioned above together with economic factors, evidently played a very important role in making or preventing conversions. But these issues, considered in themselves, hardly explain the 'historical passions' involved in changing or preserving one's ancestral religion. We have to keep under check any blind passion to be able to assess the issue of conversions ever more objectively and impartially. History means 'inquiry' not 'inquisition'. It seeks to understand not to judge and burn down historical realities. The documents also inform a careful reader about the religious passions or reactions originated by conversions.

It is important to know that Goa was surrounded by the strong Muslim Bijapur state, often hostile to Goa, despite the several friendly treaties the Portuguese made with it. The Portuguese survived for so long not only because they accommodated diplomatically with the main Indian kingdoms or because they themselves formed a cohesive group in the face of danger, but because the local Hindus had also to tolerate the Portuguese in the face of Muslim threats against themselves. The Bijapur state on its part needed Goa to sell its products.[151] We can find several concrete cases of Portuguese official accommodation and compromises with the local population. These diplomatic contracts were unavoidable and necessary to sustain the *Estado da India*. Depending on these friendly ties with the Hindu or Muslim rulers, the converts that the Portuguese made elsewhere outside their own territories could possibly be favoured by these Indian rulers. But if at times the converts were harassed by these local rulers, it was probably not so much for professing a different religion as for being held as suspects, or for siding with the political and economic interests of the Portuguese.

We havé to understand the phenomenon of conversions and the circumstances surrounding it without giving free vent to passions and religious sentiments to the extent of interfering with historical inquiry. It suffices to say here that not only were the Hindus persecuted and disfavoured most of the time, but often the converts did not receive the promised privileges and favours. Hence, the converts had neither the support from their traditional community nor from the Portuguese. Conversions did not bring miraculous social and economic opportunities. Moreover, even the Hindus who had been unwillingly converted found themselves excommunicated by their own relatives. So, it seems, the local converts had to undergo more hardships than anybody else.

Interestingly, despite severe pro-conversion decrees, the Hindus continued to be favoured and at times even more than the

Christians and ironically, even when the former opposed the work of conversions or oppressed the people. The Portuguese wanted to win the political confidence and services of the Hindus, but not always their conversion. Hindu capital, diplomatic qualities, competence and skills in business were more useful to the state than their conversion.[152] As seen earlier when rich Hindus lived in Goa its economy flourished. The Brahman Dadagi, son of Krishna, a *tanadar-mor* and *língua* to the governor was an adversary of the Christian faith.[153] But the abundant civil legislation and ecclesiastical decrees give us the impression that only the Christians were favoured, not the Hindus. Chapter five deals extensively with the decrees and instructions or the 'laws and privileges in favour of conversion' along with several reports complaining about their non-implementation.[154]

Local association or collaboration with the Portuguese normally attracted substantial benefits or privileges to the Hindus or converts alike, but only if they were people who mattered.[155] As seen above, when it came to trade, religious affiliations were downplayed, whereas when it affected directly and just one's religious beliefs preserving the puritv of the Christian (or Hindu) faith took precedence. Hence, the search for "Christians and spices" did not present itself as an inseparable project in every respect. Nevertheless, the civil and ecclesiastical authority learnt to maintain the necessary equilibrium between the temporal and the spiritual demands. Preserving the purity/orthodoxy of the faith was fundamental to create a climate for the ideal political unity so they thought, and this was exactly what the Catholic kings tried to do in Europe, but European ideals did not prove always very pragmatic to sustain the *Estado da India*.

The rivalry and conflicts between the Portuguese and the Hindus were not simply a matter of conversions and reactions to it. Rather, it was a rivalry between two politically, culturally and economically competitive groups, each one organized and justified around its own religious convictions. To fight for their religion meant upholding their cultural identity, social continuity and economic ambitions.[156] Hence, the conversion drive was only one more corollary of the entire social order, though perhaps the most fierce one. This being the case, religious goals dictated possibilities: it could create allies to support one's cultural and social claims and strengthen one's political and economic interests on the one hand, or it could increase one's enemies on the other hand. Within this framework even commercial activity could become a religious act or have its blessings. We recall that Portugal asked the pope's permission to trade with the infidels in the territories they conquered, the profit being for the work of conversion, thus making something unlawful and unchristian a spiritual act.[157] This unlawful commercial activity was justified as being necessary to sustain the work of conversion overseas.

The problems, questions, issues and methods regarding conversion varied considerably due to internal and external threats to the Portuguese empire. For instance, the royal instructions to the viceroys, apostolic zeal, state finances, local reactions, etc., differed even from decade to decade, thus establishing in turns changes, successes and reversions in conversion activity. But this does not imply that the conversion issues or the official idea of conversion varied considerably in the areas of Portuguese influence. Since the profile of Goa was distinct with a superior political status, the work of conversion took a different turn here.

By now it may be clearer to the reader that conversions depended to a very large extent on the local civil authority, and material ambitions of the Portuguese in the *Estado da India*. The Portuguese administration was more concerned about accumulating wealth quickly, which behaviour contributed to the decadence of their rule in India, already from the middle of the sixteenth century. Ironically, the Portuguese laymen blamed 'conversions' and the missionary activity, or rather, the methods used to convert the locals, for the economic and social evils in the empire. Besides, they suggested that mixed marriages had produced a 'languid population of half-breeds' who also contributed to the decline of their empire. Paradoxically, miscegenation had been the best means to create citizens for the Lusitanian colonies.[158]

When we situate our questions within the sixteenth century historical context, we see that their problems of conscience and mind-set were not exactly the same as ours today. Re-creating historical contexts, mental forms and the symbolic elements of the epoch in question is as crucial as clarifying concepts and presenting plain facts. The social and religious forms of *Gentilismo* (Hinduism) and *Mafamede* (Islam) during the sixteenth century did not have the same features as of modern Hinduism and Islam respectively, just as the mentality of Christianity of today is far different from that of *Cristandade*, simply because the historical context and the ideology that had shaped them no longer exist.

The history of conversions in Goa was not very different from that in other countries that were evangelized by other European missionaries.[159] The missionaries brought a militant evangelism, or form of Christianity which was based not on the core message of the Bible,[160] but on some of its passages which eventually became more creditable than the main message. This selective reading and practice enabled them to reconcile mamon with God.[161] This form of Christianity stressed on elaborate and magnificent liturgical ceremonies and frequent ritual participation by the local converts as means to help them to retain their faith, and attract more proselytes to it. Portuguese religious devotions became firmly rooted in Goa, and they were appreciated and respected by the Christians and Hindus alike. This was a religiosity that sought visibility — the elaborate baptismal ceremonies in big groups speak for themselves — meant not only to influence the Hindus with the power of the masters, but also to uphold the spirit of the Counter-Reformation that rejected the mystic approach to religion, as the best means of living the Christian faith as the Protestants proclaimed. Besides, what was not possible any more in Europe found expression overseas with the very Christian proselytizing instinct coming to the fore once again. Conversions were neither a spiritual conquest nor a conquest simply effected for Jesus Christ. Although the religion the Portuguese practised was far from showing examples of egalitarian values, it became a criticism of the local social conflicts and inequalities.

Hence, was conversion motivated simply by religious factors or was it just a corollary, though the most dominant one, of economic and political ends? Questions like this may become clearer when approached from a broader historical and analytical framework. Pure religious motives may be a case of conscience for men and women living in free societies in the twentieth century. However, the idea an practice of conversion within Christendom of the sixteenth century was less compartmentalized than we think. Conversions had very little to do with pure religious motives or directly with social upliftment of peoples. Catholicism here in Goa respected tradition, social inequality (caste system) and hereditary status (nobility of castes), whilst education for women was excluded. Obviously, the Portuguese did not strive at maintaining or creating institutions that did not reflect their own traditions or correspond with their interests.

Since the Portuguese were mainly preoccupied with economic gains, conversions were often seen by the non-Portuguese competing powers as the former's clever strategy for political and social control. Hence, the issue of conversions is usually explained from the economic perspective. Thus, it is argued, that the levelling down of cultures through the imposition of only one religion, was not the end but just a corollary of social alliances for economic exploitation. Conversions aimed at creating citizens for an economic project. But when the *Estado da India* was bankrupt and without almost any hope of recovery, royal funds for the work of conversion did not stop, and earlier spiritual claims continued unchanged. This is often alluded to as a counter-argument to the economic and political reductionism of the issue of conversion.

What was the ideology and pragmatism of the crown for clinging to its early spiritual and *Padroado* claims at the cost of almost empty coffers? I have found no satisfactory answer, or perhaps the answer lies in another question. Why does a good amount of contemporary Portuguese historiography reflect, or focus on, the sixteenth century historical memory of discoveries?

## The Sixteenth Century Today

What are the Portuguese historiographical claims today about the sixteenth century and why are they made in that way? Why all that interest and nostalgia for the 'golden age'? Portuguese historiography wants to maintain alive by all means the memory of discoveries and expansion as the best Portuguese identity in the face of growing national anonimity and global uniformity today. Hence, they pass many centuries by to establish a direct link between that heroic, original and epoch-making century and the present. The Portuguese pride and name boosted by discoveries, become again products to be publicized and marketed globally, just as 'conversions' and 'spices' had been marketed then. Encounter of cultures and races, and globalization, made possible by discoveries which the Portuguese claim to be pioneers, distinguish the Portuguese identity from the rest. There has to be a continuity between the present and any glorious past for historical survival. Even the kings of Portugal constantly referred to themselves as the 'perpetuators' of the policies of their 'predecessors', and as monopolists and 'masters' of commerce and conquests respectively.[162]

The sixteenth century has also been considered as the most interesting century in the history of the entire world. It should not be argued that I chose the sixteenth century to deliberately speak about the 'best' century of the Portuguese empire in the East. It is true that the documentation regarding conversions in the sixteenth century is 'original', the other centuries merely repeat the story. But what motivated me to choose this period was indeed the fact that history needs to be re-written and written by locals themselves, and re-interpreted anew. It is in the latter area that much work needs to be done, even on the much explored sixteenth century Indo-Portuguese historiography. But above all, the sixteenth century introduced significant changes in the life and behaviour of the Goans. It was a turning-point in the history of Goa.

Further, why should the subject of conversions in the sixteenth century, situated so far into the past, be re-assessed today? I believe it should, first, because the last word about it has not been said yet; second, some of the things that have been said need to be questioned to deconstruct certain myths repeated over the years and which have become as established facts; and third, many claims continue to be made, often contradictory ones, based on the events of this century. The sixteenth century need not be the most interesting for the locals as it is for the Portuguese. Nevertheless, it remains in the history of Goa as an unquestionable epoch-making as already mentioned. The sixteenth century can throw light on questions and controversies of today's interest. The Portuguese approach and ours to understand the sixteenth century events could be completely distinct. Both make claims today, but divergent ones because frameworks of analysis, interests and questions differ.

Goa of the sixteenth century may appear considerably different from Goa of the following centuries if we continue to view it from European categories: loss of Portuguese territories in the *Estado da India* to the other late-coming European nations struggling for power, and the decline of the Portuguese empire or its prosperity. Prosperity did not belong to the locals. Nevertheless, this observation does not deny the innovations and changes that the sixteenth century brought to Goa. Likewise the vicissitudes in the *Estado da India* did cause significant changes in Goa.

Goa during the sixteenth century was not an isolated geographical and historical entity, but very much affected by its neighbouring kingdoms. Goa was historically linked with the preceding and the following centuries. Likewise, our present socio-cultural traditions — or the 'Goan identity' as some would like to call it — are not dissociated from the period being reviewed. However, in spite of this close and natural relationship between that past and our present, researching on any socio-religious phenomenon so far removed from our times, is not easy.

The history of Goa in the sixteenth century cannot be understood by means of a contemporary discourse of encounter of, or dialogue between, cultures. It has to be understood from the point of view of a narrative that includes realities such as 'conquests', 'conversions', 'papal decisions', 'Moors', 'Gentiles', 'barbarians', 'infidels', 'idolaters', 'Christendom', 'good Christian customs' and 'bad customs of Gentiles', 'missionaries', 'vocations for India', etc. It is true that this sort of European mentality had created open conflicts when the rival groups met.[163] But the tendency to use a new narrative and terminology today, although so necessary to create an atmosphere for dialogue, for encounter of cultures and for a new world order, instead of conflict of cultures, cannot be easily accepted if it distorts historical facts and produces biased interpretations just to serve the interests of 'some groups'. Both tendencies are neither desirable nor necessary. What is desirable and necessary is to understand the past events for better cultural and economic cooperation today.

## Concluding Remarks

It is not possible to construct a single model for religious activities and conversions in Goa although certain actions speak louder and convincingly. Nevertheless, the issue of conversions has been usually explained as a clever mechanism of control meant to achieve economic and political goals. Rather the much-alleged need of reforms in society was not an end in itself, but to win the political loyalty of the natives for economic exploitation. Exchange of gifts, political alliances and military protection in exchange for trade, or a good price for local goods won the locals' good will. But when these methods failed to bring results, then threats, force and violence became natural. However, this perspective does not take into account the entire process and activity of making conversions.

Conversions or change of religion or new allegiances did not bring expected rewards and benefits to the converts, in spite of a large body of decrees and verbal promises to this effect. We should recall that the Marquis of Pombal, the famed Prime Minister of Portugal, had been more specific concerning legislation on granting privileges and rights to the local Christians in the middle of the eighteenth century when there was more religious tolerance, but unfortunately very little had changed for the Goans even then. How could things be different two centuries earlier? Material improvement or enhancement of status is seldom, if ever, the sole or even the dominant motive in a conversion. Dignity, self-respect, patrons who will treat them as equals, and the ability to choose one's own destiny — all these factors can serve as powerful incentives to conversion.[164]

Ever since 1498, the moment Vasco da Gama opened the sea route to India, but more precisely since 1542, when the greatest missionary of modern times Francis Xavier arrived in India, thousands of missionaries followed in his footsteps to India and elsewhere in Asia to expand the 'Christian space' or Christendom.[165] Francis Xavier in his letter of 15 January 1544, describing his conversion activity in the Fishery Coast in South India as a success, also expressed his desire to go to the University of Paris to recruit workers for this rich field.[166] But Christendom did not flourish anywhere there or in Goa as he and many others had expected. Today Goa accounts for a little over twenty-five percent of Catholics in a population of around 1 350 000 inhabitants.

"Portugal colonized big areas as in South America and Africa. But it was humanly and materially incompatible with the resources of Portugal to colonize such large areas in Asia. In India with an ancient and dissolute civilization it was not possible to found colonies as in some virgin country inhabited by savages."[167] There were several excesses and injustices, violence and exploitation as a result of the discoveries, expansion and conversion drive. But the unintended effect, namely, the coming together of the East and West or the encounter of different cultures, religions and peoples, made possible by the 'discoveries' and geographical mobility, was remarkable indeed.[168]

There are fashionable things to say in history although they may not be historically true at all, and it is unfortunate if one is carried away by this kind of fashions of the day. For this reason history needs to be re-assessed. To re-think the history of conversions with the greatest impartiality is not an easy task, and for this reason the last word in this book is not the end of the story. Dealing with conversions need not be a sensitive issue if we know how to approach it with as much historical objectivity as we can. It is easy to put it aside because it is sensitive, because it is made to be so. Forty long years have passed since the political liberation of Goa, and it is time to try to understand our history a little more objectively. But for that, it is necessary to re-create our historical contexts, as authentic as possible, with all intellectual honesty and attention to the historiography of silence.

## NOTES AND REFERENCES

1. António da Silva Rego, *História das Missões do Padroado Português do Oriente*, p. 83. C. R. Boxer, *The Portuguese Seaborne Empire*, 1415-1825, (1969), p. 66.
2. The Portuguese pioneers in the East were more tolerant than the Portuguese who came during the second half of the sixteenth century. The hardening of religious differences in Europe, resulting from the growth of Protestant heresies and from the Roman Catholic revival (the Counter-Reformation) was clearly reflected in the East during the rule of D. João III (1521-57). *Ibid.*, p. 74.
3. *DI*, IV, 293.
4. There were so many beggars in the city who forced the viceroy, Conde de Linhares, to pass a decree in 1630 forbidding them to beg. If they were caught begging, the men would be sent to the galleys and the women to work in the gun powder house. Only those who had permission in writing from the *Pay dos Christãos* could beg. *LFC*, fls. 28-29. Obviously, the religious orders became poor as well, but throughout this century there were several decrees and orders favouring conversions. *Ibid.*, fl. 66.
5. ARSI, *Goana Historia*, 34 - I, fls. 122, 215v, 217v.
6. The 'New Conquest' are territories contiguous to the 'Old Conquests'. See chapter two.
7. "O Pay dos Christãos mostra que tem havido grande omisão e abuso em se não aplicarem todos os meios decentes para a conversão dos gentios meus vassalos, e que sendo a principal obrigação dos Reys de Portugal tratarem com grande cuidado que se convertão por todos os caminhos mais efficazes e suaves. . ." This was written in 1715. *LFC*, fl. 66. It seems that force continued to be used till 1757. *LPC*, p. 349.
8. *DI*, XV, 96.
9. João de Barros, *Decada da Asia* I, (1945), p. 15.
10. *Doc*, VIII, 192.
11. B.R. Ambedkar, *Christianizing the Untouchables*, p. 9.
12. Peter Hebblethwaite, *In the Vatican*, p. 5.
13. Ranajit Guha, (ed.), *Subaltern Studies III. Writings on South Asian History and Society*, p. 308.

14. P.D. Xavier, *Goa, A Social History*, Preface.
15. The Portuguese people are a result of a long process of fusion of peoples and cultures. The earliest inhabitants that history could register in Portugal were the *celtas* (Celts) and the *iberos* (Iberians). The fusion of these two groups resulted in one of the biggest Iberian tribes, the *lusitanos* (Lusitanians). Hence, the term Lusitanian had been applied to the Portuguese people.
16. Francisco de Sousa, *OCJC*, P. 194.
17. *APO*, 3, pp. 76-77. The duty of the king was to favour conversions. AHU, *Registo de cartas*, Cod. 282, fl. 104.
18. *DI*, I, 100.
19. ARSI, *Miscellaneum Indiarum Orientalum*, 38 - II, fl. 296.
20. C. L. Monteiro de Barbuda, *Instrucções com que El-Rei D. José I mandou passar ao Estado da India O Governador, e Capitão Geral, e o Arcebispo Primaz do Oriente no anno de 1774*, p. 40.
21. *Ibid.*, p. 41.
22. C. R. Boxer, "The Problem of Native Clergy in the Portuguese and Spanish Empires from the Sixteenth to Eighteenth Centuries", p. 93. The Spanish king had also discovered a new world in 1492 and the Pope had in the following year given the same monopoly for subduing, trading with, and converting these lands in the west to Spain as it had to Portugal in the East. There was a clear cut demarcation between the territories of both the nations. Through the Treaty of Tordesillas of June 7, 1494, after much bargaining of the line of demarcation, it was finally agreed and decided that the boundary would be 370 leagues west of Cape Verde. When Portugal failed in its missions, *Propaganda Fide* was created and moved into the Portuguese jurisdiction as a rival to the *Padroado*. *Propaganda Fide* was an attempt to emancipate mission activity from the political and secular control.
23. Luis de Guzman, *Historia de las Misiones de la Compania de Jesus en la India Oriental, en la China y Japon (1540-1600)*, p. 16.
24. *DI*, IV, 777.
25. Luís Filipe Barreto, *Descobrimentos e Renascimento*, p. 103.
26. *Doc*, III, 203.
27. *APO*, 3, pp. 76-77.
28. *DI*, XVI, 67*, 196-97.

29. Luís Filipe F. R. Thomas, *De Ceuta a Timor*, p. 11.

30. "Se entendermos a cruzada do Infante D. Henrique, como esta de El-Rei D. Manuel, no sentido das cruzadas do século XII, é claro que não é licito classificar as suas expedições de cruzadas por lhes faltar a sansão canónica e o supremo comando religioso e ecuménico da Santa Sé. Não há duvida de que as grandes expedições dos descobrimentos, ordenadas e comandadas pelos monarcas, constituiam verdadeiras cruzadas políticas, ao serviço dos estados empenhados na defesa do Mundo Cristão ameaçado. E, por isso mesmo, foi sem dúvida que sempre a Santa Sé abençoou, honrrou e impulsionou as grandes horas dos Portugueses em Africa e na Ásia, justificando a luta contra os infiéis e cumulando os monarcas de honrras e proveitos, segundo o Direito contemporâneo." I. da Costa Brochado, "Joaquim Bensaúde e o Plano das Indias", p. 48.

31. "Alvorecera, porém, a Renascença, e os reinos cristãos da Europa começavam a ceder a uma nova concepção da vida internacional, desinteressando-se pelo império da Cristandade para se acomodarem comercialmente com os infiéis, dando origem a uma certa convivencia pacífica que esteve na base da grande revolução que viria a conceber a Idade Contemporanea. E assim Portugal terminou aquela sua missão, abandonado por todos os reinos cristãos, depois de ter sido lider da Cristandade durante mais de um século." *Ibid.*, p. 51.

32. A. de S. S. Costa Lobo, (ed.), *Mémorias de Um Soldado da India*, p. 146.

33. Joaquim Veríssimo Serrão, *História de Portugal*, Vol. III, p. 138.

34. Afonso Brás de Albuquerque, *Comentarios de Afonso de Albuquerque*, Tomos I - III.

35. *DI*, III, 358.

36. Luís Filipe F. R. Thomaz, *op. cit.*, p. 96.

37. "...as tiranias e os maos exenpros, que os nossos mesmos dão àquella gente nova na ffé... ao menos mande allguem por capitão que não seja tirano, se possa ser", said Fr. Nicolao Lanciloto in 1547. *DI*, I, 167.

38. "Os homens que veem à India, veem por levar dinheiro pera Portugal e não pera converter almas, immo impediunt com seu mao exemplo o fruyto que se cá pode fazer", wrote Fr. H. Henriques in 1546. *Ibid.*, 152.

39. *Ibid.*, XIII, 469.

40. *Ibid.*, XV, 737.
41. *Ibid.*, XII, 423.
42. J. H. da Cunha Rivara, *Ensaio Historico da Lingua Concani*, p. 29.
43. Luís Filipe F. R. Thomaz, "Descobrimentos e Evangelização. Da Cruzada à missão pacífica", p. 86.
44. Francisco de Souza, *op. cit.*, p. 142.
45. *Doc*, VIII, 68.
46. In 1585 Fr. Gaspar de Lisboa, a Franciscan, wrote, "Os Jesuitas são terriveis e porfiosos e sempre põem a sua no fito, apezar de quem querer." *DI*, XIV, 74.
47. Luis de Guzman, *op. cit.* p. 22.
48. *APO*, 3, p. 333.
49. *DI*, I, 47.
50. João Francisco Marques, "A Evangelização da India no Epistolário de Afonso de Albuquerque e S. Francisco Xavier", p. 245.
51. *DI*, XVI, 240.
52. *Ibid.*, XVII, 47*.
53. J. H. da Cunha Rivara, *op. cit.* p. 210.
54. *DI*, III, 710.
55. *Doc*, V, 437.
56. *Ibid.*, VI, 337.
57. *Ibid.*, V, 447.
58. BNL, *Reservados*, Cod. 176, fl. 114. A royal letter had forbidden religious orders to have private prisons for the local Christians. These prisons were meant for their disobedient and indisciplined religious members. *BFUP*, No. 2, pp. 210-12. *MR*, 2A, fls. 261-65.
59. *Doc*, X, 586.
60. *Ibid.*, IV, 361.
61. A. de S. S. Costa Lobo, (ed.), *op. cit.*, p. 194.
62. *Ibid.*, p. 221.
63. *Ibid.*, p. 192.
64. In 1591 a royal decree granted free medical assistance to the sick Hindus and Christians in Goa. *Doc*, I, 361. They also went to the villages to visit the Christians and to find out about their needs and

the Hindus seeing this concern for the Christians accepted to be converted. *Ibid.*, VIII, 53; IV, 453.

65. BNL, *Reservados*, Cod. 59, fl. 28.
66. "The conquest of the new lands, the subjugation of new peoples, were not among the designs of the Portuguese." "To spread Christianity to promote missionary activity among the peoples, to bring to them the message of Christ, was, as faithfully interpreted in the orders of the kings..." See Salazar's article in the *American Quarterly Review Foreign Affairs*, April 1956.
67. *Doc*, IV, 59-65.
68. João Paulo A. Oliveira e Costa, *A Missão de João de Brito*, p. 14.
69. *DI*, XIII, 421; *MR* 3B, fl. 302.
70. "At times a local merchant would be forced to buy a product he did not want and at a higher price, or to sell to the captain or other officials at a low price. Other merchants were forced to carry goods free on their ships, sometimes to places where they did not want to go. Forced loans were also frequent, sometimes secured by means of arbitrary arrests. The Portuguese forced contracts at fixed low prices on the Malabar rulers for the supply of pepper, but other merchants offered much higher prices. The merchants resisted." M. N. Pearson, *Coastal Western India*, pp. 23, 28.
71. BNL, *Reservados*, Cod. 866, fl. 14v.
72. Josef Wicki, (ed.), *LPC*, p. 66.
73. *APO*, 3, p. 5.
74. Joaquim Veríssimo Serrão, *História de Portugal*, Vol. III, p. 70.
75. "...favor e agmento da christandade e do desfavor da gentilidade e seus ritos..." *DI*, IV, 201.
76. "...mas tudo isto tentei muito bem: mas se a V. P. escreverem outra cousa hé ad captandas aures. Eu sou portugues e zeloso da honrra portugueza, e por isso mais nisto se me pode crer que a quem pretende contentar e encher orelhas de cardeaes com cousas estranhas, e isto quanto às terras." A letter written by a Jesuit, Fr. Fernando de Meneses, in 1579 to his superior-general, Fr. Mercuriano. *DI*, XI, 735.
77. "... para ele ver como o fazeis por meu mandado, avê-lo-ey *por bem e meu serviço.*" (Italics mine). Instructions of D. João III to Miguel Vaz, the vicar general of the diocese of Goa, regarding Christendom

in India in 1546. Artur Basílio de Sá, (ed.), *Doc*, III, 258-66.

78. *DI*, V, 229. "...Su Magestad está obligado en consciencia a procurar la conversión de aquella gentilidade, et ex consequenti a poner todos los medios necessarios y christianis;..." Information presented by Fr. Alonso Pacheco to the Conscience and Orders Board (Mesa da Consciência e Ordens) of his Majesty in 1581. *Ibid.*, XII, 254.

79. Paulo da Trindade, *CEO*, Part I, p. 284.

80. "Nas terras de Bardez não ha documentos que illustre como as cousas se passaram, mas não podia ser de diverso modo. Os Frades Franciscanos observantes, a cujo cargo ficou esta christandade, não foram tão curiosos de pôr por escripto os progressos e contradições da christandade." J. H. da Cunha Rivara, *Brados a Favor das Communidades das Aldeias do Estado da India*, p. 83.

81. "...reformar os costumes já tão diversos e apartados do primeiro modo e forma de viver, e tãobem lhe aprouve lembrar-se desta gentilidade da India, que nunqua ho quis conhecer nem onrar o seu sancto nome ategora, seguindo desdo principio dos tempos quasi ategora suas inormes maneiras de idolatrias e costumes tão monstruosos sem nunqua quererem obedecer à verdade e charidade de Jesu Christo Noso Senhor,..." *DI*, I, 50.

82. R. C. Collingwood, *The Idea of History*, p. 12.

83. H. Heras, "The Decay of the Portuguese Power in India", pp. 3-42. Frederick Charles Danvers, *The Portuguese in India*, I, p. xxxix.

84. *Doc*, XI, 598.

85. H. Heras, *The Conversion Policy of the Jesuits in India*, pp. 36, 42.

86. *Ibid.*, p. 51.

87. *Ibid.*, p. 57.

88. *DI*, XI, 274-75, 322.

89. Luis de Guzman, *op. cit.* p. 58.

90. ARSI, *Extracto das cousas*, 1a, fl. 21.

91. C. R. Boxer, *The Church Militant and Iberian Expansion (1440-1770)*, p. 95. Georg Schurhammer and Josef Wicki, (eds.), *Epistolae S. Francisci Xaverii*, Vol. II, pp. 108, 113.

92. Francisco Rodrigues, *Historia da Companhia de Jesus na Assistencia de Portugal. A Fundação da Provincia Portuguesa 1540-1560*, p. 521.

93. *DI*, XV, 109. Fr. G. Coentomani wrote to Claudio Aquaviva, superior-general of the Society of Jesus, in 1588, "...christianità di Salsete,..., la cui gente è molto indisciplinabile, ... Questa è quella terra ove martirizarno il nostro felice Pe. Rodolfo Aquaviva: è questa gente ordinariamente mal inclinata, ingrata, sconoscente, bassa, travagliosa a regere et incorregibile. Laonde entenderà V. P. quanto dificoltoso sea a soffrire li fastidii, disgosti, dispiaceri et discontentezze, che per loro impertinentie et basciezze ni dànno ogui giorno, senza poterli quasi mai regere et disciplinare, né ancora quelli che recevono..." "Questa relatione certa della gente di questa terra particolare do solo a V. P., perché a nessun altro screvo questo in India per non disanimar talvolta del fervore o convetto che in Fratelli tengono a tutti questi paesi di India, perché non é questo il mio intento." *Ibid.*, 120-21.

94. *Doc*, VII, 305.

95. José Pedro Machado e Viriato Campos, *Vasco da Gama e Sua Viagem de Descobrimentos* ("Relato Directo da Viagem de Descobrimento do Caminho Maritimo para a India, Segundo o Manuscrito Anonimo Existente na Biblioteca Municipal do Porto,"), pp. 112, 165.

96. João de Barros, *Decada da Asia*, I, (1932), p. 154. In 1500 Pedro Álvares Cabral also gave the Samorim the same reason that Vasco da Gama had given in 1498, for his coming to India. *Ibid.*, p. 183. Luís Filipe Barreto, *op. cit.*, pp. 133-34.

97. João de Barros, *op. cit.* p. 154.

98. *Ibid.*, p. 151.

99. João de Barros, *Decada da Asia,* I, (1945), p. 11. *Bullarium*, Vols. I-III, First Provincial Council, Acc. 1, dec. 1, p. 4.

100. João de Barros, *op. cit.*, p. 14.

101. *Ibid.*, p. 52.

102. *Ibid.*, p. 53.

103. *Doc*, I, 3, 16.

104. Fernão Lopes de Castanheda, *História dos Descobrimentos e Conquista da India Pelos Portugueses*, Livro III, p. 538.

105. Luís Filipe Thomaz and João Paulo Oliveira e Costa, "A Biblia e a Expansão Portuguesa".

106. Fernão Lopes de Castanheda, *op. cit.*, Livro I, pp. 78-80.

107. Luís Filipe F. R. Thomaz, "Descobrimentos e Evangelização. Da

Cruzada à missão pacífica", pp. 81-129.

108. In 1560 D. Catarina, the regent queen of Portugal, wrote to pope, Pius IV, on behalf of D. Sebastião, her minor grandson and future king of Portugal, "El-rei meu senhor e avô... pelo muito que desejou a conversão dos infieis dos reinos de sua conquista, parecendo-lhe que o meio para se isto alcançar, era os Padres da Companhia de Jesus... fundar na cidade de Coimbra um colegio para nele se criarem padres em exercicio de virtudes e letras que pudessem intender na conversão dos ditos reinos..." Francisco Rodrigues, *op.cit.*, p. 518. Instruction from the king to the viceroy, D. Luís de Ataíde, in 1568: the Portuguese should always keep in mind that the main purpose for discovering India was the expansion of the faith. Conversions should not be made by force or by any other scandalous methods. The viceroy was bound to encourage the missionaries, favour the neo-converts and see that there was a *Pay dos Christãos* in every Portuguese fortress. The same *Pay dos Christãos* was responsible for the churches, hospitals and houses of charity. He should not allow anyone to harass the Hindus and Muslims. He had the task of expelling the *jogues* from the island of Goa. He should see that justice was done to the Christians, Muslims and Hindus. *BFUP*, No. 2, pp. 173-75. *MR*, 1, fls. 137-47. *APO*, 3, pp. 1-26. *Doc*, X, 436-64. The main duty of the captains of the fortresses was to favour conversions stated a royal decree around 1585. *BFUP*, No. 2, p. 173. *MR*, 1, fls. 130-34. The king, D. Filipe, issued a decree to the viceroys and governors to set an inquiry at the end of their tenure to find out whether the captains of the fortresses had favoured conversions. There were several complaints against them about abuses and negligence of duties. *BFUP*, No. 2, p. 177-78. The main duty of the state was to expand Christendom, the king wrote to the viceroy, Matias de Albuquerque, in 1591. *BFUP*, No. 2, pp. 302-08. *MR*, 3-B, fls. 406-25. See the royal letter to the viceroy in 1604 on favouring the missionaries. *BFUP*, No. 3, pp. 577. *MR*, 9, 10, 11, fl. 2.

109. *Memória Histórico Eclesiastica da Arquidiocese de Goa,* (1533-1933), p. 106.

110. Justus Strandes, *The Portuguese Period in East Africa*, p. 50.

111. Luís Filipe F. R. Thomaz, *De Ceuta a Timor*, p. 174.

112. In Coulão in 1550, "Os Portugueses ca tratam em armas e cavalos... mercadorias com mouros e judeus e todo o genero de infieis, asi em tempo de paz como em tempo de guerra." *Doc*, VII, 36. Fr. Gaspar

Berzeu wrote from Hormuz in 1551, "Vicio publico em Ormuz - não haver nehuma differença entre o christão e o mouro, asi no comer como no beber, como no conversar de noute e de dia... e a christandade se avia de converter à lei de Mafamede." *Ibid.*, 74.

113. Luís Filipe F. R. Thomas, *op. cit.*, p. 214.

114. *Ibid.*, p. 385.

115. *Doc*, X, 68.

116. Joaquim Veríssimo Serrão, *A Historiografia Portuguesa. Doutrina e Critica. Séculos XII- XVI*, Vol. I, p. 169.

117. António Baião, *A Inquisição de Goa*, Vol. I, p. 41.

118. CEHU, *Documentação Ultramarina Portuguesa* I, p. 6.

119. Afonso Brás de Albuquerque, *Comentarios de Afonso de Albuquerque*, Vol. I, Part I, p. 72.

120. A. de S. S. Costa Lobo, (ed.), *op. cit.*, pp. 213, 229, 233.

121. Afonso Brás de Albuquerque, *op. cit.*, Vol. II, Part III, pp. 8, 13.

122. See the Provision for Commerce issued by D. Manuel I. Luis Fernando de Carvalho Dias, "As Ordenações da India", p. 23.

123. Joaquim Veríssimo Serrão, *op. cit.*, pp. 170-71.

124. BNL, *Reservados*, Cod. 866, fls. 8-8v.

125. A. de S. S. Costa Lobo, (ed.), *op. cit.*, p. 244.

126. During the first thirty years of the Portuguese presence in the East during the sixteenth century, about 2600 men left annually from Lisbon to India and after six months at sea many died. But the white population increased rapidly after the sixteenth century. Jaime Cortesão, *Os Descobrimentos Portugueses*, p. 177.

127. *APO*, 1, Part I, p. 85. A. R. Kulkarni, "Social Relations in the Maratha Country".

128. Georg Schurhammer, *Gesammelte Studien. Xavierana*, Vol III, p 117. Georg Schurhammer and Josef Wicki, (eds.), *Epistolae S. Francisci Xaverii*, Vol. II, pp. 118-19.

129. Fernão Mendes Pinto, *The Travels of Mendes Pinto*, p. xl.

130. *Ibid.*, p. xl.

131. Michel Vergé-Franceschi, *Henri le Navigateur. Un Découvreur au XV siècle.*

132. Alessandro Valignano, *Historia del principio y progresso de la*

*Compañía de Jesus en las Indias Orientales*, Vol. II, p. 23. George Mark Moraes, *A History of Christianity in India.*

133. J. H. da Cunha Rivara, *Ensaio Historico da Lingua Concani*, p. 29.

134. *DI*, I, 68-69.

135. *Ibid.*, XII, 95.

136. *Doc*, VII, 348.

137. *Ibid.*, VIII, 151-52.

138. Maria Benedita Araújo, "O «Pay dos Christãos». Contribuição para o estudo da Cristianização da Índia", p. 308.

139. *DI*, I, 153; XI, 296, 298.

140. Luis Filipe Barreto, *op. cit.*, p. 100.

141. *DI*, VIII, 583.

142. Strictly speaking a *Canarim* is a person of Kanara in the western coast of India. However, from the beginning the Portuguese used wrongly this term for a person of Goa. *Ibid.*, I, 13.

143. Paul D. Wiebe, *Christians in Andhra Pradesh*, p. 26.

144. *Bullarium*, Second Provincial Council, Acc. 2, dec. 10, p. 49.

145. Josef Wicki, "Missionskirche im Orient", p. 241.

146. *Bullarium*, Second Provincial Council, Acc. 2, dec. 12, p. 49.

147. *DI*, VIII, 70.

148. *Doc*, II, 188.

149. *Ibid.*, IV, 68.

150. "Os curumbis gente baixa e muito inimiga do nome christão." ARSI, *Goana Historia*, 33 - I, fl. 75v.

151. *DI*, XI, 364.

152. *Ibid.*, I, 68, 70.

153. *Doc*, IV, 560. The *tanadar-mor* (chief *thanadar*) was a district official who also collected taxes and commanded the native troops. S. R. Dalgado, *Glossário Luso-Asiático*, Vol. II, p. 353. *Lingua* was an official interpreter for the government.

154. Josef Wicki, (ed.), *LPC*, pp. 51-50.

155. *APO*, 4, p. 137.

156. Luís Filipe F. R. Thomaz, *op. cit.*, p. 11.

157. *Ibid.*, p. 99.

158. C. R. Boxer, *The Portuguese Seaborne Empire, 1415-1825*, (1973), p. 305.

159. "They were characterized by 'external conversion', meaning, changes coming from outside their culture (by the missionaries, soldiers, officials, teachers) with the exception of Korea. Korea is the only nation of Asia where the Catholic Church did not arrive with the western missionaries. Learned Korean laymen first experienced the Christian faith while visiting China; when they returned home they themselves spoke of it." Francis X. Clark, *An Introduction of the Catholic Church in Asia*, p. 16.

160. The New Testament was translated into Portuguese in 1681.

161. Mt 28: 19-20, Mk 16: 15; Acts 1: 8. When the missionaries followed the Bible its interpretation was rather literal as it was common at that time.

162. *Doc*, XI, 728.

163. João de Barros, *Decada da Asia*, I, (1945), p. 114.

164. John E. Clough, *Social Christianity in the Orient*, p. 279.

165. João de Barros, *op.cit.*, p. 129.

166. Georg Schurhammer, *Gesammelte Studien*, III, p. 90. Georg Schurhammer and Josef Wicki, (eds.), *Epistolae S. Francisci Xaverii*, Vol. II, pp. 166, 168.

167. A. de S. S. Costa Lobo, (ed.), *op. cit.*, p. 245.

168. Joaquim Veríssimo Serrão, *História de Portugal*, Vol. III, p. 95.

2

# GOA IN THE SIXTEENTH CENTURY

After reviewing some of the distant events and contexts directly related to the activity of conversion in Goa in the previous chapter, this one intends re-constructing in broad but sharp outlines the history and geography of Goa. This could help us to understand better the other circumstances surrounding conversions. The history of Goa can be told in many ways, but the purpose of this work is to narrate the story of conversions in its proper context. Goa, rather the city of Goa, was the centre of Christianization in the East in the sixteenth century. But the religious importance and character of this city, and of the entire territory of Goa under the Portuguese control then, can only be appreciated by re-creating the social, political and economic conditions prevaling in Goa at that time.

Goa was socially and economically a part of the Indian mainland, not an isolated territory and a mere Portuguese political and administrative city-centre. The historical documents show us that it was in constant conflict with, or in continued dependence on, the firm lands, namely, the Muslim and Hindu neighbouring kingdoms. Conquered in 1510, the city of Goa came increasingly under the direct control and influence of the Portuguese. But its other lands — the three adjacent small islands and the two districts of Bardez and Salcete — with a rural life of their own, and with more connections with the firm land than with the Portuguese authority, constituted the other face of Goa. The city of Goa although culturally and religiously very distinct from the Portuguese districts of Bardez and Salcete, was economically dependent on them. These two districts being less supervised by the Portuguese authority could entertain more direct commercial transactions, and have freer social dealings with their neighbouring territories. This seems to be a more realistic face of Goa.

It is obvious that the Portuguese looked for strategic lands in the East to suit their commercial interests. They conquered them if they could and then settled down there. Goa being a strategic point was no exception to this practice, despite strong reservations to its conquest and retention by the captains of the fleet commanded by Afonso de Albuquerque; and later the king of Portugal himself had shown some hesitation regarding its retention. Albuquerque conquered the city of Goa for its prosperity, defensible position and geographical location; in other words for its strategic position in the Indian ocean, but more importantly because it offered a natural shelter for the ships.[1] However, Goa was not spared from several sieges and attacks by the Adilshahs throughout the sixteenth century, and by the Dutch at the beginning of the following century.[2] In 1530 the city of Goa became the capital of the Portuguese empire in the East.

## The City of Goa

We have several references about the historical and cultural features of Goa, rather those of the city of Goa. Various documents speak about it as the most important and flourishing Christian centre in the *Estado da India*. It resembled any other city in Portugal.[3] Goa was a noble city and the biggest after Lisbon.[4] Luís de Camões, the great Portuguese poet who also lived in Goa during the sixteenth century, spoke about the beauty, nobility and celebrity of the city.[5] The missionary work started from Goa and then it spread to other parts of Asia. Goa was the entry point for every missionary destined for the lands of the *Padroado* and from here they moved out to preach the gospel elsewhere. In 1548 the city of Goa had more than fourteen churches, and by the beginning of the seventeenth century it counted fifty.[6] The first cathedral in the East was built in Goa in 1537, but the city had no Catholic bishop until this time. However, some bishops with the title of Apostolic Vicars passed through Goa and they ordained a few local candidates for the priesthood.[7]

Goa after becoming a political, diplomatic and administrative city-centre, from where the secular and religious activities in the East were directed, changed its face radically especially after the establishment of the headquarters of several religious orders here. Despite its 'splendour' and 'celebrity', a perusal of relevant texts tells us that Goa was just one more city among many others in the Portuguese network, but certainly the most enviable already in the first half of the sixteenth century. Nevertheless, this 'realistic' golden face of Goa alone can deceive us.

When the city of Goa became politically and militarily safer than Cochin, the former was officially made the capital of the *Estado da India* in 1530. Goa, as the viceroy's headquarters, had a far more elaborate administrative system than any other Portuguese possession in Asia, and the largest settlement of *casados* or Portuguese settlers, numbering around two thousand in late sixteenth century.[8]

The city was densely populated by *Canarins*, as the Portuguese used to call the Goans. The city had many houses of prayer or *pagodes* and innumerable idols. Everywhere there were huge water tanks made of bricks and tiles used by the Hindus and Muslims for their religious rituals.[9] Some sixteenth century writers and chroniclers mentioned the existence of splendid temples in Goa and pointed out how remarkable their architectural features were. Tomé Pires wrote that "the Gentiles of Goa had beautiful temples", and Gaspar Correia spoke about the "houses for their idols as huge buildings constructed with stone blocks and decorated with carvings".[10] The *Comentarios de Afonso de Albuquerque* mention that the Hindus had many respectable "temples with beautiful carvings". The Florentine, Andrea Corsali, described a temple in the island of Divar as a marvelous piece of architecture. It contained carved figures of extremely great perfection. Gomes Vaz, a Portuguese Jesuit Brother, wrote in 1567 about a washing tank, used for religious rituals, in the shape of a dome and with a porch of black stone at the entrace of the Verna temple, in Salcete. This porch, according to him, was of such beauty that it led him to state that he had never seen a work of such perfection anywhere, not even in Portugal. Some of the sculptures that belonged to these temples can be seen in the government museums in Panaji and Old Goa.[11]

The temples in Goa were maintained by the village communities or the *gaunkars*.[12] The *gaunkars* or village chiefs protected and looked after these temples. Each temple had its own rent or income that derived from the lands belonging to the temple itself, and these monies were used to maintain not only the building but also its personnel, namely from its priests to the temple dancing girls.[13] After the demolition of these temples from 1540, the Portuguese authority asked the *gaunkars* for the rents that belonged to the same temples to be used for other religious purposes. The former believed the latter were free now to do with the rents what they pleased. However, the *gaunkars* argued that according to their ancient customs these rents, once kept aside only for the sacred, could not be used for any other purpose. It is curious to note that it was only after some reluctance and certain conditions agreed upon that the Hindu *gaunkars* donated these rents for a new purpose. Certainly, the ancient custom alone could not have been the sole reason for this hesitation. Be that as it might the rents of the temples went to the churches and for the work of conversion.[14] The early documentation does not mention about any local reaction or even a weak protest against the destruction of the temples, but not long after we find decrees forbidding their repairs and construction of new ones. We know about the strong reaction and resistance put up by the locals when the temples in Salcete were brought down in the eighties of that century. The absence of local reactions to the destruction of the temples in 1540, may appear rather strange. Or were the locals content with migrating to the neighbouring territories as a sign of protest?

Due to religious persecution the local learned men, mostly Brahmans, left the city of Goa soon after the destruction of the temples. In 1545 one could see no temple standing in the city, but the presence of many Muslims, Hindus and bad Christians in the city of Goa was rather noticeable. These people did anything they wanted especially business, and we are made to believe that if it had not been for Fr. Diogo Borba the situation could have become still worse. Nevertheless, Goa looked like the city of Babylon.[15]

Chroniclers made the city of Goa a cosmopolitan place filled with people of different religions, nationalites and ethnic groups: Moorish, Turkish, Persian, Arabic, Ethiopian, Chinese and others, mostly Gentiles.[16] The presence of so many foreigners in the city made it look like the Rua Nova in Lisbon.[17] The Europeans marvelled at the gold chains and rings the Muslims and the Hindus wore.[18] The importance of Goa attracted merchants, royal funds and missionaries galore.

Life in Goa in the sixteenth century, but especially before 1540, was cosmopolitan with intense commercial traffic and religious tolerance; it was the meeting point of the three main religions and cultures. Soon it came to be known as the 'Lisbon of the East', with houses, storerooms, hospitals, churches, charitable houses that took every visitor by surprise. Goa was the heart of Portuguese India,[19] but in the face of the Muslim threat and great commercial competition in the Indian ocean, it could not hold its independence for long. It was necessary to defend the other strategic points in the Portuguese network in order to maintain the commercial importance of Goa. But it was equally necessary to acquire Bardez and Salcete — lands contiguous to the island of Goa.

## Bardez and Salcete

Bardez and Salcete, territories belonging to the Adilshah, ruler of the Bijapur kingdom, passed into the Portuguese hands in 1543. Now, the city of Goa was guarded by these two districts. Bardez and Salcete had been acquired in 1510, but they changed hands many times until 1543, as we shall see below.[20] Bardez to the north and Salcete to the south of the city of Goa were also known as the firm lands of Goa. These firm lands had not been ceded in perpetuity to the Portuguese. Rather, they enjoyed only the right to collect rents there. However, the Portuguese disregard for this arrangement and the total annexation of these lands by them could have been the cause of several sieges and attacks led by the Adilshahs on these territories.[21] Nevertheless, the political and administrative status of the city of Goa continued to grow, but so also did its dependence on the mainland. Bardez and Salcete supplied the city with rice, but most significantly they served the centre as buffers.[22]

The captains of the Adilshahs made constant incursions on these two territories of Bardez and Salcete, which resulted in much social unrest, poverty and migration. These invasions, obviously, impoverished the capital of the *Estado da India*. As mentioned earlier, the Portuguese regained from, and lost to, the Adilshahs, Salcete and Bardez several times. Soon after the conquest of Goa in 1510, the two districts of Bardez and Salcete were lost to the Adilshah in 1511; then Krishna Deva Raya, ruler of the kingdom of Vijaynagar, conquered these lands from the Adilshah in 1520, and offered them to the Portuguese in exchange for their friendship and for the status of the most favoured kingdom, or preference in the Portuguese horse trade. In 1521, the Adilshah re-captured Bardez and Salcete, but one of his captains donated them to the Portuguese in 1533. However, the same captain demanded them back in 1536. From 1543 the districts of Bardez and Salcete became definitively Portugal's possessions, but the Bijapur kingdom always continued to wage fierce attacks on Goa.

In 1548, during the rule of the viceroy, D. João de Castro, the Muslims entered Salcete but they were defeated; in 1557 Bardez and Salcete faced another attack; and once more in 1570 the Adilshah laid a siege to these lands for ten months, this being the worst attack on Goa. But the war ended with a peace treaty signed between the Portuguese and the Adilshah in 1571. Another war in Salcete in 1572 increased poverty and sent many refugees to the city of Goa.[23] In 1576 the Portuguese entered into a treaty of peace with the Adilshah, since the stability of the former's territory was at stake.[24] These peace treaties between the Portuguese and their neighbouring powers, obviously forced the former to concede many rights and privileges to the Hindus and Muslims residing in Bardez and Salcete.[25] Despite several peace and friendship treaties with the Adilshahs, at times the Bijapur kingdom attacked Goa destroying houses and churches. These wars slowed down or even impeded the work of conversion.[26]

The lands of Bardez and Salcete were very fertile. The rich Portuguese had appropriated the best lands and palm groves in Bardez.[27] But Salcete was by far the best piece of land that Portugal had in India, and with the most vibrant Christianity that the church could ever boast of in the East, wrote the Jesuit priest Francisco the Sousa in the middle of the seventeenth century.[28] However, many Hindus who did not show any willingness to be converted and succumb to the Portuguese pressures abandoned Salcete and went to live in the kingdom of the Adilshah.[29] Conversion work had begun in Salcete in the 1560s, and the Jesuits who had been entrusted with the task of converting its inhabitants met with great resistance from the locals.

## Social Relations

Social relations were organized on the basis of the village community and the temple. Joint family, caste and religion dictated personal and social relationships and those realities took precedence over other considerations such as government or civil matters. However, respect for the civil authority, even to the Portuguese local authority but especially to a distant king who might have appeared to them as their patron and protector, had become part of their social behaviour. After conforming to the joint family and its religion, the village community or caste duties determined the next most important social demands. Perhaps these realities were less graded or compartmentalized than they may appear here.

Since the beginning of the Portuguese rule till 1540, the inhabitants of Goa, Christians, Hindus, Muslims and others were allowed sufficient freedom to come from, and go to, the firm lands or the non-Portuguese territories. But from the year 1540 a new wave of religious intolerance gave rise to new social relations and distances.[30] Despite the distance the locals maintained from the local Portuguese authority, conflicts between them did exist which might have been aggravated from time to time.

The local Christians came immediately under the control and vigilance of the ecclesiastical and civil authority. According to a certain royal decree these Christians could enjoy the same rights that the Portuguese citizens or settlers in Goa did. But the Portuguese maintained colour-bar and social discrimination throughout their rule in all their colonies. As a consequence, the promised 'rights' and 'privileges' were often denied to the converts in practice. Only a few native collaborators, converts and Hindus, might have received some privileges. Nevertheless, Goa symbolized the unity dreamt by the European and Catholic rulers or the ideal of Christendom, the synthesis between the spiritual and the temporal, and the accomplishment of the search for 'Christians and spices'.

The caste system was not an obstacle to conversions since Christians and the Portuguese felt perfectly at home with it. Caste divisions were accepted as something naturally fair, and similar to the distinctions of rank and classes in Europe. The institution of caste could continue to manifest itself and to be upheld by the new local Christian community as something divinely sanctioned. The idea that it was contrary to the principles of Christianity did not find expression anywhere in the missionary historiography to the best of my knowledge. There is a certain criticism of it for being an obstacle to conversions and the cause of many relapses, but nothing suggests it as unfair in itself.

Ironically, caste rituals and 'superstitions' contributed for the increase of conversions. The Hindus who had been unwillingly converted found themselves excommunicated by their own caste members, and the following incident could confirm this point. One day while the main chief of a trade ate in his house, a Christian boy came in and began eating from the same plate the same food. The chief let the boy eat it without objecting to him, but not long after, this man went to the College of St Paul and requested the priests there for baptism. After seven or eight days he received baptism with his wife, his son, his sister and two of his sister's sons. The behaviour of the boy was sufficient to make some lose their caste, and to regain it they had to undergo many expensive ceremonies.[31] The missionaries used such caste superstitions to further their conversion activity.

Each village community had its own deities, and each village was almost self-sufficient in their idols as well. Perhaps this could account for the absence of reactions and group solidarity when the temples and the idols of the other villages or caste groups had been destroyed. In Goa during the sixteenth century the basic economic, social and religious unit was the village community, and within its confines almost every basic need was satisfied.

The structure of the Hindu cultic associations (*mazanias*) constituted by the members of the village community and organized on caste lines, helped to shape the new *confrarias* or confraternities (Christian cultic and social assistance lay associations), with caste differences equally and strongly present here. Caste continued to regulate the life of the converts, and it was strictly observed for the membership to the confraternities and for marriage, although it became diluted in informal and daily social dealings.

*Gaunkars* (village administrators) were the most respected and privileged group of persons in the village community or agricultural community (*gaunkaria*). They had the exclusive rights over the common property of the village community, and they could dispose of it for the benefit of the village. The religious cult depended to a large extent on these *gaunkars*. It was also around the village temple, at times the abode of an exclusive deity, that the *gaunkars* took political decisions. These *gaunkars* could be Christians and Hindus. They could belong to different castes but they were normally members from the high castes, namely, Brahmans, Kshatriyas and landed community. *Gaunkar* became socially synonymous with high status within the village community. And the *gaunkars* took the high caste non-*gaunkars* as their declared rivals. The privileges of the *gaunkar* did not cease with his conversion.[32]

What was the position and lifestyle of local women in Goa? From the following narrative we can guess the position of women in the Goan society. When a Hindu man died outside the island of Goa till 1545, it was a custom among them to ask his wife whether she wanted to re-marry or be left alone in the world, or die with her husband. If she did not wish to die in her husband's funeral pyre, her family members and others rejected her from their society, holding her for a woman of ill-repute. Then her only alternative would be to sell her body to make her own living and to help the works of the temple to which she was attached. If she opted to die with her husband, they gave in her honour a grand party with much wine, singing and dancing. Soon after the feast and under the effect of wine, her family and participants together with the widow dressed in silk clothes and with much jewelry round her neck and hands, proceeded jubilantly towards the field where a huge and deep fire-pit awaited her. Once here, the relatives approached the woman and snatched away each and every gold ornament she wore, and then a close relative induced the widow to jump into her husband's funeral pyre.[33] It was alleged that many-a-woman burnt herself willingly to join her husband, and not by force of circumstances or pressure from their own relatives, who wanted by all means to see a widow burning on her husband's funeral pyre.[34] But it seems that only the high castes followed this custom. It is a well known fact that Afonso de Albuquerque forbade this custom soon after the conquest of Goa.[35] Despite forbidding it, the practice of *sati* (widow burning) continued.[36] Religion and society taught categorically that through the widow burning act the sins of a *sati*'s husband would be forgiven, and both the dead would attain happiness in the next world as a result of his widow's devout sacrifice. Although many Hindu practices were retained by the converts, we do not have a single account of *sati* among the converts, but it is a fact that they abhored the second nuptials, a behaviour not appreciated by the religious and civil authority in any case.[37] There could have been a few cases of women becoming Christians to avoid *sati*.

It is beyond doubt that the Hindus collaborated militarily with the Portuguese since Goa was surrounded and attacked often by a strong Muslim force. A weak Portuguese rule here could spell the return of the undesirable rule of the Muslims over Goa. It may be recalled that the fall of the Hindu kingdom of Vijaynagar into the hands of the Muslims in 1565, might have led to the formation of new and closer alliances between the Portuguese and local Hindus.

## Economy

The economic life in Goa had flourished since the last years of the fifteenth century and it saw its best moments by the middle of the sixteenth century. The city of Goa became the main city port for importing horses from the Arabian and Persian Gulfs and exporting them to the Deccan and Vijaynagar regions. Several warring Indian kingdoms made many demands for these horses. But the Portuguese port in Goa had less commercial activity than those in Calicut and Cambay, which were also very active commercial cities on the western coast of India.[38]

The beautiful and famous port of Goa attracted ships carrying not only horses but also other merchandise from Mecca, Aden and Hormuz.[39] Goa had grown in fame already when the Muslims ruled it.[40] Its commercial activity boomed due to the contacts it maintained with several countries in Asia and Europe. Trade carried out between several Portuguese possessions in the East passed through Goa, an important entrepot. Goa was also a land of great rents.[41] Before 1510 Yusuf Adilshah, the ruler of Bijapur, used the port of Goa to 'import' women for his harem.[42] The importance of Goa can be appreciated by the Adilshahs' persistent moves to wrest it from the Portuguese.[43] Therefore, it was this commerce that gave Goa its privileged status, almost equal to that of the city of Lisbon, and helped the city to become a powerful political, administrative and religious centre.[44]

The period between 1510-1550 appears to be economically the most prosperous for the Portuguese in the *Estado da India*. Coins were not minted during this period, only foreign currency circulated in Goa. Food could be brought into the city without the payment of any excise duty, unlike during the pre-Portuguese rule in Goa.[45] Then with the minting of silver coins (*patações*) the value of foreign currency went up and as a result the price of food items too.[46] In 1545, the governor, Martim Afonso de Sousa, in order to tide over the economic crisis, devalued the local currency thus making life still more difficult for the poor. The Franciscans in Goa protested against such devaluation because of the hardships the people had to suffer.[47] By 1548 the city of Goa had become the most expensive place compared with any other Portuguese territory in India.[48]

Commerce was in the hands of Muslims and Hindus. The Brahmans were indispensable as interpreters, clerks and tax-collectors, since they had the people under their control.[49] There were taxes on village property, and additional taxes were levied on the merchants, money-changers, goldsmiths, laundrymen, fishermen, etc., and the Hindus alone were qualified to obtain the right to collect them. The Brahmans were economically the dominant group. The city and the rest of Goa, namely the small islands and the districts of Bardez and Salcete came increasingly under their control.[50] But, even if the Portuguese allied with the powerful Hindus of Goa, they together could not compete commercially with the Muslims.[51] The commercial alliance between the Christians and Hindus never appeared as a threat to the entrepreneurship of the Muslims.[52]

From 1560s the Portuguese control over the spice trade weakened as increasing amounts ran the gauntlet and reached the Red Sea safely. In response to this the Portuguese empire became more autonomous, their policy less concerned with the trade to Europe but more concentrated in increasing Asian trade without worrying too much about where the spices went. It is around this time that large-scale conversions began.[53]

The Portuguese being the enemies of the Muslims on all fronts, allied with the Hindu kings, the most powerful being that of the Vijaynagar kingdom. The Portuguese had a good deal of trade with Vijaynagar, especially of horses and satin, due to their friendly relations. With the collapse of this empire in 1564, the Portuguese position in India became highly vulnerable and economically poorer.[54] From an anonymous report written in 1568 and illustrated by several examples, we can judge the poor financial and economic situation caused by a bad Portuguese administration. The report also stated that Goa once boasting of its main factory in the *Estado da India* and of its port that attracted several ships to it, was almost empty by 1568.[55]

The archbishop of Goa, D. Jorge de Temudo, writing in 1569 on the ills affecting the *Estado da India* concluded that three factors contributed decisively to this state of affairs: first, the lack of justice on the part of the Portuguese captains and government officials, since the forts and factories, offices and cabotages did not go to deserving persons; second, the three year office term of the governors and other officials of the crown was rather too short to command respect from the *fidalgos* — the latter did not care to show any respect and obedience to the local authority; and third, the slow implementation of vital decisions affected negatively the empire's administration, and the prolonged idleness among the Portuguese soldiers resulted in their poor preparation for war. The majority of government officials misbehaved in their duties since they feared neither God nor the king. Their only preoccupation was to fill their pockets.[56] However, the missionaries were often held responsible for the decadence of the state: the missionary interference in matters where they had no jurisdiction and their imprudent anti-Hindu decrees and conversion policies contributed largely to weaken the *Estado da India*.[57]

The decadence of the *Estado da India* has been attributed to two external events too: one, the defeat and disappearance of the Vijaynagar kingdom which bought many horses, silk and other goods from Goa; and the other, the conquest of the kingdom of Cambay by the Mughals, which imported even more Portuguese goods than the Vijaynagar kingdom. The Inquisition of Goa that continuously forced the Hindus to abandon the city of Goa was also blamed for the decadence of the empire.[58] In 1585 Filipe Sassetti, a traveller, wrote that the custom house in Goa did not earn more than six thousand ducats when earlier it had a profit of 120 000 to 150 000 ducats. The Portuguese attributed the decadence of the *Estado da India* to several causes, they themselves being one of them. But its decline was inevitable, and later hastened by the arrival of rival European powers in the East.

Besides the first forty years, Goa had its best moments in the last decade of the sixteenth century, when there was no challenge to the Portuguese monopoly. But this was just a short- lived moment before the arrival of the Dutch and the English.[59] Despite several economic oscillations, this century has been considered as the most prosperous that the *Estado da India* had enjoyed, but this prosperity was more fictitious than real. The public coffers were exhausted almost always.[60] But interestingly the work of conversion did not appear to have been affected by these economic vicissitudes — prosperity or decadence of the empire — if we go by the number of conversions effected during this century, as we can conclude from the last chapter.

## The Religious Orders

The diocese of Goa was created in 1534 to look after the Christians and to increase the number of conversions; and in order to extend its authority and field of action it was raised to an archdiocese in 1557.[61] Until the diocese of Goa had a permanent bishop, the king of Portugal sent bishops to visit Goa and other parts in the East from time to time, to preside over functions such as ordination of candidates for the priesthood and sacrament of confirmation, but they had no jurisdiction over these territories. Frei João de Albuquerque, a Franciscan, became the first bishop of the diocese of Goa in 1538.[62]

Until 1540 there were very few missionaries and Christians in Goa. The Franciscans had accompanied the Portuguese in the first fleet that touched Goa, as chaplains of the crew, and it was the only missionary order with a royal blessing and official mandate to Christianize the East until 1542, the year of the arrival of the Society of Jesus in Goa. The Franciscans established and built their first monastery in Goa only in 1518. The Jesuits came to Goa in 1542 and a little later the Seminary of *Santa Fé* was offered to them. The Dominicans built their house in Goa in 1548. For greater vigilance, care, reform of local customs and obviously to increase the number of converts, in 1554-55 the Portuguese crown partitioned Goa to the major religious orders established here: the Franciscan, Jesuit and Dominican orders. Bardez fell to the Franciscans, Salcete to the Jesuits and the islands of Divar and Chorão were shared between the Jesuits and the Dominicans.[63] The city of Goa was shared among all since these religious orders had their headquarters here. Salcete and the islands of Chorão and Divar, the last being the most respected holy place for the Hindus because of the temple of Sapta Koteshwar here, were not given arbitrarily to the Jesuits.[64] With the distribution of a specific area or district to each religious order, Christianity in these territories acquired a relatively distinctive character.[65]

Besides the need to maximize the number of conversions, the increase of religious orders in Goa called for that territorial division. It was a common practice then to allot specific areas to the religious orders, a clever and necessary strategy to avoid scandals and conflicts among themselves. Conflicts existed between the Franciscans and the Jesuits.[66] When the Augustinians arrived in Goa in 1575, they were not welcomed by the other religious orders, except by the Franciscans.[67] This pragmatic arrangement of dividing and ruling as already mentioned also served to hide, not eliminate totally, the existing conflicts between the different religious orders that often vied with one another in the race for more conversions and royal funds. Nevertheless, despite this territorial division strong differences of opinion and praxis continued to emerge and exist amongst the religious orders. Besides, these religious groups did not always obey the royal orders or show themselves as good vassals of the king.[68]

## Goa Disputed

Goa had, earlier to the advent of the Portuguese, been a part of the Bijapur kingdom, whose rulers were the Adilshahs or Adil Khan or Idalcão as the Portuguese used to call them.[69] Goa located on the western coast of India, between the Muslim controlled north and the Hindu controlled southern areas, could become a decisive strategic point to halt the march of the Muslims southwards. Besides, Goa could also serve to control Portuguese trade and protect their fleet. It was clear that the Portuguese would not dare to venture deep inland since they were so few, and their force rested on the sea where they had weak rivals. The Indian rulers were stronger on land due to their cavalry, but without maritime force they found it difficult to challenge the Portuguese. For these reasons it became necessary to conquer vantage-points (islands) which had safe ports, and fertile land with plenty of water and food.[70] Besides these conditions their populations should also be open to conversion or at least to cordial relations, since without the local collaboration the retention of these regions would have been next to impossible. Conversions and collaboration would be easier in a territory inhabited by Hindus rather than by Muslims.

The assault of Goa was not a part of the Portuguese plans of conquests. Afonso de Albuquerque had no royal instruction to conquer it just as he had an explicit programme or orders to conquer Malacca, Hormuz and Aden.[71] The Hindu chiefs of Goa had written to Timoja or Timmaya, an exiled Hindu from Goa and now the admiral of the Honavar fleet, about how they were being exploited by the Muslim subjects of the Adilshah, and pledged support to Timoja in the event of him agreeing to help them to change this situation.[72] Timoja, informed by these oppressed Goan Hindus of the favourable conditions to oust the Muslims from the city of Goa, persuaded Albuquerque and his captains to conquer it.[73] The Hindus of Goa together with Timoja's party helped Albuquerque to conquer it.[74] Albuquerque was only supposed to help Timoja in exchange for a substantial fee for all favours received. However, the shrewd Albuquerque had personal plans for Goa to the disappointment of Timoja.

Was freedom for the people of Goa from the Muslim oppression the sole intention of Timoja when he persuaded the Portuguese to help him? Why should the Hindu chiefs, some of whom could also be merchants in Goa, help the Portuguese to expel the Muslims? Was it to free the people who were being over-taxed by the Muslims? Or was it because they wanted higher profits for themselves? Could material gains or losses be the main reason for a change of rulers, or could there be other reasons like local factionalism?[75] During the rule of Bijapur over Goa, the Hindus were taken into confidence by the sultan who placed them in high-profile posts in the local government. They had also the desired religious freedom. But could the help alone given by local Hindus to the Portuguese be sufficient for the latter to hold on to Goa? We cannot exclude the possibility of a great quantity of gold being offered as a bribe to the ministers of the Adilshah by Albuquerque, although such a move was not explicitly reported by any Portuguese chronicler.[76] The Adilshah consented the Portuguese to remain in Goa, but on condition that they should not interfere with the former's other coastal cities and districts.[77] After defeating the Muslims in Goa the Portuguese name might have risen high in prestige and courage in the eyes of the local Hindus. This might have created a favourable local opinion for the Portuguese to stay in Goa.

After the definitive conquest of Goa, Albuquerque demanded only taxes on the land that belonged to the *gaunkars*, which amounted to half of what was being exacted from them as taxes by the ruler of Bijapur. The Muslims also demanded taxes on the rents that belonged to the temple, but Albuquerque left untouched these rents expecting that the Hindus would convert soon after, and then they would donate the same rents to the churches of the villages and to the work of conversion.[78] However, he granted some patrimony of the mosques and temples to the main church in the city.[79]

The Hindus who had left the island of Goa earlier, due to political discontentment, on knowing that Albuquerque demanded only half of what they used to pay to the Muslims, and that he would also let their own chiefs govern their lands, returned to Goa.[80] The initial liberal Portuguese fiscal system changed the social and economic life in Goa.

The captains of the Portuguese fleet, who from the beginning had opposed the conquest of Goa did not want to retain it since they regarded it as a personal conquest of Albuquerque, undertaken without any mandate from the king.[81] He alone was convinced that if Goa could be retained the other conquered possessions in India would remain safe in the hands of Portugal.[82] Albuquerque conquered and retained Goa despite the lack of consensus and the displeasure of his captains with his plan. They often complained that Goa brought only significant losses to the crown's revenue.[83]

The king of Portugal asked Albuquerque to withdraw from Goa. When Albuquerque returned from his expedition to the Red Sea a royal order awaited him, directing him to discuss and decide about the retention of Goa in the council of *fidalgos*. The council, either influenced or pressurized by Albuquerque, decided on its retention, which decision displeased the king.[84] In 1542 and 1570 the possibility of vacating the *Estado da India* in favour of the conquest of Morocco was seriously discussed by the Portuguese intelligentsia and even in the council of the king.[85]

## Strategic and Geographical Features

In spite of the disagreements over the conquest and retention of Goa, the city of Goa, bordering the lands of Konkan and Kanara, fitted in well with the Portuguese plans for the strategic and central position of the city on the western coast of India. Its two rivers, the Mandovi and Zuari serving as natural and favourable obstacles, guarded the city of Goa against the enemy, thus making it a very defensible and safe land. The city of Goa proper, in the island of Goa, was rather small and surrounded by walls. The island of Goa had the shape of a triangle with its tip turned towards the west. It was 14.5 kilometres long, and in the east 9.6 kilometres wide from north to south. It had a coastline of 38.5 kilometres and was bounded on the north by the river Mandovi, on the south by the broad bay of the river Zuari, and on the east by a channel which connected the two rivers. This was the territory of Goa until 1542, and the rest was the firm land or land of infidels, which was a safe haven for the Hindus.[86]

It may be recalled that the boundaries of the sixteenth century Portuguese Goa grew and changed gradually until 1791 and it was only then that it acquired its definitive geographical boundaries. The total area of Goa under the Portuguese control in the sixteenth century consisted of the island of Goa or Tissuary (etimologically it means thirty villages or communities and the city of Goa is situated here), the three adjacent small islands — Divar, Chorão and Santo Estevão — and the two districts of Bardez and Salcete or the firm lands of Goa. Tissuary together with these three islands had been captured from the Muslims in 1510, and the districts of Bardez and Salcete later in 1543.[87] Other large territories or districts were added to Goa only in 1791. These new territories together with those conquered before 1544 gave the final shape to Goa, which the state of Goa still retains today. The former became known as the 'New Conquests' (*Novas Conquistas*) to distinguish them from the 'Old Conquests' (*Velhas Conquistas*) or those territories conquered and acquired before 1544. The Old Conquests covered an area of 755 square kilometres; the Old and the New Conquests together, which constitute the present geographical boundaries and area of the state of Goa, have 3701 square kilometres.

It needs to be said that there were hardly any conversions in the New Conquests, since it had been agreed at the moment of their annexation, that the Portuguese would respect the traditions and customs of their populations. The Christians who inhabit these areas today are migrants from the Old Conquests.[88] Similarly, when the city of Goa was conquered in 1510 and its Hindu population surrendered peacefully, they had also demanded respect for their privileges and ancient customs, and the right to continue to be owners of their land, although with only the duty of paying some taxes to the Portuguese crown.

## Concluding Ramarks

The *Estado da India* created to facilitate the Portuguese commercial activity, was not meant to be an empire with a large territory and population. Goa was not an exception to this. Rather without spices and Christians it was conquered merely to become a strategic space or a base for the Portuguese ships and a check point in the Arabian Gulf. The conquered territories proved vital for commerce, not for conversions. Goa was conquered to become a naval base, not a colony or the political capital and much less for conversion activity. The need for extra territory and local allies grew gradually. It is certain that the presence of many missionaries in Goa and the fixing of their residence here, contributed to make it a place very different from the rest of the lands under the Portuguese control. The need for social integration and population behaviour control led to the diffusion of Portuguese traditions, institutions and religion. The conquest of Goa had to be consolidated by the spiritual and cultural conquest of the Hindus. The superior and absolute claims made by the Catholic faith turned out to be one of the most emphatic features of the Portuguese presence overseas, but despite these often-made claims the Portuguese could not influence the local social and religious life as intended.[89] Most Hindus showed themselves firm in their religious practices and refused to be converted, but as the intention of the king in conquering these lands was conversion, then the destruction of their temples became inevitable together with abundant prohibitive legislation to ban Gentile rituals and ceremonies as the only means to increase the number of citizens for the empire.[90] With the destruction of the temples in the islands of Goa in 1540, the missionaries believed that henceforth the Hindus would be converted easily.[91]

We know that the Portuguese did not interfere with the religious freedom of the Hindus and Muslims in Diu, unlike in Goa. These differences arose from the fact that Goa came directly under the control and pressures of the local secular and religious authority, who wanted to erect it as the capital of the empire and as a Christian centre, while the other Portuguese possessions in India retained their specific character of commercial entrepots.[92] Goa had a distinct political and religious status. It was a case apart with a different project for it: a political project as well as a religious. Goa was not only the political capital of the *Estado da India*, it was also the 'religious capital' or centre, where several religious orders had their permanent headquarters and an enormous influence over the political affairs of the territory. As the capital of the empire it contained the headquarters of the viceroy, of the bishop, of the Tribunal of the Inquisition and of the *Padroado* in the East; it housed the Royal Hospital, the Santa Casa da Misericordia or the Holy House of Mercy and a great number of churches and monasteries. Goa became the official or legal entry and departure point for every Portuguese or European sailing in Portuguese ships.[93] This profile of Goa may help us to understand the issue of conversion better in chapters that follow.

## NOTES AND REFERENCES

1. João de Barros, *Decada da Asia* II, Part I, (1777), p. 469. Goa was prosperous because it was cool and fertile. Pissurlencar Panduranga, *Goa Pré-Portuguesa através dos Escritores Lusitanos dos Séculos*

*XVI e XVII*, pp. 30-35. The island was healthy but not the city of Goa during the months of May, October and November. Till 1570 Goa was healthy but already in 1552 its inhabitants had faced some health problems. *DI,* II, 607. There was a severe epidemic of cholera in 1543. In the first months of 1571 a severe fever killed many people in the city of Goa. ARSI, *Goana Historia*, 33 - I, fl. 244.

2. *Doc*, VII, 163. The Dutch had blockaded Goa for one month in 1603.
3. Conde de Ficalho, *Garcia da Orta e o seu Tempo*, p. 143. Goa was the main city in the *Estado da India*. *APO*, 3, p. 22. *DI*, II, 412.
4. Alessandro Valignano, *Historia del principio y progresso de la Compañia de Jesús en las Indias Orientales*, Vol. II, p. 41. "È molto bella, ornata di molti pallazzi e buone case, et non vi è casa che non habia giardino; è abondantissima di pane, riso, carne, vino della terra e vino di Portogallo, olio cossì della terra come de Portogallo, frutta della terra infinita, merangole, limoni e cedri sine fine, galline a un giulio l'una;..." "...tanta abondanza che non vi è negro né homo per povero che sia che non vesta al meno doi camise e doi para de calzoni la settimana, e muti lenzolo ogni 15 giorni:..." *DI*, XI, 364.
5. Luís de Camões, *Os Lusíadas*, X, 42. BNL, *Reservados*, Cod. 580, fl. 26. *APO*, 2, p. 138. Fidelino Figueiredo, "Viagens de um Florentino a Portugal e a India" (século XVI), p. 122.
6. Conde de Ficalho, *op. cit.* p. 140.
7. BNL, *Reservados*, Cod. 176, fls. 97-97v.
8. Anthony Disney, "Contrasting Models of "Empire" : The Estado da India in South Asia and East Asia in the Sixteenth and Early Seventeenth Centuries", p. 28.
9. Fernão Lopes de Castanheda, *História do Descobrimento e Conquista da India Pelos Portugueses,* Livros I-IV, p. 513.
10. Afonso Brás de Albuquerque, *Comentarios de Afonso de Albuquerque*, Vol. I, Part II, p. 116.
11. Panduranga Pissurlencar, *op. cit.*, pp. 40-42. Alessandro Valignano, *op. cit.,* pp. 34-35.
12. *Gaunkars* were the descendants of the original inhabitants of Goa. They were the owners of the land and administered it jointly. The inhabitants of the same village did not enjoy equal rights. The *gaunkar* family had more privileges and claimed them exclusively.
13. The rents of the temples were spent on their personnel: priests,

dancing girls, Brahmans, ironsmiths, carpenters, washermen, jesters, barbers, shoemakers, painters, etc. *DI*, I, 764.

14. *Doc*, X, 229.
15. "Porque se bem oulhais, hachareis que poucos vão da India ao paraisso, assi brancos como pretos, senão os que morrem de 14 anos pera baixo." ARSI, *Eppistolae Goana et Malabarica*, 10 - I, fl. 3.
16. *Doc*, VIII, 53.
17. *DI*, III, 114.
18. *Ibid.*
19. A. de S. S. Lobo Costa, *Memórias de Um Soldado da Índia*, p. 237.
20. We cannot exclude the fact that Bardez and Salcete were given to the Portuguese as a goodwill gesture. The Adilshah expected the Portuguese to hand over to him Meale, the Adilshah's rival and claimant to the Bijapur throne, whom the Portuguese had given political asylum and protection in Goa. *Doc*, IV, 407.
21. "Com esta vos mamdo huma carta minha pera o Ydallcão de agradecimentos da boa vontade que tem pera minhas cousas, e da com que me allargou aquellas terras firmes, e oferecemdo-lhe a minha amizade, como veres pelo trellado dela que vos emvio;..." Letter of D. João III to the viceroy, D. João de Castro. Almeirim, 8 March 1546. *Doc*, III, p. 273.
22. The subjects of the Adilshah, in Bardez and Salcete, complained to him about the ill-treatment they suffered under the Portuguese, including the destruction of their houses. This made the Adilshah lease Bardez and Salcete so that their inhabitants could live in peace. On the other hand the Portuguese also needed these territories to supply food to the city of Goa. Instituto de Investigação Científica Tropical, *Colecção de São Lourenço*, III, p. 415. "Ha hy jente nesta terra de tam mao jazigo e tão pesima inclinação que de graça folgam de dizer mall e espalhar mas novas e numqua estão senão escontra dezendo ao bem e porem ja alguns confessão que Guoa nam tem necessidade do Idalcão nem das terras firmes e se ho pam e pequeno e hay falta de vaquas que a culpa he dos que regem a cidade que com nome de reger fazem sua fazenda e emcarecem ha terra." Letter of Fr. Pero Fernandez, vicar general of the Archdiocese of Goa, to the viceroy, D. João de Castro. Goa, February 1547. *Ibid.*, p. 512.
23. ARSI, *Goana Historia*, 31 - I, fl. 247.

24. *Doc*, XI, 330. The Portuguese made peace with the Adilshah in 1575. Diogo do Couto, *Decadas da Asia*, IX, cap. xxvii.
25. Rodrigo José de Lima Felner, *Subsídios para a História da India Portugueza*, Vol. V, pp. ii, 34-43.
26. *Doc*, XI, 490. ARSI, *Goana Historia*, 31 - I, fl. 271v. Ismail Adilshah of Bijapur, from whom Albuquerque had conquered Goa, died in 1534, but the intrigues for his succession were already afoot in 1532. He had two sons, Mulu Adilshah and Ibrahim Adilshah, both equally worthless, who in turn succeeded him; but there was a strong party in the state who favoured Ismail's brother, Mir Ali. At the head of this party was a powerful nobleman originally a slave, called Yusuf of Lar who had received the title of Assad Khan and had made Belgaum his headquarters. The land on the mainland at the back of Goa was within his jurisdiction, and to purchase the assistance of the Portuguese he allowed them to occupy Salcete and Bardez, they agreeing to support Mir Ali. But the Portuguese overstepped their bounds by building a fort in Rachol.

    After the death of Ismail, Mir Ali for a time fell into disrepute and Assad Khan joined his master Ibrahim Adilshah against the Portuguese; pressure was then brought to bear to make them restore the two districts. A war continued between both for some time. When Nuno da Cunha, however, in 1538, blew up the Rachol fort, the war ended with the temporary evacuation of the two districts of Salcete and Bardez. R. S. Whiteway, *The Rise of the Portuguese Power in India 1497-1550*, pp. 231-34. It was not until December 1542, that these two district passed definitively into the hands of the Portuguese.
27. *Doc*, IV, 176.
28. Francisco de Sousa, *OCJC*, pp. Introduction, xvi. The district of Salcete had been given to the Jesuits for the work of conversions.
29. J. H. da Cunha Rivara, *Brados a Favor das Communidades das Aldeias do Estado da India*, p. 82.
30. Conde de Ficalho, *op. cit.*, p. 141.
31. *Doc*, VII, 353. *DI*, VIII, 339.
32. Leopoldo da Rocha, *As Confrarias de Goa. Séculos XVI - XX. Conspecto Histórico-Jurídico*, pp. 364-66, 375. "Feudalism in Goa, as apparently in the rest of India, is a survival of the Mohammedan period. In the old conquests, it does not exist; for the Mohammedan

period that lasted only from Yusuf Adil Shah in 1482 to the final victory of Albuquerque in November 1510. To this fortunate accident, the Old Conquests owe the survival of the community form of settlement which also extended to the New, but with feudal overlapping." D. D. Kosambi, *Myth and Reality*, p. 159.

33. *Doc*, IV, 35.
34. *DI*, X, 736. A Hindu widow had hardly any option but to perform *sati*. However, this practice depended on her status.
35. Afonso Brás de Albuquerque, *op. cit.*, Vol. I, Part II, p. 116.
36. *Bullarium*, Third Provincial Council, Acc. 2, dec. 11, p. 67.
37. J.H. da Cunha Rivara, *Ensaio Historico da Lingua Concani*, (1858), pp. 255-59.
38. Zinadim, *Historia dos Portugueses no Malabar*, p. xxviii.
39. *Ibid.*, p. 108. Fernão Lopes de Castanheda, *op. cit.*, Livro III, p. 513.
40. Panduranga Pissurlencar, *Goa Pré-Portuguesa através dos Escritores Lusitanos dos Séculos XVI e XVII*, p. 10.
41. João de Barros, *Decada da Asia* II, Part I, (1777), p. 453.
42. José Correia Souto, *Dicionário de História de Portugal*, Vol. III, p. 182.
43. João de Barros, *op. cit.*, p. 470. Albuquerque informed the Adilshah, who wanted Goa back, that he would not hand it over for any price in the world. Afonso Brás de Albuquerque, *op. cit.*, Vol. I, Part II, p. 200.
44. Raquel Soeiro de Brito, *Goa e as praças do norte*.
45. *APO*, 2, pp. 14, 142.
46. *Ibid.*, 217.
47. *Doc*, III, 279-80.
48. *Ibid.*, IV, 184.
49. Georg Schurhammer, *Francisco Javier. Su vida y su tiempo*, Vol. II, p. 295.
50. M. N. Pearson, *Coastal Western India*, p. 96.
51. *Doc*, I, 214. Raymundo Antonio de Bulhão Pato, *Cartas de Afonso de Albuquerque*, Vol. I, pp. 306-07. The Hindus and the local Christians could not compete commercially with the Muslims. AN\TT, *CC* I, Maço 16, Doc. 74.

52. The Hindus of Coromandel and the Gujaratis were great businessmen and dealt with huge capital.

53. M. N. Pearson, *op. cit.*, pp. 82-83.

54. António Pinto Pereira, *História da India em que a Governou o Visorei Dom Luís de Ataíde*, p. 35. Diogo do Couto, *op.cit.*, VIII, cap. xv, pp. 93-94.

55. António Pinto Pereira, *op. cit.* pp. 26-27.

56. Letter from the Archbishop of Goa, D. Jorge de Temudo, to the king. ARSI, *Miscellaneum Indiarum Orientalum*, 38 - II, fl. 246. António Pinto Pereira, *op. cit.* pp. 26-27. "E crea Vosa Alteza que nam he sem rezam que todos Portugueses mudam nesta terra a calidade e naçam e se fazem conformes a terra no modo de viver que nam querem senam seguir a sensualidade, dizendo: 'pera que vym a India, senão pera apanhar, e se restituir, ficarey em camisa'. Com esta entençam partem de Portugal e asi o seguem, que de todolos estados e condições que digo a Vosa Alteza, meu ver fraco que a India vay de monte a monte, que nenhuma pesoa vem pera servir Vosa Alteza nestas partes, somente com intento de seu interese, e as pesoas que ora vem de la nestas armadas todas vem pera bodas, sem armas, vistidos ricos, muitas bolsas grandes de veludo. Nam se pode manter asi a India, mas com armas e batalhas continuas, porque asi como se ganhou por forte guerra, asi se vay perdendo por nossa fraqueza, que poucas sam as somanas que nam matem dos nosos." Report of the bishop of Dume to the king. January 1522. *Doc*, I, 446.

57. Rodrigo José de Lima Felner, *op. cit.*, p. xx. A. de S. S. Costa Lobo, (ed.), *op. cit.*, p. 26.

58. Glenn J. Ames, *Renascent Empire?*, p. 60.

59. C. R. Boxer, *op. cit.*, p. 13.

60. Rodrigo José de Lima Felner, *op. cit.*, p. vi.

61. The dioceses of Malacca and Cochin were created then. Soon Goa came to be known as the 'Rome of the Orient' for its churches, monasteries, ecclesiastical establishments, and as a spiritual centre of Christendom. Through the bull *Aequum reputamus* the pope, Paul III, erected the diocese of Goa in 1534, before part of the diocese of Funchal. Georg Schurhammer, *Francisco Javier. Su vida y su tiempo*, Vol. II, pp. 144-45.

62. Georg Schurhammer, *Francis Xavier. His Life, His Times*, Vol. II, p. 146.

63. *APO*, 3, p. 825. *DI*, III, 350. *Doc*, VI, 48.

64. Panduranga Pissurlencar, *op. cit.*, p. 9.

65. *MR*, 2B, fl. 470. In 1554 the viceroy, D. Pedro de Mascarenhas, entrusted the city of Goa and its adjacent islands to the Franciscans, Jesuits and Dominicans to continue the work of conversion.

66. *DI*, XVI, 73-74.

67. BNL, *Reservados*, Cod. 59, fl. 7v.

68. J. H. da Cunha Rivara, *Ensaio Historico da Lingua Concani*, p. 29.

69. "As terras que eram dos gentios não foram tomadas pelas armas, mas entregues por concertos, que o grande Afonso de Albuquerque fez com elles quanto tomou Goa a 1ª e 2ª ves no ano de 1510. E declarando que só aos mouros fazia guerra, e a elles deitou primeiro da Cidade, e nelles depois os pos de sua espada, e da mesma maneira forão entregues as de Salsete ao Governador Martym Affonso de Souza no anno de 1543, quando o Idalcan voluntariamente lhas ofereceo, e entregou ficando huãs e outras correndo com o foro, que primeiro pagavam aos reys Gentios e Mouros em respeito dos que nunca forão bens de sua Coroa, tirando o foro..." ARSI, *Fundationes Goana*, 22 - I, fls. 59-59v. "Os da parte contraria dizem que estas terras foram conquistadas varias vezes pelas armas portuguesas no que dizem verdade, mas estas conquistas e guerras foram feitas aos mouros por pelhirem estas terras tiranicamente, porém os naturais da terra que são os canarins nunca pegaram espada contra os portugueses antes se entregaram pacificamente com declaração que lhe guardacem seus privilegios e costumes antigos os que eram serem eles senhores de suas terras pagando o foro a El-rey. Dizem mais que os Reis de Idalção fizerão doação a el-rei de Portugal de todas as ditas terras he verdade mas foi com declaração que se guardacem todos os costumes contigos os quais heram ficarem os Canarins com suas terras pagando somente o foro a el-rei." ARSI, *Fundationes Goana*, 22 - II, fls. 407, 415.

70. A. de S. S. Costa Lobo, (ed.), *op. cit.*, p. 233.

71. Malacca, the source of spices, was conquered in 1511 for being a strategic point in southeast Asia. Hormuz, in the Persian gulf an important road of commerce between the Indian Ocean and the Mediterranean Sea, was conquered in 1515. Hormuz was important since this island was a stop and shop for all the products and riches from Europe and Asia. Afonso de Albuquerque had conquered

both these territories. But the Portuguese failed to conquer Aden, another strategic point in the Red Sea, which controlled commerce that passed through it towards the Mediterranean Sea. The Portuguese crown had planned the conquest of Malacca and of those two strategic points in Red Sea as a final blow to the Muslim supremacy and their spice business. Joaquim Veríssimo Serrão, *História de Portugal*, Vol. III, pp. 117-18.

72. Afonso Brás de Albuquerque, *op. cit.*, Vol. I, Part II, pp. 104-05.
73. *Ibid.*, p. 102.
74. *Ibid.*, p. 166. João de Barros, *Decada da Asia* II, Part I, (1777), p. 430.
75. A. K. Priolkar, *The Goa Inquisition*, p. 61.
76. Zinadim, *op. cit.*, pp. 79, 100.
77. *Ibid.*, p. 110.
78. *DI*, I, 758.
79. Afonso Brás de Albuquerque, *op. cit.*, Vol. II, Part III, p. 50.
80. *Ibid.*, Vol. I, Part II, p. 155.
81. Luís Filipe F. R. Thomaz, *De Ceuta a Timor*, p. 182.
82. Afonso Brás de Albuquerque, *op. cit.*, Vol. II, Part III, p. 18.
83. *Ibid.*, Vol. I, Part II, p. 276. *Ibid.*, Vol. II, Part III, p. 50.
84. R. S. Whiteway, *op. cit.*, p. 158.
85. Luís Filipe F. R. Thomaz, *op. cit.*, p. 190.
86. *Terra firme* (firm land) was the pagan land to the north, south and east of Goa with its temples, idols, sacred tanks, custom of *sati*, dancing-girls and all sorts of idolatry.
87. One should not confuse the Salcete of Goa with the Salsette of Bassein which is an island, situated near Mumbai (Bombay).
88. During the eighteenth century when the Portuguese power was in its decline and the Maratha empire was emerging powerfully, the city of Goa needed more protection. The Portuguese decided to increase its territory upto some natural boundary. The newly acquired regions were known as the 'New Conquests'.
89. João Paulo Costa, "A colonização portuguesa na Asia", pp. 158-79.
90. *Doc*, II, 293ff.
91. *DI*, I, 759.
92. Luís Filipe F. R. Thomas, *op. cit.*, p. 253.

93. The Royal Hospital founded in 1511, was only for the Portuguese. The 'Hospital dos Pobres' or the Hospital for the Poor or local people was built later. The 'Casa de Misericordia de Goa' founded in 1516-17, helped the poor and the needy.

The monsoon determined the sailing of the ships. In September, at the close of the rainy season of the southwest monsoon, the fleet usually arrived in Goa from Portugal.

# 3

# THE IDEA AND PRACTICE OF CONVERSION

## Conversions - continuity and change

Terms such as 'conversion' (*conversão*), 'Christendom' (*cristandade*), 'making Christendom' (*fazer cristandade*), 'faith' (*fee*), 'planting the faith' (*plantar a Fee*), 'spiritual conquest' (*conquista espiritual*) and the 'affair of conversions' (*negocio da conversão)* appear several times in Indo-Portuguese historical sources under our review. Some terms other than these used in recent historiography of conversions are modified versions of these words. Besides considering the ideological and emotional force of these terms, the 'issue of conversions' needs to be understood with reference to other concepts and projects of the time, for instance,'idolatry', 'superstitions', 'impediments', 'good customs', 'Gentilism', 'infidels', 'demons worship', 'decrees and privileges in favour of Christendom', 'expansion of Christendom', unity of the 'faith and empire' and, of course, the famous project of search for 'Christians and spices'. These concepts or expressions appear together very often in the writings of the sixteenth century. Narrations on conversion have them galore.

Politically motivated or induced conversions are as old as Christianity itself. This kind of conversion became very common and socially acceptable since the state and the church officially joined hands or began working to strengthen the bond between the temporal and the spiritual realms, efforts which go back to the Roman

Empire of Constantine. The boundaries between these two powers, the state and the church, or their jurisdiction faded away. One authority would intrude into the affairs that did not concern them without any serious confusion and friction. So, whether conversions were politically or spiritually motivated was not an issue here, provided these conversions reinforced that alliance. This pragmatic arrangement between the temporal power of the emperor and the spiritual authority of the pope and bishops, this visible politico-religious alliance, dominated the medieval European history and activity. This state-church alliance gave rise to Christendom meant to sustain and expand the faith and empire. However, this single project did make double demands on those who came within the purview of Christendom. Union of powers was fundamental for the unity and defence of the faith and empire in the face of the barbarian and Muslim threats to Europe. Conversions became the most satisfactory means, and a common project for both the state and the church to achieve this unity and their own political defence. Conversions created a citizenry for the empire and the Faithful for the church, and conversely these citizens expanded Christendom and the converts strengthened the empire. The 'project of conversion' could not become a reality without the 'expansion of the empire' and vice-versa. The unity of the faith (orthodoxy) would not be possible without a strong empire (Catholic citizenry).

Although this unity had been threatened and broken often by external forces, like the barbarian and Islamic invasions in the course of centuries and later by the Protestant revolt, the idea of the unity continued to impose itself on Europe as its most urgent project. The discoveries and conquests only reinforced the European dream of unity. On the other hand, the close cooperation between the nation-states and the church helped the European countries of Renaissance to sustain their discoveries and spiritual conquests respectively. The Provincial Councils or Ecclesiastical Meetings that took place in Goa during the sixteenth century, the decrees issued by the home and local governments, the Inquisition and the *Padroado* were the main expressions of, and the means for, achieving the spiritual conquest and the unity referred to earlier. Levelling down of cultures, racial prejudices, ethnocentric attitudes, political pressures on the conquered, etc., efforts to convert the Hindus and Muslims (and the Protestants) and the execution of the common project of the unity (of the faith and empire) became the normative obsession of Portugal at this time. Even when the international political discourse began changing, the Portuguese crown and *Padroado* continued to adhere to their public discourse on the monopoly of duties and rights always in the name of the unity and expansion of the faith. Hence, continuity or conservatism rather than change characterized the idea and practice of conversion during the sixteenth century. The duty and urgency to expand the faith, so fundamental to teach 'good customs' to the locals, find frequent echoes in the Portuguese writings of the century under consideration.

There were also threats to this unity and expansion from within. Christendom as a joint venture was not an alliance without internal conflicts. Conflicts existed between the papacy and emperors or kings. Such disturbances in the state-church relations could halt the march of Christendom. They could prevent Christendom from achieving the desired results and delay the unity they planned to work together for. Favourable proselytizing or conversion policies depended on the cordial dealings between the state and the church, but by and large, agreement rather than conflict dominated this arrangement.

The common project between the state and the church which we have been dealing with was explicitly symbolized and concretely carried out overseas as search for 'Christians and spices'. The project of search for 'Christians and spices' brought the Portuguese state and the church together, and they remained together. When the Portuguese came to Goa and decided to stay here, they had weighty reasons to support Christendom and lay tall claim to their *Padroado* rights. Moreover, the government and the clergy had to sink internal differences in the face of hostile non-Christian forces. They had to make compromises with the local groups as well.

Everywhere the Portuguese went they found Hindu kingdoms and, to their surprise, many more Muslims than they ever wanted to see. This unpleasant surprise forced the Portuguese to review their original plan of 'finding Christians' — as their collaborators in the wars against the Muslims — to 'making Christians' or converting Hindus, and if possible the Muslims too. The Portuguese changed some of their preconceived ideas and began making converts to create a new citizenry for the empire or Christendom. But the idea of the unity and expansion of the faith remained unchanged . Trading with, and converting the Hindus to the faith, became the mission of the Portuguese. Later, despite the decline of trading possibilities for the empire, the missionary did not abandon the old discourse on the orthodoxy and unity of the faith. Rather it had to be shown convincingly to the other rival European nations that the Christian unity and conversions did not depend on any economic consideration or success.[1]

When the king D. Manuel declared himself 'master' of conquest, navigation and commerce, — a claim meant to be *de jure* and *de facto* — he had in mind the other rival European nations. The monarch wanted to convey to them the Portuguese exclusive right to commercial activity in the East. This declaration or claim excluded all others who could become a threat to the Portuguese interests and their Christian duties overseas, or to that single project now with stronger nationalistic features. This was a political claim with spiritual overtones. The *Padroado* was also a claim of exclusiveness of rights (and duties), especially with regard to a space interdicted to the unauthorized clergy, who could become potential danger for Christendom. This was a spiritual claim with political interests.

The church of Rome, through the popes and by its divine right, claimed jurisdiction or authority over all men and women in the world. The church thought of itself as having the legitimate right and duty to spiritually govern, teach and administer the sacraments through its agents of conversion (king and missionaries).[2] Likewise, the *Padroado* claimed spiritual jurisdiction over everybody in the Portuguese-controlled territories and beyond; and men and women in this 'area' were considered, *de facto* or symbolically, vassals of the king of Portugal.[3]

The Lusitanian official ideology underlining the 'idea and practice of conversion', therefore, cannot be simply reduced to a statement, for example, that the Portuguese wanted to convert in order 'to make vassals' to expand and sustain their empire. That ideology stated rather, that all peoples living in the Portuguese lands were already vassals of the crown much before their conversion.[4] Nevertheless, the Portuguese believed that they had the duty to make all the vassals of Portugal embrace the Christian faith, which religion in turn would give the latter the necessary protection and corresponding privileges. The vassals had to accept the 'religion' of their 'patron'. Moreover, the Portuguese also understood that only conversions could make the Hindu-vassals 'total vassals' or loyal citizens for the empire.[5] In short, conversions would give glory to God, health to souls and honour to Portugal, the patron of conversions. The more the Hindus received the faith of Christ the greater could be the power of the 'master' over his vassals and barbarian nations.[6] He could hold on to the empire with Christian vassals rather than with Muslim and Hindu ones.[7] Service to God and state were inseparable. The kings of Portugal had simultaneously become the 'masters' of, and 'patrons' in, the newly conquered lands.

The 'idea of conversion' did not have a fixed meaning. Continuity and shifts in conversion policy and praxis depended on the state budget, political needs of the *Estado da India*, local reactions to conversion, and on the church-state agreement. Continuity and change do not refer only to the methods used to effect conversions. The moral, juridical and theoretical reasons presented to justify conversions and methods of conversion did change to a certain extent during the sixteenth century. 'Conversion' was not a *fait accompli*, it was rather a process with continuity, changes, successes and drawbacks or relapses. As seen earlier, therefore, conflicts between the state and church, local collaboration or lack of it, the moods of the missionaries, the changing international situation, spontaneous reactions and planned opposition to the Christian faith contributed to changes in the 'idea and practice of conversion'.[8]

'Conversions' or *fazer cristandade* was a religious as well as a socio-political act.[9] First, conversions meant simply baptizing. Reform of Hindu customs was thought of as a natural and spontaneous consequence of baptism. Later, the act of accepting or receiving baptism implied compulsory reform of unchristian local habits. This new Lusitanian demand created a vast body of juridical sanctions and legislative measures. European Christian forms were imposed on the local Christians forcing them to abandon radically and immediately all inherited 'idolatry' and 'bad customs'. Conversion to the faith and conversion to the European culture was obligatory, a double demand indeed.

Idolatry became such an offence to God to the extent of prompting the king to eliminate it from his lands as his main duty. Innumerable decrees were passed forbidding idols, temples and practices related to idolatry. Severe penalties could be awarded to those who flouted these decrees or were proven guilty.[10] But it was equally imperative to avoid any missionary activity that could harm the interests of the state, or any act or behaviour that could scandalize the locals. Harsh methods of conversion could make the Hindus hostile to the new faith and to the Portuguese rule. However, some zealous viceroys and governors thought that by converting the Hindus even by force, they were rendering a great favour to the crown, state and God.

Portugal's missionary activity consisted in bringing civilization to others by means of reform of customs (*reformação dos custumes*). No one could be saved but by the law of Christ.[11] The Portuguese overseas had also to be instructed to live in such a manner as not to create scandals to the Hindus by their loose lifestyle.[12] The new moral and social conduct, expected from the Portuguese vassals overseas, affected the Portuguese, the converts, the Hindus and the Muslims alike. But despite a large and unambiguous legislation to favour compliance with the new social and moral order, we do not see these efforts producing the expected results.

During the Renaissance period the 'idea and practice of conversion' consisted in teaching the 'conquered other' a set of values, a morality and social norms of the 'master'; but it also implied that the 'patron' of conversions had to defend the Christians, and this was done through several institutions as well. The *Pay dos Christãos*, one of the basic institutions of Christendom, was the *Pai dos Nativos* (father of the natives), whose duty was that of protecting the converts against the ambitious schemes of, and ill-treatment by, the *reinóis* over them. The *Pay dos Christãos* was a government official with vast civil authority. He had the duty of supervising whether any local Christian was being victimized either by the Portuguese or Hindus. He had also the task of attending to their complaints and processing them.

New social institutions had to be created in Goa to integrate the Hindus who after their baptism might have to abandon their families, communities and caste — serious problems indeed of social integration. What sort of social mechanisms were devised to re-integrate the converts into society? Besides introducing a new method of large-scale conversions which solved to a certain degree some post-baptismal problems of the local Christians, there were also a number of institutions, some with the sole aim of providing them with social servives. There were also stringent decrees in favour of conversions.[13] That mass conversions facilitated the survival of some old social relationships is more than established. Group conversions allowed the individual and family converts to retain their caste and previous status. But it is equally proved that the converted group lost, to a great extent, their old cultural links by separation from the Hindu mainstream. This was due to the new relationships and demands that conversion imposed on them, and to the socio-economic structures the converts now depended upon. It was more so at the initial stage when as catechumens, neophites and converts, they were more supervised by the religious authority. Before baptisms *en masse* began, the local Christians who were rather few were very timid and felt unsafe.[14]

The crown, the civil authorities and the clergy excluded in principle forced conversion of adults, but the same did not hold good in cases of Hindu and Muslim orphan boys in the territory of Goa.[15] The story of conversions as narrated by the missionaries denies any use of force in converting individuals, entire families or villages.[16] Every accusation levelled against the missionaries about the use of force in conversions met with stiff refutation creating an embarassing situation for the plaintiff.[17] However, it is curious to observe that guards accompanied the priests and religious Brothers to the villages, when they went out to gather some people for baptism, in order to prevent any Hindu protest and unrest.[18]

When a Hindu showed some desire to be converted, the missionaries cut his *xenddi* (hair-tuft) and made him eat food cooked by the Christians, thus closing the door for him to change his mind.[19] At times the Portuguese served the Hindus with wine without the latter's knowledge.[20] They also snapped or urged the Hindus to snap their sacred thread.[21] To take away the sacred thread from a Brahman and sandal paste from his forehead could mean loss of caste.[22] Witchcraft and superstitions related to objects they wore around their neck had to be dishonoured and discarded.[23] On the other hand, if the Hindus sought baptism only to receive material favours such a request was not refused, since it was also another natural means God used to bring them to his church.[24] Religious motives could have little or no share at the initial stage of one's conversion. Nevertheless, the missionaries believed that political and material favours could not be more than just indirect incentives and factors to lead them to baptism. The missionaries held that it was only the 'divine grace' that made them Christians in any case.[25] Ironically, however, they had no doubt that 'good Christians', those without any memory of their former beliefs and without syncretic socio-religious habits but with solid devotional practices, would be a reality only in second or third generation of converts.[26]

The converts underwent an external cultural change. They were baptized with European Christian names, since no Hindu name was permitted among them.[27] A new dress code for convert men and women came into effect.[28] The local Christian men were strictly forbidden to keep long hair.[29] Food habits certainly altered. But attitudes, values, customs, language, beliefs and habits of a lifetime changed more slowly. Christianization of the names, body, dress, food, speech and the emphasis on new forms of thinking, together with more social equality and different ritualisms, might have triggered off a crisis among the first converts, rather than a sense of security and improvement. Some of these new features aimed at distinguishing and separating the Christians from the Hindus, for reasons of security of the state as well as of orthodoxy of the faith. There was also a dress code for the Hindus, paradoxically to make them less Hindu like but at the same time to be able to identify them more easily, so much so, that some Hindus cut off their *xenddi* not to be recongnized as such.[30] Besides acquiring a new cultural and theological identity the neo-converts came under a new juridical context. The converts came within the purview of the Portuguese law, duties and privileges.

The number of conversions depended on whether the viceroys and governors favoured or not the religious orders. Some viceroys and governors showed themselves very favourable to the religious orders and their activity of conversion. They gave them promptly the rents from the temple lands that had been alloted for the work of conversion. But generally, despite royal instructions to the viceroys and governors to favour conversions, the practice differed.[31] The despotism and violence of the viceroys, governors and captains who were least interested in conversion, became chronic as far as the the missionaries' complaints go.[32] For about ten years before the arrival of D. Afonso de Noronha (1550-1554), the viceroys had neglected the conversion of the Hindus.[33]

The convert was not necessarily the conquered and the subdued. The old and the new converts from the élite allied with the rulers to control others, Christians or Hindus. It is erroneous to think that the converts formed a homogeneous group and the Hindus another, or that these two groups were hostile to each other. It is well known that some moneyed Hindus allied with the Portuguese to compete with the Muslim merchants.

Scholars have approached the question of conversions from different angles, and their arguments and conclusions depend on their ideological, philosophical or theological perspective. Conversion can be understood as a response or act that requires persuasion, or as a free commitment, or as an involuntary act influenced or imposed by the social and political changes, or as an inherited factor, or as a result of divine grace. Whatever be the case, conversion produces new and visible forms of being and feeling in the convert, which are regulated by a new value system, doctrines, expected behaviour or norms of conduct, emotions, self-perceptions, etc.[34]

Generally, when we speak of conversions today it means some interior change operated by the grace of God and without material considerations, pressures or fear. In fact this has been the idea or doctrine of religious or Catholic conversion in any century. But speaking of Christendom or 'making conversions' during the colonial period, as in Goa during the sixteenth century, and 'making converts' from among peoples who already had a religion older than that of the proselytizers, the 'idea and practice of conversion', obviously, is not the same as that of today. We should also recall that Goa was not totally free from other proselytizing influences, since the Muslims and Jews were equally interested in converting the Hindus, even by buying or circumcising them.[35]

Therefore, conversion here becomes more complex and polemic. This sort of conversion is not a mere issue of personal convictions. It could offer them several economic and juridical opportunities denied by the traditional community. The locals had their own social and religious taboos to defend, but they had also to protect their own personal economic interests. Hence adjustments could have been necessary. The élite groups had much more to lose or gain, by embracing Christianity, and they might have found themselves before a greater dilemma. Therefore, for both the groups — the missionary and convert — the 'idea of conversion' would not always match with the 'practice of conversion': the missionaries made compromises and the local converts brought in their ancestral practices and beliefs by the back door.

This 'idea and practice of conversion' can help us to appreciate what happened during the sixteenth century in Goa when the people were made to move out of one religious community into another. This process had its 'betweens' and 'asides' which cannot be overlooked. It had its opponents and collaborators. But most importantly the 'affair of conversion' had its own theological — the Lusitanian empire had a divine mandate to civilize or convert the Gentiles and infidels — and philosophical justification, claims to be made and goals to be achieved.[36] The 'idea of conversion', with its ideal of the unity of the faith and empire as its main corollary, justified the 'practice of conversion', the Portuguese ideology of discoveries, their praxis, conquests, expansion and presence in their territories overseas.

## Origin of Christianity in Goa

The history of Christian conversions in Goa began with the arrival of the Portuguese here. No traces of Christianity or any material evidence of its memory was found in the land in 1510. However, from the conversion point of view one cannot speak about Goa as a stagnant or sleeping society, and then rudely awakened by the Portuguese. Before the Portuguese arrival there had been conversions to Buddhism and Islam in Goa.

The question about the presence of Christians in Goa before 1510 seems to be a settled one. The finding of a crucifix and of a copper-plate with an inscription mentioning a trinity soon after the conquest of Goa, has not been accepted as a historical evidence for the existence of a pre-Portuguese Christian community here. The copper-plate does not refer to the Christian Trinity as it was believed, but to the Hindu Trimurti.[37]

João de Barros, the Portuguese official chronicler writing in the sixteenth century, suggested that in early times, before the coming of the Portuguese, Goa had a Christian community which probably went back to the apostle St Thomas. He based this argument on the same findings. In the seventeenth century Sebastião Gonçalves argued that neither of these evidences pointed out to the existence of any Christian community in Goa prior to the arrival of the Portuguese here.[38] Later, others claimed that Christianity had been introduced into Goa by the apostle St. Thomas, but it disappeared for lack of priests, catechists and because of the Muslim persecutions.[39]

It is possible that Christian merchants from Arabia came with their Christian slaves to Goa due to the importance of its port, and stayed here for a short while. The cross found soon after the Portuguese conquest of Goa could have belonged to one of these Christians. For lack of historical evidence about the presence of Christianity in pre-Portuguese Goa, we cannot but conclude that there was no Christian settlement here before 1510.

## Three Phases of Conversion in the Sixteenth Century

This analytical arrangement is neither an attempt to periodize the history of conversions nor to arrive at simplistic generalizations. However, some striking features, events and trends do point out to some obvious changes or discontinuity in the history of conversions during the sixteenth century. Hence, we could speak about three different phases, though not totally distinct from one another. With this approach we may be able to discern a certain continuity and change between each phase. These similarities or differences could be about the number of converts, methods of conversion, decrees and privileges in favour of conversion, attitudes to Hinduism, reactions to conversion and to the Portuguese social and political demands, etc. More significantly, these phases could help us to state that noticeable shifts in the activity of conversions did occur, not only during the same century but also within the same phase; or they could help us to understand that conversions were more a 'process' with subtle distinctions that may escape any superficial analysis. I mean that much more than what had been permitted by the law did occur with the authority turning blind eye to the locals, for several practical reasons. Hence, this could serve as a warning to us that any categorical general statement made on conversions' issues concerning this century has to be taken only as a relative one. In the light of several continuities and discontinuities, intrinsic to the dynamics of conversions, which find support in facts, generalizations ought not to be taken at their face value. Hence, any absolute generalizations have to be reviewed carefully. If it is true, then our questions on conversions would necessarily change or be answered differently.

The three phases in the history of conversions in Goa during the sixteenth century can be shown thus: from 1510 to 1540, 1540 to 1580 and from 1580 to 1610. As seen earlier, continuity or change does not refer only to the methods of conversion used by the missionaries. Undoubtedly, the methods of conversion by themselves do reflect the dominant and evolving trends regarding civil and religious policies or even the historical mentality.

During the first phase, the kings of Portugal showed a great interest in conversions, but very few conversions had been made. Consolidation and justification of conquest was at stake here. In the second period the royal control over the missionaries and the Portuguese officials overseas lessened. The religious orders were actively involved in the activity of conversions. This period saw the greatest number of converts and the most overt proselytizing conduct.[40] The third phase witnessed the decline of the 'Golden Goa', but in spite of this fact conversions went on increasing in the districts of Bardez and Salcete. Nevertheless, the kings continued to be preoccupied with conversions and relapses. The missionaries appear to be more concerned about preventing relapses of the neo-converts than about making conversions. But conversions as well as group baptisms continued to take place in Goa.

First Phase (1510 - 1540). The first phase was characterized by syncretic practices and tolerant religious attitudes which lasted till 1540. Then most temples were destroyed in an attempt to implant the Christian faith. From this moment onwards idolatry and Hindu practices were officially and extensively banned in Goa. It is not true to state that the missionaries residing in Goa during this period betrayed little religious zeal, although accusations against them pointed to this direction. At this time the missionaries felt rather reluctant to interfere with the Hindu customs and religion. Political instability and the reduced Portuguese presence and force in Goa prevented any religious or social aggression. The Portuguese were neither militarily nor politically established yet. Rather they had to face constant attacks by the Adilshah's forces. Besides, they had not come to Goa with the intentions of settling down permanently. Despite this volatile situation there were some attempts to disrupt the local religious practices which fortunately did not go unregistered.

The Portuguese did not have a rigid social and religious structure yet. Hence, the laymen and the missionaries alike mixed freely and easily with the local people, behaviour that exposed them to the odium of the more oxthodox Portuguese: it was said that they were a people of loose morals and cheap behaviour. The clergy, secular and regular, entirely of young Portuguese blood, were accused of being ignorant, money-makers and of leading a dissolute life.[41] It was particularly due to, and after the Council of Trent (1545)[42] that the image of the clergy changed to a more formal and stricter one, distant from the people.

It is a fact that during this period the Portuguese authority did not interfere with the religious freedom of the locals. Hindu festivals attracted many Portuguese and local Christians as well. It may give us the impression that the converts were just inclined to such 'superstitions'. Rather the local customs were very much a part of their daily life and habits. If we take seriously the criticisms levelled by the missionaries against the local Christians, then it may be true that the first Christians were so in name only.[43]

Initially there was a great preoccupation with the moral life of the Portuguese settlers here. They remained without sacramental help and preaching, first, for being so spread out and second, for lack of missionaries. But what was still worse was the fact that the Portuguese themselves enjoyed mixing freely with the Hindus and Muslims, giving in completely to their sensual inclinations and every sort of sin. Moved by greed and desire to earn the highest returns in the shortest period of time, the Portuguese — a people normally well behaved and devout — let the idleness and riches of India corrupt them.[44] In India, one could only find robbers and destroyers of the rents of the king; and ironically, the Portuguese themselves were the leaders in this.[45] Later, the missionaries wrote that the conversion of the Hindus depended to a very large extent on the behaviour and example of the Portuguese.

The strength of the caste system and the Portuguese ignorance about the things of the Hindu religion and Indian languages for long, prevented them from making more than a few converts. The first converts were mostly the local women married to the Portuguese men, their offsprings, household slaves, servants and dependents. For these and other reasons the Portuguese made no efforts to form an indigenous clergy in Goa until 1541.[46]

Goa was exclusively Christianized by the missionaries of the Franciscan order during this period. It was the only religious order that the king of Portugal sent forth, with an official mandate, for the spiritual conquest of the East until the arrival of the Jesuits. If anyone became a Christian (very few indeed), he/she would not dare profess his/her faith openly, because the Hindus and Muslims who controlled business and the royal rents in Goa would persecute him/her. Nothing could be done about this situation since the Hindus and Muslims were favoured and respected by the Portuguese, especially by the officials of the crown.[47]

Throughout this period there was no group baptisms or mass conversions. When Francis Xavier arrived in Goa (city of Goa) in 1542, there were only about ten thousand converts here. During the first half of this century the conflicts between France and the Spanish empire that were fighting for political supremacy in Europe, did preoccupy the Portuguese kings. However, they did not show less concern about the Christian unity.[48] Portugal's neutrality in the conflict and the weakened unity prevailing in the church in Europe, probably influenced the Portuguese kings to become the champions and exemplary agents of Christendom overseas. The question of religious intolerance aggravated during the reign of D. João III (1521-1557), first in Portugal and later in Goa. This was done with the view of reviving the unity of the faith.

The Portuguese also expected that the Hindus would receive the Christian faith naturally and gradually. When this should happen, the former believed that the latter would by their own hands destroy the temples and give their rents to the churches. However, when the Hindus showed themselves firm in their beliefs, Goa experienced another set-back. Miguel Vaz and Diogo de Borba, the two persons in this period of transition to reckon with, are striking representatives of an emerging militant and intolerant mentality that would mark deeply the second phase of conversions.

With the arrival of the Jesuits in Goa in 1542, conversions increased rapidly. They devoted less time to the needs of the Portuguese; instead they gave themselves whole-heartedly to the task of converting the locals in the city of Goa. This approach opened the doors of Goa for conversions.[49]

Second Phase (1540 - 1580). Political stability in Goa and the Counter-Reformation mentality led the Portuguese to take some drastic steps in favour of conversions. Besides, the arrival of many religious orders, one competing with the other in the race for conversions, contributed to this new climate. The church hierarchy came to stay in Goa. Reform of local customs and elimination of Hindu practices as obstacles to conversion became a priority for the church militant. Since 1540 there was a great preoccupation with forming local clergy to help the missionaries. The 'rigour of mercy' began picking up its victims in the islands of Chorão and Divar from the same year, when "God remembered the people of this land, so long under the spell of the demon."[50] Bardez and Salcete had been annexed to the island of Goa in 1542, although the work of conversion began seriously here only after 1560. The missionary zeal and intolerance reached their peak in the sixties. In 1545 the king, D. João III, had given clear instructions to remove every trace of idolatry in Goa and to erect crosses at appropriate places.[51] His successor, D. Catarina, the queen regent (1557-1562), upheld these intolerant religious policies. The ban on the Hindu festivals in Goa,[52] the demolition of temples and the pro-conversion legislation were in keeping with the idea of the purity of the faith and the reform of Hindu customs as per the expectations of the Counter-Reformation and the demands of the Council of Trent. Nevertheless, syncretic practices continued to exist side by side with the new demands in spite of several efforts to eliminate or minimize 'idolatry' and 'superstitions'.

The king, D. João III, abandoned the old overseas policy started by his predecessor, king D. Manuel. A new and more pragmatic (than ideological) programme began to be implemented.[53] This pragmatism consisted in supporting the overseas project with a strong conversion drive with the view of expanding Christendom.[54] This political change resulted in the devolution of power, with initiatives of taking important decisions resting with the missionaries and private enterprise overseas. Consequently, this new pragmatism, private commercial activity and missionary work gained spectacular momentum, but not rarely the state officials, the missionaries and the private agents clashed with one another and acted in different directions at the functional or pragmatic level. Nevertheless, they seemed to agree with one another at the ideological level and on the need for more individual freedom.[55]

The missionary zeal during the second phase manifested itself in less evangelical ways. The existence of this kind of proselytism with excessive use of force, with the Jesuits in the lead, this new brand of Christendom is denied only by the apologetic mentality. The irresponsible and uncompromising zealotry obtained great support from zealous governors, but was only tolerated by the more pragmatic ones.[56] The converts and Hindus alike were subjected to severe forms of control and vigilance by the civil and ecclesiastical authorities, and above all by the Inquisition. The Office of the Holy Inquisition or state tribunal appeared in Goa in 1560.

Christendom had to expand at any cost since it needed urgently citizens to sustain the strategic regions in the Portuguese navigational network, essential for trading purposes.[57] Miguel Vaz, the untiring persecutor of 'idolaters' and responsible for the destruction of the temples in 1545, is perhaps one of the best known examples of religious intolerance.[58] Fortunately, Indo-Portuguese historiography has not silenced completely the reactions and anger of the local people against this sort of conversion drive. The Hindus, for long collaborators of the Portuguese, were now being 'officially' dispensed with from the public posts in the state, and replaced by the converts.

The Council of Trent created a new model of conduct for the clergy. The priest became a 'person-set-apart', divorced from the daily life of the people, someone who could be a model for, and rebuke the faithful. This new sort of clergy did not want to make compromises with idolatry and superstitions. Besides, the same Council sought to level down differences in Christian religious practices. It created a new and more uniform moral and social code for the Christians. Despite these demands the Portuguese laymen continued to mix freely with the local population and shared in their daily lifestyle.

After 1560, the task of preserving and instructing those already baptized was taken up on a war footing. The missionaries began instructing the local converts better, since earlier they had no opportunity to do so due to the great number of conversions, they alleged to exist.[59] Obviously, the vast number of converts was not the only or the main reason for the poor religious instruction of the first converts. As mentioned earlier, the missionaries expected that the neo-converts would learn the Christian precepts and customs as spontaneously as they would lose the memory of their ancestral religion. However, the missionaries did not take long to realize that they had to be more vigilant over the customs of their faithful, lest they might relapse into their previous social and religious behaviour. They felt they had to know the Christians personally to check their religious practices. Interference in the life of the Christians was to prevent the decline of Catholic ortodoxy. This had also been the greatest concern of the Council of Trent in Europe.[60]

The two Provincial Councils that took place in Goa in 1567 and 1575 adapted the reforms proposed by the Council of Trent to local contexts, in view of greater Catholicity and uniformity. These Councils, which were contextual expressions of the Council of Trent, shaped the clerical mentality and Catholic theology in Goa during the sixteenth century. The Protestant aggression or schism traumatized Catholic Europe, its theologians and missionaries. The Council of Trent began asserting the authenticity of Catholicism and demanding conformity with Rome, but this turned out to be illusive in Europe. Tridentine or Catholic Reformation thought it could do better overseas. The First Provincial Council (1567) re-stated, among other things, what the local missionaries had proposed earlier or were already doing, namely, the need of exerting strong social and religious pressures on the Hindus to prevent them from helping the converts to relapse to their former religion.[61]

The Provincial Council (1567) also introduced decrees to reform the local social customs as a means to increase conversions. It was during this phase that the Hindus began to lose their privileges and honours.[62] The major decisions taken by this Provincial Council were the following: the Catholic religion alone was the true one. The Portuguese crown had the duty to help in the work of conversion — rather, the secular power and the church had to work in close collaboration. The Council decreed that conversions could not be made by force or violence. No decision of the Council forced anyone to embrace Christianity. But it made the normal life of the Hindus and converts alike very difficult. The decrees of the Council need to be understood in the context of increase of conversions, and measures to curb relapses.[63] The king, D. Sebastião (1563-79), continued to insist on the Portuguese duty of making more conversions. He ordered the conversion of the Hindus, and felt the need for more teaching, preaching and confessing.[64] The decadence had set on the *Estado da India* since the reign of D. Sebastião.

From 1570, when the crown began giving more importance to Brazil, the monopoly of the sea route to India and the commerce of spices gave way to further privatization. Noble persons were authorized to operate on this route as payment for the services they rendered to the crown. The enemies of the Christian faith living next door to Portugal, in Morocco and Mauritania and the Ottoman power, constituted a serious threat to Portugal's sovereignty, which could not remain unchecked for too long. In 1573, a plan of war against the Muslims re-appeared. The Muslims doubled their attacks on the coast of Algarve in the south of Portugal.[65] Adilshah did not give up his attacks on Goa, hence instability forced the missionaries to slow down their work of conversion for a while, especially in Salcete.

Third Phase (1580 - 1610). The union of the two Iberian crowns in 1580, brought no official change in the idea and practice of conversion. The Spanish kings continued to favour the missionary activity in the Portuguese territories. They also continued to claim that the conversion of the Hindus and welfare of the new converts was their main duty.[66] With the royal goodwill the missionaries expected conversions to increase.[67] Conversions went up especially in Salcete and many churches were built in Goa around this time. After the carnage of the five Jesuit missionaries and of some locals in Cuncolim, Salcete, the missionaries hoped for a considerable number of conversions.[68] In 1596, the Spanish king, in keeping with the traditional Portuguese policies, stated again that the main reason for discovering India was to render God great service by way of preaching the Christian law.[69] By now the glory of Goa or the 'Golden Goa' had lost its lustre. The city of Goa complained of lack of funds.[70] This period was also marked by wars with the Adilshah which caused much famine and poverty.

There were some baptisms, but everything seemed very little and slow as compared with the earlier times.[71] But we are told that conversions increased astronomically in Salcete after the destruction of the temples, following the killing of the Jesuits. In 1595, the missionaries reported home an increase in conversions, information that pleased the king D. Filipe II.[72] Towards the end of the century there was a revival of conversion activity in Goa, but it was short-lived. The Portuguese *casados* or residents in Goa, who controlled the Municipal Council, being the staunch rivals to the Hindu business group, complained to the king that these people were harmful to Goa and enemies of the Christian faith: it was said that they were interested only in making money quickly, hence, the Portuguese demanded their expulsion from Goa.[73]

Members of the religious orders, especially the Jesuits, began showing some sort of moderation in their attitude towards the Hindus. They permitted the Hindus to go outside Goa to perform their ceremonies in payment of a fee.[74] Syncretism or relapses existed anyway and the missionaries could do very little about it. The religious orders were passing through difficult moments as far as finances were concerned. It was unlikely that the Jesuits, "a people against whom nobody dared do or say anything", would ever change their rigorous proselytizing policy, but for their financial hardships.[75] Conversion drive in Goa continued to find support among the Spanish kings, who issued several decrees recommending the viceroys to favour the missionaries.[76] During this period three Provincial Councils were held in Goa — the Third Provincial Council (1585), the Fourth Provincial Council (1592) and the Fifth Provincial Council (1605) — which ratified the main decrees of the previous two Provincial Councils. However, the Councils held during this phase paid more attention to the relapses of the neo-converts and measures to curb them. Despite wars with the Adilshah[77] there were some conversions in Salcete, but very few in the city of Goa. Many Hindus who resided here were merchants and had no interest whatsoever in being converted since this meant loss of their business.[78]

In chapter eight, we shall deal in greater detail with these phases vis-à-vis the practice of conversion and the various factors that provoked changes in, and ractions to, the policies and attitudes of the agents of conversion.

## NOTES AND REFERENCES

1. "A religião, que em primeiro lugar amamos e pela qual tudo se empreendia, ira ainda mais ufana calcando a própria idolatria, porque, a cada golpe da espada evangélica, caiam mil idolos dos pagodes e mil pagodes nos teatros das batalhas." Manuel de Faria e Sousa, *Ásia Portuguesa,* Vol. I, p. 57.
2. Paulo da Trindade, *CEO*, Part, I, p. 307.
3. *MR*, 3B, fl. 302.
4. *DI*, XIII, 421.
5. *MR*, 3B, fl. 302.
6. Letter written by pope, Pius V, to the viceroy of India in 1567. *Doc*, X, 251.
7. *DI*, XIII, 422.
8. "Foy Sua Alteza informado que em Bacaym e Damão e em as terras comarcãs destas cidades ha muito aparelho para se fazerem muitos Christãos e que algumas pessoas de Bacaym mais lembradas do proprio intereșse que da honrra de Deos nam somente nam favorecem esta santa obra da conversão mas ainda a desfavorecem buscando modo para inquietar os ministros da conversão escrevendo a S. A. e ao Viso Rei, e Arcebispo de Goa coisas falsas em desfavor desta obra e em outras cousas de discredito.

   Escreve S. A. as camaras e capitais destas fortalezas estranhando lhe isto muito, induzindo os ao favor desta obra declarando se lhe seu intento de proveito da India que o principal e conversão e que lhe escrevia os que nisso forem diligentes pra lho agradecer e os que fizerem o contrario pra os mandar castigar como merecem." Letter written in 1571. ARSI, *Foundationes Goanae*, 22 - I, fl. 30.
9. *APO*, 3, p. 33. D. João III saw the planting of the faith as his main duty even if it involved loss of his revenues. *Ibid.*, 1, Part II, p. 73; *Ibid.*, 3, p. 85.
10. *DI*, I, 66. "Porque a idolatria he tamanha offensa de Deus, como a todos he manyfesto, e com justiça V. A. a nam deve consentir em

suas terras, convem mamdar a Goa huma provisam que em toda a ilha nam aja nenhum pagode pubrico nem secreto, sob graves penas, nem menos o faça nenhum official de nenhuma maneira que seja, de pedra, nem de pao, nem de cobre, nem outro metal; nem façam em toda a ilha nenhumas festas gemtilicas pubricas, nem recolham em suas casas pregadores bramenes da terra firme. E que os homens que tiverem cuidado de Sam Paulo possam buscar as casas de todos os bramenes e gemtios, omde tiverem presumçam ou sospeita que estam idolos". A report on the *Estado da India* written by the vicar general, Miguel Vaz, to D. João III. Evora, November 1545. *Doc*, III, 202-04. *APO*, 5, pp. 903-04. The First Provincial Council of Goa (1567) declared an open war against idolatry and temples. ARSI, *Miscellanea Indiarum Orientalium*, 38 - I, fl. 137v.

11. *DI*, IV, 596.
12. *Ibid.*, VI, 71.
13. The Jesuits disagreed among themselves on the methods of conversion. *DI*, XVI, 59*.
14. *Doc*, XI, 811.
15. C. R. Boxer, *The Portuguese Seaborne Empire, 1415-1825*, (1969), p. 76.
16. "Hum gentio bramane honrrado vendo uma porcissão que este inverno se fazia em certa igreja para que a desse chuva porque se virem perdendo as novidades por falta dela, disse se amanha chove, pensarei que o Deus dos christãos é verdadeiro, e o seguirei fazendo christão, e choveu muito, e o brahmane não esquecido da promessa veio fazer christão com mulher e mais familia." ARSI, *Eppistolae Goana et Malabarica*, 14, fl. 73v. *Doc*, X, 126, 139, 140, 144.
17. *Doc*, X, 372.
18. Luis de Guzman, *Historia de las Missiones de la Compania de Jesus en la India Oriental, en la China y Japon (1540-1600)*, p. 56. "A conversão dos infieis sempre foi negocio de grande vagar e molestias em todas a nações do mundo. E muito mais vagarosa deve ser nesta gente pela sua grande rudeza e pouca aplicação às cousas de Deus e pouca lembraça das coisas futuras." ARSI, *Eppistolae Goana et Malabarica*, 16, fl. 180.
19. *DI*, XII, 103. *Ibid.*, IV, 692. When a boy told a priest he wanted to become a Christian the priest cut immediately his *xenddi*. ARSI, *Goana Historia*, 33 - I, fl. 183. Teotonio R. de Souza, "Xenddi Tax:

A Portuguese Version of Jizya in Goa (1704-1841 A.D.)", *Goa to Me*, pp. 106-16.

20. *DI*, IV, 808.
21. *Ibid.*, 692.
22. *Ibid.*, 781.
23. *Ibid.*, 797.
24. Alessandro Valignano, *Historia del principio y progresso de la Compañia de Jesús em las Indias Orientales*, p. 444.
25. Paulo da Trindade, *CEO*, Part I, p. 301.
26. C. R. Boxer, *A India Portuguesa em Meados do Século XVII*, p. 32.
27. *DI*, IV, 596.
28. *Ibid.*, 689. The ring of gold a Hindu woman wore on her nose was a sign that distinguished her from a Christian woman. *Ibid.*, 367.
29. *Ibid.*, 800, 807.
30. *Ibid.*, X, 471; XVI, 713.
31. *Doc*, I, 29-32; III, 313-29.
32. "Muitos mais tornariam cristãos, se fossem favorecidos dos vossos capitães, porque sayba Vosa Alteza certo que, tanto que se tornam cristãos, loguo sam tratados como cativos, e por esta causa se nom querem tornar muita gente da tera cristaam." "... que como recebem augua do Bautismo, loguo sam maltratados e desfavorecidos..." A letter written by Fr. Sebastião Pires to the king (16 December 1527). *Ibid.*, II, 143.
33. Paulo da Trindade, *CEO.*, Part I, p. 282. "O bispo, João de Albuquerque, muyto vertuoso e bom perlado he mas remyso e froxo pera o que se requere per caa. E tambem nam podera fazer mais porque os governadores querem ser reys nos poderes mas nam no sofrymento e elle he tão incolheyto que nam ousa lhes fallar senam do que elles querem e mestre Pedro que serve de vigayro geral gasta o tempo das pregações em louvores dos governadores e do contrayro nam cura e segundo dizem acha-se bem disso. E contudo nos petytorios e causas dos christãos da terra requere ao governador e faz o que pode mas mais fezera Mygel Vaaz se fora vivo. ... para requerer ao governador algumas coisas importantes acerca da conversão da gente da terra porque os padres que ca vieram da companhia tyrando mestre Francisco, todollos outros nam são capazes para isso." CEHU, *As Gavetas da Torre do Tombo*, IV, p. 415.

34. R. E. Frykenberg, "On the Study of Conversion Movements: A Review Article and a Theoretical Note", p. 128.
35. ARSI, *Fundationes Goana*, 22 - I, fl. 12v.
36. João de Barros, *Decada da Asia* I, Book VI, Ch. I.
37. Georg Schurhammer, *Francis Xavier. His Life and His Times*, Vol. II, p. 229, note 214. George Mark Moraes, *A History of Christianity in India*.
38. João de Barros, *Decada da Asia* II, Part I, (1777), p. 434-35. Georg Schurhammer, *Francis Xavier. His Life and His Times*, Vol. II, pp. 229-30, notes nos. 213 and 214. Despite the presence of Christians in South India, dating from the time of the apostle St. Thomas, or as close as in Kalina, near Bombay in the fourteenth century, Christianity did not make its appearance in Goa. *Memória Histórico Eclesiastica da Arquidiocese de Goa (1533-1933)*, p. 17.
39. Jacintho Caetano Barreto Miranda, *Quadros Historicos de Goa. Tentativa Historica*, Caderneta I, p. 103.
40. António da Silva Rego, *História das Missões do Padroado Português do Oriente*, p. 101.
41. "Eram clerigos de mau viver e exemplos." *Ibid.*, p. 541.
42. Council of Trent was the General Assembly of all the bishops of the Catholic church that was convened and took place at Trent (Italy) between 1545 and 1563.
43. *Doc*, I, 201.
44. Alessandro Valignano, *op. cit.*, p. 48.
45. *Doc*, VI, 257. "Ho noso fidallguo porque lhe pesa e querem vos dar a entender que eles sam os que mantem a Indya os fydalgos. Esta he a maneyra como vos eles enganam pera comer tudo e se queres ver a verdade disto do tempo que eu cheguey que haa dous anos vai em tres que cheguarom fidallguos naquella armada que nam traziam que comer e agora sam omens de vinte trinta mill cruzados domde sam estes dynheyros nam os ganhom elles a trautar senam que vos roubom vosa fazenda que ho fidallguo que allcansa em dous annos trinta mill cruzados nam vem ele qua pera vos servir. Este he o que vos vende." A letter written by Silvestre de Bachão to the king with news about India. Cochin, 1524. CEHU, *As Gavetas da Torre do Tombo*, III, pp. 49-50.
46. C. R. Boxer, "The Problem of Native Clergy in the Portuguese and

Spanish Empires from the Sixteenth to the Eighteenth Centuries", p. 86.

47. Alessandro Valignano, *op. cit.*, p. 47.
48. Joaquim Veríssimo Serrão, *História de Portugal (1495-1580)*, Vol. III, pp. 44-45.
49. ARSI, *Extracto das cousas,* 1a, fl. 17.
50. *APO*, 5, Part I, doc. 75, p. 161.
51. *Doc*, III, 261.
52. Josef Wicki, *LPC*, p. 65.
53. Luís Filipe F. R. Thomaz, "Descobrimentos e Evangelização. Da Cruzada à missão pacífica", p. 120. D. João III put aside the conquest of Jerusalem and of the Muslim world and discarded the medieval ideals of crusade to think above all about spices. There was a shift from suzerainty to sovereignty. The imperial project began to transform into a colonial project. Luís Filipe F. R. Thomaz, *De Ceuta a Timor*, p. 167. The king thought of India mainly in terms of commerce. *Ibid.*, p. 182.
54. Joaquim Veríssimo Serrão, *História de Portugal*, Vol. III, p. 50.
55. Anthony Disney, "Contrasting Models of "Empire": The Estado da Índia in South Asia and East Asia in the Sixteenth and Early Seventeenth Centuries", p. 32. Among the causes of the decline of the king's revenue, Simão Botelho, the chief revenue superintendent (*Vedor da Fazenda*), noticed the abuse of the grants of free carriage. A grant made to one officer was sufficient to rouse all others of similar rank to demand similar privileges, until the kings's ships sailed with nothing but cargo shipped by holders of free grants. R. S. Whiteway, *The Rise of the Portuguese Power in India 1497-1550*, pp. 295-96.
56. Conde de Ficalho, *Garcia da Orta e o seu Tempo*, p. 162.
57. *Ibid.*, p. 161.
58. BNL, *Reservados*, Cod. 175, fl. 34.
59. *DI*, V, 64, 273.
60. In 1545 the Council of Trent made a list of heresies and abuses and proposed means for counter-Reformation and reformation of morals. Provincial Councils that took place in Goa, at the recommendation of the Council of Trent, adapted the tridentine directives and objectives to particular contexts in the mission lands. The decrees

of the First Provincial Council (1567) were ratified by the king, D. Sebastião (1562-1580) and by the viceroy in the same year. *APO*, 4, p. 68.

61. Alessandro Valignano, *op. cit.*, pp. 334-35.
62. ARSI, *Miscellaneum Indiarum Orientalum*, 38 - I, fl. 137v.
63. António Pinto Pereira, *História da India em que a Governou o Visorei Dom Luís de Ataíde*, p. 27.
64. BNL, *Reservados*, Cod. 176, fl. 78.
65. Joaquim Veríssimo Serrão, *História de Portugal*, Vol. III, pp. 71-72.
66. AHU, *Registos de cartas*, Cod. 281, fl. 351v.
67. *DI*, XII, 900.
68. *Ibid.*, XII, 902-03.
69. AHU, *Registo de cartas*, Cod. 281, fls. 58v, 350v.
70. *APO*, 3, p. 136. *Ibid.*, 5, Part II, note of doc. 391, p. 489. *Ibid.*, 1, Part II, doc. 6, p. 82.
71. Letter written by Fr. Duarte de Sande. *Doc*, XII, 453.
72. *APO*, 3, doc. 140, p. 420 and doc. 175, p. 522.
73. Letter written by the Portuguese from the city of Goa to the king of Portugal in 1600. *Ibid.*, 1, Part II, p. 83.
74. *Ibid.*
75. António D'Almeida Azevedo, *As Communidades de Goa: História das Instituições Antigas*, p. 164.
76. Letter of D. Filipe II to the viceroy, D. Martinho Afonso de Castro, in January 1605, recommending protection to the bishops and religious members in India to enable them to perform their duties and increase the faith. AN / TT, *Relação de Documentos Remetidos da India*, Tomo I, p. 1. Royal letter to the viceroy, Matias de Albuquerque, in 1591 to favour the construction of new churches in the city of Goa and in Bardez. *BFUP*, No. 2, p. 196-97. *MR*, 2A, fls. 98-100. In 1597 the king ordered that the money granted annually for the baptismal dresses should be used exclusively for this purpose and that these dresses be distributed on the day of their baptism. *BFUP*, No. 2, pp. 223-24. *MR*, 2B, fl. 359. Royal letter to the viceroy, Martim Afonso de Castro, in 1605 to give every kind of help to the missionaries. *BFUP*, No. 3, pp. 513-14. *MR*, 6B, fls. 70-72. Royal letter to the viceroy, Matias de Albuquerque, to offer any help to the

religious orders engaged in the expansion of Christendom. *BFUP*, No. 2, pp. 321-23. *MR*, 3B, fls. 515-19.

77. *DI*, XI, 658, 677.

78. *Doc*, XI, 453; XII, 469.

# 4

# METHODS AND INSTITUTIONS OF CONVERSION

The frequency of group baptisms and the number of conversions performed in Goa during the sixteenth century makes one think of the methods and measures used to achieve them. We need to recall that certain methods of conversion such as the imposition of high taxation on the Hindus and Muslims, expelling those who obstructed conversions, depriving the Hindus of government jobs and all the 'decrees and privileges in favour of conversion' were as licit as they were the normal means of 'making Christendom' in the sixteenth century.[1] After all, the missionaries argued that conversions could be effected only by God, and any other consideration or means they could involve were but secondary.[2] This chapter is an attempt to show the third side of the story of conversions, or the other methods and the supporting institutions responsible for the conversion of the Hindus, and for preventing the converts from relapsing.

Perhaps, one would like to know whether generally the praxis of conversion was in tune with the idea of conversion, or whether the doctrine and policy on conversions proposed by the church was in harmony with the methods used by the missionaries to make converts. Further, we could ask ourselves whether the civil authority agreed with all the conversion methods used by the missionaries. If the Jesuits resorted to unconstitutional or illegal means to get funds for their missionary work (eg. silk trade carried on in order to support their mission), then it would not be a surprise if they also deviated from the commonly accepted methods of making conversions.[3] Interestingly, some missionary reportings do mention certain accusations made against themselves regarding the use of force, but they were only an astute device to deny the same force altogether as a malicious fabrication by the Hindus. Other missionary writings contain debates on what was permitted and what were the unlawful means. But they concluded that there had been only voluntary conversions or that they would never employ any sort of force. For certain, the Hindus criticized the missionaries for their violent methods in converting them, but the latter rebutted each and every such accusation, and held the former as unreliable witnesses and a people extremely harmful to the state.[4]

A few reports and letters written by the missionaries appear to be a self-criticism about the use of some unchristian means of making conversions. But as mentioned earlier, the conversion narratives by and large denied the use of 'forced methods'. Stories about catechumens who, not so long before offended God and now wept with joy and desire to adore the true God; or narratives telling about the successful conversion activity by the religious members such as their visits to the houses of Hindus, especially Brahmans, who expressed with great satisfaction that there could not have been a more appropriate time for Jesus Christ to enter their houses and for the demon to leave them, were the standard discourse on conversions.[5] One reads such stories *ad nauseam* in the letters written by the missionaries. Conversion narratives were very often dramatized to show how the grace of God operated in the converts despite family and caste opposition, and how the catechumens remained firm in their convictions.

Today, the issue of conversions in the sixteenth century is normally sought to be explained within the framework of the methods or means used to achieve them. Generally, in present-day debates it appears that it is not the issue of conversions *per se*, in all its facets and complexities, that becomes important and a matter of discussion, but the 'motives' behind conversions, and the 'methods' employed to make Christians. Disagreements and polemics presently emerging in discussions related to the issue of conversion have their source particularly in this narrow approach and lack of consensus among the participants regarding the definition of 'force' and 'motives'; and, of course, a disregard for any colonial frame of reference to understand complexities adds another problem to this debate on conversions. Obviously, there will always be differences in interpretation of terms. Force, direct or indirect, in effecting conversions has often been highlighted or downplayed, precisely because of the difficulty in accepting the 'definition of force' of the opponent, not to say anything about vested interests of each group involved in this debate. This is not a new problem, since the question of force in conversions was also being discussed even by the missionaries themselves during the sixteenth century. Then, many complaints and accusations levelled against one another were directly related to the methods of conversion or more precisely to 'force' used in conversions. The missionaries argued that when there was a decree permitting a particular action, there was nothing unlawful in performing that action. Curiously, at first sight it appears that the debate was not between the pro-conversion and the anti-conversion stands but on proper methods of conversion. But on further perusal, it seems that it was not only conversions or the methods of conversion *per se* that made the debate on conversions a sensitive and polemic one then, but also the 'frequency' of group baptisms and the great 'number' of conversions, even if they were not made by coercive methods.

It is one thing to demonstrate that the missionaries opposed aggressively traditional culture and converted people by force, and quite another thing to conclude that conversions caused radical changes in the Goan society. Syncretism is a good example about the survival of things 'local' despite several decrees against them. Syncretism also shows that in spite of religious conversion, forced or free, the converts continued to be influenced by their former customs. Christendom still needed the Inquisition and several Provincial Councils to teach them its so-called civilized Christian behaviour. Obviously, one can study the methods of conversion without paying any attention to their context and consequences. But this would be distorting historical facts and consequently nonsensical. Hence, to avoid further distortion, the methods and institutions that sustained conversions need to be understood, having in view their total context and religious demands.

Conversions, regardless of the methods employed by the missionaries, found also great local resistance and opposition.[6] This aspect has not been systematically dealt with due to insufficient historical evidence about it, since the missionaries would not report reactions to conversions so easily. However, even a superficial reading on conversion material will reveal a strong local opposition to missionary interference and the subsequent Portuguese violence to curb this reaction. To be able to fully exploit this interesting aspect in the history of Goa, one requires to have an unbiased perspective towards documents and not an apologetic approach to history. The people were not passive recipients and vassals at the mercy of the missionaries; the missionaries accepted the fact that reactions against conversions were, by no means, negligible; and reactions did not come only from the high castes. Those who could not resist, and those who expected better life, succumbed without fully abandoning their old customs, and this adjustment knew no caste bar.

The missionaries used the same methods of conversion wherever they went, with greater or lesser initiatives and interests, depending on human and financial resources, royal support and local reactions. The methods adopted by one religious order to 'make Christians' did not differ substantially from those of the other. And the methods used in Goa during the sixteenth century were far from being an innovation, since they had already been tried in some parts of western coast of Africa, where the missionaries had been working during the last few decades of the previous century. The Portuguese entered, conquered and maintained Goa with a cross in one hand and a sword in the other. This was no exception as far as Portuguese territories overseas are concerned, since this was a normal practice of any Catholic power. Paradoxically, when the prosperity of Goa began declining from the middle of the sixteenth century, the missionaries felt the need to exert the greatest pressure on the people. Perhaps an exigency, for more citizens to defend Goa, dictated different strategies of conversion at this time.[7]

It is also useful to understand how the use of force in conversions was legitimized by the missionaries in general, and in Goa in particular. How could the Christian conscience reconcile the use of force with the principles it professed? We should not forget that we are confronting the conscience of Christendom, of war against infidels, of cultural ethnocentrism and of the Counter-Reformation. In Europe the methods used by the counter-reformers to end the unpleasant situation created by the Reformation that threatened Christendom with the defection of many of its followers, proved weak. Moreover, a conscience of conquest, domination, the projection of Christendom and its expansion with heroic feats, all in the name of reforming customs and converting infidels, prevailed in Europe and elsewhere.[8] In this context several theological and ideological positions were proposed to justify and promote a certain sort of praxis for the counter-reformers.

The common missiological positions during the sixteenth century stood, as Bartolomé de las Casas (1484-1566) the leading theologian of the time also did, for only peaceful means in conversions, like persuasion by means of reasoning and a free invitation of the will. Another missiological current argued, and the theologian, Juan Ginés de Sepúlveda (1490-1573), was one of its firm proponents, against the direct use of force but held that indirect force could be exerted, since it was a natural and divine duty and absolutely lawful to correct men who walked toward their damnation. If persuasive methods failed, then force would be useful.[9]

From the above discussion we could group the methods of conversion used in Goa during the sixteenth century in three broad categories: conversion by coersion, convenience and by conviction; or more broadly into 'weak methods' and 'strong methods'. Likewise, there were 'weak measures' and 'strong measures' to prevent relapses of the converts, but this we shall see especially in chapter eight on 'Syncretism in the Life of the Christians'.

## 'Strong Methods' of Conversion

The Hindus complained to the Portuguese authorities that their sons and relatives were being forcibly converted and deceived, and that some of them were even in the custody of the missionaries.[10] Food that would make one lose caste was immediately given to those who wished to become Christians.[11] Some religious Brothers, many of them former soldiers, showed an excess of zeal for the cause of conversions.[12] They went out to the villages to catch their 'preys', meaning, Hindus to be converted. The village chiefs and high caste Hindus on whom the conversion of many locals depended, became their favourite 'preys'.[13] Historical sources suggest that the conversion of Brahmans and local soldiers would be more profitable to the Portuguese state.[14] Some friars gave large sums at the cost of the king's revenue to entice the Hindus to the faith.[15] Portuguese soldiers baptized people they held captive.[16] Such methods of conversion created tensions within the local community.[17] However, some conversions had all the signs of being forced but that was not the case. At times some Hindus, who wished to become Christians but were afraid of their relatives, pretended to be victims of forced conversion to avoid being dishonoured by their own relatives.[18] Everything was pre-planned and decided between the priests and these Hindus.[19] At other times when a Hindu wanted to be converted, he himself ate together with the Portuguese.[20] A certain Hindu had requested a priest to baptize him, but the latter perceiving the lack of Christian instruction in him refused him baptism. This same Hindu threatened to accuse the priest to the ecclesiastical authorities of neglecting his duty.[21] The Provincial Councils forbade the use of real or feigned force to bring anyone to the church.[22]

Some conversion methods, including conversion decrees, generated polemic not only between two different religious orders but also within the same order. Disagreements regarding the methods of conversion existed among the Jesuits themselves. Certain methods were not acceptable to all the missionaries, although these objectionable methods often seemed to be more effective than many decrees granting privileges to the locals.[23]

In 1561 a charter of the king forbade the Hindus to perform their religious ceremonies. If they were caught in possession of idols they could be arrested, declared guilty for breaching the law, and then for fear of punishment they often asked for baptism. Some of the guilty were taken to the College of St Paul and after providing them with shelter and food prepared by the Christians they lost their caste, remaining thus without any hope of regaining it. This act defiled them permanently in the eyes of the other Hindus. Thus left without any alternative these people were instructed in view of baptism. Some Hindus complained that this was tantamount to forced conversions, but the priests counter-argued saying that to baptize them was an act of mercy, since they themselves asked for it in exchange for the punishment they deserved by law.[24]

The feast of the conversion of St Paul (January 25) was a special day chosen for group baptisms. Just before this day the Jesuits went through the streets of the Hindu quarters accompanied by their black slaves to gather candidates. When the slaves caught the fugitive Hindu they smeared his lips with a piece of beef, thus causing him to lose caste and become untouchable. Conversion to Christianity was now his only option. The Hindu priests devised soon an 'antidote' by which the untouchable could regain his caste.[25]

A report in 1595 tells us that conversion of infidels in India was not effected generally by preaching and catechetical instruction, but by preventing their idolatries, punishing them for these practices, denying favours to the Hindus and granting them to the new converts. These means had been approved and ratified by the Provincial Councils held in Goa, by the decrees of the kings of Portugal and by the viceroys.[26] Miguel Vaz, the vicar-general of the archdiocese of Goa, and Diogo Borba, a secular priest, are the best representatives of 'strong methods' and noted persecutors of idols and idolaters.[27]

Emigrations in Goa have been associated with forced conversions; however, not every emigration was the result of harsh Portuguese policies of conversion. That the Hindus were not always driven out of Goa on refusing to become Christians becomes clear after reading several accounts written by travellers in the sixteenth and seventeenth centuries. In 1583, for instance, John Huighen Van Linschoten stated that the city of Goa and its surroundings had countless pagans of many denomination, i.e. Hindus, Jains, besides many Muslims and Jews. We know that only some people had been asked to leave Goa.[28]

It is unquestionable that there had been emigration due to harsh methods of conversion. But some emigrations resulted from the prevailing system of property relations in the village communities, and from the financial situation the Portuguese regime had created which led to the imposition of heavy taxation on the Goan peasants, who were then forced to migrate with their families to the firm land where there were better opportunities.[29] Simão Botelho, *Vedor da Fazenda* of Portuguese India, wrote to the king in 1552 saying that some missionaries wanted to convert the Hindus by force, to the extent of even harming them and compelling them to migrate.[30] The Hindus left Salcete because permission was not granted them to perform their ceremonies.[31] In 1556 the absentee *gaunkars* from Navelim village in the island of Divar were invited to return to Goa within a fixed period of time, and take charge of their abandoned properties; defiance would mean loss for good of their property, as it had already happened in other villages.[32] Earlier some *gaunkars* had run away from their villages for fear of conversion.

The request made by Azu Naik, a Hindu, to the king in 1548, to end forced conversions in Goa, which would allow its inhabitants not only to live in their lands peacefully and in freedom to carry on their customs but also in turn would help to increase the rents of the crown, was not taken seriously.[33] Muslim merchants made an agreement with the Portuguese on coming to the port of Goa so that their slaves would not be forced to change their religion.[34] In 1595 some Portuguese merchants had been accused of snatching violently some slaves belonging to the Muslims and retaining them with the pretext of wanting to convert them.[35] No serious study on Goa in the sixteenth century denies the use of force in conversions. Its frequency and intensity, however, is much debated. I think that the most convincing argument about the existence of strong or forcible methods in conversions does not rest so much on the 'making' of conversions (or its numbers) as on the 'breaking' of (many) temples and idols from 1540 onwards. It is interesting to see the legislation on this regard. The next two chapters on the 'Decrees and Privileges in Favour of Conversion' and 'Decrees on Temples, Idols and Orphans' attempt to summarize the vast legislation in favour of Christendom.[36]

## 'Weak Methods' of Conversion

The most ordinary means to attract the Hindus to conversion were charity, kindness and social service; intensive and constant preaching, confessions, admonitions, judicial penalties, catechetical instruction and indulgences; appeal to emotions, fantasy and senses through the relics of saints, lives of saints, hymns and promises of eternal salvation. It may be recalled how D. Aleixo de Meneses used his pompous retinue to persuade the Syro-Malabar Christians of Kerala to join the Latin church. They had never seen such magnificence before. It was perfectly licit to use 'human means' or favours at the beginning, but later they would not be needed, when the converts came to know about the grace they had received from the Christian religion, thought the missionaries.[37]

The missionary practice of going out to the villages to meet the people started in 1560, and it proved to be one of the most successful means to win converts. It was expected that the care the religious Brothers showed to the catechumens and the new converts would move many to the Christian faith.[38] In 1518 Friar António suggested to the king, D. Manuel, that if a small gift of rice was given to the converts, many Hindus would also feel inclined to accept baptism.[39] However, in the same year the bishop, Duarte Nunes, wrote to the king informing him just the opposite, namely that it was not easy to make conversions, particularly due to the deeply rooted customs and convictions of the people.[40]

The conversion of one member of a family could lead the others or the entire family to join Christianity.[41] It was often the love for their sons and relatives, who had become Christians earlier, that was the motivating factor for others to also ask for baptism; and conversely, the converts tried to convince their Hindu family or relatives to receive baptism. Probably, the priests instructed them to act likewise. Others, deprived of alternative, under the direct or indirect pressure of the royal and ecclesiastical decrees, converted for their own convenience.[42] According to the missionaries, it was necessary to use all the human means and favours within their reach to make Christians; however, these means and favours constituted only secondary and temporary ingredients in any conversion.[43]

## The *Confrarias*

Confraternities or *confrarias* were lay associations, essentially of religious character, founded for the spiritual formation of the new converts. The members of a confraternity were called *confrades* and these confraternities excluded women from their membership. These associations had also various charitable features. Moreover, these confraternities or associations of the converts helped the Christian public cult, and worked to influence the Hiṇdus to conversion. They certainly contributed as much for the increase of religious devotion among the new converts as for preventing relapses. These confraternities in Goa were modelled after the confraternities in Portugal; but in the colonies they assumed a distinctive character to adjust better to the religiosity and needs of the local Christians.

The creation of confraternities in Goa was directly related to the growth of conversions. They appeared first in the monasteries and gradually in the churches. Hence, each religious order might have founded several confraternities. They tended to be organized around caste considerations and not surprisingly they were addressed to caste rivalries and tendencies too. Conflicts of economic and social nature were not absent between them. There were conflicts of economic order between the confraternity of 'Misericordia de Goa' whose members were only Portuguese and the other confraternities.[44] The interference by the Confraternity of Mercy in the welfare service to the converts carried out by the Confraternity of S. Miguel created conflicts between them.[45]

Already in 1511 we hear about confraternities or pious associations working mainly to foster the Christian cult in Goa and promote the holiness of their *confrades*. They were in harmony with the original aim of these confraternities that consisted in preserving the faith of the Christians. Later, they began working for the increase of converts and *confrades*, but at the same time they continued to protect the new converts. Those who joined the confraternities could gain spiritual favours, indulgences and graces. It was believed that the Hindus, on seeing the privileged condition of the Christians and their own misery, would soon convert to the Catholic faith.[46]

Since the city of Goa had many Christians and a considerable number of convents, it was but natural for these religious houses to become the first nuclei of confraternities. As the work of conversion went on spreading out to the islands of Goa and districts of Bardez and Salcete, several other confraternities emerged in the newly built churches there.[47] Each confraternity had its own statutes (*regulamentos*) by which they regulated the activity and devotional life of their *confrades*. Besides the general orientation common to all confraternities, each one showed some distinctive features in its statutes.

The first Constitutions of the Archdiocese of Goa (1568) classified the confraternities into two categories: one, all those confraternities that fostered the religious cult, and in the other category were those confraternities that looked after the maintenance and repairs of the churches and their properties.[48] These confraternities, besides being dedicated to the welfare of the Christians as specified and demanded by their statutes, also suggested that the confraternities should be organized around caste or race considerations, which arrangement often resulted in social conflicts. Hence, we see for instance, two types of confraternities instituted by the Jesuits: one for the Portuguese and the other for the local Christians, but this had been in force only for a short while.[49] In 1606 we hear of a confraternity for the Brahmans in Margão, Salcete.[50] The king did not permit the Jesuits to found a confraternity for the Portuguese soldiers in 1595.[51]

The confraternity of 'Conversão à Fé' or 'Holy Faith' had the following statutes for its chief office-bearers: they had to forbid the Hindus to build new temples or repair the demolished ones; they had to keep the civil authority informed when the Hindus ill-treated the Christians; they had to check whether the new converts lived and worked honestly; in other words they had to discourage idleness among them to prevent the Hindus from criticizing Christianity. The official members of the confraternity were obliged to advise and punish the converts when required, and if necessary they had to help the poor with the confraternity funds. They were obliged to see also that the converts received support from their Hindu parents and relatives, and that they had a share in their family inheritance. To promote the interests of the Christians in dispute was another duty of the chief *confrades*. The statutes required them to visit and help the sick spiritually and corporally, to accompany the dead, and to care for the orphans and destitutes. They had to be on the alert for Muslims and Jews trying to buy Hindu boys to circumcise them, but if a boy was found with these people he had to be freed immediately, and the culprit punished with exile. The chief officials had to see that government jobs did not go to the Hindus but to the Christians alone. It was licit to impose taxes on the Hindus and Muslims and grant the Christians many favours.[52] These were some of the duties and works of charity the administrators or the chief *confrades* of the confraternities needed to keep in mind and execute. We could summarize the obligations of the *confrades* thus: they should work for the increase and defence of the Catholic faith in such a way as to protect and favour the Christians in all things,[53] so that on seeing the favours bestowed on the converts the Hindus might be converted.[54] Portuguese or local Christians, but only noblemen, could become officials in the confraternities. The officials of the confraternity of 'Conversão à Fee' (Conversion to Faith), known also as 'Confrarya dos Comvertidos', (Confraternity of the Converts) were requested to become godfathers to the Hindus who wanted to convert in order to favour them.[55]

Each month the *confrades* had to attend a meeting held by the confraternity, during which its president spoke about a saint of that month exhorting them to imitate his exemplary life. The *confrades* participated in the mass on every solemn feast day.[56] Certain confraternities demanded of its members daily thirty minutes of mental prayer, examination of conscience, and prayers for the important intentions of the church, elimination of heresies, propagation of the Catholic faith, and for peace and harmony among the Catholic princes. Imitation of the virtues of Our Lady was encouraged too. A *confrade* could be dismissed from the confraternity if he did not fulfil his obligations, or for any immoral behaviour.[57]

The confraternity of 'Our Lady of the Annunciation' was instituted to teach the young students to progress in their spiritual life through participation in the sacraments.[58] Fraternal charity and concern for others stood out as the main objective of the confraternity of the 'Eleven Thousand Virgins'.[59] Its *confrades* were obliged to visit the sick, console the prisoners, help the needy and perform other similar charitable works. Plenary indulgences could be gained by all those who confessed, received communion, and became *confrades* in the confraternity of the 'Santíssimo Sacramento'.[60] In 1552, seventy two *confrades* of the confraternity of 'Santa Ursula' had been chosen and sent out by a priest to investigate and report back about the public sins in the city of Goa, and also about the needs of the poor people. This was rather easy to do, since these *confrades* lived in different quarters in the city. They were also requested to inform the priest about any weakness they might detect in their relatives, friends and neighbours.[61] The rosary was recited on Saturdays, and during the lenten season everyday, perhaps in most confraternities. Confraternities were founded to pray the rosary.[62] The confraternity of the 'Irmandade de Misericordia' or 'Brotherhood of Mercy' performed many works of charity like keeping deposits, giving credit, helping the poor, the sick and the imprisoned, or like sustaining the abandoned children, giving young girls in marriage, receiving repentant women, ransoming captives, protecting the orphans and the widows, etc.[63] This confraternity was formed exclusively for the Portuguese settlers in Goa. It devoted more time to charitable works than to the propagation of the faith. In 1595, the statutes of the confraternity of 'Misericordia de Goa' ordered four men to go through the city thrice a week at night, with a bell shouting: "Christians, helpers of Jesus Christ, remember the souls in purgatory and those in mortal sin, and help them with one Our Father and Hail Mary for God to have mercy on them, and for the forgiveness of your sins, as well. Amen."[64]

Confraternities were maintained by voluntary contributions or alms given by the faithful. Each church had its confraternity, and the latter gave to the church everything it needed for the divine cult, like chalices, candles, mass vestments, etc.[65] The *confrades* contributed financially for the Christian festivals, and saw to it that they were celebrated regularly to strengthen the Christian faith and embarass the Hindus. Favours of a social character granted by these confraternities might have led some to embrace Christianity.

## The *Pay dos Christãos*

The institution or office of the *Pay dos Christãos* or 'Father of the Christians' appeared for the first time in Goa in 1537.[66] The *Pay dos Christãos* was founded in all Eastern territories under the Portuguese control but especially in India. This institution was created and financed by the government. Its nature was always more secular; nevertheless, it dealt with religious matters too.[67] The *Pay dos Christãos* was a man responsible for conversions as well as for the catechumens and the new converts. He had the duty to protect, preserve and instruct the local catechumens and the converts living in India, and elsewhere in the Portuguese territories overseas. We have already stated that most local Christians were poor and totally at the mercy of the Portuguese authorities. At times some Portuguese settlers fined and ill-treated them for insignificant reasons, and this proved to be sufficiently dangerous or harmful for the converts. Relapses could easily follow if the converts were left unprotected.[68]

It would be useful to spell out here other responsibilities of the *Pay dos Christãos*. This person had the duty to visit the catechumens and Christians in their villages and take note of how they lived. He should prevent them from having any dealing with the Hindus. Besides, he was supposed to be a spokesman for the local Christians before the viceroys and the civil authority. He should act as an arbitrator to settle disputes and complaints of the converts. He had to favour, pacify or punish the new converts whenever necessary. He ought to be a defender, in a fatherly manner, of the Christians in and out of court. The *Pay dos Christãos* had to find some Portuguese willing to become godfathers and benefactors to the catechumens.[69] He had the power to take decisions on behalf of the converts, and had a strong say in matters relating to government jobs for the local Christans. The allocation in those positions depended to a very large extent on the recommendation the *Pay dos Christãos* gave to the governor.[70] In certain cases the liberty of the Hindus depended on the information sent by the *Pay dos Christãos* to the Portuguese authority. He had also the duty to take the census of the Christians.

The 'Father of the Christians' had to prevent idolatrous practices, punish culprits, and work for the salvation of souls of the Hindus too.[71] But the religious instruction of the catechumens and their baptism became an important responsibility of the *Pay dos Christãos*, since he was incharge of the houses for catechumens. There was a great concern to show that the catechumens received an adequate religious instruction before their baptism in order to dispel questions, doubts and accusations regarding forced conversions. The catechumens besides receiving instruction in the Christian faith also learnt to fight "blind and idolatrous Hindu practices".[72]

Conversions took place in small numbers, and the local Christians were scattered even in the land of the Muslims; hence, they suffered frequently at the hands of the Hindus and others. One should not think that the institution of the *Pay dos Christãos* had been created essentially to protect the converts against the tyranny and injustice done against them by the Hindus, Muslims and by the Portuguese; or that its main duty consisted in settling disputes and differences that existed among those communities; or that it sought to solve problems of the local Christian community; or that it granted to the converts many favours or privileges.[73] This institution was created to promote the conversion of Hindus and to gather catechumens and illegitimate children of Hindu parents for baptism. Christian education was imparted to these candidates to enable them to earn their own living.[74] Some *Pays dos Christãos* had higher proselytizing schemes than others. One can imagine the people's opposition to them when they came to the village to investigate scrupulously about the existence of any Hindu religious practice. Needless to say that the care and protection given to the catechumens and the converts depended on the character and interest shown by the *Pay dos Christãos*. But generally he was respected by the Christian community.

The *Pay dos Christãos* was far from being an almighty and kind father. He was supposed to be a guardian to the Christians, but at times he acted more like a policeman than like a benefactor. He found little favour with the Portuguese officials and did not draw a big salary.[75] Generally the information the *Pay dos Christãos* gave to the Portuguese authorities regarding government jobs for the local Christians was respected. However, at times when the civil authorities disregarded this information, government offices were given to rebellious, scandalous and disobedient Christians, complained a *Pay dos Christãos*.[76]

The different religious orders in Goa had been playing the role of the *Pay dos Christãos*. The *Pay dos Christãos* was a Jesuit in Salcete, and a Franciscan in Bardez, but each religious order had a *Pay dos Christãos*.[77] He could be a married man with a family; if so, then his wife would take care of the female catechumens.[78] The *Pay dos Christãos* had become an important institution or figure, and was indispensable to expand and sustain Christendom in the Portuguese Eastern territories. The *Pay dos Christãos* disappeared from Goa when the houses for catechumens became extinct here in 1842.[79]

## The Hospital: a bait for conversions

The health facilities or services the Portuguese offered to the local Hindus and Muslims might have contributed to their conversion. Many Hindus were treated in the hospital for the locals and subsequently converted. Notably, during the war with the Adilshah, the Muslims destroyed many houses and all the churches in Salcete, but they caused no damage to the hospital saying that it was the house of God and charity.[80]

We find references to a hospital in Goa as early as January 1511. It may be recalled that the Portuguese ships arrived in Goa with many dead and sick people. This hospital attended only to the Portuguese. However, it probably also admitted some locals who lived in direct contact with the Portuguese, or those who had become helpers or associates of the Portuguese. We hear of another hospital built at the request of D. João III in the city of Goa in 1549 for the poor local converts.[81] Perhaps there was one more hospital in Goa for the locals ordered by the Portuguese.[82] Later the king, D. Sebastião, ordered a hospital for the locals with the best local physicians, since the converts often complained that after their conversion they were neglected.[83]

The sick Hindus, after coming to the hospital, received some Christian instruction, and those at death's door were baptized. Others, after recovering, went to stay in the College of St Paul to prepare themselves for group baptisms.[84] When a sick Hindu stayed at the hospital he had no other alternative but to eat with the Portuguese, which act made him an outcaste. There was no hope for such a man of regaining his caste or continuing to have contacts with the other Hindus.[85] Even if one took some medicine from the Christians one would lose caste.[86] In this fashion the hospital served as a bait to attract conversions, since many Hindus came there for treatment.[87]

The hospital for the locals received only men, and poor Christians who had no other place to go, or sick Hindus inclined to become Christians.[88] One day a Hindu had been beaten up by the villagers and at the same time disowned by his own relatives. Finally, he sought help in the hospital and showed willingness to become a Christian. The hospital staff treated him with great care and attention, and after receiving some Christian instruction he was baptized. When a sick Hindu woman wanted to become a Christian, she was kept in the house meant for female catechumens, in the care of a virtuous and charitable old lady. There could be a hundred woman catechumens in this house. The physical and spiritual healing went together in the hospitals.[89]

The Jesuit hospital at Margão in Salcete treated many Hindus, and a few, after seeing this sort of charity, were converted willingly.[90] Others, after being cured from dangerous diseases, asked for baptism with their entire household.[91] Some Hindus, unable to get remedy for their illnesses, asked for baptism. And many were converted when, after the accident in the gunpowder factory in 1562, they were taken to a hospital.[92]

Probably due to the hospital services and the attention rended here some Hindus, who for a long time had been offending God as the missionaries put it, became Christians in one hour, to the missionaries' surprise and consolation.[93]

**Jubilee: incentive to convert others**

The local Christians, and even some Portuguese, took great advantage of the jubilees by working for conversions.[94] A jubilee was a special occasion, or a definite period of time, during which the Christians could gain indulgences or spiritual favours if they performed specific deeds laid down by the jubilee, for example, converting a Hindu. In order to gain these indulgences some people worked with enthusiasm to make a convert.[95] Further, to benefit from the jubilee, the faithful had to do some works of charity like teaching catechism to the local Christians.[96] In 1569 an indulgence was offered to those who helped the houses for catechumens.[97] The jubilee of 1551 granted by pope, Julius III, arouse great enthusiasm among the Portuguese. There was another jubilee in Goa in 1558 which lasted for forty days. A jubilee could last for a full year, as in 1575.[98] Any Christian, Portuguese or local, could gain, or avail of, favours during a jubilee.[99]

The jubilee of 1564 granted indulgences to all those who converted a Hindu or Muslim. After announcing the jubilee the number of conversions increased.[100] Unusual fervour became visible not only among the Portuguese men and women but also among the local poor women eager to win indulgences for themselves and others.[101] A certain Christian woman had converted two Hindu persons. Unable to share her jubilee gains with her sick daughter — since such transfer of merits was unacceptable by the rules of the jubilee — the woman was determined to find for her daughter another person willing to be converted, so that the girl might also benefit from the jubilee.[102]

Perhaps in Goa, as it happened in Cochin, the Portuguese

who normally never cared for religion, at the time of the jubilee worked hard to make converts to the extent of even paying the Hindus to become Christians and other similar things.[103] But the merits of a jubilee could not be acquired by buying, since such a practice was unacceptable to the church.[104] A certain God-fearing man, who had worked sincerely to convert a Hindu to avail of favours of a jubilee, did not succeed in his intent. When he asked a priest whether he could gain it by buying the conversion of a Hindu it was outrightly refused.[105] If the jubilee required conversions and the power of persuasion failed, then other doubtful means might have been used to gain indulgences. Therefore, the jubilee must have caused many Hindus to flee from Goa.[106]

## Public Disputes: refutation of Gentile errors

The European tradition of theological and philosophical disputes had been introduced into Goa in the sixteenth century. We hear about several disputes with the Hindus, Muslims and Jews in Goa.[107] Public theological and philosophical debates with the Hindus and Muslims were normally held to convince them of the lies and falsities of their religion. This might have incensed them but they were reprimanded if they failed to attend, and intimidated into doing so. According to the missionaries the mere refutation of the Hindu errors or religion sufficed to prove the truth of the Christian religion, and prepare the Hindus to accept the church's doctrine.[108] The missionaries also believed that through arguments and reasoning one could come to the knowledge of God, and of Christianity as the true religion. Hence, with many arguments they presented their point of view.[109] A young and honest hermit, but skillful and discreet, wanted to have a dispute with the Catholic priests about his own religion and caste, but to the surprise of all those present, the dispute ended up by convincing the hermit of his errors. As a sign of his defeat or of his new convictions, the hermit burnt all the objects he had of his old religion in the presence of many Brahmans who had participated in the debate, to their bitter resentment and disapproval.[110]

It is difficult to imagine that the Brahmans and *jogues* (*yogi*) asked for disputes only to be mocked at, and to be put to shame. The Hindus and Muslims, obviously, never won any such disputes. Disputes could have taken place among the Christians themselves to show the errors of Hinduism to the neophites and catechumens. Perhaps the Hindus were compelled to be present at these disputes and to question their own beliefs. The missionaries challenged the Muslims and Hindus with visits to their houses, writings, exhortations from the pulpit, and preaching against them.[111] Hindu religious books were translated in order to learn their falsities and then refute them.[112] D. Gaspar, bishop of Goa, wrote many books to confront the Quran, but no copy of these books seems to have survived.[113] Christian doctrine was disputed in the houses for catechumens too.[114]

### Catechist Boys: catechists to adults

The conversion of some Hindus depended to a large extent on their converted children. Francis Xavier was convinced of this. Hence, he strongly recommended the instruction of young boys.[115] The young converts, by their reasoning and exemplary life, persuaded many Hindus to change their ancestral cult for the true one. To see these boys draw others to baptism was a motive for great rejoicing and consolation to the missionaries.[116]

Children were made to teach catechism (Christian precepts) to others, but some priests objected to this method, arguing that the lofty mysteries of the Christian faith could not be entrusted to children. The schools taught the boys good Christian customs, in turn expecting them to influence their parents who were still under the spell of their former idols. Men learnt better when instructed by these boys.[117] Moreover, they discouraged the Hindus from embracing Islam. Without doubt, it was easier to convert children than the adults.[118]

The boys who knew catechism well were chosen to dispute the Christian doctrine among themselves, and those who answered the questions satisfactorily won prizes.[119] They sang the doctrine on the streets everyday while going to, and leaving, their schools which immensely confused the Hindus.[120] At times one could see two hundred such boys singing the Christian doctrine even better than the sons of the Portuguese.[121] Now these convert children disowned their former gods.[122] And when the priests asked them whether they remembered anything about their former idols and rituals, the boys answered negatively.[123] It is interesting to know that perhaps many parents of these boys continued to remain Hindus.

The teachers wanted these children to assemble together in each village everyday in the evening to study the doctrine in groups. With this sort of exercise some local women and boys, even those who could hardly speak the Portuguese language, learnt the Christian doctrine perfectly.[124] The teachers made use of a catechism book, written in the form of a dialogue in the local language to instruct the school boys, and on Sundays and holy days it was recited in the churches with great profit for the Christians.[125]

The students of the College of St Paul had the duty to teach the Christian doctrine at night to the servants of their household, as well as to all others who did not know it, and they did it with enthusiasm.[126] However, if they omitted this duty even for a single night they confessed it, despite the consequent punishment they would receive from the priests.[127]

## Catechism: first instruction then baptism

In principle the adult Hindu or Muslim should not be baptized without first being submitted to a test. This test consisted in showing that he/she knew the Christian doctrine well, and that one was able to perform acts worthy of baptism. The motives of the person were also observed closely. Although there were several group baptisms and hasty baptisms too, it was understood that the candidate had been instructed individually before the baptism, if not, soon after it.[128] But there could have been cases of people learning only some Christian precepts before receiving baptism, after which they stayed in the house for catechumens for further instruction.[129] Here the local Christians were taught according to each one's learning capacity.[130] The tenets of the Catholic religion insisted on a good faith formation to the adults before their baptism.[131] But did the catechumens, especially when pressed by the demands of group baptisms, (or the neo-converts), learn anything when catechism (Christian doctrine) was conveyed to them in common and for a short while? When prayers were taught to a group it was noticed that not all in it knew them, but to make sure that everybody had learnt the prayers sufficiently well, each person was individually asked to recite them.[132] Ignorance of the Christian doctrine led to the printing of a manual on it, for catechetical purposes, after which many converts learnt better what they could and ought to do, and about sins.[133] Christian instruction was imparted to them in the churches every Sunday.[134] Singing and music in the churches were also meant to attract the Hindus to them. However, very few turned up there.[135] Catechism was taught to the girls in the morning, and to the boys in the afternoon, in the churches.[136] In 1546 D. João III urged the viceroy, D. João de Castro, to build schools in Goa, in localities where Christians resided, to instruct them in the faith and to compel the Hindus to attend the preaching.[137]

Traditional European theater and dramas of religious character, staged for catechetical and didactic purposes, had themes normally related to the virtuous lives of saints.[138] Religious meetings organized in the villages or schools provided instruction to the Christians, and the Hindus were also obliged to attend them.[139] The priests asked the viceroy to make it compulsory for the Hindu Brahmans to be present at the College of St Paul every Sunday in order to hear about their ignorance and superstitions.[140] The First Provincial Council (1567) ordered the Hindus to hear sermons, but this order met with a rebuff.[141] Failure to comply with this order attracted reproof.[142] Whether these sermons could ever convert or affect anyone may be questioned; however, we are told that once after hearing a forceful discourse delivered by a Brahman convert against Hinduism, some Brahman Hindus present there felt very embarassed, but went away just as they had come.[143]

During the sixteenth century thousands of booklets on the Christian doctrine were sent to Goa in order to teach its population. They were also meant for teachers to instruct the ignorant secular priests to read, and for the boys to learn the Christian doctrine and how to read as well.[144] The latter learnt not only the Christian doctrine but also 'good customs' as part of their Christian formation.

In 1575 Alessandro Valignano, a Jesuit superior, gave some guidelines to his fellow Jesuit missionaries regarding religious instruction to the catechumens and local Christians. First, he reminded them that they should teach what the catechumens and neo-converts should believe in, namely, the articles of faith and the sacraments. This teaching included what they should do to keep themselves away from sins and Hindu customs, and the Christian works they ought to perform. Moreover, the catechumens and the neo-converts ought to learn about the reward or punishment they could receive for their actions. It was also necessary to dispel any false opinion they might entertain, by showing them the errors and wickedness of the Hindu religion, and by telling them that Christianity alone was holy and reasonable. Second, the missionaries had to show them that the Christian law had been examined, approved and decided by all the learned in the world and by the great councils as being the only true religion, and that it alone could lead anyone to salvation. Third, examples and miracles, from the life of martyrs and apostles and the persecutions they suffered at the hands of infidel rulers, had to be communicated to the catechumens and neo-converts.[145] These guidelines stressed that the missionaries should not be too hasty in baptizing Hindus without first giving them a sound Christian instruction and testing their intentions and sincerity. Valignano's arguments for a solid instruction to the catechumens rested on his experience that many who desired to become Christians did not always come with the right motive, and baptizing them in this state could hardly make them abandon their superstitious customs. He also alleged that some converted only to marry Christian women, but no sooner had they got married than both went to live among the Hindus, and still worse she turned to her husband's superstitions.[146] These instructions to the Jesuit missionaries was nothing new in 1575; rather, they summarized what was normally believed and practised during the entire sixteenth century. Catechism was taught to the poor before giving them alms, but in practice a sound catechetical instruction did not always precede baptism.[147]

**Processions: to foster devotion**

Solemn processions galore in Goa, were staged especially to create and elicit devotion in, and from, the faithful.[148] Likewise, solemn religious festivals helped devotionally the new converts and even some Hindus to be converted.[149] We can think of the famed processions of the *Corpo de Deus*, of the *Rosário* by the Dominicans, the procession of the *Senhor dos Passos* by the Augustinians and many others conducted by the different religious orders.[150] Confraternities and chapels fostered the local cult and used it to have processions, which in turn helped to keep the faith of the people alive.[151] Folkloric element became part of religious cult and processions since Goa had very few occasions to offer its people good secular entertainment programmes.[152] These glamorous processions tried to impress on the masses the superiority of the rulers, and to exploit their religious feelings.The innumerable churches and their stately size also symbolized the power and riches of the patrons and masters.

The Italian traveller, Pietro Della Valle, informs us that he had never seen in any other country in the world so many processions as in Goa. Each one of the numerous religious orders in the city of Goa organized several processions. These religious orders enjoyed great power and being very rich they could afford to entertain their devotees. He remarked that these processions might have been commendable from the religious point of view; however, they proved improper in a place like Goa, surrounded by enemies constanly at war with it.[153] Despite this, the people idle and eager for spectacles awaited joyfully these occasions, and gave themselves whole-heartedly to them when they took place which, unfortunately, made them neglect other more important duties.

Besides these Christian solemn ceremonies meant to attract the Christians and the Hindus alike to the faith, there might have been also other feasts of secular character to satisfy the locals.

The *Foral de Salcete* speaks of a Hi¬du theater called *Zagor* performed in Goa during certain festivities.[154]

## Local Language

From the very beginning the missionaries, especially the Jesuits, were convinced about the need to promote the local languages at their colleges. The Jesuits ensured that the young boys from different nations who frequented the College of St Paul did not forget their own mother tongue. They expected these boys to teach the Christian faith to others when they returned to their countries of origin, after their studies. In order to become fluent in their mother tongue, their teachers ordered each student to practise it twice a day.[155] Ironically, most missionaries preached and taught the Christian doctrine through interpreters chosen from among the boys of this college. Missionary work through interpreters did not achieve the desired results. Hence, some missionaries believed that if they knew the local languages they could do a better job. But many showed great reluctance to learn them.[156]

It is sufficiently clear that all the five Provincial or Ecclesiastical Councils held in Goa during the sixteenth and beginning of the seventeenth centuries, urged the religious and secular clergy to learn the local languages, since without which the work of conversion would meet with many set-backs.[157] The Second Provincial Council (1575) went so far as to demand from a candidate for the priesthood the knowledge of the local language.[158] There was a royal letter in 1598 encouraging the religious to learn the local language.[159] However, curiously but not surprisingly, many locals were excluded from the priesthood on account of the difficulty they had in learning the Latin language, which had always precedence over the local languages in the seminaries. Despite a number of decrees ordering the missionaries to learn the local languages, the important question regarding how many in fact knew the local languages still remains without a satisfactory answer. But without advancing numbers we can state that very few indeed knew or were willing to learn them. The missionaries continued to teach and preach through interpreters.[160]

But teaching and preaching through interpreters brought poor results as has been pointed out earlier.[161] Experience showed them that one person who knew the local language could do much more work than ten others who did not know it. Besides, the one who knew the language was highly respected not only by the Christians, but also by the Hindus.[162] When the work of conversion had begun in Bardez and Salcete the need to learn Konkani (language of Goa) was increasingly felt.[163]

We have reportings about some missionaries who appeared to have mastered the local language.[164] But we should not forget that several accounts written by the missionaries aimed at pleasing, edifying and convincing their superiors and others about their religious zeal. Hence, the exaggeration of numbers, especially when the missionaries were accused of neglecting their proselytizing duties, was not uncommon. We also read that some Franciscans learnt the local language and became excellent masters of it. One of them wrote the Christian doctrine and the mysteries of the Catholic faith in the local language, in poetry form in about two thousand verses, for the Christians to sing and thereby strengthen their faith, and to open the eyes to the Hindus.[165] Some missionaries preached in Konkani, and those who knew it a little could hear confessions. The Franciscans were aware of the need to learn the local language.[166] They gave the impression that they knew it rather well, but we are told that during the seventeenth century they were responsible for the official suppression of Konkani, allegedly to continue to administer their own churches.[167] Earlier, the bishop of Goa had demanded from all the parish priests in the diocese the knowledge of the local language as an indispensable condition to administer the parishes.[168]

We hear in 1575 that the local language was also being taught at the Jesuit school in Salcete.[169] They wanted to write books in Konkani but unfortunately this project never saw the light of day.[170] The Jesuit priests and Brothers learnt languages at the College of St Paul.[171] Here, a *Canarim* student taught the religious Brothers the local language.[172] A letter written in 1576 informs us that three Jesuit priests knew the local language rather well. Hence, they could produce better results than many others who did not know it.

Those who did not know the local language preached with the help of interpreters.[173] But we also hear that around 1587 not more than five Jesuit priests knew the local language;[174] in 1593, only five priests could preach in Konkani.[175] Interestingly, a Jesuit wrote that it would not be possible to learn the local language if they did not reside among the locals, but he soon added that the Jesuits themselves disliked staying among the *Canarins*.[176] Fernão Guerreiro, a Jesuit himself, reported that all the Jesuit priests residing in Salcete in 1603, knew the local language.[177]

At the group baptisms the priests delivered a sermon in Konkani.[178] Children learnt the Christian doctrine with the help of booklets written in Konkani by the inmates of the College of St Paul. Ordinarily, sermons were also delivered in Konkani.[179] The catechumens were instructed through Konkani in the houses for catechumens.[180] Some religious Brothers taught them through the local language.[181] A Portuguese lady gave catechism lessons in Konkani, which she spoke fluently.[182] When we read that the Christian doctrine was taught in the local language it could also mean that it was done so through interpreters.[183] These interpreters were often boys from the College of St Paul. Many local boys and women knew the Christian doctrine fairly well in Portuguese language too.[184]

Preaching and teaching could be done throught interpreters, but not confessions. It appears that only hearing confessions could motivate the missionaries to learn the local language. But it was not so, since confessions were also heard through interpreters despite reports stating that all the priests heard confessions in Konkani.[185] In 1561, hardly any priest was able to hear confessions in Konkani due to the ignorance of the language.[186] To confess through interpreters had no precedent, rather it was not a norm in the church, hence this method was questioned.[187]

The articles of faith might have been transmitted to the catechumens in their own language. But the idea that only the Catholic religion was considered as the true one and the Latin language the best medium to convey it, made it impossible for the missionaries to find parallel or similar concepts in other local languages and cultures to express the mysteries of the Christian faith, if at all this was attempted in the mission fields.[188] European and missionary ethnocentrism and linguistic difficulties prevented them from learning local things. If books were written about Indian things they were simply to prepare future missionaries, and to refute the errors of idolatry. Some Hindu sacred books were translated to find out their errors and to challenge the Brahmans.[189]

The service of interpreters to declare the doctrine to the converts was never dispensed with.[190] Churches needed interpreters to teach the doctrine to the new converts.[191] The College of St Paul prepared local interpreters to work for the missionaries. After the missionaries learnt a little of the local language or began using interpreters, conversions increased.[192] The need for interpreters continued to be felt throughout the sixteenth century.

The missionaries are often held responsible for the decadence of Konkani in the sixteenth century. Although this constitutes another point for discussion, it would not be totally out-of-place to mention here that during the following century a few books were written in Konkani, especially by the Jesuits. The knowledge of the local language had become necessary to assume ecclesiastical posts, such as those of the parish priest during the last quarter of the seventeenth century, as already mentioned. This exigency proved to be too serious an obstacle to the ambitious plans of the missionaries who, for too long, had assumed the reins of power without the knowledge of the local languages. The missionary solution to this new and unpleasant situation was nothing short of demanding the suppression of the local languages. Then in 1684, a decree issued by the viceroy, D. Francisco de Tavora, and soon after ratified by a royal decree, suppressed Konkani in Goa and the local languages in other territories under the Portuguese control. Later, some blamed only the Franciscans for the decree on the suppression of local languages. This accusation, however, is questionable since the reading of events and context appears to be vitiated. But going by facts, all the religious orders seemed to have profited from this obnoxious decree.

Based on the facts mentioned above, today, one could perhaps argue and make a general remark that the Goan Christians developed a separate linguistic identity by alienating themselves from their own mother tongue in favour of Portuguese, both as a language of education and communication till very recently. But how many have done so?

## Conclusion

The official and traditional doctrine of the church never approved any sort of forced or feigned conversion. Catholic theology held that conversions were entirely the work of God. The convertor could be only God. Undoubtedly, the sanctity of the evangelizers — the instruments of God's grace — was extremely important especially in the case of conversion of Hindus, who were little inclined to arguments and reasoning. Hence, a much better moral behaviour and lifestyle was expected from the Christians and missionaries overseas, than from the clergy and faithful in Europe.

The First Provincial Council (1567) decreed that no force should ever be used to bring anyone to the faith.[193] The Second Provincial Council (1575 ) was against forced methods for the following reasons: first, it was scandalous and incited the people to join together and revolt against the Portuguese; second, if ten converts could be made by force many more potential converts could be lost; and third, converts made by force ran away to the territory of the Adilshah. The viceroys and the government officials did not approve of any 'strong method' for the revolts and social unrest it created.[194] Fr. F. Cabral wrote to Portugal informing not to send men with excessive religious zeal to the missions, since these people were very harmful to the work of conversion.[195]

The king of Portugal referring to the methods of conversion in 1568, stated that conversions should be made with temperance and love, namely, without any scandal or use of force, for methods other than these could prevent the majority from joining Christendom. Moreover, while attempting to instruct the Hindus in the faith they should be told that their conversion could bring them not only salvation, but also several social privileges or advantages.[196] Again in 1588, the king rejected the use of force, direct or indirect, in order to avoid scandals.[197] Nevertheless, royal decrees such as the prohibition of the Hindu ceremonies or the statute demanding that the orphans should be taken away from the care of their Hindu relatives for instruction, had to be implemented strictly. It was necessary, however, to give the impression to the Hindus that the missionaries had no part in these decisions.[198]

The city councillors and government officials held the Jesuits responsible for the migration of many local Christians to the territory of Muslims, which move had caused a considerable loss to the crown revenues. Due to harsh proselytizing methods some catechumens ran away. When the Hindus, who had left Goa earlier, were requested to return by the Portuguese authority, the Hindus demanded from the priests some assurance that they would not be made Christians by force. They also sought government counter-guarantees, as for instance to be able to practise their religion freely. There was so much discussion on this matter among the missionaries — on whether religious freedom should be granted to the Hindus in general — to make it disgusting to the governor.[199]

People may embrace or change to a particular religion when it appeals to them, but religious activity beyond the limit gives diminishing returns. When the priests spoke about conversions the Hindus hardened themselves and shunned the missionaries; whereas when they spoke only about the glory of God and of things of the other life, without telling them to become Christians, they themselves asked for baptism.[200] The intention of the Hindus who asked for baptism was not examined. After being instructed the missionaries held that it was sufficient to hear from them that they wanted to become Christians for the love of God.[201]

Perseverance of the converts amidst difficulties and even persecution need not be necessarily a valid argument in favour of voluntary conversion of these people. Just as syncretism and relapses do not point necessarily to forced conversion of the relapsed, however, force could have been used initially but not continually.

Although the missionaries who came to India did not have the necessary theological preparation to respond to new culture, their own social analyses of the Indian reality convinced them that certain local cultural and religious elements could hardly be made to change. Preaching and teaching alone would not suffice. Favours had to be granted to the converts. The only way to make many Christians was to favour them very much, Francis Xavier wrote to D. João III in 1548.[202] If the king did not demand from the Portuguese and government officials their personal attention to the activity of conversions, if he did not enforce threats and punishment against those who neglected this duty, then the endless decrees in favour of Christendom would be of no value. However, Francis Xavier had no hopes that such attention would ever be given to the work of conversion overseas.[203]

Finally, in the face of 'decrees and privileges in favour of conversion' often adverse to the intrests of the Hindus, many preferred to convert rather than to migrating or losing their lands. If the Hindus complained to the secular authority that conversions were effected by force, the latter had to refer the matter to the ecclesiastical authority, who then examined and decided about it. The ecclesiastical decision was final, decreed the First Provincial Council in 1567.[204]

## NOTES AND REFERENCES

1. *Doc*, III, 7-8.
2. "...conversão das almas é cousa de Deos..." *DI*, XI, 12.
3. *Ibid.*, XV, 324-25.
4. Josef Wicki, (ed.), *LPC*, p. 146. ARSI, *Eppistolae Goana et Malabarica*, 14, fl. 68.
5. Luís de Guzman, *Historia de las Misiones de la Companía de Jesus en la India Oriental, en la China y Japon 1540-1600*, pp. 59-61.
6. *Doc*, VIII, 299-301.
7. *APO*, 3, p. 5.
8. BNL, *Reservados,* Cod. 176, fl. 97v.
9. *La Iglesia en America: Siglos XVI-XX,* pp. 28-29.
10. *DI*, VI, 402; VIII, 76; XIII, 422; XV, 647; XVIII, 870-71. Luís de Guzman, *op.cit.,* p. 61.
11. *DI*, VIII, 60f.
12. *Ibid.*, XV, 581. When a boy manifested his desire to become a Christian the rector of the College of St Paul cut immediately his *xenddi* (hair-tuft). ARSI, *Goana Historia,* 33–I, fl. 183.

13. *DI*, VII, 67.
14. *Doc*, I, 152.
15. Rodrigo José de Lima Felner, *Subsídios para a História da India Portugueza,* Vol. V, p. xx.
16. *Doc*, VII, 33.
17. *DI*, IX, 280.
18. *Ibid.*
19. *Ibid.*, IV, 342, 648.
20. *Doc*, VIII, 58.
21. *DI*, IV, 343.
22. *Bullarium*, Second Provincial Council, Acc. 2, dec. 1, p. 47; Third Provincial Council, Acc. 2, dec. 23, p. 70.
23. *DI*, XV, 580-83.
24. *Ibid.*, V, 64-65. C. R. Boxer, *The Portuguese Seaborne Empire 1415-1825*, (1973), p. 71.
25. C. R. Boxer, *The Church Militant and Iberian Expansion, 1440-1770*, p. 100.
26. *Bullarium*, First Provincial Council, Acc. 2, dec. 1. *DI*, XVII, 84, see note 7.
27. Rodrigo José de Lima Felner, *op. cit.*, p. xx.
28. H. Heras, "The Decay of the Portuguese Power in India", p. 23.
29. Teotonio R. de Souza, "The Voiceless in Goan Historiography. A Case for the Source-Value of Church Records in Goa", p. 120.
30. CEHU, *Gavetas da Torre do Tombo*, V, p. 320.
31. *DI*, XI, 262.
32. *APO*, 5, doc. 556, p. 602.
33. *Doc*, IV, 454.
34. *Ibid.*, XI, 337.
35. *BFUP*, No. 2, pp. 317-21. *MR*, 3B, fls. 490-95.
36. *Doc*, II, 343.
37. ARSI, *Extracto das cousas*, 1a, fl. 3.
38. *Doc*,VIII, 53.
39. Friar António wrote to the king in 1518, "Pareceme, Senhor, que se mandardes fazer huma asinada esmola de aroz a estes gentios que se fizeram cristãos, que em proviso muitos se converterão." *Ibid.*, I, 354.
40. P. D. Xavier, *Goa: A Social History*, pp. 115, 117. C. R. Boxer, *The Portuguese Seaborne Empire 1415-1825*, (1969), p. 70.

41. *Doc*, VIII, 214.
42. *Ibid.*, 299.
43. *DI*, III, 357-58.
44. *Ibid.*, II, 476-77. 'Misericordia' was an welfare institution or charity organization.
45. *BFUP*, No. 16, p. 796.
46. Leopoldo da Rocha, *As Confrarias de Goa. Séculos XVI-XX. Conspecto Histórico-Jurídico*, p. 4.
47. *Ibid.*, p. 275.
48. These properties came to be known later as *fabrica da igreja*. *Ibid. Doc*, X, 654.
49. Leopoldo da Rocha, *op. cit.*, p. 275.
50. ARSI, *Goana Historia*, 33 - II, fl. 212v.
51. *BFUP*, No. 2, pp. 206-10. *MR*, 2A, fls. 245-57.
52. *Doc*, III, 3-12.
53. *Ibid.* Leopoldo da Rocha, *op. cit.*, pp. 5-6.
54. Sebastião Gonçalves, *Primeira Parte da História dos Religiosos da Companhia de Jesus e do que fizeram com a Divina Graça na Conversão dos Infieis na nossa Sancta Fé Catholica nos Reynos e Provincias da India Oriental*, p. 122.
55. *Doc*, III, 4.
56. Leopoldo da Rocha, *op. cit.*, p. 152.
57. *Ibid.*, p. 153.
58. *Ibid.*, p. 16.
59. *DI*, II, 476-78.
60. Ana Cannas Cunha, *A Inquisição no Estado da India - Origens (1539-1560)*, p. 264.
61. *DI*, II, 476-77.
62. Leopoldo da Rocha, *op. cit.*, p. 35.
63. Edward Grey, (ed.), *The Travels of Pietro Della Valle in India*, Vol. II, pp. 382-83.
64. Georg Schurhammer, *Francisco Javier. Su Vida y su Tiempo*, Vol. II, p. 287.
65. ARSI, *Miscellaneum Indiarum Orientalum*, 38 - II, fl. 295v-96.
66. Josef Wicki, (ed.), *LPC*, p. x. The office of *Pay dos Christãos* came into existence by a royal decree in 1532-33. António da Silva Rego, *História das Missões do Padroado Português do Oriente*, p. 201.

67. Josef Wicki, (ed.), *op. cit.*, p. 16.
68. *Doc*, IV, 564.
69. *DI*, XVII, 86. ARSI, *Miscellanea Indiarum Orientalium*, 38 - I, fl. 139. *BFUP*, No. 1, p. 49.
70. Maria Benedita Araújo, "O «Pay dos Christãos». Contribuição para o estudo da Cristianização da Índia", pp. 306, 313.
71. Josef Wicki, (ed.), *op. cit.*, pp. 14, 16.
72. *Doc*, XII, 738.
73. Maria Benedita Araújo, *op. cit.*, p. 305.
74. "Determinaram os reis desdo o principio da Cristandade neste Estado para promoverem a converção dos gentios houvesse um Padre Pay dos Christãos para buscar e descobrir os cathecumenos, e uma caza aonde os recolhese para serem instruidos nos mistérios da nossa santa fé - se achavão os ditos Padres na posse de recolherem na dita caza todas a crianças illegitimas, isto é, nascidas de mãys gentias que não estavão cazadas legitimamente, e de darem as ditas crianças o santo bautismo contra a vontade das proprias mãys e ainda dos gentios que dizião erão seus pays, e procuravão depois para as mesmas crianças huma Christam educação, e algum modo de viver com que, se quizessem, pudessem ganhar a sua vida temporal e não perderem como os outros a vida eterna". Josef Wicki, (ed.), *op. cit.*, p. 350.
75. *Doc*, III, 521.
76. ARSI, *Eppistolae Goana et Malabarica*, 15, fl. 174v.
77. Paulo da Trindade, *CEO*, Part I, p. 127.
78. *Doc*, III, 521. Josef Wicki, (ed.), *op. cit.*, p. 16.
79. We recall that the Jesuits had been expelled by the Marquis of Pombal in 1759. Later, at the time of the constitutional monarchy in 1834, all the religious orders were also expelled from Goa and the East. *Ibid.*, p. x.
80. *DI*, XI, 267.
81. *Ibid.*, I, 104. *Doc*, VI, 45. "Porque, pera o effeito da comversão da gente desta terra serve muyto verem usarmos com elles todalas obras de misericordia e obrigação, pera que man tenhão cousa de dizer, que depois que se comvertem a nosa santa ffé não temos cuidado delles, porque se adoecem não nos curamos e se morrem não nos enterramos, como geralmente diziam, ffoy ordenado o esprital pera a gente da terra,... Pello quall os mordomos terão muy espiciall cuidado de prover o dito esprital, pera serem curados quanto

ffor posyvell todolos pobres que vierem a elle, que forem christãos pera esta maneira, acrecentando o que pello tenpo se mais poder ffazer." "Averá senpre ffysico da terra dos milhores que ouver..." This was written in 1546. *Ibid.*, III, 359.

82. ARSI, *Miscellanea Indiarum Orientalium*, 38 - I, fl. 140.
83. ARSI, *Fundationes Goana*, 22 - I, fls. 19v-20.
84. *Doc*, VIII, 390.
85. *Ibid.*, 300.
86. *DI*, VIII, 339.
87. *Ibid.*, IV, 737; X, 737.
88. *Doc*, IX, 466, 91.
89. *Ibid.*, IX, 91. *DI*, V, 609.
90. *Ibid.*, XII, 423; XI, 651.
91. *Ibid.*, VI, 120.
92. *Doc*, IX, 116.
93. *Ibid.*, IV, 747-48.
94. Sebastião Gonçalves, *op. cit.*, p. 91.
95. *DI*, II, 42-43, 187-88. Sebastião Gonçalves, *op. cit.*, p. 91.
96. *DI*, IV, 275.
97. *Ibid.*, VII, 660.
98. *Ibid.*, IX, 192.
99. *Ibid.*, VI, 402.
100. *Doc*, IX, 374.
101. *Ibid.*, 421, 427.
102. *Ibid.*, 372.
103. *Ibid.*, 434.
104. *DI*, VI, 368.
105. *Ibid.*, IX, 372.
106. *Ibid.*, 411.
107. *Ibid.*, II, 261.
108. J. H. da Cunha Rivara, *Gramatica da Lingua Concani Composta pelo Padre Thomaz Estevão*, p. LV.
109. Fernão Mendes Pinto, *The Travels of Mendes Pinto*, p. xl. *DI*, XVI, 320.
110. Luis de Guzman, *op. cit.*, p. 61.
111. BNL, *Reservados*, Cod. 176, fl. 102. *DI*, III, 727.
112. *Doc*, VI, 470. Maria Benedita Araújo, *op. cit.*, p. 309.

113. BNL, *Reservados*, Cod. 176, fl. 102v.
114. *DI*, VII, 400.
115. *Ibid.*, III, 367. A catechist was an instructor of the Christian doctrine.
116. *Ibid.*, XVIII, 882.
117. *Ibid.*, III, 317.
118. *Doc*, VI, 47.
119. *DI*, XII, 612; XVII, 366.
120. *Ibid.*, III, 735; V, 273. *Doc*, X, 89.
121. *DI*, IX, 305.
122. *Ibid.*, VIII, 325.
123. *Ibid.*, VII, 68.
124. *Doc*, X, 89.
125. *DI*, XVIII, 890.
126. *Doc*, VI, 49.
127. *DI*, VI, 609.
128. *Ibid.*, IV, 367.
129. *Ibid.*, V, 606. The local Hindus and Muslims had to be instructed in the Christian doctrine for 20 days before receiving baptism. *Bullarium*, Third Provincial Council, Acc. 2, dec. 26, p.71.
130. *DI*, IV, 185.
131. *Ibid.*, I, 604-05.
132. BNL, *Reservados*, Cod. 176, fl. 118v.
133. Alessandro Valignano, *op. cit.* p. 353. Booklets on religious or devotional content (*cartilhas*) were printed at the printing press in the city of Goa. José Wicki, "Ainda o IV Centenário da Primeira Imprensa de Goa", pp. 557f.
134. *DI*, XI, 271.
135. *Ibid.*, XVI, 853.
136. *Doc*, V, 50.
137. *DI*, I, 106.
138. *Ibid.*, XV, 3*. In 1572 they performed a tragicomedy representing the first imprisonment of Saint Paul. ARSI, *Goana Historia*, 31 - I, fl. 271. Mario Martins, "Teatro Sagrado nas Cristandades da Índia Portuguesa, século XVI".
139. *Doc*, III, 265.
140. *Ibid.*, VII, 345.
141. ARSI, *Miscellanea Indiarum Orientalium*, 38 - I, fl. 139.
142. *DI*, IV, 423.

143. *Doc*, VII, 348.
144. Isaías da Rosa Pereira, "O ensino da doutrina cristã nos séculos XIII a XVI", pp. 361, 363.
145. *DI*, XI, 13.
146. A. Valignano elaborated these guidelines thus: "E não sejais muito faceis em bautisar sem verdes que estão bem doutrinados, porque como ainda os christãos são muito fracos e os que se querem fazer christãos ordinariamente não vêm como devião na intenção, quanto mais se fazem desta maneira christãos, mais difficultosos são a os tirar de seus gentilicos custumes e superstições: quanto mais que ordinariamente os que se querem fazer christãos não hé senão pera casar-se com alguma molher, a qual depois levão antre os gentios, ou torna com seu marido a suas gentilicas superstições; porque acompanhada a molher fraca na fee com hum marido que se pode chamar gentio, não se pode esperar senão que aja de tropeçar. E por isto tende muito tento em fazer os ditos christãos, a antes de se casar dêm fiança segura de viver antre os christãos com suas molheres." Guidelines given by A. Valignano in 1575. *Ibid.*, 21.
147. Sebastião Gonçalves, *op. cit.*, p. 95.
148. *Bullarium*, Second Provincial Council, Acc. 3, dec. 4.
149. *DI*, IV, 189.
150. Leopoldo da Rocha, *op. cit.*, p. 156.
151. Confraternities were institutions imported from Portugal which spread quickly due to the existence of similar structures among the Hindus.
152. Leopoldo da Rocha, *op. cit.*, p. 163.
153. J. A. Ismael Gracias, "A India em 1623-24. Excerptos das Memórias do viajante italiano Pietro della Valle", p. 20. Fr. Luís Fróis wrote from Goa in 1557, "Esta cydade parecia toda huma religião, porque todos os dias os religiosos de todas as ordens fazian precisões..." *DI*, III, 708.
154. Panduranga Pissurlencar, *Goa Pré-Portuguesa através dos Escritores Lusitanos dos Séculos XVI e XVII*, p. 44.
155. *DI*, I, 121.
156. *Ibid*, 184.
157. *APO*, 3, p. 826. *Doc*, XI, 600.
158. *Bullarium*, Second Provincial Council, Acc. 4, dec. 4 p. 47.
159. *BFUP*, No. 2, p. 248. *MR*, 2B, fls. 470-71.
160. *DI*, IV, 356, 646, 753; VIII, 65, 88. *Doc*, X, 98.

161. *DI*, II, 382.
162. *Ibid.*, X, 242, 245, 246, 291, 467.
163. J. H. da Cunha Rivara, *Gramatica da Lingua Concani*, p. LVII.
164. *DI*, VIII, 68, 338, 339.
165. *Doc*, V, 406.
166. Paulo da Trindade, *op. cit.*, p. 296.
167. J. H. da Cunha Rivara, *Ensaio Historico da Lingua Concani*, (1858), pp. 255-59.
168. Délio de Mendonça, "The Suppression of Konkani Language in 1684", pp. 1-14.
169. *DI*, X, 732.
170. ARSI, *Eppistolae Goana et Malabarica*, 16, fl. 180.
171. Luis de Guzman, *op. cit.*, p. 56. *DI*, V, 274.
172. *Ibid.*, VI, 111.
173. *Ibid.*, X, 468.
174. *Ibid.*, XIV, 468.
175. *Ibid.*, XVI, 180.
176. *Ibid.*, X, 617; XIV, 648.
177. Fernão Guerreiro, *Relação Anual das coisas que fizeram os Padres da Companhia de Jesus nas suas Missões,* Vol. II, p. 355.
178. *Doc*, V, 405.
179. *Ibid.*, XI, 490; XII, 738. *DI*, V, 273; X, 734; XI, 273.
180. *Ibid.*, XII, 417.
181. *Doc*, X, 98.
182. *Ibid.*, 249.
183. *DI*, XI, 273.
184. *Ibid.*, 90.
185. *Ibid.*, 5, 273f; XVII, 295. J. H. da Cunha Rivara, *Ensaio Histórico da Lingua Concani*, p. 225.
186. *Doc*,V, 417; X, 99.
187. The Jesuits heard confessions of the people through interpreters in Brazil. José Oscar Beozzo, "O Diálogo da Conversão do Gentio. A evangelização entre a persuasão e a força", p. 561.
188. *Doc*, X, 498.
189. *DI*, IV, 201, 336.
190. *Ibid.*, IX, 277.
191. *Ibid.*

192. *Ibid.*, XV, 14, 290.
193. *Bullarium*, First Provincial Council, Acc. 2, dec. 10, 36.
194. *DI*, XV, 581.
195. *Ibid.*, 583.
196. *APO*, 3, pp. 3, 9.
197. *DI*, XIV, 879.
198. *Ibid.*, 863,
199. *Ibid.*, XV, 581.
200. *Ibid.*, XVII, 385.
201. *Ibid.*, V, 230. "He verdade que os mais dos gentios se convertem per occasiões que nos não somos obrigados a examinar basta que quanto pedem o baptismo e o recebem ja instructos nas cousas da fee dizem que o fazem por amor de Deos." Letter from the Archebishop of Goa to the king of Portugal in 1561. CEHU, *As Gavetas da Torre do Tombo*, III, p. 191.
202. *Doc*, IV, 18.
203. *Ibid.*, 18-19. "Eu, Senhor, não estou de todo determinado a ir a Jappão, mas vay-me paresendo que sym, porque desconfio muito que não hei-de ter verdadeiro favor na India pera acrescentar a nossa sancta fee, nem pera conservação da christandade que está feita." *Ibid.*, 199.
204. *Bullarium*, First Provincial Council, Acc. 2, dec. 34, p. 13.

# 5

# DECREES AND PRIVILEGES IN FAVOUR OF CONVERSION

## Privileges for Lusitanian Citizens

The vast body of decrees and privileges in favour of the converts and Christendom proved to be the most 'successful' means to compel and attract the Hindus to conversion and prevent the local Christians from relapsing or falling back. The missionaries believed that to increase the number of converts it was urgent and absolutely necessary to help the Christians, and disfavour the Hindus. It was certainly easier to do the latter but it was also dangerous. Help to Christians came often late or almost never. Nevertheless, granting substantial privileges to the Lusitanian citizens went hand-in-hand with the promulgation of some drastic measures and decrees against the half-citizens — Hindus and Muslims — of the empire. Favours and disfavours could be considered as the two inseparable sides of the conversion strategy, meaning that anything that favoured the 'affair of conversion' was good enough to be made into a decree.

Several documents inform us that those drastic decrees that prevented Hindu rituals, their bad social customs, unhealthy human dealings, etc., aimed at facilitating conversions or favouring converts. The refusal of an invitation by the Hindu civil servants to be converted led the Portuguese authority to pass a decree on their exclusion from the government offices, and another decree on the reservation of these jobs only for the converts. For instance, the job of rent collection, rent that belonged to the crown, had to be leased out only to Christians. There were many complaints that the most profitable government positions had been for long in control of Hindus to the detriment of conversions. Favouring Hindus without any hope of their conversion proved to be a great disservice to conversions.[1] Besides, the Portuguese authority, among other things, forbade the Goan Hindus to perform their ceremonies in and outside Goa, since such practice prevented their own conversion and discouraged the new converts as well.[2] Obviously, the most affected groups, especially the Brahmans, reacted and flouted these laws.[3] But did all these 'decrees and privileges in favour of conversion' really favour the Lusitanian citizen-vassals? Whether the Hindu losses were gains to the converts will be discussed in this chapter.

It is clear that some Portuguese and Hindus, mainly the rich and the powerful Brahmans, oppressed the Christians in the island of Goa. Some Hindus worked hard to win back to Hinduism some converts, especially by embarassing them. However, the care and support these converts received from the missionaries prevented their relapse.[4] It was imperative to take stock of the situation and promulgate some laws for the welfare of these converts.[5] But it is beyond doubt that despite the 'decrees and privileges in favour of conversion' or Christendom the Hindus, particularly the Brahmans, continued to be the recipients of many privileges and to occupy the best positions in the government administration till 1557. We read that after this year the Christians began to have preference in government jobs and to acquire more social privileges.[6] But this is far from being an honest appraisal of reality.

The 'decrees and privileges in favour of conversion' may appear as an euphemism for anti-Hindu customs, law and freedom. But according to the Portuguese mentality and arguments they were not anti-Hindu decrees. More often than not they could in fact be so. However, to be consistent with the terminology of our sources, I prefer to use the same expression. It needs to be said that many decrees have only the resemblance of being pro-conversion since they were anti-Hindu, but they did not have anything to do directly with conversions. Rather these decrees were issued for the defence and security of the state, or to tie up its fiscal deficit or raise revenues for the crown. However, the Hindus being richer than the Christians were obviously prejudiced by these decrees as we shall soon see.

Conversions in a colonial context have been associated either with force or favours of material and social nature. This chapter may give us an overall view of some relevant decrees and privileges in favour of conversion, their origin and implementation in concrete contexts and moments. These favours or privileges could embrace both the Hindus and Christians. As stated earlier, their purpose could be either to effect conversions or prevent relapses. The privileges granted to the Lusitanian citizens by the royal or civil decrees and charters could be in the form of jobs, gifts, lands, posts in public services, dispensation from tax payment, civil rights, social emancipation for slaves, women, etc; they could be just alms for the poor converts,[7] free medical assistance[8] or dresses for their baptism.[9] Some privileges, like the baptismal dresses for the catechumens, created some serious problems later when the empire became moribund. Many Hindus who were inclined to conversion and were even ready for it, refused baptism when the administration failed to provide them with these dresses. They went back to their former practices.[10]

Decrees and official letters speak repeatedly about penalties for breach of any law in favour of conversion. These penalties could vary from simple fines to life imprisonment: the transgressor could be sent captive to the galleys, and loss of property or personal belongings in favour of the crown was not uncommon.[11] An informer or approver could be rewarded with half of the goods confiscated from the accused, the other half being for the state.[12] The penalty depended on the nature of the offence. For instance, the penalty for the breach of the law of D. Sebastião in 1564, forbidding any Hindu or Muslim to persuade another person to convert to his own religion, could mean for the former the loss of his property and remaining captive for the galleys;[13] and the same kind of punishment was reserved for the relapsed new convert.[14] The local Christians could be severely reprehended for their errors and those who did not pay any heed to the decrees on conversion, were threatened with the fires of hell or even with excommunication.[15] The new converts, poor as they were, had to pay fines for the slightest offences. The poor Hindus were at the mercy of the whims of the Portuguese authority, and they were frightened of baptism.

Some decrees may appear rather strange when read outside their socio-political context, as for instance, the decree of the governor, António Moniz Barreto, in 1574, forbidding the Hindu pundits and physicians to move about in the city of Goa and its outskirts on horseback, sedan-chair or palanquin. In 1575 this prohibition was extended to the use of the parasol too. The breach of this decree could attract a fine of fifty *pardaus* and loss of these objects or goods.[16] The edicts regulating the number of pages, employees to harness horses, slaves to carry umbrellas (or a nobleman's retinue), and the use of palanquins were primarily meant to make personnel available to fight at the time of war, and to levy additional taxes. The political and military security of the Portuguese state being constantly threatened by its neighbouring rulers, forced the issuance of a decree forbidding fully-covered palanquins for women in Portuguese-controlled areas bordering regions of the Hindu and Muslim kingdoms.[17] Some statutes attempted to control lavish habits or lifestyles, since they harmed the rents of the crown and service to God. In order to curb abuses of high spending in dressing, a certain decree decided against the use of silk, brocade or linen clothes and such other luxuries in Goa. Dressing habits should be without any sort of extravagance or fashion as a measure to reduce state expenses.[18] In 1548 there was a huge expenditure of money on silk clothing, embellished with gold and silver, and on other items not so common in this land. To continue to maintain this lifestyle, they had to sell their arms, cheat the Christians and Muslims and trade with the enemies of the faith.[19] In 1575 the Second Provincial Council demanded moderation in customs and correction of excesses to exalt the name of Christ and to reform irreligious practices.[20]

The local converts and the foreign Christians residing in Goa had to dress in a manner that enabled anyone to recognize them as such, or more concretely, the First Provincial Council upheld that a foreign Christian should wear a cap or carry a parasol to be distinguished from a Hindu, or that no Hindu or Muslim could dress like a Christian. But often the commoners, Christians and Hindus, wore a dress consisting of only one piece of cloth.[21] Moreover, a Hindu woman should also be distinguished from a Christian woman in dressing. Whenever the former came outdoors she had to place a piece of red cloth on her uncovered shoulder, and in case she failed to conform with this prescription, she would be fined.[22] Brahmans were forbidden to wear the sacred thread.[23] Some decrees might appear strange and foolish to us. However, in order to understand these decrees, we need to keep in mind the continued Portuguese preoccupation not only with preventing communication between the Hindus and Christians, but also with eliminating every Hindu sign or custom that could remind the converts of their former practices.[24]

Conversion was a result of various forces at play that kept changing according to historical demands and several other considerations. It is clear that even a superficial reading of the sixteenth century documentation can give us the impression that most Hindus converted because they received, or better they had been promised, favours or material benefits from the Portuguese; or that they were forced to convert due to harsh anti-Hindu legislation, and that they did so for convenience rather than for the love of the new religion; or that the converts were saved from relapsing due to the privileges they received from the Portuguese, or threats from the ecclesiastical authorities. In short, these decrees and privileges in favour of conversions may appear to us today as mere enticements to conversion or discouragement to falling back and nothing more.[25] However, the sixteenth century ideology and argument that justified the need of a comprehensive legislation, cannot be reduced, simplified and made to conform to our present day first impressions derived from a slipshod reading of the historical narrative in question.

It is obvious that the immediate purpose of these decrees and privileges in favour of conversion was to increase the number of loyal citizens for the Lusitanian empire; or to prevent relapses; or to persuade the Hindus to convert, and punish those who obstructed the work of conversion. Briefly but most importantly, the sixteenth century argument that justified the sizeable body of 'Decrees and Privileges in Favour of Conversion' rested on the assumption that the increase of conversions was necessary to enable Portugal to fulfil entirely its duties and obligation, entrusted to it by the pope.[26]

The repetitive nature of this kind of legislation or ratification of most decrees and privileges in favour of conversion, led some historians to doubt and question about their execution, and the seriousness of the law enforcers in this regard. It is difficult to ascertain when and how consistently, and strictly they were implemented. Nevertheless, to suggest that the Goan people remained unaffected on account of this legislation is tantamount to distorting basic facts. It is certain that the implementation of these decrees and privileges and the application of penalties varied widely in time and places. Personal status of the locals, political and economic conditions of the state, are other relevant factors that can help us to understand the implementation of this legislation.[27] But the crux of the problem still remains unanswered, namely, whether the innumerable royal and other decrees and letters in favour of the Christians *de facto* favoured and provided privileges to the converts.[28] What follows is an attempt to answer this question.

## Social Privileges

Local information sent to the crown and to other authorities in Portugal conveyed that those who became Christians were always, and in all things, favoured with justice. This information stressed that the converts were treated well, that no rigorous method was used against them, and that even those guilty in light matters were not punished but simply rebuked.[29] The Portuguese overseas also reported that from 1545 no fines had been imposed on the offending Christians but only healthy penances.[30] These are but a few examples about the treatment meted out to the converts. However, there is much documentary evidence to show that what was reported to the king was not the whole truth. Misinformation was deliberately sent to Portugal. The royal orders, for instance, promulgated in

1513 and ratified in 1559 and 1563, granting the same legal and civil rights and social privileges the Portuguese settlers enjoyed in Goa to the local converts, were hardly taken seriously by the local administrators and governors.[31] Expectations in Portugal that these privileges would move the Hindus to the Catholic faith rose higher.[32] By this royal decree the local Christians could legally claim all the rights a Portuguese citizen enjoyed in Goa. But would such claims, if ever encouraged, be entertained by the civil authority?[33]

We need to evaluate in what manner the conversions and the civil legislation related to them affected the social and economic life of the local Christians (and of the Hindus and Muslims too) in Goa. What were the social and economic conditions, before and after, of those who embraced Christianity? Did the converts lose their traditional social rights as a result of their abandoning the ancestral religion? These issues and a few others will be considered in this chapter.

The converts could have changed their traditional occupation more easily, especially the most socially degrading ones, but their social and economic situation might not have changed considerably. They remained within the same caste and were not favoured as they should have been by the Portuguese authority. The local Christians had no chance of occupying positions of importance, as for instance, at the level of municipal administration of Goa. But an Eurasian had better opportunities here. However, there were some opportunities for the more ambitious in religious life than outside in the world. In Goa many secular clergy recruited from among the *Canarins* (sons of the soil), and educated at the Seminary of Santa Fé of the Jesuits or in the seminaries of the other religious orders from 1550, were mostly Brahmans who, after their conversion, had lost their traditional profession and status. They found it easier to regain some lost social prestige, especially in clerical life or among the European-born clergy, although in subordinate positions.[34]

From the above observations we can conclude that after conversion, the Hindus lost their traditional social rights and place within their own community. In other words they were despised by their own families and caste group. That they were despised and treated even worse than local ordinary soldiers by the Hindus and the Portuguese alike, was a recurring complaint made by the missionaries.[35] These social injustices suffered by the converts were responsible, to a large extent, for the crown's decrees in favour of conversions, or else the converts would succumb to their family and group pressures. The Portuguese, obviously, had no other alternative but to protect them if they wanted their collaboration and to increase the numbers of the Lusitanian citizen-vassals.

When the Brahmans became Christians they had much to lose at the beginning, especially their honour and respect among the Hindus, but gradually they were able to recover their fortunes among the Portuguese. Not a few Brahmans became Christians in Goa.[36] If the Portuguese tried to create here a new social order with little consideration for old traditions such as caste honours or social hierarchy, it would certainly not attract the high castes to conversion. However, this could be remedied if the crown and governors gave to the prospective candidates to baptism many privileges, honours and protection and denied them to the obstinate Hindus.[37] We have already seen how clerical life restored to some their lost honour and social privileges.[38]

Considering the unstable situation of most of the new converts, it is hard to accept as a fact that they ever looked down upon their Hindu neighbours, as alleged at times, due to their newly acquired post-conversion status, believed to be higher by those who claimed the superiority of the Christendom.[39] It is more probable that the Brahman Christians looked down upon the non-Brahman converts, and that the former continued to behave in a superior and more arrogant manner.

Slaves, after their conversion, could become as free as any Portuguese citizen. A provision issued by the viceroy, D. Constantino de Bragança, in 1558 granted freedom to the slaves who were converted. The decree ordered their immediate release from slavery, without any obligation of debt on the part of the convert slaves to their foreign owners.[40] However, some Portuguese bought slave boys on the pretext of giving them a Christian instruction, but they were sold to the Muslims for a higher price. "Thus to earn four more *pardaus* these slave boys were lost to the demons", complained the missionaries.[41]

We come across another decree stating that the Christians could not sell their Hindu slaves to any Muslim or any other infidel.[42] There are also clear instances that despite the decree granting freedom to the convert slaves, vassals of the king, the Portuguese continued to retain them as slaves, whereas the Hindus and the Muslims had to surrender their convert slaves without the right to any indemnity.[43] Moreover, the Christian slaves were forcibly taken away from their Hindu owners for running the risks of renouncing their belief. A Christian slave could only change over to another Christian household to prevent any control by the Hindus over him. The situation regarding the slaves who fled from Bijapur to Goa and became Christians was regularized in the Treaty of 1571 with the Adilshah. Probably this treaty favoured the slaves who were converted.[44] At times conversion became a haven for the slaves of the Muslims and Hindus.[45] If a slave wished to be converted he was examined for three or four days by the priests, and after ascertaining his devotion and freedom of his decision, he began learning the things of the faith.[46]

The local Christians, obviously, did not receive indiscriminately the same kind of favours and attention from the Portuguese. The *honrrados* or caste Hindu converts were the most privileged. The majority of Christians found themselves in an inferior social and economic position vis-à-vis the Hindus and the Portuguese. Evidently, this was not because conversion impoverished them, but because of their pre-conversion inferior status. More often economic and social disadvantages were causes for conversion rather than its consequence. After baptism the converts found themselves in a third social group or category. This third group did not survive so much on the Portuguese privileges as perhaps on the cordial relations with, and the good will of, their Hindu neighbours. Those who were converted were normally from among the underprivileged groups, and this is what gave them the status of 'dependent citizens' within the empire.[47] Obviously, conversion did not necessarily and immediately change one's social and economic condition.

## Economic Privileges

### (a) *Inheritance Rights of the Converts*

If the converts were subjected to social discrimination by their families and caste, it seems logical that they were also denied any property or inheritance rights.[48] A convert, then a social outcast by Hindu custom, lost all his/her inheritance rigths. But, since the majority of the converts were poor, we can conclude that they did not lose much, or did they? Be that as it might, he/she lost his/her place within the joint family, which satisfied one's economic needs. Therefore, it was not so much the loss of inheritance that mattered but the psychological pressures exerted by the joint family on the convert. There might have been tensions in the family when a member of that family showed an inclination to be converted.[49] Experience showed that many converts abandoned the Christian faith not long after their baptism, hence the issuing of decrees on inheritance rights.[50] Henceforth, no Hindu could disinherit his son just for becoming a Christian.

The *Foral* of 1526 — a charter with laws and privileges for the locals — established that when a Hindu died without an heir, his property should go to the king; even if his wife and daughters were alive they could not inherit it. In 1545 Miguel Vaz wrote to the king that this custom of taking the property of the deceased was a great injustice.[51] Then, the governor, Martim Afonso de Sousa (1542-1545), ordered that only the movable goods of the deceased, not exceeding the value of fifty *pardaus*, could go to his Hindu wife and daughters. In order to oblige the Hindus to support financially the members of their families who converted, it was suggested that a convert daughter should be entitled to receive the same amount of inheritance as a Hindu son,[52] or that a married Hindu woman on becoming a Christian should acquire the same rights as those of her Hindu husband, over the household property or inheritance, just as per the law in force in Portugal.[53] But it seems that the law regarding the inheritance rights as prescribed by the *Foral* of 1526 continued to be observed even in 1548. It was argued and suggested to the king that if the converts could inherit some property, there would probably be more Hindus open to receive baptism. No harm would ever result to the crown revenue, since many of these properties or lands were of little value. The valuable properties had been appropriated long before by those who already had much land.[54]

In 1557, we find a royal decree stating that the convert women and their female children could inherit property in the absence of a male heir.[55] The property of a Hindu who died without a son, had necessarily to go to his Christian wife and daughters even if they were still Hindus but intented to convert. In the absence of Christians in that household the property would go to the closest relatives of the deceased, if they were Christians or wished to convert.[56] In 1559 the viceroy, D. Constantino de Bragança, passed another decree allowing female converts to inherit from their parents, to the exclusion of the other Hindu heirs.[57] Then one more stipulation in 1562 permitted a convert woman estranged from her hindu husband to claim all her ornaments back and half of her husband's property.[58]

The land that belonged to the Muslims before the conquest of Goa had become the property of the crown. However, the Hindus who converted were allowed to retain their land. The Hindus had also retained some lands they had not declared.[59] In 1574 a decree by the archbishop of Goa, Dom Gaspar, established that the lands belonging to the crown and whose value did not exceed two hundred *pardaus* could be distributed among those who were converted.[60] The poor new converts asked for the property of those Hindus who had been expelled from Goa and who had taken their wives along with them. At times the Hindu householders sent their wives and family members along with their wealth to the firm land, but the men remained behind expecting a change of fortune.[61] In 1575 the governor, António Moniz Barreto, issued a decree that set aside the wealth and property of the expelled Brahmans for baptismal dresses for the catechumens.[62] However, later in 1585 the decree by the viceroy, D. Duarte de Meneses, stated that the property of the absentees or expelled Hindus should be handed over to their closest relatives but just to be looked after, until such time as when the former returned.[63]

## (b) *Exemption from Taxation to Converts*

The bailiffs (*meirinhos da igreja*) dealt with the people harshly and demanded money from them. They also extracted some money from the poor Christians as penalties for doing some work on a religious feast day. It was the opinion of the learned that the bailiffs should have no authority to impose pecuniary penalties on the converts. Instead, they could impose only healthy penances on them. However, pecuniary fines could be imposed on the Portuguese or foreign Christians, which money could be used to maintain churches, monasteries, colleges and to support the needy converts.[64]

Since the Hindus did not have to pay tithe-taxes, they paid other taxes as Hindus instead. But when these people converted they were obliged to pay the tithe-taxes, remaining thus at the mercy of the tax-collectors, mostly Hindus. Some persons ran away to avoid paying taxes.[65] Requests were made to exempt the converts from paying taxes for a period of fifteen years, which could also work as an incentive for more conversions.[66]

In 1561 the king had been informed that many Hindus were not attracted to the Christian faith for fear of having to pay new taxes on their lands and farms. Those who had become Christians were reeling under this heavy taxation and could not fulfil their obligation. Hence, it was suggested that all the converts should be exempted from paying taxes.[67] Then, in the same year, the king issued a decree favouring the converts with a tax-free period of fifteen years, with effect from the date of its issue.[68] This decree was ratified in 1581 by king, D. Filipe I.[69] Later, in 1594 it was decreed that the converts should not be taxed in addition to what they were already paying.[70] More concessions continued to be offered to the local Christians. Again, in 1597 the king granted a further exemption from taxation for a period of another fifteen years to the local Christians in Salcete, and this law embraced even those who had already enjoyed a tax holiday earlier.[71] In the following year another royal resolution declared that the converts and all those who converted should be exempted for life from paying the tithe-tax. Further, the king asked the opinion of the learned in India whether the Hindus should be made to pay the tithe-tax instead, in addition to the taxes they were already obliged to pay for the lands they cultivated.[72]

It is necessary to recall that most Christians came from poor economic and social strata. Hence, it is not likely that the property inherited by, or the privileges of inheritance to, a convert, made a great difference to his/her economic and social condition, even when the Hindu family saw its traditional inheritance rights go to its converted members. It is also necessary to ask whether the privileges and decrees — if we believe they were often granted and implemented respectively — safeguarding the rights of the converts vis-à-vis the privileges of the Hindus and Portuguese, created tensions for the converts. The converts did not appear to have improved their economic position in any visible manner as to command respect from the Hindus and others. The jobs of tax-collecting, offices of great profit could hardly be held by the local Christians, for they could not afford to buy these offices. Most sources of government revenue in Portuguese India were given out by the crown to the highest bidders, who generally happened to be Hindus.[73]

## Other Decrees and Privileges

The converts found themselves in extreme material privation.[74] We have seen that they were exposed to constant caste and family reprehensions and allurements, which were too strong occasions for them to abandon their new faith. The converts, especially those who depended on their Hindu or Muslim families, needed protection and material favours to remain firm in their belief. Privileges and favours to the weak Christian minority enabled them to live relatively safe among the Hindus.[75] The missionaries sought to protect the converts where the Hindus showed themselves more arrogant and a threat to the former, as in Margão in Salcete.[76] Therefore, the crown enacted several other decrees to favour the converts, to prevent their relapses and to entice or force the Hindus to change their religion.

It is undeniable that these decrees might have promoted social mobility, especially for the *honrrados* (nobles); however, the majority of converts continued to be neglected. But it is equally unquestionable that when these privileges were not granted, most converts did not abandon their faith. Relapses did happen of course but not strictly for not receiving the promised favours and privileges.[77] These laws in favour of converts did not necessarily imply disfavour to the Hindus, not only because many of them were hardly-ever implemented in favour of the Christians, but also because the Hindus continued to be favoured with the expectations that they would convert one day. Besides, the Portuguese needed the skills, services and capital of the Hindus to hold the empire.

Many decrees and privileges issued by the kings and governors should not be viewed as being exclusively for Goa. Rather many were applicable to all the territories under the Portuguese control.[78] However, there were a few of them specifically for Goa. It is possible that the Christians in Goa could be more favoured than those living in Hindu-ruled territories, like Cochin or Ceylon (Sri Lanka) or even in other Portuguese-controlled territories;[79] but the Portuguese expectations and demands vis-à-vis the Goan converts were also greater. Interestingly, the Portuguese demanded and expected from the Hindu and Muslim rulers respect and favours for the Christians living in their territories, particularly if the Portuguese had economic interests or factories at stake here.[80] Unfortunately, often the Portuguese would not reciprocate or favour the Hindus living in their acquired territories, certainly not as far as their legislation is concerned. Disfavours to the Hindus residing in the Portuguese-dominated territories however, were not so intensive and extensive all the time.

The decrees introduced in Goa during the sixteenth century reflected a combination of favours, disfavours and penalties to both Hindus and Christians. Perhaps, the most violent penalty for breach of some decrees, was the sending of the culprit to the galleys or loss of his property just, for example, for performing a Hindu ceremony.[81] It has been suggested that such penalties — and many such others — were hardly imposed on the accused, since evidence in support of the execution of such penalties is lacking.

Ignorance of the decrees was no excuse for one's illegal

actions or omission of the lawful ones. The Municipal Council had to make summaries concerning decrees and letters and communicate them to all.[82] The royal decrees were proclaimed in public places in the city of Goa.[83] They were probably also communicated to the Christians in the churches. The crown often reminded the civil authorities overseas to stringently implement them.[84] It is obvious that some decrees aimed simply at protecting the territorial integrity of the empire and had little to do directly with conversions. Rather, these decrees in favour of the state were supposed to end any political opposition to the Portuguese rule.

Several other decrees were issued to protect the converts against the influence of the Brahmans and government officials who oppressed the converts.[85] The local Christians were at the mercy of the Portuguese captains and factors, who had civil jurisdiction over them. The civil authorities, instead of favouring, ill-treated the local converts. The captains used their powers mainly to exploit the local Christians. The documents inform us that such attitude towards the converts was one of the main causes for many Hindus and Muslims to shun the new religion. Hence, it was suggested to the king that nobody should have any authority over the converts, except those who had a mandate from the king himself. Probably, the offices of the *Pay dos Christãos* and of the Judge of Orphans were created to correct those malpractices.[86] The quick increase in conversions demanded more officials of justice, like the Special Judges for the local Christians.[87] Unfortunately, these judges also began oppressing the converts.[88]

It is certainly not easy to distinguish all the motives or re-create the contexts that prompted the Portuguese authority to produce this vast body of decrees, or even to separate the decrees meant to favour the converts from those ones meant to disfavour the Hindus (or favour their conversion). In order to grasp the complex implications and applications of the decrees in favour of Christendom, they have to be viewed not only from the perspective of conversions but also from the socio-political context of Goa in the sixteenth century, which was also a result of this legislation. They have to be assessed, of course, in relation to a broader context, namely, the *Estado da India*, since these decrees and privileges were not issued exclusively for the territory of Goa.

At times some distant event in the *Estado da India,* which had no direct impact in Goa, could influence a governor to issue a decree which in turn would be applicable to Goa too. Decrees in favour of Christendom were not necessarily in favour of Christians. Many decrees were supposed to favour the conversion of the vassals of the king of Portugal, rather than simply favour the already converted. The Hindus, just as the Christians, were vassals of the crown. Following this argument or principle of vassalage even the Hindus were obliged by natural duty and law, let alone civil, to worship the only God, creator of heaven and earth and of the whole universe.[89] Hence, any Hindu ceremony practised by any Lusitanian vassal, was considered as an offence to God. Such acts became aggravated when performed in the presence of Christians. Correction of this was a decree of the queen regent in 1559 abolishing all the Hindu, Muslim and Jewish ceremonies in Portuguese territories overseas.[90]

The Hindus were not always disfavoured. Albuquerque favoured the Hindus, as often he did the Muslim merchants, for their valuable assistance to him in capturing Goa. He did not interfere with the customs and laws of the Hindus. Albuquerque had only forbidden *sati* or the burning of widows, but only in the city of Goa. No matter how praiseworthy and humanistic his act might have appeared then, it must have been enough to incense the local Hindus against the Portuguese, for *sati* according to the Hindus in the sixteenth century — being one of the most important religious act for the future happiness of a married man and wife — had to be performed at any cost. Their strong beliefs in the after-life and the value of *sati* as a requisite for it, prompted the Hindus to work hard to abolish the anti-*sati* decree. And if they had to perform *sati* they would not spare any effort to do it secretly.[91] In 1585 the Third Provincial Council mentioned the existence of a strong tendency among the Hindus to revive the widow burning custom.[92] It appears, therefore, that the anti-*sati* act was no favour done to the Hindu society by this tolerant and humanitarian governor. *Sati* continued to be practised openly outside the city of Goa, namely, in the other islands of Chorão and Divar and in the districts of Bardez and Salcete, where the anti-*sati* decree was not yet in force. Prohibition of *sati* was extended to these last two districts only during the rule of D. Constantino de Bragança (1558-61).[93] Only then the ban became total in Goa. A severe penalty awaited those who encouraged it, consisting in loss of property and life imprisonment.[94] The Jesuits always kept a strict watch to prevent the Hindus from performing any *sati*-related act. In 1557 three women were saved from committing *sati* and became Christians.[95] Even around 1585 the Hindus wanted their widows to burn themselves and shave their heads.[96] In 1575 the Second Provincial Council had already forbidden Hindu widows to shave their heads.[97]

Be that as it might, Albuquerque is esteemed for having favoured the Hindus. Nevertheless, he wanted to see Christianity flourishing in Goa. The *Foral* of 1526 left most local religious and social practices undisturbed. But it is doubtful that the changes made in the issue of inheritance by that *Foral* as already seen, pleased the Hindus.[98] The *Foral* also allowed the Hindus to take their oath on their idols.[99] In 1532 the king modified the decree on taking oaths regarding matters that had no records. The royal decree allowed the Hindus to swear only on the temple of Bandora.[100] Again, the *Foral* of 1534 respected religious freedom of the Hindus, but upheld the prohibition of *sati*. Goa and its three neighbouring islands had many temples. Hindu marriages and all the other festivals continued to be celebrated with all the ritual elaboration and noisy processions.[101] Subsequently, further decrees ratified the *Foral* several times until many 'decrees and privileges in favour of conversion' made the *Foral* obsolete.[102] It was also the spirit of the Counter-Reformation and the need to increase the number of converts that inaugurated a new and violent proselytizing period. But this was not to be always so.

The Hindus continued to be favoured despite the anti-Hindu decrees. In 1542 Krishna, the Hindu chief *thanadar*, negotiated with the sultan of Bijapur on behalf of the Portuguese and got him to cede Bardez and Salcete to the Portuguese.[103] In 1545 Anu Synay, a Brahman, who opposed conversions and tyrannized the people with full support of the Portuguese administration, served as a goods-broker (*corretor das mercadorias*) in Goa.[104] The government officials needed the services and the capital of Brahman and Muslim merchants. Some Portuguese wanted Hindus in the offices of profit in the state, such as collection of rents.[105] Besides, the Portuguese did not like the new converts to be their partners or to have the same privileges and rights as they themselves had. It is certain that even the governors did not want the converts to enjoy the same privileges as the Portuguese did.[106] But how did the local authority expect the converts to behave when the king himself wanted them to enjoy the privileges of Portuguese citizenship? The Portuguese alleged that the converts considered themselves 'equals' to the Portuguese and refused to do jobs that were not according to their new status, like working in the fields. But these converts were not prepared to assume administrative jobs, whereas Brahman converts could supply these services better. Some Brahmans who had become Christians showed great allegiance to the Portuguese, but they might not have been sufficient in number to be able to service the entire state machinery.[107]

In the affair of conversions, promises and favours went hand in hand. At the beginning it was believed that the social contacts with the Portuguese would suffice to motivate the Hindus to baptism. By the same logic or due to the contacts with the western culture, it was expected that the converts would lose most of their ancestral cultural and religious traits, and consequently become stronger in the faith. But when this did not happen decrees were implemented to create the expected results. The Portuguese were too few to influence religiously the Goan society, and there were no plans to regularly send missionaries to India. Most missionaries who came here went back after serving the Portuguese. It was only in 1598 that the king informed the prelates or religious superiors and religious members stationed in India not to return to Portugal due to many inconveniences created by their absence in Christendom of India.[108]

The villages continued to be administered by the Hindus in 1541, as they were still their chiefs.[109] In 1543 a great part of the rent (*renda*) of the island of Goa was in the hands of Brahman Hindus, Muslims and Portuguese. The rent of washermen, for instance, was leased to one Pêro de Lisboa for 250 *pardaus* on the condition that no one else could earn his/her living i. e. washing clothes without an agreement with this *rendeiro* or tax-collector. The *rendeiro* had to pay the government the stipulated amount to get this right.[110] The local Christians were in no position to pay and become a *rendeiro* and they did not possess the necessary shrewdness to control the services and goods of others. Nobody could exercise an office without buying the licence from the rentier or crown. In 1548 the majority of the leaseholders or royal tax-collectors were Hindus. Hence, they had the people under their control.[111] Trade in Goa was in the hands of Muslims and Hindus, and the Brahmans were indispensable as translators, secretaries, accountants in government offices, etc.[112]

In 1545 the governor, Martim Afonso de Sousa, passed a provision at the request of the vicar-general, Miguel Vaz, forbidding the Brahmans to serve any official person of the crown. In 1546 favours and honours were offered to the Hindus who were also oppressed by some local tax-collectors, as incentives to change their religion.[113] The new converts had not been taken seriously even by 1547, because there was no zeal among the Portuguese in Goa. As a matter of fact, the Brahman chiefs, who obstructed the work of conversion, had to be expelled from Goa at any cost. Miguel Vaz added that the Hindus who were inclined to be converted were just waiting for this occasion. Expelling the Brahmans would help these prospective converts to overcome the social stigma associated with conversion; perhaps that move would also spare both the parties much dishonour.[114]

Information belonging to the year of 1550, tells us that the powerful Muslims and Hindus continued to serve in government posts and to receive support from the Portuguese.[115] Besides, the tax-collectors, who happened to be Portuguese and Hindus, used their position of profit to exploit, despise and oppress the people, especially the Christians.[116] Due to this situation the converts did not dare manifest themselves openly as Christians. Those who wished to receive baptism did not come forward for the little respect and support they received from the Portuguese and Hindus.

One reads in the letters written by the missionaries that the exemplary life and preaching of Francis Xavier changed the moral conduct of the residentes in Goa, and that the converts began living as good Christians. Thereafter, Goa had become morally and religiously very different from what it was before the arrival of Xavier.[117] It has been suggested that the misconduct of the Portuguese living in Goa before the arrival of Francis Xavier here in 1542 had been exaggerated, just to match the narrative of the miraculous change brought about by him. The purpose of this exaggeration was only to highlight the virtues and power of the saint. Nevertheless, the king of Portugal, hopeful that some drastic measures would increase conversions, explicitly forbade idolatry in his territories in 1550.[118]

Despite the new legislation in favour of conversion, the Hindus continued being chiefs of the land and nobody could stop them from celebrating their festivals publicly. They had gained so much in power and favours from the Portuguese to be sufficiently emboldened to persecute the Christians till 1557.[119] That the officials of the king favoured the Hindus in these acts, is evident from several reports left by the missionaries.[120] When the missionaries persuaded the governor, Francisco Barreto (1555-1558), to put an end to the privileges and favours the Hindus enjoyed, the governor issued provisions to this effect.[121] From 1557 a number of royal decrees were issued against the Hindus, especially the harmful Brahmans holding government jobs. This measure was also prescribed and supported by the Canon Law, the law of the church.[122] These decrees stated that government offices should be reserved exclusively for the converts.[123] In 1559 the king, D. Sebastião, ratified the citizenship decree of 1513, that stated that the local converts in Goa and those desirous of conversion could enjoy the same privileges and rights as did the Portuguese settlers here.[124] In the same year he passed another law ordering that no official of justice or finance could keep Hindu assistants, but only Christians. Any Portuguese official who did not comply with this order could lose his office, and the Brahmans and infidels found in the job could be imprisoned and forfeit their property.[125] It was expected that this measure would force the Hindu *gaunkars* to convert.[126] It may be recalled that this happened when D. Constantino de Bragança (1558-1561) — one of the most fanatical or zealous viceroys the *Estado da India* ever saw during the sixteenth century — governed Goa. Bragança excluded from his government all the Brahmans and took Christians in their stead.[127] Preference for Christians in public offices formed part of measures to entice the Hindus to be converted too.[128]

Some of these decrees caused occasionally a great uproar among the Hindus, local merchants and the Portuguese as well, to such an extent that it seemed almost impossible to enforce them.[129] Due to the harsh policy on conversion the Hindus threatened to abandon the city of Goa, and a few others tried in vain to bribe the Portuguese authorities and the governor to revoke the anti-Hindu provisions.[130] Alessandro Valignano wrote saying that this policy proved to be the turning point in throwing open the doors to conversion in Goa. Many Hindus who had been waiting for many years to become Christians came forward to receive baptism now.[131] From then on the Christians began living differently. Before, they lived like exiled people,[132] but from this moment onwards they began convincing their relatives about the benefits they could enjoy on becoming Christians.[133]

The Brahmans did not stop raising obstacles in the path of conversions, and for this reason the king insisted on the need to expel such harmful people. But the local Portuguese authority did not take seriously the royal advice.[134] Promises and threats were made, publicly and secretly, so that the Brahmans should change their mind, but to no avail. Discussions and disputes with them to convince them on the truth of the Christian religion were equally futile. It was next to impossible to convince the Brahmans that they were wrong.[135] No sooner the Brahmans responsible for lack of conversions were expelled than several baptisms followed.[136] Where there were no Brahmans, there were more conversions.[137] The law of expulsion from Goa embraced members of any caste, carpenters and blacksmiths alike if proven guilty of obstructing conversions.[138] This decree affected only the harmful Hindus, but not their families.

These drastic measures against religious freedom, left some Hindus with no option but to ask for baptism if they wanted to retain and remain in their lands in 1560. Not a few in a number of villages were converted for this reason.[139] But many Hindus left Goa. As soon as D. Constantino de Bragança completed his tenure as governor in 1561, the new governor felt that the social and economic situation of the state was so precarious that he recalled the Hindus who had abandoned their lands, promising them to restitute their land and property.[140] The island of Goa and the other adjacent ones had become uninhabited, the fields inundated due to the river blockage and other damages caused deliberately by those who had left the land in anger. The order demanding their return within a fixed period of time also established that in default their property would be confiscated in favour of the converts.[141] Due to these pressures the Hindus returned and the persons responsible for those damages asked for pardon and offered themselves, with many relatives and friends, for baptism. Hence, the argument that the Hindus embraced the faith to enter government services or not to lose their lands is not totally untrue either. Several reports inform us that some Hindus were just waiting for someone to take them to the College of St Paul and that it was so easy to convert them. Even the school-boys played the role of missionaries on such occasions. "Thus the faith triumphed", wrote Francico de Souza in *Oriente Conquistado a Jesus Cristo pelos Padres da Companhia de Jesus da Provincia de Goa.*[142]

Substitution of Hindus by converts was preferable to protect the latter economically and socially and from relapsing.[143] But at the same time the Hindus also continued to receive privileges to become more receptive to conversion. Subsequently, in 1568 the king wrote that justice should be administered equally to all his vassals, Christians, Muslims or Hindus,[144] but equality and justice understood in the context of favouring conversions.[145] A royal decree in 1571 proposed that the job of interpreters should be given to local Christians understandably, if they were capable of it.[146] Again in 1572 the king ordered that all his vassals, the new converts and others, should be treated with justice.[147]

Many decrees in favour of the converts followed in 1572, but very few were implemented. Ironically, more taxes were levied on them resulting in many injustices and tyrannies and also loss of crown's revenues. Christians were compelled to become sailors in the Portuguese galleys, contrary to the royal orders issued in 1560. They were made to work in the fortification of Banesterim.[148] But on the other hand, the Hindu *gaunkars* were forbidden to enter the village assemblies when there was a sufficient number of Christian *gaunkars* in the village to form the quorum. Some Portuguese believed that this measure — which deprived the Hindus of their traditional honour — would persuade or pressurize them to convert.[149] But this sort of treatment only infuriated them. Further, no Hindu or Muslim could stand as a witness against a Christian when Christians could do so, because they were considered as unreliable people.[150]

A royal letter in 1580 decided on the urgent need to favour and honour the converts and those Hindus who showed some inclination to be converted, and to refuse such favours to those who remained adamant in their idolatry and abominable errors. Those who obstructed the work of conversion should be punished severely. The Hindu festivals with idolatry in plenty, especially in Bardez and Salcete, were banned for attracting many new converts to them, and for causing a great harm to conversions.[151] In 1587 the king ordered further privileges and favours for the local Christians.[152]

In 1594 a royal letter reminded the viceroy, Matias de Albuquerque, to observe all the instructions regarding prohibition of public Hindu ceremonies.[153] Another royal letter in the same year explicitly stated that no Christian *gaunkar* should ever be forced to work in the galleys. It demanded a fair treatment for the inhabitants of Salcete, who had complained that the Treasury officials did not respect their laws and privileges.[154] Further, in 1599 the king expressed that all the local Christians should be favoured and helped according to their capacities and interests.[155] He also proposed an inquiry into the manner in which the Christians, Muslims or Hindus treated their slaves, since he had been informed that they punished the latter severely; if proven guilty they would be punished according to the Portuguese laws pertaining to homicide of free citizens.[156]

In 1598 the viceroy, D. Francisco da Gama, diplomatically passed certain provisions granting some religious freedom to the

Hindus which turned out to be very harmful to the work of conversion.[157] In the same year the archbishop of Goa informed this viceroy that his predecessor had implemented some controversial decrees in favour of the Hindus regarding their temples and ceremonies, which should be withdrawn immediately.[158] Perhaps given the option to choose between preserving the converts or converting the Hindus, the former took precedence. The Portuguese argued that if the converts were neglected they would eventually be lost to their former customs. Moreover, the difficulty they encountered in making more converts and the need to hold intact the state, might have prompted the viceroy to issue some lenient decrees, which granted certain liberties to the Hindus. The civil authorities sensed that the missionaries and clergymen were unable to attend to the needs of all converts, not because of lack of clergymen in Goa.[159] It is probable that the missionaries were not interested in the welfare of the converts. Whether more religious freedom had been granted to the Hindus is debatable, but the fact remains that even the most fertile land in Goa, the land in Salcete, remained uncultivated due to the Hindu exodus just before the turn of the century.[160]

In 1600 the king issued another order to exclude the harmful Brahmans from the job of factors, but those useful to the state or with diplomatic links with the neighbouring rulers could be retained.[161] We find in the same year the Hindus managing the crown's revenue collection, when there were Christians to do such job. This right was leased to the Hindus with the royal attorney's approval.[162] Complaints went from Goa in 1600 that the Christians continued to be harassed indiscriminately by the revenue-collectors, mostly Hindus, with the protection of the Treasury officials.[163] Despite requests to expel the enemies of the Christian faith from Goa in 1602 and the royal order to empower the Christians with collecting the crown's rents in 1604, the Hindus continued to be in control of these jobs even in 1605.[164] Despite the crown's insistence to give the local Christians government jobs, the local authority argued that the converts did not qualify for these jobs, because they did not have the necessary knowledge and skills or any business sense.[165] Hence, the continued Portuguese complaint that they could not serve the king and do justice to their offices without the Hindu collaboration.[166]

In 1604 a royal letter asked for the opinion of the bishop of Goa and of other learned persons, on the advantages of granting some freedom to the Hindus or letting them celebrate their religious ceremonies on payment of a fee, which could be spent exclusively for the work of conversion.[167] Obviously, no religious freedom was officially granted to the Hindus, however, it appears that by this time there was more religious tolerance to perform local rituals. The Jesuits began permitting the Hindus in Salcete to go to the firm land to perform their ceremonies on payment of a fee, but such permission had no explicit government approval.[168] The Portuguese knew that without the Hindu collaboration commerce in Goa would suffer or come to a stand still, but even this fact never allowed the latter to erect officially their temples, a necessary condition for many exiled Hindus to return to Goa. It is certain that the Hindus were never allowed to build or rebuild their temples, but it is probable that the Portuguese permitted things to happen surreptitiously. This compromise was so necessary for the stability or even survival of the state by the turn of the sixteenth century.[169]

The Hindus had no official permission to perform their ceremonies even inside their own houses. But on the other hand they had to be prevented from going outside Goa, where they could entertain all sorts of superstitions more freely. As a result the Hindus were gradually allowed to celebrate their festivals in Goa, but only indoors provided these ceremonies did not harm the converts.[170] Since it was absurd to celebrate a marriage ceremony in secret and without frolic in Goa, they continued to go to the kingdom of the Adilshah. But when the ceremonies were celebrated in Goa they were obliged to inform the priests who would send one of their assistants to keep watch on them.[171] Hindu marriage ceremonies were banned where the Christians lived.[172] In 1639 the viceroy, Pêro da Silva, authorized the return of all the Brahmans or Hindus of any other caste who had been forced to abandon Goa, for whatever reason, but that did not mean that any legal religious freedom had been allowed to them.[173] In 1647 many Christians left Goa either because of the ill-treatment meted out to them by their

Hindu neighbours or because of their 'natural inconsistency' or relapses.[174] Christians were neglected after conversion.[175] One can arrive at a general impression from the historical documents that the Hindus continued to be preferred, for being more capable and profitable to their masters, in governament jobs even after 1657.[176] The exclusion of Hindus from the village councils in Salcete was suggested again in 1699,[177] and in the same year the decree to favour the Christians with government offices was ratified once more.[178] During the seventeenth century the Hindus continued to serve as brokers in the city of Goa, in every commercial business related to Europe and India, and every change in this situation proved harmful to commerce and collection of royal rents.[179] The viceroy proposed to the king of Portugal in 1694 that the widows and the sons of local soldiers who died in war at the service of the crown, should enjoy the same privileges as did the Portuguese in Europe.[180]

Even despite the existing relative religious freedom, at no time until the middle of the eighteenth century did the Portuguese officially permit the construction of temples in their territory.[181] It was only after the acquisition of the 'New Conquests' — in last quarter of the eighteenth century with the Portuguese agreeing not to interfere in religious and social customs there — that no more anti-Hindu decrees were issued in the 'Old Conquests'. By then the situation for the Hindus and Christians had changed a good deal in the 'Old Conquests'.

I hope that this is a more impartial reading of the decrees and privileges in favour of conversion. I hope that with this perpective we may be able to re-create a more realistic history of conversions in Goa.[182] The next chapter discusses 'Decrees on Temples, Idols and Orphans' which were directly related to the 'Decrees and Privileges in Favour of Conversion or Christendom'.

NOTES AND REFERENCES

1. *DI*, IV, 200-01.
2. *Ibid.*, 206.
3. *Doc*, VI, 346.
4. *Ibid.*, 345.
5. *Ibid.*, 346.
6. *Ibid.*, VII, 327-64; IV, 318.
7. A royal charter in 1519, granting alms to the poor converts. *APO*, 5, p. 41.
8. *Ibid.*, pp. 44-45.
9. *LFC*, fl. 12v. A royal decree to give clothing to the Hindus who converted. Almeirim, 25-1-1571. *BFUP*, No. 1, p. 36.
10. *MR*, 2B, fl. 359.
11. *APO*, 4, p. 12.
12. *Doc*, VIII, 8.
13. *BFUP*, No. 1, p. 48.
14. Josef Wicki, (ed.), *LPC*, p. 194. *Doc*, IX, 340.
15. *DI*, VII, 67.
16. *BFUP*, No. 1, p. 18. *Doc*, XI, 285; XII, 286. *APO*, 5, doc. 773, p. 899.
17. *Ibid.*, 1, Part II, p. 186. These decrees could also be applied to the Portuguese.
18. *Ibid.*, 3, p. 143.
19. Ana Cannas da Cunha, *A Inquisição no Estado da India - Origens (1539-1560)*, pp. 257-58.
20. *Doc*, XI, 294.
21. *Ibid.*, IV, 125.
22. *Bullarium*, First Provincial Council, Acc. 2, dec. 39, pp. 15, 34.
23. *Ibid.*, Second Provincial Council, Acc. 2, dec. 5, p. 65. There is an interesting information about the sacred thread of the Brahmans. *DI*, III, 728.
24. See how the Hindu ceremonies were prohibited. *Ibid.*, IV, 321. "...encomendando-lhe tãobem que se chamem polos nomes de christãos e não de gentyos." *Ibid.*, 596.

25. Josef Wicki, (ed.), *op. cit.*, p. 132.
26. *LFC*, fls. 8, 11.
27. In 1581 the governor, Fernão Telles, ratified all the provisions in favour of conversion. *Ibid.*, fl. 29. Letter from D. João V to the viceroy, D. Vasco Fernandes César de Meneses, to implement rigorously all the laws in favour of conversion. Lisbon, 1714. *BFUP*, No. 1, p. 64.
28. Josef Wicki, (ed.), *op. cit.*, pp. 32, 285-87. Letter from the king to the viceroy, D. Francisco Mascarenhas. February 1582. *APO*, 5, Part III, doc. 820, p. 989.
29. *Ibid.*, 3, pp. 9, 72. Decree by the governor, António Teles de Meneses, empowering the *Pay dos Christãos* with the authority to arrest delinquent Hindus and Christians. Goa, 13-8-1540. *BFUP*, No. 1, p. 55.
30. Ana Cannas da Cunha, *op.cit.*, p. 233.
31. *BFUP*, No. 1, p. 59. Law of D. Sebastião ratifying the privileges to the local Christians in 1563. *Ibid.*
32. Josef Wicki, (ed.), *op. cit.*, p. 38.
33. *Ibid.*, p. 285. In 1774 the Marquis of Pombal's decrees to the Portuguese local authorities to favour the Roman Catholic Indians over and above the *reinóis* fell on deaf ears. It is difficult to see how the decrees issued during the sixteenth century in favour of the Christians could produce a better response on the part of the local authorities. "A christandade da terra é tão desfavorecida assim do eclesiastico como secular, somente pelos religiosos que não podemos mais que falar e os christãos são timidos e por certo que nenhum se convertera se a Inquisição se entender nelles e virem que castigam algum por ella." Letter from Fr. Baltazar Dias, rector of the College of St Paul, in 1555. CEHU, *As Gavetas da Torre do Tombo*, V, pp. 71-72. Royal decree by the queen granting the local Christians the same privileges enjoyed by the Portuguese settlers in Goa, in 1559. *BFUP*, No. 1, p. 32. This decree was ratified several times. *Ibid.*, p. 32-33. One of these privileges reads that the local Christians could not be imprisoned, except for some serious crimes, however, the nature of these crimes was not specified. *Ibid.*, p. 43.
34. C. R. Boxer, "The Problems of the Native Clergy in the Portuguese and Spanish Empires from the Sixteenth to the Eighteenth Centuries", p. 98. *Bullarium*, Third Provincial Council, Acc. 4, dec. 3, p. 77.

35. Letter written by Fr. Sebastião Pires to the king of Portugal in 1527, "Em Goa muitos mais se tornariam cristãos, se fossem favorecidos dos vossos capitães, porque saiba Vosa Alteza certo que, tanto que se tornam cristãos, logo sam tratados como cativos, e por esta causa se nom querem tornar muita gente da tera cristaam... que como recebem augua do Bautismo, loguo sam maltratados e desfavorecidos." *Doc*, II, 143. "Escravos que se convertem fiquem forros sem por elles se pagar couza alguma a seu donos." Josef Wicki, (ed.), *op. cit.*, p. 173.
36. *DI*, VIII, 70.
37. *Ibid.*, IV, 9.
38. C. R. Boxer, *op. cit.*, p. 98.
39. P. D. Xavier, *Goa. A Social History*, p. 21.
40. *LFC*, fl. 34. *BFUP*, No. 1, p. 46.
41. *Doc*, III, 211.
42. *DI*, I, 74.
43. *Doc*, IV, 457. *Bullarium*, First Provincial Council, Acc. 2, dec. 16, p. 10. A great number of slaves worked at the College of St Paul in Goa. ARSI, *Extracto das cousas*, 1a, fl. 16.
44. *DI*, XVIII, 665. *APO*, 5, Part II, p. 827.
45. *Doc*, V, 300.
46. *LFC*, fl. 15v. In an auction Christian slaves had compulsorily to be sold to Christians. Josef Wicki, (ed.), *op. cit.*, p. 173. A decree by the queen stated that, slaves belonging to foreign Gentiles on converting had to be sold to the Christians. Lisbon, 24-3-1559. *BFUP*, No. 1, p. 37. But there was another royal decree in 1533 ordering freedom to the slaves, vassals of the king, on becoming Christians. *Ibid.*
47. *DI*, I, 761.
48. Anthony D' Costa, *Christianisation of the Goa Islands (1510-1567)*, pp. 119, 148-50.
49. *Doc*, VII, 281.
50. Josef Wicki, (ed.), *op. cit.*, p. 119.
51. *DI*, I, 71.
52. *Doc*, III, 208.
53. Francisco de Sousa, *OCJC*, p. 129.

54. *Doc*, IV, 175.
55. *BFUP*, No. 1, p. 60.
56. Josef Wicki, (ed.), *op. cit.*, p. 290. This decree was ratified in 1573. *LFC*, fls. 22, 57v. *Doc*, VII, 264-66. Royal decree permitting a Hindu woman (and her daughter(s)) to inherit property of her deceased husband, if she converted within six months from his death. Lisbon, 15-3-1583. *BFUP*, No. 1, p. 40.
57. *APO*, 5, Part I, doc. 304, p. 410.
58. *Ibid.*,5, Part II, doc. 427, p. 514.
59. Paulo da Trindade, *CEO*, Part I, p. 357.
60. *BFUP*, No. 1, p. 39.
61. Decree by the viceroy, D. Constantino de Bragança, ordering the Hindu jewellers to bring back their wives, and property, they had sent to the firm land. If they refused to obey the order they would have to leave the island of Goa within a certain period of time. Goa, 8-6-1560. *Ibid.*, p. 49.
62. *Ibid.*, p. 51.
63. *Ibid.*, p. 42.
64. *Doc*, III, 210, 198.
65. CEHU, *As Gavetas da Torre do Tombo*, IX, p. 26.
66. *Doc*, III, 209.
67. *Ibid.*, IX, 613.
68. *MR*, 1, fl. 78. Josef Wicki, (ed.), *op. cit.*, p. 57. *BFUP*, No. 1, p. 34.
69. *Ibid.*, p. 35.
70. *MR*, 2A, fl. 274.
71. *BFUP*, No. 1, p. 163. *MR*, 1, fl. 78. *BFUP*, No. 3, p. 416. *MR*, 5, fl. 50.
72. *BFUP*, No. 2, p. 252. *MR*, 2B, fl. 484.
73. M. N. Pearson, *Coastal Western India*, p. 103.
74. *LFC*, fl. 23.
75. *DI*, VII, 66.
76. *Ibid.*, VIII, 70.
77. Archana Kakodkar, "Shuddhi: Reconversion to Hinduism in Goa".
78. In Mombasa in 1613, two hundred bags of rice used to be distributed

annually among the Christian converts to prevent their relapses and to attract potential converts as well. Additional enticement was offered to the converts throughout the Eastern Empire as for example, exemption for fifteen years from all government and church dues. Justus Strandes, *The Portuguese Period in East Africa*, p. 153.

79. Royal decrees issued in 1513 and 1559 were first applicable only to Goa. Later in 1571 they were extended to all Portuguese territories. *Doc*,VII, 271-72. Royal decree. Lisbon, 1-3-1571. *LFC*, fls. 1-2. *BFUP*, No. 1, p. 74.

80. Rodrigo José de Lima Felner, *Subsídios para a História da India Portuguesa*, pp. ii, 32-35. In 1605 the ruler of Cochin showed little empathy towards the Christians. He harassed those who wished to be converted. He took away their property and destroyed some churches. "Muytos deixam de se comverter em Cochim e em Ceilam, porque lhe os reis tomam as fazemdas despoes de bautizados." *Doc*, III, 222. In Cranganore it had become a custom to deprive the converts of their property. The Hindu princes used these tactics as warnings against conversions without however, creating bad relation with the Portuguese. *Ibid.*, IV, 3. In the Moluccas the Muslim king would take away the property of those who converted and persecute them till death. *Ibid.*, II, 14.

81. *LFC*, fl. 7v. A man who dressed like a woman and vice-versa, or wore masks outside festival time, could be punished severely. *Ordenações Manuelinas*, Tit. xxxi, p. 90.

82. *LFC*, fl. 9.

83. *Ibid.*, fl. 22v.

84. *Ibid.*, fl. 2v.

85. Hindu tax-collectors tyrannized the Christian people. *APO*, 1, Part II, p. 118.

86. *Doc*, IV, 251, 270.

87. *Ibid.*, III, 79, 530.

88. Royal decree to the captains of Bardez and Salcete to prevent injustices done by the tax-collectors and by the Judge of the Orphans against Christians. Elvas, 20-2-1581. *BFUP*, No. 1, p. 38. There was a decree issued by D. Sebastião forbidding the judges to arrest the converts and deal with their complaints. Goa, 11-12-1573. *Ibid.*, p. 45. By order of the king there was a special judge for the local Christians, who dealt with their grievances and crimes. This judge

was nominated in order to avoid delays in processing those cases. *LFC*, fls. 12, 59-60.

89. *Ibid.*, fl. 72v.

90. *Ibid.*, fl. 7.

91. *DI*, III, 727.

92. *Bullarium*, Third Provincial Council, Acc. 2, dec. 11, p. 67.

93. *DI*, III, 406. Afonso Brás de Albuquerque, *Comentarios de Afonso de Albuquerque*, Vol. II, p. 20. In 1560 the viceroy, D. Constantino de Bragança, notified by a decree that no Hindu woman, living in the islands of Goa, Bardez and Salcete could commit *sati*. Decree issued by the viceroy, D. Constantino de Bragança, forbidding *sati* in the villages of Candolim, Calangute, Nagoa Pomburpa, Saligão and Sirula; in Bardez, Salcete and Goa. Pangim, 1558. *BFUP*, No. 1, p. 46. Decree by D. Constantino forbidding *sati* in 1560. *APO*, 5, Part I, doc. 353, p. 458.

94. *LFC*, fl. 34v.

95. *Doc*, VI, 354.

96. *Bullarium*, Third Provincial Council, Acc. 2, dec. 11, p. 67.

97. Shaving of the head was a sign that they could not marry and according to the Provincial Council such attitude also prevented the conversion of widows. *Ibid.*, Acc. 2, dec. 10, p. 67.

98. The *Foral* of Afonso Mexia in 1526 decided that the property of a deceased Hindu without heir should revert to the crown even if the deceased was survived by his wife and daughters, brothers and relatives. At this time the Hindu succession law created conflicts and disputes among the Hindus, and the *Foral* sought only to resolve these conflicts. Later the widows began inheriting their husbands' property, but only if they were Christians, or intended to be converted within six months from their husbands' death. *APO*, 5, Part I, pp. 118-33.

99. *Ibid.*, p. 126.

100. Georg Schurhammer, *Francis Xavier. His Life, His Times*, p. 231. The *Foral* of 1526 respected polygamy of Hindus, burning of corpses, religious ceremonies and their oath-taking methods. Later in 1532, the oath taken on any temple or sacred object was forbidden due to malpractices and disregard for the oaths taken. The Hindus were not always serious about it. Then, only the oath taken on the

temple of Bandora became acceptable by Portuguese law. The concerned Hindu parties were asked to take the oath on a temple called Uzzo, another name for Bandora, while declaring that what they were saying was right. Such oath was taken when there was a lawsuit or disagreement among the Hindus regarding inheritance of immovable goods or disputed property in a village, or when there was no witness or any written document to establish the truth. *Doc*, II, 350-51. "Foral dos usos e custumes dos gancares e lavradores de Goa" of 1526. CEHU, *Gavetas da Torre do Tombo*, IX, p. 23. "...todos os que nella vivem (Cidade de Goa) virão que os gentios quando se per elles queria provar alguma cousa lhe era dado juramento em huma folha derva, a que chamão betele, e em bosta de boy ou vaca, e em sal, uzandosse por esta maneira, parecemdo que por serem gentios entre elles era verdade o que assy juravão, o que he sabido que he muyto pello contrayro, e se fizerão, muytas falsidades, e se derão muytas sentenças injustas; querendosse saber a maneira que se devia de ter pera delles se saber a verdade, se soube que somente em huum pagode, que se chama Bamdora, dizião a verdade; e aqueixandovos disso ao Governador, e por se elle emformar na verdade, e achamdo que era assy, vos passou hum seu Alvará, que todo juramento, que se desse aos ditos gentios, seja no dito pagode de Bamdorá..." Letter from Goa to D. João III, in 1532. *Doc*, II, 209-10.

101. *DI*, III, 407, 727.

102. Georg Schurhammer, *Francisco Javier. Su vida y su tiempo*, p. 294.

103. Anthony D' Costa, *Christianisation of the Goa Islands 1510-1567*, p. 27. *Tanadar-mor* (chief thanadar) administered and collected taxes. Krishna had three government jobs when the Portuguese in Portugal could hold only one. *Doc*, II, 196.

104. *Doc*, III, 205. *DI*, I, 69.

105. *Ibid.*, VII, 59. A royal decree ordering the rents of the crown to be given to the Christians. The highest bid made by a Christian in an auction was to be taken as the last and final bid. Almeirim, 1561. *BFUP*, No. 1, p. 37. Another decree by governor, Antonio Moniz Barreto, in 1575 stated that the Hindus holding the job of revenue collection of the lands should leave this post in the hands of Christians or Portuguese officials. *Ibid.*, p. 49.

106. *DI*, III, 357.

107. "Alguns bramenes e neiqebarys (village administrators, captains of the native troops) são tornados cristãos e serviram Vossalteza neste cerqo de Goa bem e fiellmente." *Doc*, I, 152.

108. *BFUP*, No. 2, pp. 237, 242. *MR*, 2B, fls. 430-35, 446. The king did not permit any missionary to return to Portugal in 1606. *BFUP*, No. 3, pp. 513-14. *MR*, 6 B, fls. 70-72.

109. António da Silva Rego, *História das Missões do Padroado Português do Oriente*, p. 221.

110. Josef Wicki, "Mais Documentos de Miguel Vaz Coutinho Primeiro Vigário-Geral de Goa (Princípios de 1545)", pp. 146-51.

111. Georg Schurhammer, *Francis Xavier. His Life and His Times*, p. 231. António da Silva Rego, *op. cit.*, p. 206.

112. The order that the rents of the king should be leased out to Christians alone and not to the Hindus, went unattended till 1558. *DI*, IV, 201.

113. *Doc*, II, 196. *Ibid.*, III, 207.

114. *Ibid.*, 205, 532. As voluntary conversion involved certain loss of prestige in the locality, men from high caste used to come to an understanding with the missionaries so that the latter might simulate acts of violence or coersion and the former feign resistance. Rui Gomes Pereira, *Goa: Hindu Temples and Deities*, p. 15.

115. Georg Schurhammer, *Francisco Javier. Su vida y su tiempo*, p. 299.

116. Sebastião Gonçalves, *Primeira Parte da História dos Religiosos da Companhia de Jesus e do que fizeram com a Divina Graça na Conversão dos Infieis na nossa Sanca Fé Catholica nos Reynos e Provincias da India Oriental*, Vol. I, p. 109.

117. Sebastião Gonçalves, *op. cit.*, p. 109.

118. "Eu El Rey vos envio muito saudar. Como sabeis a idolatria he tamanha offensa de Deos, que não devo eu consentir que a aja nas terras dessas partes, que são de meu senhorio, e porque são informado que na ilha de Goa ha alguns pagodes publicos e secretos..." *Doc*, IV, 507.

119. Alessandro Valignano, *op. cit.*, p. 344.

120. *Ibid.*, p. 345.

121. *Ibid.*, p. 346.

122. Josef Wicki, (ed.), *LPC*, p. 104. *LFC*, fls. 19v, 20. *APO*, 5, Part III, doc. 821, p. 989. Royal decree forbidding a Hindu to occupy any public office according to the Canon Law of the time. Lisbon, 3-4-

1582. *BFUP*, No. 1, p. 39.

123. *Doc*, VII, 215-16. *APO*, 5, Part I, pp. 319-20. Decree by the king, D. João III, in 1557 prohibiting Portuguese officials to avail of the services of Brahmans, instead to use only the services of Christians. *BFUP*, No. 1, p. 50. Decree by the governor, Francisco Barreto, in 1557 forbidding officials to make use of the services of the Brahmans and to reserve government jobs for only the Christians. *LFC*, fl. 39v.

124. *Ibid.*, 7693, Vol. I, fls. 56-56v. "Dom Sebastião pretende que sejam favorecidos que a ella (fé catholica) se convertem, e a muita necessidade que tem de favor e ajuda temporal para se converterem e permanecerem nella os que estão debaixo da pertenssão de seus pais e parentes gentios ou mouros, pellas muitas reprehensões, induzimentos e occaziones que lhes dão para se não converterem e sendo convertidos, para deixarem a fé que muitos por isso deixão, e depois de a ter recebida." Letter written in 1559. *Ibid.*, fl. 23. *Doc*, VII, 280.

125. *LFC*, fl. 5v. *Doc*, VII, 215-16, 267.

126. Josef Wicki, (ed.), *LPC*, p. 109. *APO*, 5, Part II, doc. 575, p. 612.

127. *DI*, IV, 318-19. "Mas porque el Viso-Rey Don Constantino fué sempre mui entero en el favor de la conversión de los infieles, y para más libremente los induzir a la fe vedava todas las ydolatrías en toda la ysla de Goa, y castigava los ydólatras y favorecía a los que se conbertían a la fee, y daba lo que hera necessario para lo gasto de los catecúmenos para que se vestisen al modo de los christianos, occasione accepta comensaran a murmurar, unos diziendo que se azían los christianos por fuerça, otros que gastavan el dinero del Rei con negros, otros que se despoblavan las tierras y se deminuían las rentas del Rei,..." Letter from Nunes Barreto to the superior-general of the Society of Jesus, Diogo Laynez. Cochin, 1562. *Ibid.*, V, 486.

128. *Ibid.*, VIII, 65-66.

129. Alessandro Valignano, *op. cit.*, p. 346. *DI*, V, 66-67. The Portuguese suffered losses with the expulsion of Brahmans. *Doc*, VIII, 301.

130. Alessandro Valignano, *op. cit.*, p. 346.

131. *Ibid.*, p. 247.

132. "E com estes favores vai a christandade em muyto cresentamento, de modo que á já muy poucos gentios, e com ho numero dos christãos já será agora mayor que o numero dos gentios, se tem

agora por onrra antre elles fazer-se hum christão, ho que antes se tinha por grande vituperio, e com isto há já pouco que fazer em a conversão destas ilhas. Todo o mais do trabalho que agora temos hé em cultivar ho que está feito. Prezará Nosso Senhor que cedo virão ao baptismo os de Bardêz e Salsete..." Letter from Fr. António de Quadros to the king of Portugal. Cochin, 1561. *DI*, V. 67.

133. *Doc*, VI, 347.

134. *DI*, I, 69; VI, 116.

135. *Doc*, VIII, 58-59.

136. Decree by the viceroy, D. Constantino de Bragança, ordering the expulsion of Brahmans from Goa. Goa, 2-4-1560. *Ibid.*, 59.

137. *DI*, VI, 116.

138. *APO*, 5, Part. II, doc. 575, p. 612.

139. *Boletim Eclesiastico da Arquidiocese de Goa*, Ano IV, no. 7, p. 275.

140. *Doc*, IX, 615.

141. *APO*, 5, Part II, p. 488.

142. Francisco de Souza, *op. cit.*, p. 145.

143. *Doc*, III, 207, 223-24, 316, 526, 532; VII, 215-18. Agricultural land to be leased preferably to the Christians according to a provision on December 4, 1567. Maria Benedita Araújo, "O «Pay dos Christãos». Contribuição para o estudo da Cristianização da Índia", p. 314.

144. *APO*, 3, p. 5. AHU, *Registo de cartas*, Cod. 281, fls. 353, 356.

145. *APO*, 3, p. 10.

146. *LFC*, fls. 49-49v. *BFUP*, No. 1, pp. 36, 55. This decree was ratified by D. Filipe I in 1582. *Ibid.*, p. 40. In 1545, Fr. Diogo Borba had requested Fr. Simão Rodrigues to intercede before the king so that "os officios da India de lingoas, naiques, se dem aos naturaes christãos destas partes e não aos gentios..." *Doc*, III, 245.

147. *Ibid.*, XI, 254.

148. *Ibid.*, 252. Decree by the viceroy, D. Antão de Noronha, in 1565 about taking first the Hindus for sailors, and only then the Christians. *BFUP*, No. 1, p. 47.

149. *Doc*, X, 213. Village assembly or *gancaria* was the local body that discussed and settled village issues. In 1573 the Christian *gancars* of Salcete had preference over their Hindu counterparts in the village assemblies. Another decree by the governor, António Moniz

Barreto, forbidding the Hindus to hold any village assembly when Christian *gancars* were absent. *BFUP*, No. 1, p. 52.

150. Josef Wicki, (ed.), *LPC*, p. 146. "Estes negros nunca falam verdade". *Colecção de São Lourenço*, III, p. 520. "Canarins pessoas notadas de falsidade e mentiras e como a taes esta ordenado que não sejam admitidos a testemunhar a cousa alguma, nem se receberão informações e testemunhos desta ma gente." ARSI, *Eppistolae Goana et Malabarica*, 14, fl. 68.

151. *Doc*, XII, 643.

152. *APO*, 3, p. 72.

153. *BFUP*, No. 2, p. 213. *MR*, 2A, fls. 273-74.

154. *BFUP*, No. 2, p. 213. *MR*, 2A, fls. 273-74.

155. *BFUP*, No. 2, pp. 269-72. *MR*, 3A, fls. 188-96.

156. *BFUP*, No. 1, p. 165. *MR*, 1, fl. 95.

157. *MR*, 2B, fl. 471.

158. *APO*, 3, p. 827.

159. *Ibid.*, p. 120.

160. *Ibid.*, 5, Part II, pp. 489-90, see the second footnote.

161. AHU, *Registo de cartas*, Cod. 282, fl. 17.

162. Francisco de Sousa, *op. cit.*, p. 142. *APO*, 1, Part II, p. 106, 118.

163. AHU, *op.cit.*, fl. 43v.

164. *BFUP*, No. 3, p. 572. *MR*, 8, fls. 177-79. *APO*, 1, Part II, pp. 118, 185. *BFUP*, No. 3, p. 585. *MR*, 9, 10, 11, fl. 48.

165. A. K. Priolkar, *The Goa Inquisition*, p. 186.

166. *DI*, III, 719.

167. *BFUP*, No. 3, pp. 577-78. *MR*, 9, 10, 11, fl. 4.

168. *APO*, 1, Part II, p. 97.

169. *Ibid.*, 6, Suppl. II, doc. 49, p. 156; doc. 57, p. 184.

170. ARSI, *Goana Historia*, 34 - I, fl. 215v. In 1624 another provision stated that the Hindus could not be allowed to celebrate their marriage ceremonies in public, not even outside Goa, but only at their houses. "Não se poderem fazer casamentos dos gentios entre os fieis mas que se façam em suas casas (uma provisão). Se os gentios vão fora de Goa isto é um prejuizo ao Estado, porque lá na terra dos mouros eles podem usar mais livremente das superstições

de modo que a oportunidade que se tem de os converter cá perde-se." Josef Wicki, (ed.), *LPC*, pp. 248-50.

171. Paulo da Trindade, *op. cit.*, p. 286.

172. *APO*, 6, Suppl. I, doc. 511, p. 1200.

173. *BFUP*, No. 1, p. 54. "Manda o V. rei Pêro da Silva em 1639 que todos os bramanes gentios, ou de outra qualquer casta que seja, que e temor da converção violenta se ouver passado a terra firme, os asegura en nome de Sua Magestade pera que se possam vir livremente para esta cidade de Goa e pera todas as mais ilhas adjacentes, adonde não serão constrangidos por pessoa alguma de nenhuma calidade, e poderão viver sem receio debaxo das leis e provisões de Sua Majestade." Josef Wicki, (ed.), *op. cit.*, p 251.

174. ARSI, *Goana Historia*, 34 - I, fls. 222-23.

175. *Ibid.*, 34 - II, fl. 497.

176. *Ibid.*, 34 - I, fl. 222; 34 - II, fls. 497.

177. *MR*, 63, fls. 265-66.

178. *Ibid.*, fl. 296.

179. *Ibid.*, 63, fls. 458-60.

180. *Ibid.*, 58, fl. 329.

181. Josef Wicki, (ed.), *op. cit.*, p. 327.

182. *MR*, 54, fls. 146-47v.

# 6

# DECREES ON TEMPLES, IDOLS AND ORPHANS

## Decrees on Temples and Idols

Least said soonest mended. However the story, although sometimes disagreeable, needs to be told to the contentment of one's curiosity. It is normal to think that force began to be used to expand Christendom when conversions by mild means proved a failure. Although this may not always be true, the destruction of temples and idols speak for themselves.[1] The magnificent Hindu temples had to be substituted by even more sumptuous Christian buildings to bring about greater confidence among the new Lusitanian citizens. These building besides illiciting devotion from the converts also aimed at increasing the number of adherents to the religion they represented.[2] Alessandro Valignano has left for us a detailed description in lofty terms about these Hindu temples or their architecture in Goa.[3] The missionaries believed that the destruction of the temples would serve as the greatest punishment to the Hindus. This would deter their religious zeal.[4] And the priests concluded that the number of conversions increased rather quickly after the destruction of the temples and idols.[5]

The main temples in almost every village had been founded by the village community, and a fraction of the income from the best lands in the village was always set aside for the building maintenance and for the temple personnel.[6] The Brahmans controlled the temple patrimony or land, and the temple priests leased them out and collected their rents. The temples functioned not only as places of worship and learning for the privileged, but around them fairs were also organized especially at religious festivities. The temples played a decisive role in the economic life of the village. Moreover, the temples functioned as centres where the village chiefs discussed crucial issues relating to the village and took decisions.[7] Local allegiance was given to the village temple. The *gaunkars*, members of high castes or the privileged groups, owned the land, hence they obviously controlled the temple and the allegiance of the people. In order to safeguard the traditional rights of the Brahmans and their monopoly in the village community, it was said and believed that anyone who usurped the land from a Brahman, even an inch of it, would be lost forever in hell. The Brahmans of Goa being very rich and powerful projected themselves as a united group, despite their internal differences. This was done to keep the others under their sway, and no matter what sort of efforts the viceroys made to change this situation they proved futile.[8] But after the destruction of the temples the land changed hands, and the traditional power relations suffered lasting modifications. For instance, the destruction of the temples in Goa disrupted the traditional clerical power and the core of economic order organized around the temples.[9] The priests, Brahmans, dancing girls, kolvonts and other temple personnel found themselves out of their jobs and displaced, and the tenants who cultivated the lands that belonged to the temples had perhaps no other alternative but to leave the land or be converted, in order to continue to cultivate the land and live on it.[10] Much of the rent for the crown came from the rich lands that belonged to the temples.[11]

We are told that for a long time before the destruction of the temples, the Hindus lived under the spell of the demon and their idols.[12] The Hindus were at the "service of the demon", wrote João de Barros, the Portuguese official chronicler, in the sixteenth century.[13] The missionaries also believed that the temples that stood on the Portuguese-controlled territories offended God and weakened the faith of the converts. Besides, the "Hindus were fanatical in their practices", which made their conversion almost impossible.[14] Temples were occasions for the new converts to remember their previous falsities and to cause relapses, since some of them lived very close to these temples.[15] More importantly, the multiplicity of the Hindu deities could hardly help social integration and local vassalage to the crown, so believed the Portuguese. Hence, to erase every trace of Hinduism, often Christian monuments were erected on the ruins of the destroyed temples where the idols had been worshipped before;[16] and at times solemn crosses were planted in those places.[17] The existence of churches in the villages turned out to be another excellent means of making conversions.[18]

Despite Cunha Rivara's often quoted statement that "in the first heat of conquest the temples in Goa were destroyed", whatever he meant by the 'first heat', the fact remains that no systematic and officially approved destruction of temples took place before 1540.[19] However, some mosques had been demolished soon after the conquest of Goa in 1510.[20] Later, the convert Fabian Gonçalves himself destroyed all the temples and houses of idolatry in Goa, wrote Miguel Vaz in 1543.[21] It had been calculated that the temples brought down in the islands of Goa numbered 160: twelve in Chorão, eleven in Divar, six in Jua, one in Vamsi and the rest in Tissuary.[22] The Franciscans contributed to the demolition of three hundred temples in Bardez, where false gods were worshipped.[23] Salcete accounted for a little more than two hundred temples, but we read that 280 to 300 big temples were destroyed here in 1566-67.[24] The destruction of the temples in Bardez and Salcete was completed in 1567, we were told.[25] But this does not correspond with facts or other reports. Portuguese captains and soldiers, together with some religious Brothers, brought down these temples. Some priests used to be present at the moment of their destruction.[26] The Portuguese decrees on the destruction of temples and idolatry embraced territories other than Goa as well. In another Salsette near Bassein (not in Goa) when 10150 souls received baptism two temples were demolished.[27] In Thana twelve temples saw the same fate.[28] Temples were also brought down in Hormuz.[29] In Congo the missionaries asked the Portuguese captains to destroy the local idols and to celebrate the occasion in style.[30]

Some idols from the destroyed temples were thrown into the river and others found their way to the foundry-work for producing candle-holders and other objects for the churches.[31] Since not all the public and private idols had been confiscated or destroyed in Goa, in 1546 the king ordered a search in the houses of suspected Hindus.[32] They found more than eight hidden idols in Salcete in 1599.[33] Due to the religious persecution, the Hindus began painting their deities on leaves and on coconuts, since it became easier to conceal them when searches took place.[34] Some idols were taken away to the territory of the Muslims.[35] Curiously, a certain priest in Goa wanted to get hold of some idols to break them as a remedy for his headaches.[36]

For several years the church had exclusively paid its attention to the Portuguese, but after 1540 it began concentrating on the needs of the converts and on the conversion of the Hindus. Many chapels were in dire need of finacial assistance, and were even in danger of being neglected or abandoned, whilst some were already suffering this fate. Moreover, the people who had been converted, poor as they were, had to be helped lest they despaired and abandoned their new faith altogether. The missionaries believed that the Hindus without their temples might willingly embrace the Christian faith,[37] and the temple rents would considerably benefit the churches and chapels, and the new conversion drive. However, after the destruction of the temples these lands continued to be in possession of the *gaunkars*, who alleged that they were not obliged to pay more rents to the crown than what the *Foral* had stipulated. Moreover, the *gaunkars* stated that no one but they themselves had any claim over the temples' property, even over their movable goods, jewelry and money.[38] In 1541 the *Vedor da Fazenda* (chief revenue superintendent), Fernão Rodrigues de Castelo Branco, persuaded the *gaunkars* to donate the rent of the temples to the work of conversion. Strangely, we read that the *gaunkars* did not object to this request, instead they seemed only desirous to help the Portuguese.[39] Eventually the property of the temples was taken over by the government.[40]

It can be argued that when the majority of the population in a particular village were converted, the temples became dysfunctional here, hence their inevitable destruction. This kind of argument does not find support in our documentation. However, there could have been a few such cases.[41] At Daugim when almost all its inhabitants had been converted, the converts themselves broke down the temple and asked for a church to be built in its stead.[42] In 1545 there were no temples but many Hindus, Muslims and bad Christians residing in the city of Goa.[43] There were over five thousand converts and about forty thousand Hindus in the island of Goa in 1548.[44] In Goa most temples were destroyed in 1540 with much uproar and unrest. It was not easy to demolish the temples in Salcete because many Brahmans and *jogues* (*yogis*) living there prevented it.[45] In the same district we hear of a big temple which the king of Portugal could not, or did not dare to, destroy till 1563, since this place was a stronghold of Hinduism and Islam.[46] Hence, everything points to the fact that the destruction of temples preceded the conversion of villages.

There was some debate and even disagreement among the Portuguese regarding the destruction of the temples. Some Portuguese argued that with the destruction of the temples the rent for the crown had diminished, but the zealots counter-argued saying that it had only increased.[47] It may be true that the destruction of the temples brought immediate material profit to the crown, but the adverse effects were increasingly felt when the Hindus began abandoning Goa in great numbers as a result of these and other harsh conversion policies.[48] Besides, some sort of uneasiness and reluctance brewed among the local Portuguese authorities when they were compelled to implement the royal decrees regarding the destruction of temples and idolatry, etc., because of the violence and local reactions they caused. The local civil authorities disagreed with the decrees of the king, but since it was unchristian to permit temples in their own territory, Portuguese prudence allowed the Hindus to practise their religion and customs in disguise.[49] Summarizing these arguments, we can conclude that the expansion of Christendom, which did not come about so easily or just as the missionaries wished it would happen, led to the destruction of the temples.[50] The destruction of the temples to control their patrimony and rents was of no less importance.

It is beyond any doubt that the destruction of the temples in the islands of Goa took place in 1540.[51] Historical sources offer us no consensus on who ordered it and those involved in the first destruction of the temples. The king, D. João III, the vicar-general, Miguel Vaz, Fr. Diogo Borba, and even a local convert were mentioned as being directly responsible for, and involved in, their demolition. But what is important for us to know is that despite the destruction of the temples in Goa in 1540, a vast number of decrees ordering the destruction of the remaining standing temples, and a ban on rebuilding them, were issued subsequently.

In 1545 Miguel Vaz requested the king of Portugal to endow him with extensive power to enable him to cleanse the land from its temples.[52] There were several decrees on the destruction of the temples and idolatry which we need to consider. We shall examine some decrees that forbade the construction of new temples and the repairing of the old ones throughout the sixteenth century and even thereafter.[53]

In 1546 the viceroy, D. João de Castro, ordered all the temples to be pulled down.[54] In 1548 a royal decree considered it illegal to possess idols.[55] Another decree of the governor, Jorge Cabral, in 1549 banned the construction of temples and mosques.[56] D. Catarina, queen regent of Portugal, banned Hindu ceremonies in the Portuguese-controlled territories in 1559.[57] Further, D. Antão de Noronha by a decree in 1566 forbade the Hindus to build or repair any temple without his permission. The penalty for breach of this decree was the destruction of these temples anew.[58] The Brahmans reacted and complained that their gods could not remain at the mercy of destructive climatic elements, but the viceroy refused to entertain their complaints. The Hindus began transferring their idols to the Muslim territory, and when the temples were gradually abandoned their lands became the patrimony of the churches.[59] The ban on temple construction continued. In 1576 no temples could be constructed or repaired without the consent of the viceroy.[60] On the other hand the Jesuit missionaries did not permit any Hindu temples and ceremonies in Salcete. The Hindus were ready to donate thirty thousand *pardaus* for the permission to perform their ceremonies freely.[61] In 1579 they appealed again, but the missionaries objected saying that if such a permission was granted to them, it would certainly spell the end of Christendom.[62]

In 1580 a decree by the governors of Portugal did not allow the existence of temples in Bardez and Salcete.[63] D. Filipe I ratified the ban on Hindu temples and banned public ceremonies with another decree in 1581.[64] In the same year the king withdrew from the captains and viceroys the power to give permission to build temples, and controlled it himself.[65] These are the summaries of various decrees related to Hindu temples and idols that I could find.

## The Question of Hindu Orphans

The decrees issued by the kings and viceroys to facilitate the conversion of orphans, the reasons behind them and the means to execute the same decrees deserve some attention. These decrees were as controversial as they were important for the expansion of Christendom. Not less was the interpretation of the term orphan. I think that we can assess the sixteenth century decrees more profitably if we situate them in relation to other decrees of the same nature issued in the subsequent centuries. Hence, the presentation of other orphan-related issues pertaining to the following centuries.

The number of decrees produced about the Hindu orphans should make us wonder at the concern and necessity to modify and ratify the same decree several times over, in the course of the sixteenth century and even thereafter. It needs to be clearly stressed that just as the decrees on the temples and others, the decrees on the orphans were not applicable exclusively to the territory of Goa. I did not find any other decree on the orphans after 1754. We already know that by then some religious freedom had been granted to the Hindus in Goa.

The body of decrees ordering the separation of a Hindu orphan, less than fourteen years of age, from his home, to be baptized even if he/she had mother or relatives seems to have had a great impact on the work of conversion. Reactions and even violence were not absent when the decree was implemented. The decree further stated that if a Hindu widowed mother could not provide a good education for her son, he would not be returned to her after his conversion.[66] It was believed that this decree motivated many a widowed mother and her relatives to ask for baptism almost every day.

Local reactions and social unrest prompted this decree to be slightly modified in the course of the century. Be that as it might, some letters and reports would have us believe that the conversion of orphans posed little local and individual resistance. However, facts do not support this pretension. Social unrest and reactions did take place especially when the fatherless boys were also separated forcibly from their mothers, and kept in the houses of Christians to be instructed and baptized.[67]

With slight modification of details the decrees on the orphans could be read thus: an orphan boy/girl could be taken away from his/her Hindu mother, and given in the care of a Christian tutor or placed in a house for catechumens by the Judge of the Orphans, if their mothers had no intention whatsoever of making them Christians. After instructing the orphans in the Christian faith they were kept away from their relatives and from any harmful Hindu influence. The decree further stated that if the orphans persisted in their old beliefs while in the care of the tutors, they would be sent home without any pressure or violence.[68] However, if the mother expressed the desire to become a Christians her son or daughter could remain with her. It was necessary to have a dispatch from the viceroys or from the Judge of the Orphans to take an orphan away from their relatives. As a precautionary measure some officials of justice had to be always present at the place on the occasion of taking an orphan away from his mother, so that everything went off without creating any violence or resentment.[69]

The decree on orphans issued by the governor, Francisco Barreto (1555-1558), in 1556 seems to be the first official order. It reads that an orphan of Hindu parents of less than fourteen years of age, even if he/she had mother or close relatives, could be taken away and kept with a Christian tutor. The orphan would remain with the Christian tutor till the age of reason or fourteen, after which he could freely decide about his religion.[70] This law remained in force in its essence in Portuguese India till 1677, bringing a rich harvest of boys and girls to the church.[71]

Probably, the Hindu reactions and fear of escalation of disturbances compelled D. Catarina, the queen regent, to modify the decree mentioned above in 1559. The new decree read that only Hindu orphans without father, mother, grandparents and other relatives and aged less than fourteen years could be taken to the College of St Paul to be educated and baptized; later suitable jobs would be given them.[72] In 1564 the viceroy, D. Antão de Noronha, on behalf of the king, D. Sebastião, ratified the queen's decree of 1559. Freedom to choose one's religion on completing the age of fourteen years stood valid.[73]

The clergy present at the First Provincial Council held in Goa in 1567 asked the king to apply the Portuguese civil law concerning orphans in the East too, and this request was granted.[74] The Portuguese law defined that a boy of less than fourteen years of age and a girl of less than twelve years without father, even if he/she had mother, grandparents or great-grandparents, or even if he/she had been married and with a consumated marriage, was an orphan.[75] This law was adopted by the same Provincial Council with the view to implementing it in Goa and elsewhere.[76] It was a reversal of the 1559 and 1564 decrees on orphans.

The decree on orphans adopted by the First Provincial Council with the royal approval was ratified in 1571.[77] Further orders in 1575 urged the College of St Paul to instruct the Hindu orphans from Bardez and Salcete. Hiding the orphans or taking them outside Goa became a common practice, but this could attract punishment like being sent to the galleys, or loss of all their property.[78] The governor, Fernão Teles de Meneses, upheld all the previous decrees passed in favour of Christendom and at the same time ratified the decree on orphans in 1581.[79] Another royal decree in 1582 ordered the handing over of Hindu orphans to the College of St Paul.[80]

It is certain that disagreements on the issue of orphans surfaced among the clergy and the local authority; nevertheless, we are made to believe that the decree continued to be implemented without relaxation. The Portuguese discussed the decree from the point of view of civil rights and natural law. Some argued that by civil right the state could take away the sons from the Hindu mother. Further, by civil right the child could be taken away from the arms of the widowed mother who married again, or lived in scandal. Could a child not be taken away from a Hindu mother to avoid that he should be lost to idolatry, asked the missionaries. Moreover, since the Hindus did not observe, or rather were incapable of observing, even the natural law — as they themselves proved by their constant visits to the firm land to worship idols and perform their ceremonies — the punishment meted out to them for the breach of natural law was justifiable, because any worship was due only to the true God. The question became more acute for the more scrupulous missionaries, particularly when the orphans were baptized before the age of reason.[81] The less scrupulous and the hardliners argued that taking the orphans to a house for catechumens against their will was not tantamount to making them Christians by force, since there was a royal decree ordering their baptism. Hence, there could not be violation of civil rights or natural law in anyway.[82] The fact that the decrees on orphans motivated the father, or mother, or relatives of the orphan to be converted seemed to have been the most convincing argument in favour of baptism for orphans for the scrupulous and unscrupulous alike.[83] After all, this was precisely what the decree aimed at.

The Second Provincial Council (1575), probably to appease the Hindus, made it clear that the orphans were taken away from their mothers not to be baptized before the age of reason, but rather to be brought up with good habits.[84] The decree of the governor, António Moniz Barreto, ordered that all the orphans should be reported to the College of St Paul, and those who hid them could be punished with exile and loss of property in favour of the catechumens.[85]

At the beginning of the seventeenth century the archbishop, D. Aleixo de Meneses,[86] decreed that only orphans without father, mother and grandparents could be taken away from the Hindus. He held that to do otherwise would be tantamount to infringing natural law. The Franciscans, and possibly the Jesuits, disagreed with this opinion and suggested a stricter decree on orphans, which would force their mothers and other relatives to accept baptism. A consensus on this matter proved difficult, for the archbishop was unwilling to change his mind. Subsequently the matter was presented for discussion at the Fifth Provincial Council that took place in Goa in 1606. The Council, after much debate, favoured the stand of the Franciscans. It decided that after the death of the father, the fatherless boy had to have a tutor who, as the representative of his late father, would be responsible for his education. He could also decide about the child's baptism. The Hindu mothers continued to hide their sons after the death of their fathers.[87] It was reported in 1605 that some mothers preferred to sell their own children to other Hindus, rather than hand them over to the Christians to convert them.[88]

In 1646 the viceroy, D. Felipe Mascarenhas, stated that the death of his/her father made a child an orphan, irrespective of his/her mother, grandparents or other family members being alive or not. This orphan could be baptized even if its family objected to it.[89] Normally, an orphan had a Christian tutor who was like a guardian to him/her until the age of fourteen years, before which he/she could not inherit any paternal property. This decree repeated what the First Provincial Council[90] had determined, and what had been ratified by the viceroy, D. António de Noronha, in 1567. The decree of Mascarenhas only expressed the wishes of the Fifth Provincial Council (1606), which affirmed that the consent of the Christian tutor was sufficient to baptize an orphan, even before the age of fourteen, regardless of its mother's and relatives' opinion.[91]

In 1672 and 1674 the king opposed forced baptisms of the sons of Hindus, except in the case of orphans.[92] Rich Muslim and Hindu merchants fearing conversion of their sons after their death abandoned the Portuguese-dominated territories. In 1678 another decree — abrogating the decree passed by D. Filipe de Mascarenhas in 1646 — permitted only the adoption of orphans without maternal and paternal relatives. This new decree, which in fact conformed with the law of D. Sebastião or that of the queen regent (1559), did not allow the taking of the fatherless orphans away.[93] The clergy considered this new law as reactionary and contrary to the spirit of conversions. Those who opposed conversions of orphans died prematurely as a punishment from God, so preached the missionaries. Due to harsh conversion laws the Hindu and Muslim businessmen and merchants stopped coming to Goa. Trade and commerce declined each day.[94]

It was noticed that when the orphans grew up they returned to their former Hindu practices; hence it was decided that no force should be exerted on them.[95] But the question of orphans dragged on even to the beginning of the eighteenth century. Probably, some over-zealous missionaries had taken a few boys away from their families, alleging that they were truly orphans or children of illegitimate unions. Even in the case of genuine orphans the priests could be very selective, choosing especially the rich ones. This excess of zeal or ambition scandalized the Hindus and discouraged their conversion. Orphans girls, less than twelve years of age, could also be taken away to a house for catechumens, although this is not mentioned explicitly in historical documents. The *Pay dos Christãos* entered the Hindu houses and took the children away from their mothers, a behaviour condemned by the king who demanded a strict adherence to the law of 1678.[96]

A provision issued by the Goa inquisitors in 1706, stated that every orphan should be reported to the *Pay dos Christãos* and those who hid them would be punished.[97] In 1709 the *Pay dos Christãos* issued another order to gather the orphans at a house for catechumens.[98] In the same year a letter by king, D. João V, recommended the viceroy, D. Rodrigo da Costa, to verify certain complaints that the former had received from the Hindus regarding their orphans. Further, the king ordered the viceroy to return the fatherless boys to their mothers. By then it became necessary to ask the orphans in the presence of their Hindu mothers whether they desired to become Christians.[99]

In 1715 the Portuguese authorities issued a warning not to use force to baptize orphans.[100] Another decree by the viceroy, D. Luís de Meneses, in 1718 warned the relatives of the orphans against taking them away from Goa.[101] In 1750 a ruling decided that no Hindu orphan could be made Christian against his wishes, and that his Hindu relatives had necessarily to know about the orphan's free consent in case he was to be baptized.[102] The excessive preoccupation of the missionaries with the baptism of orphans, brought to light another royal decree in 1754. It discussed whether the custom of taking illegitimate Hindu children to a house for catechumens should continue.[103] Whether the decrees favouring (read forcing) the conversion of fatherless boys had been always taken seriously throughout these two centuries is a disputed matter.

What were the main reasons for issuing the decree on orphans and the means used to implement it? The missionaries argued that if the adult person did not wish to go to heaven willingly or forcibly, at least their children should go hence their baptism.[104] As seen earlier, the widowed mother or her relatives had to take her son to a house for catechumens or to the *Pay dos Christãos*, but if they failed in this duty they could be penalized even with expulsion from Goa.[105] However, not all the orphans were taken away from their mothers or relatives despite rigorous orders.[106] The Hindus tried to bribe the Portuguese authorities to allow them to hide their orphans.[107]

It may be recalled that when the king of Portugal, D. Manuel, had issued an order to separate the Jewish children from their parents in Portugal, some Jewish parents preferred to kill their children rather than to lose them to the Christians.[108] Did something similar occur in Goa? It seems that when a Hindu woman lost her natural rights over her children after the death of her husband, and when she did not succeed in taking her children to the firm land, she preferred to kill her children rather than subject them to this cruel law of separation.[109] Did this really happen? When things became difficult for them, the Brahmans threatened to leave the city of Goa, but many women and relatives without any alternative converted to stay together with their children.

As mentioned before, some scrupulous priests doubted whether it was ethically right to baptize a Hindu orphan of less than fourteen years of age against the wishes of his mother. However, most missionaries agreed in principle that if the orphan persisted in his ancestral beliefs he should be sent home. This served to dispel doubts about forced conversions. The Judges of the Orphans and some others incharge of the orphans had been accused of letting some orphans return to Hinduism.[110]

The property or inheritance of the orphans was used up by their relatives on themselves, said the First Provincial Council. The stepfather and the mother of the child spent all the wealth of the orphan before he could reach the age of reason.[111] Whether the property or orphan's inheritance share was taken away along with him, when he was separated from his relatives, or at the time of his baptism is not clear. However, it seems that in many cases, a boy on becoming an orphan was immediately baptized, in total disregard for the spirit and letter of the decree on orphans.[112] There was a good amount of money destined for the orphans, but those responsible for it, especially the Judges of the Orphans, lent it to their friends; so much so that when the orphans needed some money nothing was available.[113]

We are informed that in Goa in 1516, there were seventy orphans of alliances between the Portuguese and prostitutes, slaves and other women.[114] The House for Orphans was founded in the city of Goa in 1553 to shelter local orphan boys and *mestiços*, offsprings of mixed marriages, whose fathers had died at the service of the crown. They were educated to be virtuous persons and to help the priests (of the Society of Jesus) in the activity of conversion.[115] Here the orphans learnt about the Christian commandments, the articles of faith and the mortal sins.[116] There were normally a hundred orphans in the house and they wore a white uniform with a coloured cross on their chest. This house was supposed to have developed into a college for orphans, but it did not. It functioned in the care of the Jesuits in the same College of St. Paul, as there was no separate building for them.[117]

In Pomburpa village, in Bardez, the Franciscan church of Madre de Deus had a college for orphans, and some of its inmates became priests. It is probable that at Reis Magos, in Bardez, there was also a college for orphans as per the provision of D. João III on the Hindu orphans, but we hear of another college for orphans at Reis Magos only in 1576.[118] These orphans learnt humanities, Christian doctrine and good habits.[119] We have seen that only the talented orphans were admitted to the College of Santa Fé or St

Paul to study arts, but the less gifted ones were given jobs according to their abilities. A few learnt how to read and write after which they were kept in the houses of Portuguese men. Some Portuguese orphans joined religious order and became priests.[120]

The main reason or justification for the decrees on Hindu orphans was the protection and education of the orphans — they had to be kept away from idolatry as early as possible or before becoming contaminated by it;[121] the decrees also helped the expansion of Christendom.[122] The number of decrees does not suggest that they were relunctantly implemented. Likewise, we cannot conclude that they were always implemented with the same rigour, or that their infringment brought the prescribed penalties. The documents are silent on details and facts, probably because interests, facts or praxis were in conflict with the very law; perhaps because each and every decree on orphans was not clear to, or significant for, the missionaries. However, such legislation cannot be overlooked while assessing the methods of conversion in Goa during the sixteenth century.

## Conclusion

We have discussed the twists and turns of the decrees and privilges in favour of conversion in this and in the previous chapters. Very often the Portuguese authorities deliberately failed to implement the decrees and privileges in favour of the converts, or better, in favour of conversions. At times the enforcing agents lost all sense of justice either due to excessive religious zeal or personal ambition to earn more and quickly. Leaving aside these and other reasons or the poor implementation of these decrees, it was expected that the Hindus on seeing the favours being granted to some and disfavours to others might soon be converted.[123] At times decrees in favour of conversion and decrees against the Hindus might have produced the same hoped-for results, but both were not necessarily the same thing as I have consistently affirmed. In any case, it was licit and ethically justified to make Christians by any means.[124]

Many Hindus showed great repugnance and resistance to accept the Christian faith, whereas others were attracted to it for the great many favours they could receive.[125] Despite the force used and decrees issued in favour of conversions, the missionaries could just prevent the Hindus from performing their ceremonies publicly in the city of Goa, since it came directly under the control of the Portuguese and the missionaries. They could do very little about it in Bardez and Salcete. Here the Hindus continued to perform their ceremonies and no one was able to stop them.[126] Even in the city of Goa they celebrated their festivals and ceremonies by night.[127]

The Portuguese policy or means employed to make Lusitanian citizens, namely, decrees, religious instruction, privileges and penalties defined what the locals could retain and what they had to abandon from their own culture. Decrees were one thing and their implementation another thing. The missionaries understood very well that the neo-converts would not be able to remain firm in their faith without favours and privileges, but we also know that the missionaries often complained to home authorities that the converts were not favoured by the local officials. Conversions could not depend simply on the good will of the Portuguese authorities, which was rare. Hence, something more than decrees and privileges was necessary. This was to be the Catechumenate period and continuous religious instruction.[128]

In brief, the missionaries held firmly that no adult Hindu or Muslim could be baptized without being submitted first to a test. The catechumens had to show by deeds that they were worthy of baptism. Although there were group baptisms and hasty baptisms, the missionaries alleged that they had been instructed individually before baptism, or soon after it.[129] Houses for catechumens for Christian instruction were essential to strengthen the loyalty of the neo-converts as we shall see in the next chapter.

## NOTES AND REFERENCES

1. António Baião, *A Inquisição de Goa*, Vol. I, p. 25.
2. *Ibid.*, pp. 7, 25, 36-37.

3. Alessandro Valignano, *op. cit.*, p. 81.
4. *DI*, VI, 617-18.
5. *Ibid.*, XII, 254.
6. The word *pagode* could mean a 'temple', a 'feast', an 'idol' or a 'gold coin' (gold pardau=360 reis). *DI*, IV, 204; I, 66, note no. 2. *Pagodes* were idols and demons. *Ibid.*, V, 358-59: "Las casas onde están los ídolos y bragmanes llámansse pagodes." Georg Schurhammer and Josef Wicki, (eds.), *Epistolae S. Francisci Xaverii*, Vol. I, p. 171.
7. A. Lopes Mendes, *A India Portugueza*, Vol. II, p. 66.
8. Alessandro Valignano, *op. cit.*, p. 374.
9. The Aryan onslaught had dispossessed the original inhabitants of their properties depriving them of their gods and temples too.
10. The temple received the income of *kolvonts* (dancing-girls) who lived in the temples. *Doc*, VI, 470.
11. ARSI, *Miscellaneum Indiarum Orientalum*, 38-I, fl. 111. Doc, II, 294.
12. *Ibid.*, 293 ff.
13. João de Barros, *Decada da Asia*, I, (1932), p. 104.
14. *DI*, VII, 388.
15. *Ibid.*, 396.
16. *Memória Histórica Eclesiastica da Arquidiocese de Goa*, p. 105.
17. *Doc*, X, 292.
18. *DI*, VIII, 331.
19. J.H. da Cunha Rivara, *Ensaio Historico da Lingua Concani*, p. 13. J.H. da Cunha Rivara, *Gramatica da Lingua Concani,* p. XLIX.
20. *DI*, VII, 395. "Faço saber aos que este virem como querendo nosso senhor lembrar-se desta terra e gente della, que de tantos tempos estava sujeita ao demonio, e seus Pagodes, houve por seu serviço inspirar em muitas pessoas destas Ilhas pera se converterem á sua sancta fé, e que os Pagodes fossem derribados, e desfeitos de todo, sem ficar nenhum em todas ellas,...." Goa, 1541. Written by Fernão Rodrigues de Castello Branco, chief revenue superintendent *(Vedor da Fazenda). DI*, II, 293.
21. "E per sua mão (de Fabiam Gonçalves, lascarym) foram destroydos e tirados todos os pagodes e casas de idolatrya que avy'a em Goa, domde se seguyo não ser nelas o Senhor Deus maes deservido, e aver se remda pera sostimento do colegyo, domde esperamos ser tamto servido." *Lascarins* were fighting native soldiers of the crew. Letter from the vicar-general, Miguel Vaz, to the king in 1543. *Doc*,

II, 343.

22. Panduranga Pissurlencar, *Boletim do Instituto Vasco da Gama*, 68 (1952), pp. 37-41.
23. *Doc*, V, 408.
24. *DI*, XII, 919; VII, 387, 391; X, 734.
25. *Doc*, X, 298.
26. *DI*, VII, 394-95. Many temples were pulled down in Bassein in 1551. *Doc*, IV, 64.
27. *Ibid.*, V, 403.
28. *Ibid.*
29. *APO*, 3, p. 99.
30. João de Barros, *Decada da Asia,* I, (1932), pp. 104, 109.
31. *DI*, VII, 395.
32. *Doc*, IV, 507. In 1559, "Hum homem principal de huma aldea, depois de feito christão, descobrio certos pagodes de pedra, mui bem lavrados, que os gentios na mesma aldea tinhão enterrados debaixo do chão. Foi la o Pe. Pero de Almeida e desenterrados, os fizerão em pedaços, e o mesmo fizerão depois outros christãos e, descobrindo estas manqueiras dos gentios, e particularmente se achou hum enterrado junto de um tanque de agoa, que era o padroeiro desta ilha, Gounato por nome, donde a ilha se chama Guoa, segundo suas historias." *Ibid.*, VII, 356.
33. *DI*, XVI, 9.
34. *Ibid.*, IV, 203.
35. *Ibid.*, VII, 63.
36. *Ibid.*, V, 359.
37. *Doc*, II, 293ff.
38. From the beginning the *gancars* had set aside the best land in the village for the expenses of the temples, over which they themselves had no rights. The Brahmans received the rents of these lands, kept them apart for the service of the cult, but after the destruction of the temples the rents should have necessarily reverted to the *gancars*. *Ibid.*
39. *Ibid.*, 293, 295.
40. J. H. da Cunha Rivara, *Gramatica da Lingua Concani*, p. L. The rent accruing from the temple lands were allocated for the ordinary expenses of the churches, hospitals, dresses for catechumens, salary of the church guards, *Pay dos Christãos*, parish priests, native priests who heard confessions of the local Christians in the villages, catechists, etc. *DI*, VIII, 553; IX, 276; XI, 276-77; XII, 86, 594;

XIV, 538. Anthony D'Costa, "The Demolition of the Temples in the Islands of Goa in 1540 and the disposal of the Temple Lands", pp. 161-76.

41. *Doc*, V, 415; III, 147.
42. *Ibid.*, II, 103. "... tanadarya de Daugym, omde novamente se fez huma casa de Nossa Senhora, da ymvocação da Madre de Deus, cousa muyto devota e de gramde romagem, no propeo lugar omde estava ho pagode, o qual os mesmos gemtyos dele ho quebraram per suas mãos, pidimdo casa de Nossa Senhora e sam quasy todos cristãos..." Letter from Miguel Vaz to the king in 1543. *Ibid.*, 343.
43. *DI*, I, 45.
44. *Ibid.*, 253, 408.
45. ARSI, *Miscellaneum Indiarum Orientalum*, 38 - I, fl. 111.
46. *DI*, VI, 255-56.
47. *Doc*, IV, 64.
48. *DI*, VII, 396.
49. *APO*, 6, Suppl. 1-2, doc. 49, p. 156.
50. *DI*, I, 66.
51. "E como o intento da conversão dos infieis fosse o que mais obrigava a El-rey nosso senhor a conquistar estas partes da India, tendo já conquistada esta ilha de Goa, e os moradores della quietos, e seguros na sua vassalagem, querendo pôr em effeito esta sua tenção tão sancta, sendo informado que muitos destes moradores erão já christãos, e os outros estavão firmes na crença de sua gentilidade por se consentir que fizessem seus ritos e cerimonias nos paguodes que adoravão, mandou que os ditos paguodes fossem derribados, e os não houvesse em toda a ilha de Goa e seus termos, nem se consentisse ao gentio fazer nas terras de seu senhorio nenhuma cerimonia gentilica, pera com este rigor de misericorida os obrigar a se esquecerem do culto gentilico, e se converterem a nossa santa fé, como tinham feito e fazião muitos que já erão convertidos, e em comprimento desta tão santa obra se desfizerão e derribarão os ditos paguodes no anno de quarenta." *Ibid.*, 759.
52. *Ibid.*, 66.
53. Anthony D'Costa, "op. cit.", pp. 161-76. *DI*, I, 759, 793.
54. *LFC*, fl. 30v. "El Rey lhe mandava que nam sofresse na ilha de Goa pagodes publicos nem secretos, que castigasse ... todo o official que fizesse ou lavrasse... idolo algum." *DI*, I, 66-67, note no. 2.
55. *BFUP*, No. 1, p. 45.
56. *Ibid. LFC*, fl. 31.

57. *Ibid.*, p. 35. *DI*, IV, 328, note no. 30. *APO*, 5, Part I, p. 389. *Doc*,VII, 284-85.
58. *BFUP*, No. 1, p. 50. *DI*, VI, 671, note no. 2.
59. *Doc*, X, 73, 103.
60. *LFC*, fl. 41.
61. *DI*, X, 870.
62. *Ibid.*, XI, 262, 692.
63. *BFUP*, No. 1, p. 35.
64. *Ibid. Doc*, XI, 728. *APO*, 5, Part III, pp. 977-78.
65. *DI*, XII, 920. "...procurar a conversão da gentilidade, e aumento das christandades das partes e conquistas da India, evitarão e proibirão por suas cartas e provisões os pagodes ceremonias, e ritos publicos gentilicos, nem de mouros nas ditas partes e terras da India que são de meu senhorio, nem que os capitães ou VisoReis das ditas partes possão para isso dar licenças..." *APO*, 5, Part III, pp. 977-78.
66. Francisco de Souza, *op. cit.*, p. 131.
67. *Bullarium*, First Provincial Council, Acc. 2, dec. 13, p. 9. Paulo da Trindade, *op. cit.*, p. 375.
68. *Doc*, XI, 754. Paulo da Trindade, *op. cit.*, p. 370. Francisco de Souza, *op. cit.*, p. 129.
69. *APO*, 5, p. 1266.
70. Francisco de Souza, *op. cit.*, p. 129. *APO*, 6, Supplements I-II, doc. 48, p. 155 and doc. 12, p. 46.
71. Francisco de Souza, *op. cit.*, p. 129.
72. Lisbon, 23-3-1559. *APO*, 5, Part I, p. 385. *BFUP*, No. 1, p. 38.
73. *LFC*, fl. 61. *Doc*, IX, 311. "...:hey por bem e mando que a ley que ElRey, meu senhor e avô, que esta santa gloria haja, fez per que mandou que os filhos dos gentios que nestas ilhas e cidade de Goa, e nas partes da India ficarem sem pay e sem mây, e sem avô ou avó, ou outros ascendentes, e que não forem de idade que possão ter entendimeto, ou juizo de rezão, se tomem pera serem doutrinados e bautisados pelos Padres da Companhia de Jesus." *APO*, 5, Part II, doc. 523, p. 577. (D. Antão de Noronha attributed this decree to the king D. João III.)
74. Paulo da Trindade, *op. cit.*, p. 371.
75. *Ibid.*, p. 357. *Doc*, VII, 273-74. Only after the age of fourteen could a boy, and a girl after twelve years, be permitted to marry according to the laws of the church, since by then they were considered fit to administer their property. Being able to administer one's property made him/her an independent and adult person.

76. *Bullarium*, First Provincial Council, Acc. 2, dec. 13, p. 9. Francisco de Souza, *op. cit.*, p. 129.
77. *LFC*, fls. 18-19.
78. *Doc*, XII, 282.
79. *BFUP*, No. 1, p. 44.
80. *Ibid.*, p. 38.
81. Francisco de Souza, *op. cit.*, p. 132. According to the Portuguese, by natural law a boy who was able to administer his property, which was supposed to be when he completed the age of fourteen, became an adult.
82. *DI*, VII, 130.
83. Francisco de Souza, *op. cit.*, p. 132.
84. *Bullarium*, Second Provincial Council, Acc. 2, dec. 4. Francisco de Souza, *op. cit.*, p. 130.
85. Goa, 2-3-1575. *BFUP*, No. 1, p. 50. Royal decree about orphan, sons of Hindus to be taken to the College of St Paul. Lisbon, 3-4-1582. *Ibid.*, p. 38.
86. D. Aleixo de Meneses was the archbishop of the archdiocese of Goa (1595-1609) and governor in the *Estado da India* (1607-1609).
87. Paulo da Trindade, *op. cit.*, pp. 371-73.
88. *APO*, 1, Part II, p. 158.
89. 12-10-1646. *LFC*, fl. 61.
90. *Bullarium*, First Provincial Council, Acc. 2, dec. 13, p. 9.
91. *Ibid.*, Fifth Provincial Council, Acc. 2, dec. 7, p. 114. *APO*, 6, doc. 584, pp. 1265-66. *BFUP*, No. 1, p. 61.
92. *MR*, 38B, fl. 202.
93. *BFUP*, No. 1, p. 61.
94. Francisco de Souza, *op. cit.*, pp. 132-33.
95. *LFC*, fl. 63 "Muitos dos orphãos baptizados depois de crescidos tornavão a usar dos ritos de sua gentilidade, devendo ser a conversão dos gentios pellos meyos suaves da ley de Christo e pregação, em que se deviam empregar os missionários da India, e não com as violencias com que se faziam contra vontade de suas mãys e avós, de que rezultava auzentarem-se pera terras estranhas, por se verem avexados, buscando outros domicilios, com que ficava a Igreja sem esperanças que podia ter, de trazer ao gremio della estas almas, se viverem entre os fieis." Josef Wicki, (ed.), *LPC*, p. 312.
96. *APO*, 6, Suppl. I-II, doc. 48, p. 155. *Doc*, VII, 273.
97. *BFUP*, No. 1, p. 62.
98. *Ibid.*, p. 63.

99. *Ibid.*
100. *APO*, 6, Suppl. I-II, p. 46.
101. *BFUP*, No. 1, p. 65.
102. *LFC*, fl. 80v.
103. *BFUP*, No. 1, p. 67.
104. Alessandro Valignano, *op. cit.*, p. 65.
105. Josef Wicki, (ed.), *LPC*, pp. 283, 304. "He para dar graças ao Senhor ver meninos que ainda mamão ou podem mamar, que escasamente sabem falar, dizerem e ensinarem a doutrina." *Doc.*, IV, 229.
106. Sebastião Gonçalves, *Primeira Parte da História dos Religiosos da Companhia de Jesus e do que fizeram com a Divina Graça na Conversão dos Infiéis na nossa Sancta Fé Catholica nos Reynos e Provincias da India Oriental*, Vol. I, p. 130.
107. ARSI, *Goana Historia*, 34 - I, fl. 216v. *DI*, XIV, 298.
108. Joaquim Veríssimo Serão, *História de Portugal*, Vol. III, p. 17.
109. *APO*, 4, p. 92.
110. *Bullarium*, Third Provincial Council, Acc. 2, dec. 13. Francisco de Sousa, *op. cit.*, p. 129.
111. *APO*, 1, Part II, pp. 152, 184.
112. Francisco de Sousa, *op. cit.*, p. 130. *Bullarium*, First Provincial Council, Acc. 2, dec. 13, p. 9. *Doc*, XI, 730-32.
113. *Ibid.*, IV, 483-84.
114. *Doc*, I, 287.
115. Luis de Guzman, *op. cit.*, p. 56.
116. *Doc*, IV, 453; XII, 754-55.
117. *DI*, II, 467.
118. Paulo da Trindade, *op. cit.*, p. 288.
119. *DI*, X, 53.
120. Sebastião Gonçalves, *op. cit.*, p. 130.
121. *DI*, IX, 307.
122. *APO*, 5, Part II, doc. 532, p. 577.
123. *DI*, I, 781.
124. *Ibid.*, 783.
125. *Ibid.*, XVI, 322-23.
126. *Ibid.*, V, 66. *Ibid.*, VII, 62.
127. *Ibid.*, IV, 321.
128. *Ibid.*, 200, 647. *Doc*, X, 19.
129. *DI*, IV, 367.

# 7

# CATECHUMENS AND GROUP BAPTISMS: LOCAL CHRISTIAN BELIEFS

## The Catechumenate

The missionaries often wrote to their superiors in Europe saying that two things were necessary to reform local customs and expand Christendom: more missionary preachers and houses for catechumens (Christians-to-be under instruction). More missionary preachers to instruct the Hindus in the Christian faith without which many souls would be lost.[1] Although letters written by the missionaries conveyed the need for more preachers in the field, as a matter of fact there was more preaching in Goa than what was necessary. Houses for catechumens became very active with the rapid increase of conversions.[2] The adult catechumens needed to be instructed in the faith for some days before receiving baptism, since without this instruction normally the converts relapsed easily.[3] Relapses often occurred soon after their baptism, especially in those converts who lacked a solid Christian formation. Hence, the importance of the catechumenate or a period of faith formation for the prospective Christians, prior to their baptism, and for the neo-converts.

The houses for catechumens or the institution of the catechumenate contributed greatly to the increase of conversions. They prevented relapses by strengthening the faith of the converts too. Besides, the difficulties that the Hindus and Muslims showed in accepting the Christian faith, demanded a testing period under constant care and supervision.[4] The catechumenate was supposed to cut off all the roots of Hindu practices and idolatries while they were being prepared for baptism.[5] This test, or religious and social surgery, could be better performed in the house for catechumens. Moreover, some neophites or new converts who had not received an adequate initiation before their baptism, stayed in these houses for further Christian instruction. The missionaries were of the opinion that if the locals were instructed consistently, they would make very good Christians. Nevertheless, the missionaries, not rarely, failed to instruct these catechumens as they ought to have been. The kings of Portugal, informed of this negligence, often reminded the missionaries of their duties.[6] However, the most serious problem was not that many adults received baptism with very little or no religious preparation at all, but that many catechumens, desirous to receive baptism but unable or unwilling to stand a long testing period, soon turned back to their former practices. At times the catechumens themselves delayed their baptism as a sign of little interest to become Christians.[7] Were these people made catechumens by force?

We find several examples of Hindus being refused baptism for lack of proper Christian instruction. Again, from the accounts written by the missionaries, one can easily gather how they perceived the entire process of changing one's religion or becoming a Christian: 'conversion' could be effected only by God, then followed 'religious instruction' and finally 'baptism'. It was supposed to be invariably conversion-instruction-baptism in keeping with the church theology of 'making Christians'. Once in 1563, while a priest prepared himself to baptize some catechumens at the door of the church, a Hindu jeweller walked up there and on noticing this ceremony he requested the priest to also baptize him then and there. The priest advised the jeweller to wait for the next baptismal ceremony, since he had no religious knowledge yet.[8] Edifying missionary letters are replete of such stories: without Christian instruction no baptism was granted. But missionary praxis did not adhere scrupulously to the teachings of the church. Complaints from India together with the constant royal warnings or reminders cautioning not to effect baptisms without the faith instruction, explain better certain historiographical silence and the missionary praxis of 'making Christians'. The missionaries often alleged that the main cause of several relapses was the converts' ignorance of things of the faith. In 1545, the council of the learned in Portugal fearing the great risk the neo-converts faced of relapsing into their former practices, suggested to the king the urgent need for instructing these Christians and catechumens more carefully.[9]

From 1559 we find the earliest charters granting several privileges, exemptions and subsidies to the houses for catechumens.[10] These houses possessed great wealth as a consequence of alms and donations made by the Portuguese noblemen, especially those who became godfathers[11] to the converts, and the rich local converts.[12] The king allocated annually for the expenses of the catechumens a rent of seven hundred *cruzados*[13] in addition to other rents that once belonged to the temples.[14] The administrators of the houses for catechumens looked for rich persons who could stand as godparents to the noble catechumens, and some of these godparents became generous benefactors of these houses as well. The catechumens were provided with everything they needed so that they could concentrate better on learning the Christian doctrine.[15] But there were moments when these houses passed through great financial difficulties, to the extent of discouraging many catechumens or to even making them turn back.

(a) *The Houses for Catechumens*

There were a few houses for catechumens in Goa. Each religious order had several houses.[16] The first house for catechumens was founded in 1540 in the College of St Paul in the city of Goa.[17] The *Pay dos Christãos* was in charge of this house. The new converts, men and women of all ages, and some persons who were being instructed to receive baptism stayed in this house.[18] Men and boys stayed in one part of the house and learnt the mysteries of the Christian faith until the moment of baptism. Hindu and Christian boys attended catechism lessons together probably in this house too.[19] In another part of the house virtuous Christian women taught women and girls the Christian doctrine. In 1557 there were two houses for catechumens in the city of Goa — one in the College of St Paul for men, and the other outside the college for women. Catechumens from various nations were housed here: *Canarins*, Muslims, Ethiopians, Malabaris, Malaysians, Chinese, etc.[20]

When the hospital for the locals was built near the College of St Paul in 1559, the women wishing to become Christians were kept here with their children to learn catechism. As mentioned before virtuous women instructed these catechumens.[21] If a sick woman asked for baptism she was taken to the house for catechumens.[22] Local noble women also learnt the Christian doctrine at the houses of respectable married Portuguese people in the city of Goa.[23] The Jesuits founded another house for catechumens near their College at Margão in 1582. The Jesuit hospital for the poor in Margão also instructed its patients.[24] The Franciscans also had their houses for catechumens. We find houses for catechumens in many territories under the Portuguese control.[25] However, the churches and chapels were the ordinary places for the catechumens and Christians to assemble.

Some Hindus or prospective converts, stayed in the house for catechumens for a brief instruction of three days, after which they were sent to work at the houses of Portuguese families. This was supposed to be a further testing period to see whether they could persevere.[26] Other candidates stayed in the house for catechumens for about two or three months.[27] The catechumens, besides residing with honest Portuguese families, were also entrusted to the care of local Christians.[28] Probably, it was difficult to find honest custodians among the Portuguese in India, going by several missionary reports describing their social and religious behaviour.[29] The noble catechumens were kept in the care of rich Portuguese persons, who eventually became their godparents and bestowed on them several favours.[30] It was customary to offer dresses to the catechumens, according to the status of each candidate, on the day of their baptism.[31] Often the godfathers sponsored these dresses for their godchildren. D. Constantino de Bragança had his own godchildren, whom he dressed and sheltered with great care to the extent of embarassing the Hindus. The Portuguese *fidalgos* had also their godchildren.[32] After baptism the neo-converts returned to their homes with the instruction to bring others to baptism.[33]

It may appear rather strange to hear that many neo-converts went back to live with their own parents and relatives who continued to be Hindus. Would they not be disowned by the latter? Considering it to be true that some or almost all the neo-converts, on leaving the houses for catechumens, went back home, then we have to examine some interesting problems here. Could the neo-converts continue their Christian practices in such 'hostile' environment? What about the neo-converts polluting the Hindus? Could it be that the entire household or villages converted at the same time?[34] Not always, since there was a decree demanding from the Hindus financial support for their Christian relatives. Perhaps some did not go back to their homes. Where else could they stay? Normally, the boys after baptism were given back to their parents;[35] similarly the women returned to their homes.[36] The factor that decided the future residence of a new convert was his/her status and faith. Those sent back home were persons of high standing, and who had given sufficient proofs that they would not abandon their new faith.[37] These neo-converts received help like some jobs or other benefits.[38] Some convert women after acquiring some religious knowledge stayed with Portuguese families, and in turn they continuously exhorted other women from this household to pray.[39]

It was not unlikely that the new converts found themselves in an uncomfortable and difficult situation vis-à-vis their Hindu family and relatives. Under these circumstances the houses for catechumens served them as a safe haven. They could indeed become houses of refuge or rescue for the converts.[40] At times boys running away from their parents, wives from their husbands, slaves from their owners, and men sought shelter in these houses. They eventually became Christians.[41] It was necessary to shelter the new converts since their own families would not accept them again. If nobody paid any attention to their sad plight, the weak converts would succumb to social pressures and return more easily to their former customs.[42] The houses for catechumens had their immunity, and those preparing for baptism here could find solutions for their innumerable problems.[43] The prisons in Goa were full of insolvent Hindus and local Christians, and surprisingly they preferred to remain in prison rather than at liberty, at the mercy of their creditors.[44] Conversion, or simply the desire to receive baptism meant access to the house for catechumens or the possibility of getting immunity, and therefore, served as a convenient alternative to life in prison. Perhaps a few who wanted to escape paying taxes chose conversion. Hence, the houses for catechumens, besides being a place where the Hindus, Muslims and new converts received the Christian instruction, also served to shelter and protect those whose motives for staying there were not always above suspicion.

(b) *Examination of Motives*

Abundant historical evidence gives us the impression that the missionaries spared no pains to instruct and prepare the catechumens for baptism. Before 'making them Christians' they wanted 'to make them catechumens'.[45] Before admitting any person to the house for catechumens the missionaries examined his/her true intentions and watched carefully his/her social dealings. The priests doubted the candidate's sincerity and motives to become a Christian.[46] The test for admission in the case of the Jews and Muslims were still more rigorous.[47] In 1559, Fr. Pero d'Almeida told a person who desired to become a Christian, "You, being a Moor, will not stay with the Gentiles in the house for catechumens, nor will you step into the church; get yourself ready to undergo two years of trial before baptism".[48] Some Muslims, obstinate men as they were in their customs, were made to stay longer in the house for catechumens.[49] Since, the Muslims, Jews, and *jogues* (yogis) relapsed more easily, their scrutiny and preparation could often last for three or four months.[50] Stricter methods were used with these people, who were more unreliable and faithless, in order to remove every trace of their blindness.[51] But the Muslims rarely converted as they were obstinate and hardened in their beliefs.[52]

In 1550, the need was increasingly felt to multiply the houses for catechumens, since many converts returned to their former idolatrous practices without any fear.[53] However, some missionaries argued that many more Hindus would convert if they were immediately baptized without wasting time with their catechumenate: the catechumenate turned out to be the main reason for many Hindus to refuse baptism.[54] Despite this argument, in 1559 it was necessary to close the College of St Paul for some time in order to free its teachers and students to instruct the catechumens, since there were so many awaiting baptism.[55] Although the catechumenate period scrutinized the intentions of the catechumens and laid great stress on faith instruction, the need to increase the number of Christians and to preserve them was equally felt.

Teaching the Christian doctrine to the Hindus and neo-converts was not the sole purpose of the houses for catechumens. They also aimed at correcting or 'curing' the erring Christians. The fallen converts were brought to these houses to be rehabilitated, and they were retained here till they showed signs of having abandoned their errors completely.[56] Meanwhile, many abandoned the catechumenate and the Christian faith either due to personal reasons or to external social pressures. To counteract any natural tendency and social pressures that encouraged relapses, a vast number of decrees in favour of the new converts and punitive measures for their breach had been created as has already been seen. Those, for instance, who had freely asked for baptism and then left the faith, mocking thus the Christian religion, could be punished with two years in the galleys.[57]

While undergoing the testing period the catechumens could not entertain any conversation with the Hindus, or with any other persons who could mislead or dissuade them from becoming Christians.[58] It was necessary to prevent the new converts from having familiar dealings with their Hindu relatives too. It would be difficult for a neo-convert to remain a good Christian and live among the Hindus simultaneously. Hence, it was suggested that the Hindus from the city of Goa should live apart in the islands of Divar or Chorão.[59] Moreover, the boys preparing for baptism had to be kept away from any danger of being deceived by the Hindus, or being taken away by their relatives.[60] Not infrequently, their relatives came to the houses for catechumens and took the boys away to the firm land.[61]

(c) *Unwilling Catechumens?*

The First Provincial Council (1567) decreed that all the Hindu orphan boys and girls, irrespective of their mothers', grandparents' or other relatives' consent, should be baptized.[62] The Hindus began taking their orphans to the territory of the Muslims knowing it to be illegal. According to the missionaries this defiance was very harmful to the propagation of the faith.[63] In order to foil their plans, the *Pays dos Christãos* went in search of these boys and girls and forced them to stay in the houses for catechumens. But to countermine the move of the *Pays dos Christãos,* the relatives of a girl, when sensing that she could become a victim of the decree on orphans, declared that she was already married according to their rituals; hence she was no more an orphan. But this argument did not prevent the *Pays dos Christãos* from taking the orphan girls to the house for catechumens.[64] Hindu girls were married even before completing the age of twelve years, the minimum age for a girl to contract a legal marriage according to the Portuguese civil law.

Once some Brahmans suspected that a Hindu teenage girl had been taken to the house for catechumens to be baptized by force; but on scrutiny it was found that she had accepted Christianity on her own.[65] Some religious Brothers from the College of St Paul were constantly on the lookout for people to fill the houses for catechumens.[66] Some Hindu boys after being captured by the Portuguese soldiers near the island of Divar were sent to the house for catechumens, resulting not only in their baptism but also in those of their parents and relatives.[67] But not all came to the house for catechumens in the same manner. The missionaries took great pains to show that the Hindus were there of their own accord. Stories about free conversions were attempts to disprove the existence of forced conversions, since there was a great deal of accusations against the missionaries of using forcible methods.[68] Despite the catechumens' willingness to become Christians as frequently reported by the missionaries, these catechumens had to be kept

away from dangerous contacts with the Hindus, who were all out to convince or pressurize them to change their minds.[69] When the priests went to the villages to gather catechumens, a soldier and a guard had to accompany them to avoid any scandal, unrest and violence.[70] The incident about the villagers beating up the religious Brothers when they planned to take a Hindu orphan away, is a clear instance of mixed methods of conversion.[71] There were catechumens in almost all the villages in Goa. The religious Brothers from the College of St Paul, who went through the villages in search of catechumens, became known as 'the hunters'.[72]

### (d) *Method of Christian Instruction*

The *Pay dos Christãos,* the person responsible for the catechumens, had a helper or attorney who preferably was a married man so that his wife could look after the female catechumens too.[73] The attorney had the duty to find jobs for the catechumens and solve their lawsuits and petitions and was like a father to them.[74]

The house for catechumens of the Jesuits in the city of Goa was the most important and with the greatest number of people awaiting baptism. A religious Brother or a catechist looked after the needs of the catechumens and instructed them in the Christian doctrine, first together and then each one separately.[75] When a Brother was not availale, a boy who knew the doctrine well taught them.[76] The catechumens spent most of their time memorizing the Christian doctrine. They were instructed according to their capabilities and qualities.[77] A priest instructed them in the mysteries of the faith and the power of the cross as a help to them against the devil.[78] But the boys also learnt good habits, besides unlearning the bad ones, through examples, advices and threats of punishment.[79] They studied cases of conscience to dispel ignorance.[80] The priests argued that those who did not learn these things would soon be lost to the bad customs of the place.[81]

When the Hindus first entered a house for catechumens, the priest-in-charge of it persuaded them to abandon every superstition and to detach themselves from their old customs. To achieve this, he exhorted them against the deceits of the devil and that no salvation could ever be possible through him. This kind of instruction was carried on throughout their testing period, and after learning these things they themselves confessed that they had erred for too long, showing thus their willingness to accept the new law till death. After a while, they gradually learnt other Christian precepts according to a certain catechism booklet composed for this purpose.[82] First, the catechumens learnt to make the sign of the cross, which the Christians use against the devil. The neo-converts feared a good deal that some evil would befall them for disowning their ancestral religion, hence they made the sign of the cross with great devotion, believing that it had a special power against the devil.[83] Then they learnt the main prayers and beliefs: the Our Father, the Hail-Mary and the Creed; the Ten Commandments, the Works of Mercy, the Capital Sins, the Seven Sacraments, the Theological and Cardinal Virtues. The psalms and hymns were also taught in Latin and Konkani.[84] Moreover, the catechumens learnt about confession, exhortation, admonitions, litanies, salves, sung mass, and their Sunday and feast day duties and obligations. They could participate in the mass until the moment of the offertory, when they had to leave the church.[85] They were warned to avoid swearing since it offended God and harmed their souls.[86] Many neo-converts who before knew only how to offend God, now confessed their sins in great detail.[87]

The Christian doctrine was taught to all twice a day, in the morning and evening, and a priest instructed them once a day. It was also taught individually according to the needs of each catechumen.[88] Before baptism they were further tested by making them serve in the houses of Portuguese to ascertain if they would persevere, since the converts did not spontaneously accept the Christian faith.[89] Nevertheless, they had to be favoured precisely for their natural weakness in things Christian, and for the ill-treatment they constantly suffered at the hand of the Portuguese.[90] Besides, there were several discussions on the Christian doctrine in the houses for catechumens for their inmates. The boys also discussed the Christian doctrine among themselves and had conferences in Konkani on the same.[91] The catechumens were kept unoccupied and every need was provided for to enable them to learn the doctrine well.[92]

Could it be that caste sensibilities and cultural prejudices were ignored in the houses for catechumens? Sharing the same roof and the same food and the same utensils would certainly affect their future social relations. It is probable that the houses for catechumens weakened caste rigidity and diluted caste and religious ritualisms as well. If after baptism the neo-converts lived with their family, or whether on becoming a Christian one earned for himself/herself the status of a social outcaste, the fact that abundant legislation was necessary to protect the Christians against social and economic discrimination remains incontestable.

### (e) *The Problem of Dresses for Baptism*

It is clear by now that no baptism was supposed to be administered without giving the catechumens a good Christian instruction. Later, when new dresses for baptism were not presented to the catechumens, they began saying that they were least interested in baptism.[93]

Godparents gave their godchildren, the catechumens, dresses for baptism but due to the expenses incurred by the godparents, the government began offering them these dresses. The status and the caste of the catechumens determined the quality of the dress.[94] There was a lot of competition in dressing the catechumens for their baptism. Sometimes the religious Brothers who were responsible for dressing the catechumens on the day of their baptism, offered them rich silk clothes. This certainly would displease their benefactors, for what was spent on one catechumen in this fashion could suffice to dress up modestly seven or eight of them for the baptismal ceremony.[95] It became a custom to dress the catechumens for their baptism in Portuguese fashion.[96] The missionaries performed group baptisms with all solemnity until they were prevented by delays in presenting these baptismal dresses and poor state of the economy.[97]

When the state took upon itself the duty of dressing the catechumens it did not find this task very easy, since neither the local officials were interested in helping with conversions nor had the government coffers sufficient money. The crown had set aside a certain amount of money for the religious orders to spend on baptismal dresses, but it was not always handed over to them as stipulated, for the Treasury did not have funds. Due to long delays in offering the catechumens these dresses many returned to their old customs. Waiting for baptismal dresses had already become a well-established custom, and the catechumens refused baptism without new dresses.[98] The missionaries themselves had instructed the catechumens to get rid of every Hindu trace, hence they refused baptism in their old Hindu dressing. In Salcete in 1569 there were two thousand catechumens, already instructed, awaiting their baptismal dresses and baptism for two years, since no one came forward to give them the much-demanded dresses.[99] Again, in the same place in 1573 two thousand catechumens were waiting for baptism for the same reason, because they were accustomed to see the other catechumens shedding their Hindu dressing.[100] In Chorão in the same year about six hundred catechumens waited for these dresses.[101] In 1580 other catechumens refused to be baptized without receiving new clothes.[102] In Salcete in 1595 there were a thousand catechumens, but many of them could not be baptized for lack of special dresses.[103] When earlier the viceroy, D. Constantino de Bragança (1558-1560), had donated some money to the houses for catechumens for dresses, some Portuguese accused him of making conversions by force, and others complained that he spent the rents of the king on negroes.[104] There were thousands of conversions during his tenure as viceroy in Goa.

When it became difficult to dress the catechumens in Portuguese style, it was suggested that they could wear any other dress of the land for the baptismal ceremony.[105] To prevent further delays and relapses, the missionaries decided to favour individual baptisms without waiting for solemn group baptisms.[106] The catechumenate period had become an obstacle to many Hindus willing to be converted.[107]

The catechumens were neither Hindus nor Christians. But granted that the catechumens lost their traditional status, it is important to keep in mind that some of them turned back when the new religion did not appeal to them immediately. The houses for catechumens could give us the impression that all those who resided here did so at their own request. Separation of catechumens from their caste and kin was necessary at the beginning, but impossible and unavoidable later.

The catechumens showed themselves more inclined towards the Hindu practices, not only during their testing period but even after imparting to them the Christian faith. After all, the catechumens were more Hindu than Christian.[108] A report in 1567 informs us that the adult catechumens continued to behave like Hindus: they kept long hair (hair tuft) and needed to be constantly reminded to wear shirt, coat, shoes, hats, doublet, little coat, underpants to look like Christian persons with the Holy Spirit indwelling in them.[109]

The catechumenate as a time of faith preparation for baptism may be as old as Christianity itself. However, it is difficult to fix precisely the year when the catechumenate as a well-organized institution first appeared in Goa. Probably it was founded in 1540. However, some would like to think that it was founded soon after the conquest of Goa in 1510. The last and the only house for catechumens that survived closed down in 1842 when there was almost no candidate in Goa.

## Solemn Group Baptisms

Till 1557 the catechumens were baptized in simple private religious ceremonies, either in the main centres of Christianity or where the catechumens resided. Later, the missionaries started baptizing many catechumens together so that such occasions might serve as an example to the Hindus. This was the beginning of group baptisms or *batismo geral,* which was conducted with all the solemnity of the occasion. The Hindus were astonished with what they saw at these baptismal ceremonies, since many favours were bestowed upon the neo-converts.[110] These religious solemnities did not only encourage other Hindus to come forward to receive baptism, but they also edified the local Christian community.[111]

The pompous Hindu religious festivals and their magnificent temples astonished the missionaries.[112] As a counter-attraction to these Hindu festivities, group baptisms began to be celebrated in well-decorated churches, with feasts, games, music, dancing, frolic and pealing of bells. Besides, the Portuguese tried very hard to impress upon the locals the superiority of their own religion.[113] The missionaries wrote to Europe informing that many Hindus embraced Christianity merely on seeing the solemnity of the Christian celebrations.[114] These solemn festivals created great devotion among the people too.[115] It is not surprising to know that there might have been minor solemn baptisms almost every month, but it has been calculated that there was at least one major solemn group baptisms every year in Goa, so that by the turn of the sixteenth century three fourths of Bardez and more than half of Salcete had been converted.[116] In 1608, Bardez had around forty seven thousand Christians.[117] Salcete reached the figure of forty thousand Christians in 1607-08.[118]

Generally, ten to twenty catechumens received baptism every Sunday and on holy days.[119] In 1557 the Jesuits started the practice of group baptisms, and soon in 1559 the Franciscans and the Dominicans followed suit.[120] The first group baptisms by the Jesuit initiative, although with a few converts, was celebrated with much pomp. The governor himself had proposed a group baptism for one hundred and ten catechumens, for greater fervour and devotion among the Christians and to serve as an embarassment to the Brahmans.[121] A letter written in 1557 tells us that 1081 catechumens had been baptized, an achievement indeed, compared with the previous years when only thirty or forty had been converted.[122] Likewise, it was reported that the Franciscan friars performed their group baptisms with great display, but without true devotion and genuine conversions.[123]

Not everything went well with these baptisms. D. Gaspar, the archbishop of Goa, forbade group baptisms in Goa in 1561, prompted by some complaints he had received. He heard that conversions had been effected by unchristian methods. But the same archbishop re-introduced them in 1563.[124] Then, in the same year seven hundred catechumens dressed like Christians were baptized in the College of St Paul.[125] In 1588 the Jesuits were forbidden to organize group and solemn baptisms, despite their argument that the solemnity of such occasions helped to challenge the Hindu beliefs and to animate the new converts. If these baptisms were celebrated quietly not many would be converted.[126]

In 1592 a curious and astonished friar asked another how the Franciscans could possibly make so many conversions in Bardez. The reply was that no force was used to convert anyone; rather, all those conversions were just a result of preaching and taking the Hindu orphans away from their relatives to be baptized.[127] The baptism of one person led to that of some others; subsequently, the baptism of some led to the baptism of many others in a village. Entire families received baptism with their servants. It was calculated that about two thousand Hindus had received baptism in the College of Reis Magos in Bardez, in 1597. At the same place there were eight group baptisms between 1600 and 1603, during which seven thousand were converted. In 1594 Claudio Aquaviva, the superior-general of the Society of Jesus, appealed to the moderation of the Jesuits during their religious festivals and solemn group baptisms conducted in the College of St Paul.[128]

In 1605 the king discouraged group baptisms on hearing certain complaints that they were not conducted according to the norms established by the Provincial Councils. The king was informed that these baptisms were effected without sufficiently instructing the catechumens.[129] The missionaries, especially the Franciscans, had failed to adequately instruct their catechumens. When group baptisms re-started, the Franciscans, decided to celebrate these occasions with more publicity and in the presence of the viceroy, the archbishop, all the magistrates and noblemen. These dignitaries besides being a people who could bear witness to the work and devotion of the Franciscans, which had been slighted earlier, could also contribute generously to these celebrations and dresses for baptism for the catechumens.[130] With impressive statistics on conversions these friars hoped to convince the king about their seriousness and fervour in their missionary duties. Evidently, without the good offices of the king and viceroys their financial situation could have worsened.

Viceroys, noblemen, political and clerical authorities, other important persons and a great number of people of the city attended these solemn group baptism.[131] Some group baptisms were postponed because the viceroys wanted to be present at these ceremonies.[132] Godfathers, persons who acted like sponsors at the baptism and benefactors thereafter, played an important role in conversions. The governors and Portuguese dignitaries used to become godfathers to the noble converts, mainly to the Brahmans who were like the Portuguese *fidalgos*, persons of social standing and rich, and to *gaunkars* who were like the chief magistrates or *regedores*.[133] Many *honrrados* or noble persons received baptism.[134] The viceroy, the archbishop and many noblemen took upon themselves the task of dressing the new converts for baptism. They contributed according to their own financial means and personal devotion.[135] But a few converts prepared for baptism at their own expense. Some silk merchants, the richest in the city of Goa, were converted in 1573. They dressed in silk with red boots and golden swords, so much so that they looked like Portuguese soldiers.[136]

The godparents had cordial relations with their converted godchildren. The former offered gifts and protection to their godchildren and the later gave their loyalty to their benefactors.[137] A Brahman, for the honour he had received from the viceroy, began opposing the other Hindu Brahmans soon after his conversion, to the extent of asking the archbishop to expel them from Goa for some wrongs they had done.[138] The godparents also protected the converts from the Hindus. Those who were of marriageable age were given in marriage. Jobs were given to the boys and their services were paid for. Some of them worked with mastercraftsmen at the latter's workshops. Many persons took their godchildren to their homes and gave them necessary means to settle in life.[139] In 1540 Fr. Diogo Borba requested any devout person wanting to help as godfather in the work of conversion, to register his name in a book so that on seeing this the Hindus might also convert.[140] Noble catechumens were named often after their own godparents.

The missionaries held that baptism removed all irregularities, including homicide, except bigamy.[141] But facts show that if a prisoner converted he would not be set free.[142] Those condemned to death did not escape the gallows after receiving baptism.[143] Despite receiving baptism a man who had been accused of treason was condemned to death.[144] The Hindus who were condemned to death by the state were persuaded to become Christians before dying, and the priests would not leave them before baptizing them. However, they preferred to die in the law of their ancestors, which had guided all their life.[145] Others after being arrested by the Inquisition asked for baptism.[146] Some Hindus asked for baptism for fear of punishment, but if the judges and the captains did not grant them pardon they refused to become Christians. If the arrested Hindus were not baptized while in prison, they were not likely to accept baptism when at liberty. Some of these arrested persons had been converted forcibly by giving them ritually polluted food.[147] If both, husband and wife converted, immediately after their baptism they would be married according to the Christian rituals at the entrance of the church.[148]

Group baptisms, celebrated with great solemnity, began in 1557 and increased rapidly. We can imagine in 1581 solemn baptisms with four hundred catechumens all dressed in Portuguese fashion.[149] As has been said earlier, group baptisms, encouraged the Christians and restrained the Hindus; besides, they edified not only those in India but also in Europe.[150] The missionaries were unanimous that the various solemn religious ceremonies performed in Goa contributed to the growth of the faith, since they moved greatly some Hindus to conversion and embarassed others. These festive occasions gladened the new converts and helped them to feel more committed to the Christian religion; besides, they helped to distract the local Christians from the Hindu festivals, which they had forsaken not too long before.[151] Where the Hindus were more obstinate and adamant to conversions there more fanfare was displayed.

Gradually, due to the difficulties to gather catechumens together to instruct them, it was decided to baptize them in simple ceremonies.[152] Local reactions and social unrest forced the missionaries to discontinue group baptisms, so much so that a soldier had to accompany the religious Brothers when they went to the villages to gather catechumens.[153] But from time to time these solemn group baptisms were celebrated in Goa.

## Religious Beliefs and Devotions of Converts

We are informed that the converts were weak in Christian practices, but their faith and devotional life was highly commended.[154] The local Christians believed that the sacrament of confession could cure them of their physical illnesses. They also trusted in the healing power of the holy water. Some converts from the island of Divar, bitten by poisonous snakes, became well after drinking holy water.[155] For the neo-converts, baptism was a solution for some physical illnesses. Hence, one need not be surprised when some of them received it several times (according to the Christian teaching one can receive it only once in one's life time).[156] They had great devotion to St Anthony and addressed their needs to him. Even some Hindus came to Goa to ask for help for their ills through the saint's intercession.[157] Whenever a saint's solemnity was celebrated the converts took part in it, and they asked the priests to celebrate masses in honour of the saint's.[158] These Christians showed great respect and attachment to holy images which they wanted to have at home, and before which they prayed. A poor convert had in his house a beautifully-decorated portrait of a king which he mistook for a saint's, and he thought himself a devout man with this 'holy picture'. Another man had five playing cards, which he had also mistaken for holy pictures, arranged in the shape of a cross on the wall of his house and it served him as an oratory.[159] Holy pictures and crucifixes were given to the Christians for their devotion.[160] They also had devotion to the rosary and to Our Lady.[161]

Normally the neo-converts showed more devotion, zeal and frequency to the sacraments and other signs of true Christian life than many Portuguese residing here.[162] Whenever there was a feast in memory of a saint, the local Christians could be seen in great numbers in the churches participating in the mass with great devotion. They fasted and gave alms, whereas the Portuguese scandalized them by eating meat and not observing any abstinence during the lenten season.[163] The exemplary life of the converts, something to marvel at, caused much confusion to some Portuguese.[164]

The mass was celebrated almost daily in all the parishes,

and the priests were obliged to make the Christians attend it on Sundays and holy days.[165] During the Sunday mass in all the churches the Christians received some instruction,[166] and after the mass matters pertaining to the faith were taught to the local men and women, and to the Portuguese too, through interpreters.[167] They learnt the Christian prayers: the Our Father, the Creed, the Salve Regina, the Ten Commandments and other prayers. The converts confessed during the lenten season and whenever they needed it.[168] But the local Christians could not receive the sacrament of communion even during the Easter season. The parish priest gave this sacrament only to the nobles and important persons, excluding the others from it.[169] The reason for this exclusion was not of a racial or social nature, but because of serious abuses in its reception. The neo-converts were unfamiliar with its demands and lacked sufficient preparation to receive the eucharist.[170] We should recall that the reception of this sacrament before 1550 was so rare in the Catholic church, that whoever approached it outside the lenten season was taken for a hypocrite.[171] Perhaps the neo-converts frequented the sacrament of confession oftener than the sacrament of communion.[172]

The chief Christian families sent their children to the church everyday to learn the gospels. As they had much faith in the holy water they sent for it from the churches and used it constantly in their needs, and in return they offered oil for the churches' lamps.[173] The boys sang the Christian doctrine while grazing their cattle, and working in the fields. These boys, who not long before their conversion had "sticks and stones for their gods", now began worshipping the true God.[174] Likewise, the local converts disowned their former idols, which they had abandoned not long before.[175] The Jesuits made use of holy images in the churches and chapels and resorted to the narration of miracles. The veneration of the image of the Child Jesus in the church of the College of Rachol is an example of a popular devotion in Goa. The local Christians performed their penances to extremes, at times resorting to discipline[176] and scourging, which they believed to be acts of true devotion, causing much astonishment to the Muslim and Hindu community.[177] When in 1572 the Adilshah came to attack Goa, the

Christians began offering many prayers and sacrifices and frequenting the sacraments; processions were led through the villages and city; fasting, prayers and the use of discipline in the monasteries and religious houses had increased.[178]

Credulous people, easily susceptible to emotion and fantasy, the Goan Christians of the sixteenth century with a simple and sincere faith, let the missionaries exploit their sentiments. The fiery sermons, the virtues of saints, the different forms of popular piety which included prayer, sacramental life, the cultivation of virtues, the idea of holiness, indulgences and privileges granted by the popes, appealed greatly to their Christian imagination and beliefs.[179] In chapter nine, 'Syncretism in the Life of the Christians', we shall examine other local religious beliefs condemned by the church for being unchristian, and against the purity and unity of the faith.

The institution of catechumenate, therefore, had become one of the pillars of the conversion activity. Group baptisms or mass conversions became possible to a very large extent due to the houses for catechumens, where their inmates acquired new religious beliefs and a Christian identity.

## NOTES AND REFERENCES

1. *DI*, III, 114.
2. *Ibid.*, X, 279.
3. *Doc,* IV, 558.
4. *Ibid.*, VII, 97.
5. *DI,* VII, 325.
6. Paulo da Trindade, *op. cit.*, Part I, p. 327.
7. *DI,* XVI, 324.
8. *Ibid,* VI, 125; VIII, 67.
9. *Doc,* III, 199.
10. Viriato A. C. Albuquerque, "Casa de Catechumenos em Goa", p. 362.
11. Godfather/godmother is a person who pledges, when a person is baptized, to take an active interest in his/her welfare. Godchild is a

person for whom a godfather acts as sponsor at baptism. The godchild is a protégé/gée of the godfather.

12. *Ibid.,* p. 364.
13. *DI.* X, 54.
14. *Ibid.,* IX, 276. *Doc,* XII, 756.
15. Josef Wicki, (ed.), *LPC,* pp. 24, 50.
16. *DI,* III, 210-11.
17. *Ibid.,* I, 759.
18. *Ibid.,* IV, 209.
19. *Ibid.,* V, 258.
20. *Ibid.,* VI, 121.
21. *Doc,* VI, 48; IX, 467. *DI,* III, 371, 720-21.
22. *Doc,* IX, 116.
23. *DI,* III, 720f. Young female catechumens were entrusted to respectable Christians to teach them the Christian doctrine. *Ibid.,* VIII, 69.
24. *Doc,* XII, 789. *DI,* X, 54.
25. There were houses for catechumens in Cochin (*DI,* XVIII, 901), Tuticurim (*Ibid.,* 914), Bengal (*Ibid.,* 672), Bassein (*Ibid.,* 895), Daman (*Ibid.,* 898), Thana (*Ibid.,* III, 591, 692), Mozambique (*Ibid.,* V, 397), Malacca (*Ibid.,* 672).
26. *Doc,* VII, 97.
27. *DI,* III, 350, 720-21.
28. *Ibid.,* IV, 322.
29. Georg Schurhammer and Josef Wicki, (eds.), *Epistolae S. Francisci Xaverii,* Vol. I, pp. 281-82.
30. Josef Wicki, (ed.), *op. cit.,* p. 16.
31. *DI,* IV, 322.
32. *Ibid.,* 212.
33. *Ibid.,* 323-24. Francisco Pyrard de Laval, *Viagem de Francisco Pyrard de Laval,* p. 47.
34. An entire village in Mormugão, in Salcete, with about 577 inhabitants, was baptized in 1573. *DI,* IX, 303.
35. *Ibid.,* VIII, 45.

36. *Ibid.*, III, 772.
37. *Ibid.*, 576.
38. *Ibid.*, VIII, 45.
39. *Doc*, IX, 249. *DI*, VI, 122; XI, 274-75.
40. *Ibid.*, IX, 280. In Malacca, captives who wanted to gain freedom ran away from their non-Christian masters and sought shelter in houses for catechumens. *Ibid.*, V, 672.
41. *Ibid.*, III, 720-21. *Doc*, IX, 446.
42. *DI*, IV, 213-14.
43. *Bullarium*, Fifth Provincial Council, Acc. 2, dec. 31, p. 119.
44. *APO*, 1, Part I, pp. 12-13.
45. *DI*, IV, 209; X, 734.
46. *Ibid.*, 287.
47. *Doc*, IX, 249. *DI*, VI, 122.
48. *Ibid.*, IV, 429.
49. *Ibid.*, VIII, 583.
50. *Ibid.*, XVII, 86; III, 210-11.
51. *Ibid.*, VIII, 45-46.
52. *Ibid.*, IV, 429.
53. *Ibid.*, II, 126.
54. *Ibid.*, IX, 307.
55. *Memória Historico Eclesiastica da Archidiocese de Goa*, p. 54.
56. *DI*, VIII, 45-46.
57. AHU, *Registo de cartas*, Cod. 281, fl. 203. *Bullarium*, Fifth Provincial Council, Acc. 2, dec. 30, p. 119.
58. *DI*, XVII, 86.
59. *Doc*, IV, 558.
60. ARSI, *Extracto das cousas*, la, fl. 25.
61. ARSI, *Goana Historia*, 33 - I, fl. 75v.
62. *Bullarium*, First Provincial Council, Acc. 2, dec. 13, p. 9.
63. Josef Wicki, (ed.), *LPC*, pp. 308-16.
64. *Ibid.*, p. 238.
65. *DI*, VIII, 76.

66. *Ibid.*, VIII, 61.
67. Francisco de Sousa, *OCJC*, p. 158.
68. *DI,* XI, 274-75, 322.
69. Josef Wicki, (ed.), *op. cit.,* p. 19.
70. DI, XVIII, 652. The *meirinhos* treated the locals harshly and fined them too. (*Meirinho* was an officer whose duty was to arrest malefactors). *Ibid.*, I, 73.
71. *Ibid.*, XVIII, 658.
72. *Ibid.*, XII, 138.
73. Josef Wicki, (ed.), *op. cit.*, p. 15.
74. *Doc*, XII, 738.
75. *DI,* IV, 166.
76. *Ibid.,* II, 352.
77. Alessandro Valignano, *op. cit.*, p. 348.
78. *Doc*, IX, 248.
79. *DI,* III, 351.
80. *Ibid.*
81. *Ibid.,* 576. "A casa de catechumenos em Margão onde os meninos aprendem doutrina e bons costumes, a ler e escrever e posto que se tenha bom cuidado deles todavia nollos furtam seus parentes e os levam para terra firme pera que deixem a fé." ARSI *Goana Historia*, 33 - I, fl. 75v.
82. Probably the catechism booklet used to instruct the catechumens was the one prepared by Francis Xavier. Tomás Estevão, *Doutrina Cristã em Lingua Concani*, pp. 3-4.
83. For more details see on Christian instruction to catechumens. *DI*, IV, 166-77; III, 722.
84. *Ibid.*, XVI, 394.
85. *Bullarium*, Fifth Provincial Council, Acc. 2, dec. 29, p. 119.
86. *DI,* II, 410.
87. *Ibid.,* 114.
88. Josef Wicki, (ed.), *op. cit.*, p. 20.
89. *Doc,* X, 97.
90. *DI,* III, 576.

91. *Doc*, X, 90, 302.
92. *DI,* III, 350; XII, 414, 609.
93. *Ibid.*, VI, 612.
94. *Ibid.,* XVII, 86.
95. *Ibid.,* XII, 138.
96. *Ibid.,* X, 736.
97. *Ibid.*, XVII, 306.
98. *Ibid.*, IX, 278.
99. *Doc*, XII, 357. *DI*, VI, 612; IX, 278.
100. *Ibid.*, 277, 306.
101. *Ibid.*, 306.
102. *Doc*, XI, 593ff.
103. *DI*, XVII, 295, 306.
104. *Ibid.*, V, 486.
105. *Doc*, XI, 600.
106. *APO*, 3, p. 718.
107. *DI*, IX, 307.
108. *Ibid.*, XVIII, 653.
109. *Doc*, X, 249.
110. *DI*, IV, 284.
111. ARSI, *Miscellanea Indiarum Orientalium*, 38 - I, fl. 140.
112. Paulo da Trindade, *op. cit.,* p. 84.
113. *DI*, IX, 303. ARSI, *Goana Historia*, 33 - I, fl. 184v.
114. ARSI, *Eppistolae Goana et Malabarica*, 14, fls. 71-72v.
115. *Ibid.,* 10 - II, fl. 313v.
116. Paulo da Trindade, *op. cit.,* pp. 297, 326, 334. *DI*, IV, 222.
117. Archille Meersman, *The Ancient Franciscan Provinces in India, 1500-1835*, p. 157.
118. Fernão Guerreiro, *Relação Anual das cousas*, (1611), p. 1.
119. *Doc*, X, 305.
120. *DI*, III, 721.
121. *Doc*, VI, 348.
122. Alessandro Valignano, *op. cit.,* p. 349.

123. J. H. da Cunha Rivara, *Gramatica da Lingua Concani*, p. lxxiv.

124. Fr. Nunes Barreto wrote that the archbishop of Goa, relying on misinformation and complaints sent by some Portuguese who had stated that conversions were being effected by force, began disfavouring the way conversions were made till then. He stopped group baptisms. This move created adverse conditions for the work of conversion. However, Fr. N. Barreto added that less force was being used to make converts than what the theologians and canonists had established as permissible. Letter from Nunes Barreto to the superior-general of the Society of Jesus, Diego Lainez. Cochin, 1562. *DI*, V, 485.

125. *Ibid.*, VI, 122. *Doc*, X, 105.

126. *Ibid.*, XVI, 39.

127. Paulo da Trindade, *op. cit.*, p. 326.

128. ARSI, *Extracto das cousas*, la, fl. 16. "Y se ha de aver processión, es neccessario que se haga con algunas danças y fuegos y músicas, porque, como nosotros no cantamos como otros clérigos y frades, si esto le falta será tan insípida nuestra processión que nadie verná a ella; mayormente que los desta tierra se mueven mucho por lo exterior assí como los portugueses como los nascidos acá y mucho más los christianos naturales de la tierra, que tienen necessidade de los fomentar con cosas exteriores assí de gozo como de tristeza, porque los gentiles hazen sus fiestas gentílicas con mucha más solenidad." *DI*, XV, 208, 218.

129. Paulo da Trindade, *op. cit.*, p. 327.

130. *Ibid.*

131. ARSI, *Eppistolae Goana et Malabarica*, 14, fl. 73v. *Doc*, VI, 198-99; VII, 332-34, 298-323, 245-47; X, 305. Luis de Guzman, *op. cit.*, p. 59.

132. *DI*, VIII 587.

133. *Ibid.*, X, 469. Sebastião Gonçalves, *op. cit.*, p. 121.

134. *DI*, IV, 428.

135. Luis de Guzman, *op. cit.*, p. 59. The viceroy, Constantino de Bragança, had his own godchildren whom he dressed and sheltered with great care, to the extent of causing much embarassment to the Hindus. The noblemen also had godchildren. *DI*, IV, 212. The viceroy, D. António de Noronha (1571-1573), became godfather to

many converts. *Ibid.*, IX, 303.

136. *Ibid.*, 303.
137. Luis de Guzman, *op. cit.*, p. 56.
138. *DI,* V, 608.
139. *Ibid.,* IV, 213.
140. Sebastião Gonçalves, *op. cit.*, p. 121. *DI*, I, 778.
141. *Ibid.*, XIV, 894.
142. *Ibid.,* XV, 530.
143. *Ibid.*, XVIII, 876. ARSI, *Goana Historia*, 33 - I, fl. 179.
144. *DI,* XI, 569.
145. *Ibid.,* V, 604.
146. *Doc,* VII, 302. *DI*, XV, 657.
147. *Ibid.*, X, 287.
148. *Ibid.*, IV, 324.
149. *Ibid.*, XII, 416.
150. *Ibid.*, X, 289.
151. *Ibid.*, XII, 413; VI, 119.
152. *Ibid.*, X, 289.
153. *Ibid.*, XVIII, 652.
154. *Ibid.*, IV, 184f, 222; V, 274.
155. *Ibid.*, XVIII, 664. *Doc*, X, 110. *DI*, V, 275.
156. *Ibid.*, 277-78.
157. Paulo da Trindade, *op. cit.*, p. 287.
158. *DI,* V, 275.
159. *Doc*, VIII, 216.
160. "Nos christãos se vee muito zelo da fee e devação às cousas de Deos, e afeição aos sacramentos, e, a mais dela, gente simples e que facilmente tomão o que lhe dizem. Dos filhos principalmente se espera grande fruito por serem tirados das idolatrias ò tempo que ainda delas não sabem nada, e asy se vee pola bondade de Deos, porque são tão domesticos e afeiçoados á doutrina e a quem lha ensina, que parece que nunca souberão outra cousa." Letter written by Fr. Eduardo Leitão to the superior-general of the Society of Jesus. Goa, December 1573. *DI*, IX, 307; XI, 258.

161. *Ibid.*, V, 275.
162. *Ibid.*, IV, 797; V, 274.
163. *Doc*, VIII, 417-18.
164. *Ibid.*, 416.
165. *Ibid.*, 53.
166. *Ibid.*, 415.
167. *DI*, V, 273f.
168. *Doc*, II, 300.
169. Leopoldo da Rocha, *op. cit.*, p. 25.
170. *Ibid.*, 166.
171. Sebastião Gonçalves, *op. cit.*, p. 109. "Em este Collegio (de São Paulo) vão em muyto crescimento as confissões . . . e este he o principal fruyto desta terra porque como a gente antes andasse desacustumada era isto ao principio tam estranho nelles que huns pelo descustume outros por seguirem a natureza da mesma terra o fazião muy raro. E por isso logo ao principio ouve nelles esta maneira de repugnancia. Mas vierão se tanto a affeiçoar que j'agora non ha dia que nesta igreja non haja muitas confissões. Muytas pessoas destas são de cada sabbado se confessarem e cada domingo tomarem o Santo Sacramento. Em a doctrina christãa se faz muyto fruyto... que em nhua terra se faz com ella mais fruito que nesta (City of Goa) porque ao menos em os moços se ve claramente . . . . De maravilha se achara moço de dez anos pera baixo que a nom saiba de cor toda e pela melhor cumprirem asi por si mesmos... que asi pelas ruas como em casa e em igrejas defendem todas aquellas cousas em que conhecem que se pode offender Deus Nosso Senhor . . . e asi pareceo sempre ca ao nosso bendito padre mestre Francisco que destes moços dependia a salvação de seus pais e mais pois que com tanta efficacia encomendou esta instrução delles." Letter with news about India to the priests and Brothers of the Society of Jesus in Europe. Goa, December 15, 1555. CEHU, *As Gavetas da Torre do Tombo*, V, p. 62.
172. *DI*, VIII, 339; V, 275.
173. *Ibid.*
174. *Doc*, X, 102.
175. *Ibid.*, VIII, 485.
176. Self-inflicted bodily punishment meant to achieve spiritual self-

perfection or to gain a particular grace or favour from God.

177. *DI,* XVIII, 880.

178. *Doc*, XI, 84. "Era una grande compasión y lástima ver los christianos pobrezitos que vivíam de labrar sus heredades y palmares dexarlo todo, no traiendo consigo más que sus pobres vestidos, porque, quitandoles quatro palmos de tierra que labran, no les queda más de hazienda. Por otra parte su constancia y amor a nuestra santa fee consolava mucho." *DI*, XI, 226. "... en medio de los trabajos y muertes, dar a muchos constancia para morir en la confissión de la fee, porque, a revuelta destos alborotos, tomaron algunos christianos los moros y exercitaron en ellos sus tyranías, y a algunos mataron y a otros, vencidos del interesse, después de muchos tormentos que les dieron para los tornar moros, los dieron a resgate." These events took place during the war with the Adilshah in Salcete, but they were written down in 1578. *Ibid.*, 263.

179. Leopoldo da Rocha, *op. cit.*, p. 10.

# 8

# CONVERSIONS: RESISTANCE AND CONSEQUENT IMPEDIMENTS

## Conversion Policy: continuity and change

After discussing the 'idea and practice of conversion' for the unity of the faith and empire, and examining the different means and institutions of conversion including the decrees and privileges in favour of Christendom, this chapter purports to elaborate and unfold the activity of conversion according to its three phases that I had proposed in chapter three. This will enable us to evaluate continuity and change in the affair of conversion, namely, acceptance of, and reactions to, the policies, praxis and efforts related to the making of a new citizenry in Goa. Continuity and change in making conversions can be appraised in a fairminded manner only vis-à-vis the political changes in Goa, its economic prosperity and stability, the religious zeal of each viceroy or governor and, of course, vis-à-vis the activities of the Tribunal of the Inquisition. And the moods of the missionaries cannot be excluded from this framework.

It may be recalled, however, that often a liberal conversion policy did not necessarily imply that the governors had less religious zeal, or even that the period affected by such policies was religiously changing. Likewise, one cannot easily conclude that the severe religious decrees were always widespead in time and space, even in Goa. Smooth political functioning of the state and an economically-viable colony demanded some liberalization, or a little less religious intolerance. While this chapter unfolds and examines in three phases the activity of conversion in Goa during the sixteenth century, we need to keep in mind the relevant changes that took place in the 'idea and practice of conversion'.

(a) *Pragmatic Religious Tolerance (1510-1540)*

To conquer Goa, in Muslim possession before 1510, the governor, Afonso de Albuquerque (1509-1515),[1] began exploiting the existing disaffection and conflicts among the Goan Hindus. Soon after its conquest he allied himself even more with them to also eliminate his Muslim rivals. Subsequent to Goa's conquest, the destruction of mosques by the Portuguese followed but simultaneously and strangely they showed considerable respect for the Hindu religious freedom. Then the granting of a few important concessions and privileges to the Hindus, or rather restoring to them their traditional rights which the Muslims had once deprived them of, probably made most Hindus well-disposed towards the new rulers. The Hindus might have thought of the Portuguese rule as lighter, and even more tolerant, than the rule of the Adilshah.[2] And the Muslims continued to live peacefully in Goa despite the slaughter by Albuquerque during its second conquest.[3] Nevertheless, if Albuquerque exhibited tolerant views, such does not seem becoming of any sixteenth century Iberian political leader or conqueror. The oft-repeated Albuquerquian tolerance was more pragmatic than ideological. Initially, when the *Estado da India* needed capital and human resources, the Hindus provided both to a very large extent, but had they been persecuted, the Portuguese, obviously, would not have been able to elicit their indispensable assistance.[4] Ironically, later, despite religious and social persecution, trading partnership and even military collaboration between the Hindus and the Portuguese did not cease throughout the sixteenth century.

It is beyond any doubt that the initial tolerance was only one of the Albuquerque's clever political strategies meant to consolidate his conquest. I think that this quality of the second governor of the *Estado da India* has been exaggerated. We need to consider that during Albuquerque's rule there were very few missionaries or that most religious orders were not yet established in Goa. Later on, the missionaries were known for encouraging and pressurizing governors and viceroys to issue several decrees in favour of conversions. As a matter of fact, despite pressures from many religious quarters to issue strict laws in favour of Christendom many viceroys and governors withstood them, perhaps due to force of circumstances, making themselves as 'tolerant' if not even more so than the famed Albuquerque. Such tolerance was also determined by the need to preserve the *Estado da India*, especialy when its safety was at stake. Political conditions, commercial demands, religious orders, private enterprise and several other considerations dictated government strategies and policies, including those regarding conversions. But all this had very little to do with benefitting the masses. Unfortunately, the initial respect for property rights, for corporate organization and religious freedom of the locals did not last long; just as the hostility towards the Muslims did not continue for much longer.

During the first years of the Portuguese rule, temples, sacred trees, tanks used for religious rituals, sacred cows, stones carved with the images of snakes and bulls were permitted, or rather tolerated, in Goa. Hindu priests and dancing girls of the temple exercised their duties and profession without any interference.[5] But the stone gods and goddesses depicted with a man's, monkey's, lion's or elephant's head and with several arms might not have pleased a few missionaries already living in Goa during the early years. The island of Goa was full of temples and idols, and its annual festivals attracted many local Christians and Portuguese as well.[6] These places of false cult filled with temple girls and public immorality could not be permitted in a Christian territory for long, since they were a grave offence against God.[7] During the so-called tolerant phase, there had been several requests to the Portuguese authority to end this unchristian situation, but they were not seriously attended to. The official mission of removing idolatry had to wait till 1540, when the destruction of several temples took place as a service done to God and to the king.[8]

When some Brahmans and *Neiqebarys*[9] became Christians, the missionaries expected thenceforth that the common folk would soon embrace Christianity. Efforts were made to convert other village chiefs with promises of favours and material gains.[10] Besides, the missionaries strongly believed that the religious discussions they held with the Hindu priests would lead them to the true faith. But when the Hindus began showing themselves adamant and refused to accept the Christian arguments, the missionaries hardened themselves and did not stop condemning the Hindu repugnance to reason things out, their mean attitudes and superstitions. The priests attributed this behaviour to the demons whom, the missionaries felt, the Hindus worshipped.[11]

Although the Hindus were left free to practise their religion and traditional customs, these things were certainly disagreeable to the missionaries. The priests had a keen interest in ending idolatry in order to begin their work of conversion. António do Louro, a Franciscan, admitted that he had discussed with the governor, Lopo Soares (1515-1518), about introducing new methods to convert the Hindus. However, the governor excused himself and requested this Franciscan to discuss the matter directly with the vicar-general of the diocese. Louro did not pursue the matter further. We know for certain that this friar had suggested to the king the creation of separate quarters only for the Christians, to prevent them from mixing freely with the Hindus.[12] He also insisted that the king ought to forbid any *jogue*[13] from entering Goa, since these people incited the masses to follow Hindu practices. Moreover, he proposed that the new converts should be favoured with alms of rice, which would also serve as a strong incentive for more conversions.[14] Before the destruction of the temples in 1540, there were probably more than two serious requests in the city of Goa to exile harmful Hindu elements and destroy their temples.

It is an acceptable fact that no temple had been brought down during this tolerant period, but already in 1518 a great part of a big temple in Divar island had been destroyed, and the Franciscans had asked for its stones to build their monastery.[15] In the same year a friar had placed a few crosses inside some temples.[16] The *jogues* had been forbidden to move about in the villages without restrictions, for they used to go about telling stories and lies of their religion and influencing people with their relics. This could not go unchallenged and unchecked. Through arguments the Hindus had to be brought into the Christian fold.[17]

The bishop of Dume complained to the king in 1522 that the Hindus living in the islands of Chorão and Divar adored the enemy of the cross in their temples. Their festivals attracted many local Christians and Portuguese alike.[18] He added that it would be a great service to God if these temples were destroyed and churches built there. Whoever wanted to live in these islands would have to become a Christian, otherwise he/she should be asked to leave the islands, which he/she was unlikely to do. The people were so attached to their lands that they could not even think of abandoning them. The bishop also reported that it would be rather easy to convert the Hindus.[19]

The reluctance of the Hindus to spontaneously embrace Christianity disappointed and angered the missionaries. When the priests wanted to gather Hindu boys from the villages to impart religious instruction, they had to go out accompanied by guards to do the job.[20] The conversion of the adult turned out to be much more difficult than they had ever expected. But when conversions took place, generally the men made the initial move and the women usually followed their example. The women were more ignorant of the Christian doctrine than their husbands, but the former excelled in religious devotion. Conversion of children could have been easier, but some missionaries carried away by their own scruples doubted the validity of baptism to a Hindu minor boy/girl, though often they cared little about this sort of scruples.[21]

The first converts were those who were directly in contact with, or dependent on, the Portuguese, like their local wives, mistresses, slaves, helpers at the forts and factories, widows, orphans, *solteiras* meaning prostitutes, etc. If, however, many Hindus had no difficulties in receiving baptism, their own relatives or the Brahman chiefs prevented them from taking the final step.[22] In 1541 it was suggested that if the Brahman chiefs of Goa —

Krishna, Loquu and Anu Synai — the main opposers of conversion work, were invited to Portugal and retained there for two years on the pretext that the king needed some information from them about Goa, perhaps many people would become Christians in their absence. In case these Brahman chiefs refused to convert while in Portugal, or soon after returning, they should be asked to leave Goa. It was almost certain that they would prefer conversion to being forced to abandon their land,[23] despite the fact that most Brahman Hindus preferred to lose their lands than leave their religion.[24] Krishna, the main chief of the Hindus, had given word to the Portuguese officials that only after seeing the king would he become a Christian. He saw the king but did not keep his word.[25] Anu Synay did not convert either. Loquu did convert, but only after his arrest by the Portuguese.

After Loquu became a Christian conversions increased.[26] The baptism of Loquu proved an interesting publicity for conversion. He was one of the chiefs of the Brahmans and while in prison he had asked for baptism. It was reported that after his baptism a few Hindus decided to follow suit.[27] Loquu, baptized as Lucas de Sá, was made the chief *thanadar* (*thanadar-mor*).[28] The missionaries continued to hope that entire villages would not take long to follow the example of their own converted chiefs.

These relatively-tolerant attitudes prevailed during most of the first phase of conversion in Goa (1510-1540).[29] No group baptisms had taken place yet, just very few conversions here and there, for even if some Brahmans were converted the peasants were not. Baptism even of many Brahmans, as in a particular village in 1573, did not affect or influence the Brahmans or peasants in another village due to the self-sufficient and the insular character of each village community.[30] The agents of conversion did not take long to understand that the greater the number of Brahmans living in a village, the less the chances they had to convert the people there. Brahman Hindus prevented conversions aggressively.[31]

Before 1540 conversions were effected through mild or peaceful methods. The churches and the chapels were meant more for the Portuguese than for the local converts. Till then the Christians and Hindus had enjoyed greater freedom, since rigorous vigilance and religious instruction did not preoccupy the missionaries as it would do later. This freedom, the missionaries argued, caused a lot of uncontrolled hatred and discord among the Christians in the city of Goa.[32]

The work of conversion was taken up on a war footing when the Portuguese decided to remain in Goa and make it their empire's capital. Outposts in areas bordering the Hindu and Muslim territories needed personnel for their defence, and conversion of soldiers here and in other strategic regions was necessary. But the locals were not easily entrusted with the defence of the Portuguese-controlled lands. They were potential threats. Besides, they were a people with little force and few skills in warfare.[33] Frontier parishes were not alloted to the local clergy to work in. It was rightly said that when sufficient trust was not placed on the local priests, the people could not have expected a different treatment from the church authorities and the white clergymen.[34]

### (b) *Militant Conversion Drive (1540-1580)*

This period experienced severe anti-Hindu decrees — 'decrees and privileges in favour of conversion or Christendom' as I called them — which were long overdue according to the missionaries, for cleansing the land from its superstitions and idolatry. Hinduism had worried the missionaries earlier, but they could do almost nothing against it. Probably, there was more activity of conversion during this phase than during the other two phases together (1510-1540 and 1580-1610). We have already mentioned that the destruction of the temples began in 1540, but not all of them had been pulled down then.[35] Churches, chapels and crosses substituted them. The converts put crosses in their courtyards, where hitherto they had their idols.[36] The inhabitants of Daugim, after their conversion in 1543, destroyed its temple and asked for a church.[37] I did not find any other report about a similar case.

A pastoral letter written by the bishop, D. João de Albuquerque, in 1544 urged all the parish priests to teach the Christian doctrine to the converts, preach in public and exhort the people to frequent the sacraments of confession and communion.

Besides, he ordered the creation of a school in each church to teach the Christian faith.[38] But the Hindus, with their customs and lifestyle so different from those in the Christian world, never wanted to love, know and obey God; instead they preferred to follow their immoral customs.[39] To change this situation, in 1546 D. João III ordered a search in the Hindu houses suspected of possessing idols. He also prohibited Hindu festivals and Brahman preachers in Goa. Around this time the overzealous Miguel Vaz, the vicar-general of the diocese of Goa, returned from Portugal with extensive royal powers to carry out his plan of cleasing the land of idolatry. However, the king requested Miguel Vaz to use persuasion rather than any scandalous means, and to urge the neo-converts to behave like good Christians.[40] Despite the sudden death of Miguel Vaz, mourned intensely by the Christians and the Hindus alike strange as it might appear, the conversion drive did not slow down. Rumours had gone round that Miguel Vaz had been poisoned at the initiative of some Brahmans, since he had come from Portugal with the royal mandate to cleanse the land of its idolatry, and to expel harmful Hindus from the city of Goa. We are informed that the Brahmans were so shrewd that if they wished to kill a hundred persons by poisoning, they could do so without any difficulty.[41] In 1550 a law ordered the destruction of all the remaining temples in the territory of Goa, and it also forbade the Hindu cult in public. The Hindus waited to re-build their temples and make new ones, but there was no provision to this effect. Rather, the Brahmans who abused the Christians could be punished. This law paved the way for expelling the Hindus from public services.[42] In spite of the law forbidding the Hindu rituals in the city of Goa, they were allowed to perform their ceremonies privately in the island of Divar. Stone idols and sacred trees carefully protected could still be seen in front of their houses, especially of the Hindu/Brahman chiefs.[43]

Between 1551 and 1554 the local nobles, rich clerks, Brahman merchants, doctors and wealthy businessmen, all great contributors to the revenues of the king, abandoned their houses and lands and went to live outside Goa. Interestingly, many neo-converts also left Goa. The reason for this drastic move had been forced conversions by the priests.[44] The Jesuits began harassing the Hindus by cutting their hair tuft, forcing them to eat beef, and to go against their 'superstitions and idolatries', despite objections raised against such methods by the Dominicans and Franciscans.[45]

The Christians who had remained in the city of Goa, after the rest had migrated, were robbers and drunkards. They began dressing and living well only after their conversion, but refused to work. These people preferred to lead an idle life whereas earlier as Hindus they had to take up any kind of job, and were rather poor. Our historical sources inform us that many people came to Goa just to benefit from this comfortable lifestyle or to have free clothing and food, and a few of them had even asked for baptism thrice, hoping thus to receive some favours each time. The priests, guided by their excessive zeal to serve God, had failed to understand the shrewdness of these people yet. Later, the priests began demanding some surety from those who came from the firm land to be baptized.[46] Those Christians who showed tendencies to idleness could be punished if proved incorrigible.[47] They were taught good customs and virtues: how to work, till the soil, sow paddy as per the custom of the land, and how to live honestly by their own work. The poor Christians also received some monetary help.[48]

We are informed that when the village chiefs and Brahmans were converted the people followed them;[49] and that after expelling these obstinate chiefs or converting them, it had been easier to convert the rest.[50] When the Brahmans were expelled from Goa, the Christians found some relief and the *gente meuda dos gentios* (poor Hindus) came forward to become Christians. This certainly caused anxiety to the Hindu élite.[51] When it was not easy to make conversions some pleasant surprises did occur at times. To the astonishment of the missionaries, some rich Muslims and Hindus, wearing plenty of gold rings and chains, came to the city of Goa from different parts to become Christians in 1554.[52] Some Hindus who had fled from Goa due to the religious intolerance returned and became Christians.[53]

The rigorous policies of the viceroy, D. Pedro Mascarenhas (1554-1555), against the Hindu and Muslim public ceremonies might have forced more people either to convert or to migrate. He promulgated several laws in favour of conversion and ordered them to be read on the streets of Goa. These orders banned all the Hindu ceremonies in Portuguese territory, and demanded the separation of Hindu orphans from their relatives so that they might be brought up in Christian customs. The Hindus began reacting against these policies. In 1555, the situation worsened so much so that the Hindus threatened to leave Goa. When the governor, Francisco Barreto (1555-1558), arrived in Goa, he had no other alternative but to suspend the decrees that harmed the state, thus slowing down the conversion drive.

Till 1556 very few had become Christians in Goa, and the Muslims outnumbered the Portuguese. One of the reasons for few conversions in Goa and in other parts of India till then, was the continued ill-treatment meted out to the converts by the Portuguese.[54] The governors hardly favoured the converts, but contrary to the royal instructions the same Brahmans who encouraged Hindu practices received great many favours for their talents and shrewdness, which in turn benefitted and enriched the powerful Portuguese officials in Goa. Many Portuguese officials argued that they could not perform their duties without the assistance of the Hindus, an argument the missionaries outrightly refuted.[55] If this favouritism continued the Christian faith would hardly attract anyone to it.[56]

The Hindus, through the good offices of their Portuguese dependants, began persuading the governor, Francisco Barreto, to allow them some religious freedom in order to avoid any social unrest. This governor held that these anti-Hindu laws had been necessary only at the beginning to introduce and establish the Christian faith, but since it was already firmly rooted in Goa, he argued, these decrees could even prove harmful to the state's prosperity if observed strictly. Thus Francisco Barreto putting aside all precautions, and carried away by his personal interests, revoked the law banning the Hindu Brahmans from public services.[57] He also allowed, by other decrees, certain practices that had been forbidden earlier by the king and the bishop of Goa. Further, he permitted the Brahmans to conduct their marriage and burial ceremonies in public, and gave them freedom to practise *sati*. Then, the Hindus began celebrating their feasts with much pomp and display of their idols and idolatry. The decree that granted freedom to a convert slave was repealed. Now a Hindu could retain the money accruing from the sale of his Christian slave. The missionaries insisted that the decree granting freedom to convert slaves served as the greatest incentive for their conversion.[58] The Franciscans, Dominicans and Jesuits, unwilling to reconcile with the stand of this governor, protested vehemently against these decrees and decided to send jointly a memorandum to the king to abolish the new decrees. To the annoyance of the Jesuits, the Franciscans and the Dominicans refused to sign the memorandum. In spite of this the Jesuits did not relent their proselytizing campaign; instead, they pressed the governor to implement the former orders that had withdrawn all concessions enjoyed by the Hindus.[59] Henceforth, the Hindus nursed an unwavering hatred against the Jesuits.[60]

The governor, Francisco Barreto, under severe pressure, did not take long to issue other decrees favouring conversions. Substitution of local Christians for Hindus in government posts followed. The new converts could inherit from their parents and from the Hindus soon after their baptism, if the latter did not have natural heirs.[61] The local Christians began receiving privileges in accordance with the previous decrees in favour of Christendom.[62] The large number of conversions in 1557, probably motivated by favours granted to the converts by the governor, led the missionaries believe that soon the entire island of Goa would become Christian.[63] With this victory over the harmful Brahmans the missionaries felt more encouraged to wage a "spiritual war against the demon".[64]

In spite of the severe decrees, we find the Hindus performing their marriage ceremonies secretly by night in the city in 1558.[65] Another reason for a drop in conversions and for some revival of Hindu customs in Goa was a certain disagreement between the archbishop, D. Gaspar, and the Jesuits.[66] But during the rule of D. Constantino de Bragança (1558-1561) conversions increased extraordinarily. It is almost certain that during the entire sixteenth century no other viceroy or governor displayed so much prozelytizing zeal as D. Constantino de Bragança.[67] God continued to favour the work of conversion in these parts of India, especially in Goa, wrote the missionaries.[68]

The viceroy, D. Constantino de Bragança, implemented mercilessly all the decrees in favour of conversion. He promulgated a few more, even stronger than those of his predecessors. He passed a decree in 1559 ordering the destruction of the remaining temples and idols.[69] Bragança expelled the harmful Brahmans from Goa in 1560.[70] To those who had immovable property he gave one month to sell it; the others had to leave Goa immediately. In default they would be sent to the galleys after forfeiting their goods. Under the same threat he ordered all the goldsmiths, who had taken their women folk and children and goods to the firm land, to bring them back to the island or abandon the land.[71] In 1559, Bragança prohibited Hindu widows from committing *sati* in the city of Goa, its neighbouring islands and in the districts of Bardez and Salcete. Anyone who was found guilty of helping a woman to commit *sati* could be made captive and lose lands.[72] Further, no *jogue* was allowed to enter the island, for they had become a constant danger to the neo-converts.[73]

The Hindus, especially the Brahmans, possessed great power and assumed airs of arrogance.[74] When the decrees began to be implemented the Brahmans refused to accept their fate. Instead, some tried all the possible means to change the mind of Constantino de Bragança and others waited for his tenure to end. Their efforts availed them nothing. Then they closed their shops and persuaded the cultivators to destroy the dikes in the paddy-fields to allow the salt water to fill them. After doing this they decided to leave Goa. They declared that forced conversion compelled them to take this decision.[75] Surprisingly, after the Hindu merchants abandoned the city and the cultivators refused to work, religious intolerance grew still worse so much so that in 1559 the state ratified all the decrees in favour of conversion.[76]

After the expulsion or migration of the Hindus in 1559, the city of Goa contained very few Hindu inhabitants. The missionaries expected that the remaining Goan Hindus would accept the faith before the next contingent of ships arrived from Portugal.[77]

However, there would always be foreign Hindus in the city who came from various parts of the world, to trade in this competitive city port.[78] Muslims and Hindus continuously asked for baptism, though only little pressure was exerted on them. Since these people lacked Christian instruction and came from distant lands, the priests told them to return accompanied by someone, preferably known to the priests, who could stand surety on their behalf.[79] Curiously, a Hindu who wanted to become a Christian, but perhaps prevented by social constraints to take this step, cut deliberately a sacred tree or *ariqueira*, used by the Hindus in their religious festivals. To cut an *ariqueira* was unlawful. Hoping to secure his conversion, he went to meet with a priest and accused himself of this act to compel the priest to report this wrongdoing to the local authority.[80] The previous chapters contain a few stories on conversions as narrated by the missionaries, some of them exaggerations for dramatic effects, to show that they brought no direct pressure to bear on the Hindus.[81]

In 1560 after some Hindus converted at Carambolim and as this village was quickly turning Christian, seventy Brahmans and others from here on perceiving that they could not escape conversions much longer, came together to deliberate on what action to take.[82] Despite differences of opinion the majority suggested that they should move out from Goa with their families. However, the opinion of an old Brahman prevailed. Knowing well that the priests and the viceroys would not stop harassing them, the old man proposed that they should abandon their vain idols and become Christians, to be able to live and work peacefully and receive favours from the Portuguese government. They asked for some priests to teach them the Christian doctrine. But curiously, after their baptism, the demon they adored before appeared continuously and reminded them about their former religion.[83] The people of Carambolim decided to become Christians in 1560 for, as they believed, the Jesuits sooner or later would force them to convert.[84] When in the same year the districts of Bardez and Salcete reported several conversions, it created a feeling that very shortly every trace of Hinduism would be wiped out from Goa.[85]

During the three-year rule of Constantino de Bragança more

than twenty thousand Hindus were converted in the city of Goa and surroundings.[86] This viceroy prized the conversion of the poorest Hindu more than all the riches.[87] More conversions took place during his three-year tenure (1558-1561) than ever since the conquest of Goa till 1558.[88] From this statistical information we can imagine how whole-heartedly or fanatically he might have favoured the work of conversion in Goa. Nevertheless, conversions among the common people proved rather slow.[89]

The rule of Bragança was marked by a rigorous anti-Hindu drive which depopulated Goa. One cannot think of a more violent policy of conversion which proved harmful to the state and crown revenues during the sixteenth century. It was during his rule or in 1560 that the *Tribunal do Santo Ofício* better known as the Tribunal of the Inquisition had been established in Goa. With the departure of this viceroy in 1561, many Brahmans returned to Goa. The Portuguese laymen, who opined that the use of force in conversions was irrational and violated human rights, invited them to return to Goa, since their presence or services were indispensable to the state.[90] The next viceroy, D. Francisco Coutinho (1561-1564), passed a decree restoring to the Hindus their confiscated goods, and invited them to the island of Goa in 1561.[91]

In 1561 D. Franscisco Coutinho after discussing with, and most likely pressurizing, the archbishop, theologians, jurists and learned men, agreed that the de-population of Goa and the subsequent abandonment of the fields, a result of his predecessor's decisions, had harmed the state considerably. This viceroy's move, supposedly in favour of the state, permitted the Hindus to return to Goa and the restoration of confiscated property.[92] This was possible partly due to pressures exerted by some influential Portuguese who supported a more liberal policy of conversion, but which the missionaries opposed uncompromisingly for being favouritism to the Hindus. The archbishop of Goa, D. Gaspar, misguided by some Portuguese who succeeded in convincing him that force was used to convert, began disfavouring the work of the missionaries, wrote Fr. Nunes Barreto in 1562. This, obviously, slowed down the expansion of Christendom.[93] D. Gaspar mentioned about some disorders in the methods of conversion, but this being sorted out, the work of conversion proceeded as per the law of the church.[94] Fr. Barreto did not deny the use of force in conversions, but he added that whenever it had been used, it was negligible if compared to what the theologians and the canonists approved as normal and ethical.[95] The Brahmans never stopped opposing the work of conversion. They persuaded the neo-converts to abandon their faith, as a result no solemn baptism could take place for two years for lack of catechumens. The missionary enthusiasm diminished significantly.[96]

The king had reminded the viceroy about the importance of conversions since it was the most urgent duty of Portugal.[97] Hence, attempts to expel all the Brahmans from Goa, who indulged in anti-Christian activities, intensified in 1563. However, those who did not oppose conversions and served the state as tillers of the land, doctors, carpenters, ironsmiths, shopkeepers and tax-collectors were permitted to remain in the city. At this time the viceroy issued orders to expel Hindu physicians and mechanics if they proved harmful to the state. Warned of their arrest, the Brahmans had no alternative but to sell their property and abandon the city. No public edict had been issued regarding expelling the harmful Brahmans, for it had to be carried out without creating any unrest in the city.[98] The decree did not aim at specific castes, but at all suspected of undermining Christendom. When the harmful Hindus left the city, the missionaries could perform a solemn group baptism. We are told that, henceforth, the work of conversion went on unopposed.[99] The viceroy, D. Francisco Coutinho, and the archbishop, D. Gaspar, resolved to favour conversions again.[100]

In 1566 the viceroy, D. Antão de Noronha (1564-1568), despite his religious zeal, issued an order recalling the exiled *gaunkars* of Navelim in Salcete with the assurance of returning their confiscated property if they tilled the soil.[101] During the government of Noronha the First Provincial Council (1567) took place. It issued several intolerant decrees to increase conversions and prevent any kind of syncretism among the new converts. However, the king, D. Sebastião, urged the same viceroy to avoid scandals and occasions that could bring discredit to the Christian faith, because such situations would make the Hindus more adamant to the reception of the faith, and easier for the neo-converts to abandon it.[102] In fact, a more serious moral and social behaviour was expected from the missionaries, Portuguese laymen and local Christians alike in overseas Portuguese territories than in Portugal. In the former places greater emphasis was laid on 'good examples', a *sine qua non*, to attract the Hindus to the Christian faith. The conversion of several Brahman chiefs in 1567 strengthened the missionaries' conviction that soon many others would enter the church.[103]

A great number of temples still standing in Bardez and Salcete in 1567 offended God, complained the missionaries. When the work of conversion had begun in these lands, four or five years earlier, the priests had demolished some temples here. However, later, fearing further disorders and scandals, they tried to pull down a few only at a time under the pretext that they were doing so for some wrong the Hindus had committed.[104] The viceroy, D. Antão de Noronha, had ordered his troops to destroy about two hundred temples in Salcete in retaliation for an attack on the new converts by the Hindus.[105] The archbishop stood for the expulsion of the Hindus from Goa, for government posts exclusively for the Christians, and for the exclusion of Hindu *gaunkars* from the village councils when there were Christian *gaunkars* to replace them.[106]

When D. Luís de Ataíde (1568-1574) became viceroy, the king, D. Sebastião, gave him instructions to work for the increase of conversions, to administer justice, and conquer whatever he could.[107] Although conversions had precedence over the conquest of lands, the former could not be achieved without the latter. Since 1570, when the crown turned its attention to Brazil, the Portuguese authority in Goa was alarmed with its already-reduced personnel to defend the *Estado da India*. It was during the rule of the viceroy, Luís de Ataíde, that the Adilshah laid siege to the city of Goa in 1570-71, lasting for about ten months.[108] The siege made life in the city and the activity of conversion extremely difficult.[109] Poverty had increased with the loss of many Portuguese ships.[110]

When earlier in 1569 the same viceroy had issued a decree forbidding the reconstruction of the destroyed temples, the Hindus in Salcete refused to comply with it and reacted rebelliously. The matter was taken to the archbishop of Goa for his verdict.[111] To permit the Hindus to re-build their temples, he argued, would be tantamount to a great scandal to Christendom, shame to the Christian name and to the Portuguese image in the East.[112] The law forbidding the reconstruction of temples was also notified in Bardez, in 1567.[113] Further, the viceroy forbade the Hindu teachers and doctors to teach and practise respectively in 1574.

The Second Provincial Council (1575) dealt with issues like the divine cult, increase of faith, prevention of relapse, moderation in customs, correction of excesses, exaltation of the name of Christ among the Hindus and Muslims, reform of customs, etc.[114] Henceforth, all the Hindus were forbidden to move on horseback, in sedan or palanquin, or carry an umbrella in the city of Goa. Those who had the permission to collect the rents of the crown were pressed to relinquish these jobs in favour of Christians, as per the ruling of the Provincial Council and law of the king. The harmful Hindus, still at liberty in Goa, had their lands confiscated. The administrators of confraternities received additional juridical power to decide some cases and to imprison any Hindu found guilty, and the latter had no right of appeal after the former's verdict. They were also invested with authority to make inquiries about idolatrous practices.[115]

In 1575 the Jesuit priests agreed unanimously that no direct or indirect force should be used to convert Hindus: no Christian food should be forced on anyone as means of making him lose caste. Orphans should not be taken away from their relatives, nor should the idol-makers be imprisoned, for such methods created hatred against the priests and scandalized many Hindus. No public or secret threat should be employed against anyone. Rather the priests could admonish and show the erring person the charges he/she could incur to his/her body and soul. This would be more effective if done secretly to avoid accusations against the Jesuits.[116] The captains could be informed about those who made idols or performed Hindu ceremonies to be punished accordingly. Moreover, the Jesuits deliberated that some inquiry was necessary about the life of the catechumens to ascertain their seriousness.

Group baptisms were encouraged not only for the euphoria they elicited from the local Christians, but also as a reprimand to the Hindus. Group baptisms edified those in Europe too.[117]

The governor, António Barreto, stated in 1576 that no force should be employed to convert a slave belonging to a Muslim.[118] The ill-treatment meted out to many convert slaves by their owners led the governor to issue a decree by which a convert slave would have to be sold only to Christians, a law supposed to prevent these slaves from returning to their former idolatry, or running away to the land of the Muslims. Another decree permitted a convert to divorce his Hindu wife and marry a Christian woman. If later, however, his first wife converted she became his legitimate wife, hence he had to take her back which meant that he had necessarily to leave his second wife, with whom he could have been living for many years. To change wives this way was not only impossible but also impractical, scandalous and an impediment to conversions. Many Hindus shunned becoming Christians, knowing that after living with another woman for fifteen or twenty years they would have to go back to the first one.[119] It is interesting to know whether they debated this issue just for argument's sake or whether there were some cases of converts divorcing their Hindu wives. But facts point out that entire families or even villages normally converted together, and that any decree in favour of conversion, no matter how scandalous it might have appeared to the locals, was always valid and justified by the missionaries.

In 1579 due to the war with the Adilshah the work of conversion were at a standstill, especially in Salcete which had earlier seen the flourishing of Christianity. Christians from Salcete left their lands and came to the city of Goa. In spite of several privations they showed great courage and faith.[120] Conversions in the city of Goa and the island had become rare by this time since the Hindu merchants, ever more preoccupied with their own business, hardly felt inclined to accepting baptism, which could spell the end of their trade.[121] Hindu *gaunkars* supported the Muslims when the latter invaded Bardez, but the former were equally quick to help the Portuguese repair the damages caused by the Muslims.[122]

### (c) *Conversions or Political Stability (1580-1610)?*

During this phase, preserving the faith of the neo-converts seemed to be as important as converting the Hindus.[123] At times the former concern appears in historical sources to have precedence over the latter. At this stage, local reactions made the work of conversion rather difficult, especially in Salcete, as sections two and three in this chapter dealing with resistance and impediments will show. Now, the real decadence showed how fictitious the prosperity of the Portuguese Empire in the East was. The existence of many adulteries, disorders, scandals, unnecessary expenditure in dressing and lifestyle or going about in the city accompanied by many servants was alarming.[124] The viceroy, D. Duarte de Meneses (1584-1588), complained of lack of funds in Goa, as a result of Hindu migration, expulsion or decrease in rents and taxes.[125]

In 1590 the Hindus, unable to bear the tyranny of the Portuguese who took away their lands, left Goa for the firm land.[126] When the bishop resolved to collect new tithe-taxes from the Christians, some Portuguese remarked that the local people, ambitious as they were and being people who would not hesitate to sell even their parents for a little money, would not pay the taxes. Moreover, nobody would think of becoming a Christian to pay additional taxes.[127] The lands in Salcete, once the best in the Konkan coast and densely populated, appeared almost uninhabited at this time, not only because of the wars with the Adilshah but also because of the Portuguese policy of religious persecution.[128]

From 1597 till 1603 Christendom suffered a set-back due to many scandals, injustice, disorders and ill-administration of judges. Surprisingly, even some Goan Christians preferred to live in the territories of the Adilshah.[129] Another ban on local ceremonies and idols did not deter the Hindus and the Muslims from committing many offences against God. They worshipped their idols and celebrated their religious rituals publicly in the city of Goa. Brahman preachers, the people responsible for this situation, had to be expelled at all costs from Goa.[130]

The Hindus continued to go to the firm land, where many of them had their families, to perform their ceremonies despite the government prohibition. The Jesuits always considered this practice unlawful; however, they did not stop the Hindus from leaving Goa. The Jesuits began imposing a new tax on those who wished to go to the firm lands, instead of letting them go there unopposed to perform their ceremonies. These outspoken missionaries argued that since it was nearly impossible to convert the Hindus or to stop them from doing what they pleased, they could at least pay in that way for the works of conversion. Nobody dared contradict or proceed against the Jesuits. But rumours went about that the Jesuits began caring for money more than for the work of conversion, a thing that in the past they prized so zealously.[131]

The political argument stated that if the state promulgated strict laws against the public ceremonies of the Hindus, they would stop coming to Goa to trade. Those laws would result in a big loss to its economy. Therefore, it would be wise to let the Hindus practise their rituals secretly.[132] On the other hand, the missionaries argued that since the Hindus persecuted and ill-treated the Christians, stricter measures should be imposed on them. The Portuguese threats against the Hindus or vice-versa, or an external threat, evidently, brought salient compromises and changes of policy and praxis, as any good diplomacy for survival demands. However, it was imperative to show to the crown and other authorities in Portugal that faith or Christendom was the main Portuguese concern overseas; just as it was equally imperative for the crown to continuously advertise its 'most important duty' before the other European nations. But often this 'most important duty' had no priority over political pragmatism. It remained only on paper, since several decrees and privileges in favour of conversion were not executed as they should have been by the local law enforcers. Each time the Portuguese decided to implement any harsh anti-Hindu statute the locals reacted and revolted against it. The continuous pressures from the religious orders on the reluctant Portuguese authority to implement decrees in favour of conversion and the urgent need of preventing the political and economic decadence of empire, created serious differences of opinion and conflicts among the Portuguese themselves. The local authority insisted that in the interest of the king's revenue and service to God the local traders should not be forced to leave Goa. Generally, the governors and the viceroys did not oppose royal orders or instructions, but in practice they adapted or discarded them according to the political and economic situation of the state.

Conflicting information on the activity of conversion should caution us about the complexity present in the history of conversions. Around 1590 it was reported that conversions went on increasing.[133] But we are also told that since the religious Brothers stopped going out on Sundays to teach the Christian doctrine as they used to do before, entire Christian villages turned again to Hinduism.[134] In 1591, during the rule of the governor, Manuel de Souza (1588-1591), Christianity was at a low ebb, and where the Portuguese abounded conversions were very meager. The viceroy, Matias de Albuquerque (1591-1597), favoured conversions to such an extent of not paying heed to the complaints of the Hindus; instead, he sent them to the galleys for breach of law.[135] This could be another exaggerated report to please the home authorities and to attract distinctive honours for himself. The king, D. Filipe II, congratulated Matias de Albuquerque for his zeal in the activity of conversion.[136] But in 1596 the king showed his displeasure with the work of conversion carried out by the Franciscans. He had received complaints about the Franciscans' negligence of their duties. However, the Franciscans were quick to clarify any doubt on this regard.[137]

The viceroy, Aires de Saldanha (1600-1605), showed interest in spreading the faith. He became godfather to many converts.[138] D. Aleixo de Meneses, an Augustinian archbishop of Goa and also its governor (1608-1609), lamented to the heads of religious orders in Lisbon in 1609, that the Augustinians lacked that militant spirit so essential to make conversions; therefore, the moment had arrived for them to accept into their religious orders *mestiços* or Eurasian canditates.[139] The other religious orders did not fare better as they were also in a state of decline and weak, except the Jesuits who did not think of returning to Europe as the other religious did, added the archbishop.[140] As has been mentioned earlier even the Jesuits had changed their approach to the Hindu practices and religion by the turn of the sixteenth century. We could perhaps suggest from the above evidences that what happened in the field of conversion at the end of the century was not exactly the same as witnessed during the 60s of the same century.

## Resistance

From the outset the locals opposed the missionaries and conversions. Unfortunately, these facts have remained on the dark side of history. Nevertheless, we can find scattered here and there in our historical sources traces of reactions to religious intolerance. Local resistance, disagreeable to missionary work could not be reported; but when narrated, the story ended up with the missionaries overcoming every resistance to the embarassment of the enemies of the faith. Such reportings hardly reveal the entire story. The accounts about local resistance have to be suspect.

The Hindus resisted conversion in Goa and its islands.[141] It was alleged that the Hindus poisoned D. João de Albuquerque, the first bishop of Goa, when he began cleansing the land from its idolatry.[142] Invariably, the missionaries attributed this resistance to the hardness of the Hindus and their refusal to convert. However, we know that it was not only the policies of conversion that destabilized the socio-economic life in the village community, and the traditional power relationships. It is unquestionable that conversion or the very duty of converting had more than religious consequences. With conversions some had much to lose or gain; others were able to retain their status, property and privileges; but the majority though poor did resist, consciously or unconsciously, change of religion and social customs.

Conversion gave a person Lusitanian citizenship, but not always Lusitanian rights and privileges. It gave them more Lusitanian duties. The well known singular story of the free conversion of the daughter of Meale, a Muslim and claimant to the throne of Bijapur, and the resistance put up by her family to prevent her conversion, tells us the different political interests at stake under the religious garb.[143] Likewise, we can see more than pure religious motives behind many schemes devised by the Brahmans to hinder the conversion of the Hindu folk.

The islands of Divar (the hub of Hinduism) and Chorão had a population of about three thousand inhabitants and thirty temples. The hold these temples had over these people made their conversion almost impossible. Ganesh, just one of the many Gods they had, took the central stage and attracted many pilgrims to its temple, even from distant lands. All the means the viceroy and the missionaries used to convert them proved futile. With the Brahmans governing these islands no hopes of their conversion remained. The missionaries decided that, "the common people could not continue to live under the influence of the demon much longer".[144] They offered prayers and masses for their conversion, preached to them and did penances too. When the work of conversion had begun in the islands of Divar and Chorão in 1540, all the temples were destroyed.[145] Then a few months later, after the Brahmans and many islanders had been baptized, the situation changed radically.[146]

Divar famed for one of its temples, attracted many Hindus eager to gain indugences. Even after its destruction the Hindus continued to assemble at this place to receive the indulgences it conferred upon them. The Brahmans, surrounded by the new converts, convoked a meeting to decide whether it would be wiser to become Christians or abandon the island of Divar, since the law of Christ had already reached their doorsteps. Some of those present at the meeting said that it was the will of God that they should become Christians as the time was ripe for them to change their religion. Others, however, objected to the idea of changing their old practices, and preferred to abandon their land to disowning the law of their ancestors.[147]

The Hindus, who did not want to convert, abandoned the islands with their families and went to live among the Muslims. The government handed the property of those who left Goa over to their convert relatives. Often, before migrating, they decided that at least one member of the same household should stay behind and become a Christian to be able to retain their property without Portuguese harassment. This strategy left open the possibility for them to return some day when the situation changed. Some of those who had left the island, knowing very well that no change would occur in the conversion policy, had no other alternative but to return and become Christians. However, to show that the local Christians prized their new faith more than any material gain or property that had been handed over to them, they were made to go out to convince their Hindu relatives to return to the village and take possession of their confiscated property again.[148] Moreover, we are informed, that despite the hostility and ill-treatment that the Christians suffered from their Hindu relatives, the former found it worth suffering for the conversion of their relatives. But when provoked, the Christians stood together and even retaliated with the destruction of their temples.[149]

The Brahmans created many difficulties for the missionaries in Bardez too. Later they themselves together with others asked for baptism.[150] There were approximately three hundred temples in Bardez, around five in each village. After their destruction churches were built, and crosses planted, in their places.[151] In 1561 in Candolim, in Bardez, the Hindus destroyed a cross erected by the Franciscans, as a reminder or warning against conversions. In the same village the Hindus also beat up a Franciscan friar when they sensed that he had come with the intention of destroying their idols;[152] the Christians retaliated by stealing some idols from here.[153] But when quarrels took place between the Hindus and Christians, normally the latter had much to suffer. There were many quarrels between Hindus and Christians.[154]

In 1564 the inhabitants of Rachol, in Salcete, resisted conversions.[155] Angered by the missionary activity they burnt down a church and its images.[156] One of the reasons for the war in Salcete in 1577, was the ban on Hindu ceremonies and on building their temples.[157] The Hindus created other difficulties, like for instance delays in the entry and delivery of goods to the city, and threats of abandoning the land if their orphans were forcibly taken away for baptism.[158] However, the most famous case of violent resistance or disturbance happened in Cuncolim, in Salcete, in 1583.

Salcete, a territory under the Portuguese control since 1542, had sixty-six villages and around eighty thousand inhabitants. Two villages, Cuncolim and Assolna bordering the land of the Muslims, were inhabited by a daring Hindu population. They paid rent whenever they felt they should, and only after consulting their idols to the annoyance of the Portuguese authority. Moreover, they also continued to build temples, despite a banning-order, and refused to give up their idolatry. For a long time the missionaries found it impossible to convert them.[159] The Hindus, besides opposing and challenging the priests, used to join hands with the Muslims against the Portuguese and destroy churches in Salcete.[160] It was only when the viceroy, D. Constantino de Bragança, began bestowing some favours on the inhabitants of Salcete that the missionaries could make a few conversions.[161]

On one occasion in 1567, when the community of Loutolim disobeyed Diogo Rodrigues, the captain of Rachol fort in Salcete, he ordered his soldiers to burn a temple in this village. The local community appealed to the Portuguese authority against the captain, who was judged guilty and made to re-build the temple.[162] But the temple was never re-built as a decree forbidding the re-building of temples came to light then.[163] Consequently, the viceroy, D. Antão de Noronha (1564-1568), ordered Diogo Rodrigues to burn down all the remaining temples he could find in Salcete. In 1567, when the Hindus were unaware of the viceroy's plans, the captain with a good number of soldiers destroyed two hundred temples without giving them any chance to protect the temples. After this incident the number of Christians grew to twelve thousand, and the missionaries felt more encouraged.[164]

After the destruction of the temples, the Hindus offered to the viceroy, D. António de Noronha (1571-1573), a huge amount of money to obtain permission to re-build them. They almost had it but for the Jesuit priests whom the Hindus hated and held responsible for conversions and the destruction of their temples.[165] They eventually implored to the king and to the Tribunal of the Inquisition for permission to re-build their temples. Needless to say that the Hindus did not have the much-sought permission, because the missionaries accused them of resorting to false statements in their petition. Further, the missionaries argued that if the Hindus in Salcete had some concessions others would ask them too, and what had been achieved with much pain would be lost easily.[166] The affected Hindus held the Jesuit priest, Afonso Pacheco, responsible for the ban on Hindu customs.

The Hindus could not react openly against the missionaries, but they took every opportunity to destroy the churches and residences of the priests with the help of the Muslims, when the Adilshah invaded Salcete. In 1578-79, there was another war between the Portuguese and the Muslims.[167] After the war, with the establishment of peace, the Hindus and Christians returned to Salcete and the activity of conversion proceeded normally. The churches were reconstructed but the Hindus went on burning them down.[168]

Five villages in Salcete (Assolna, Cuncolim, Veroda, Velim, Ambelim) neighbouring the Muslim territory continued to refuse to pay tribute to the Portuguese. They re-built the temples again and conducted their festivals and rituals publicly without permission. The viceroy, Francisco Mascarenhas (1581-1584), wanting to teach them a lesson ordered the destruction of all the temples they had re-built, together with some houses and fields, without giving them any possibility to defend themselves. Fr. Pedro Berno, also a Jesuit, was present when the temples were brought down, and he himself destroyed many idols with his own hands.[169] The Hindus had not yet forgotten the past events, and the Brahmans, who with the destruction of the temples and idols had lost their honour and privileges, took the opportunity to instigate the population by reminding them of the many offences committed against their gods.[170]

In 1583 Fr. Rudolfo Aquaviva, as the chief of the mission, together with four more Jesuits received orders from their superior to go to Salcete to maintain law and order and to effect more conversions. They also planned to erect more churches. They chose Cuncolim village to make their first survey of the situation. Rudolfo Aquaviva, Afonso Pacheco, Francisco António, Pedro Berno and Brother Francisco Arana (some of them mentioned earlier), together with some local Christians went to Cuncolim. They found this village as an ideal place to build a church.[171] The Hindus, on perceiving the intentions of the missionaries and remembering the injuries inflicted upon them and their idols, threw themselves like

hungry wolves on the priests standing there like lambs, killing them and the local Christians who had accompanied the priests.[172] R. Aquaviva and his companions were killed because they wanted to convert the Hindus, destroy their temples and build churches here, reported another Jesuit missionary.[173] One of the villages was depopulated for some years, because their inhabitants had gone to reside in the land of the Muslims. They held on so stubbornly to their idolatry and would not hesitate to kill those who came to convert them; but surprisingly, one day, they themselves invited the missionaries to teach them the Christian doctrine.[174] Conversions increased to twenty thousand in Salcete in 1588.

There were some unresolved issues regarding ownership rights of disputed lands between the old residents (*gaunkars*) and the late Hindu settlers in the villages. The latter accused the former of usurping their properties. This issue would certainly be settled in favour of those who converted, and if so we cannot exclude the possibility of many *gaunkars* and non-*gaunkars* becoming Christians only to retain the disputed lands. Conversions increased astronomically so-much-so that in some villages one could hardly see a Hindu. Salcete counted more than thirty thousand Christians and thirteen churches in 1596.[175] We have also an information stating that till 1607 a great part of Salcete had not yet been converted.[176]

Surprisingly, some Christians turned hostile towards the Portuguese. The missionaries explained that this behaviour was mainly due to the fact that the Portuguese had conquered their lands and also to the arrogance or lack of Christian humility among the Portuguese themselves, and towards the locals.[177] The local Christians hated the conquerors of their lands, because the former were not yet strong in their faith, so judged the Portuguese, and they wished that the Adilshah could re-conquer it.[178] Curiously, a local Christian chief together with some Hindus had planned to kill all the rector priests residing in Bardez in 1614. However, an elderly lady discovered the plot in time and denounced them to a rector. The priests could hardly believe that even the local Christians harboured such ill-feelings against them.[179] And the proud Portuguese oppressed the poor Christians in Bardez, Salcete and the islands, and the latter cried for justice.[180]

From what has been said so far about conversions in Goa, we can conclude that they did not seem to have been a smooth affair. The Hindus resisted and reacted obstinately against any initiative of conversion. Conversions created turmoil among the Hindus, hence they had to be effected after taking all the necessary precautions, and at times in total secrecy. In Salcete, the Hindu priests in particular and the Hindus in general sought to destroy at all costs everything that the missionaries had achieved, including dishonouring and persecuting the new converts. The Hindus shunned the Christians to the extent of not offering them a glass of water even in case of extreme necessity. It was necessary, therefore, to build a hospital there for the Christians, now considered as outcastes by the Hindu community. Such was the hatred that the Hindus felt against the law of God and those who received it, so the missionaries believed.[181] Hence, their discourse presented the Brahmans as the main obstacle to conversions, the Muslims as fanatics, and the Hindu peasants as an easy lot to be converted, and still easier to be deceived by their own religious leaders.[182]

It must be evident to all that the Goan Hindus reacted against the missionary interference subtlely and overtly. But so did other peoples, victims of the Portuguese policy of forced conversions. Goa in particular and India in general did display a developed cultural and religious identity, but it was not simply for this reason that people had reacted against forced conversions. For instance, in West Africa, Congo, Guiné, S. Tomé and Príncipe the missionaries had also faced great opposition from one group or other. The local kings or chieftains by accepting the religion of the powerful — in our case Christianity — could attain commercial and political advantage over their local rivals, and consequently they could achieve the desired objectives. Likewise, if the Portuguese denied them support, the locals did show feelings of hostility towards any move to convert them.[183] The Angolans resisted conversions until the Portuguese permitted them to trade in 1560.[184] There were moments in the history of Japan when it was contrary to their ancestral customs or forbidden by the local military rulers to preach the gospel there, hence the missionaries were kept out from Japan.[185]

Local internal conflicts were not absent in Goa. Conflicts between two or rather three élite groups — the missionaries, *fidalgos* and landed Hindus — each one seeking dominance and fulfilment of their ambitions decided conversion policies too. However, for a thorough study on conversions it is not enough to assume the interests of these rival groups and keep the rest of the people, local peasants and lower castes, out in the dark. Unfortunately, missionary historiography has given prominence to the élite groups and hardly any attention to the rest. The missionary documentation, by and large, attributed most religious and social resistance to the high castes; whereas, the peasants were seen as more receptive to conversions but, at the same time, more naturally inclined to superstitions and syncretic practices. It may be true that the caste people resisted their own conversion and that of the others much more aggressively than the masses; however, more work needs to be done in this area in order to arrive at a more convincing argument.

## Impediments

The missionaries called 'impediment' or 'inconvenience' every planned local resistance to their work of conversion. These terms could also signify all kinds of difficulties the missionaries encountered in the field, which could be either due to the unpleasant situations created by the Portuguese themselves or to the deficient state laws, resulting in lack of conversions. I have used the same terminology to describe several hurdles in the path of the missionaries.

The ignorance of the blacks, as the Indians were called, their lack of reasoning power, their idolatry and superstitions, attachment to laws and customs of their ancestors made it extremely difficult to convince them about the truth of the Christian religion.[186] Their idolatry, which prompted them to adore sticks and stones, blinded their reasoning. Generally, each family had its own private deity or idol.[187] Some Hindus adored a kind of man with some peculiar qualities and others adored animals, like oxen, elephants, etc., according to the favours they received from them or the dangers they had been protected from. Apart from these private idols, the Hindus had a few others in common, namely, the gods of War, Sowing, Fortune, Life, Death and the supreme god, whom they adored in several forms with offerings of rice, goats, sheep and other sort of things, to protect them and their properties. All these things created by the demon constituted serious obstacles.[188] All these idols had their own temples, priests and their annual solemn festivities.[189] It was inconvenient to tolerate such Hindu ceremonies and rituals, for they reminded the converts of their earlier life. Hence, these activities should be forbidden in public, but if they should be performed, they had to be conducted privately and with moderation.[190]

The presence of Brahmans and a large number of Hindu priests, who tirelessly taught the people about their religion, constituted another serious impediment to conversions. Further, the over two hundred temples in Salcete was also an impediment to reckon with.[191] These Brahmans and the village chiefs prevented the missionaries from entering the villages to preach the gospel, and the locals showed themselves so obstinate, that even with great efforts only a few were converted. The task of preserving the faith of the converts was still more difficult. From 1560 the overzealous viceroy, D. Constantino de Bragança, took this matter into his hands. He forcibly removed all the impediments against conversion, changing radically that situation. Henceforth, with the viceroy's favours and support, two thousand Hindus accepted baptism and five churches were built in Salcete.[192]

When the rich and the noble Hindus converted they became poor and the others scoffed at them. They lost everything they possessed. Likewise, the Hindu merchants lost their business after becoming Christians.[193] Even the Portuguese held them in contempt for losing their previous influence and prestige.[194] The greed exhibited by some Portuguese laymen to quickly acquire riches for themselves was another impediment; their licentious life was the despair of the missionaries. But the behaviour and attitude of the Portuguese towards the locals was harmless when compared with that of the Muslims.[195]

The rich and powerful Muslim merchants, who had settled in Goa for commerce and trading, persuaded and forced its inhabitants to embrace Islam, and they harassed mercilessly those who became Christians. Mosques had been built all over the island of Goa.[196] The synagogues, mosques and temples holding their public festivals weakened Christendom. They lowered the image of the Christians and the prestige of the Portuguese in the East.[197] However, the Portuguese laymen preferred the local Muslims and Hindus to Christians, because they traded without any sense of ethics. They had also links with their rich relatives living outside Goa. When they became Christians they were of no use to the Portuguese, since their relatives refused to have any dealings with them. The converts and the missionaries had constant communication among them, hence the missionaries could have a firm control over the behaviour and conscience of the Christians.[198]

The main inconvenience to conversions was the undue importance the Portuguese gave to the Hindus and Muslims residing in the Portuguese-controlled territories. Due to the decisive role that they played in the economy of the state, the Portuguese permitted them to live according to their rituals and idolatry. The converts came inevitably under their influence to the extent of losing the little they had learnt.[199]

The Portuguese created difficulties and opposed the work of conversion by accusing the priest of using force to make converts. The former complained that in forcing one Hindu to convert, the missionaries scandalized one thousand Portuguese.[200] The Portuguese, especially the chiefs of the villages, forced the poor Hindus to work on their lands, however, after their conversion they could not be exploited so easily, observed the missionaries.[201]

It was inconvenient to show undue interest in the conversion of the Hindus or to want to convert them with favours; for instance, by acquitting and satisfying them, since after becoming Christians they normally repented of their decision. It was also improper to convert Hindus by depriving them of their respect, honour and privileges, for this was tantamount to coercing them to embrace the Christian faith. The consequences of such conversions were often quick relapses. The missionaries needed to keep in mind the need for moderation at the time of making conversions.[202]

It was also contentious to give Christian food to the Hindus who asked for baptism, in order to make them lose their caste immediately and to hasten their conversion. They suffered shame from their relatives who forced some of them to return to Hinduism. Even the old Christians, despite being charged guilty in the *autos-da-fé* for apostatizing, did not show signs of a strong faith. Hence, it was suggested that the Hindus should remain free or without losing caste until the moment of their baptism.[203]

Demanding taxes from Christians was an unfortunate inconvenience.[204] When the parish priests visited the new converts, the former fined the latter for their own profit. This scandalized the Christians and made the Hindus laugh and mock, saying that the neo-converts had gained nothing; rather they were obliged to pay now what they did not as Hindus. Since the people were poor and miserable this was no small impediment to conversions.[205]

Group baptisms with a large number of people proved to be very inconvenient, since the people taking part in them were ill-prepared religiously due to the hurry in conducting these baptisms. Consequently, individual baptisms were recommended at the church of the village where they resided.[206] The missionaries perceived that the lack of churches in the villages created several inconveniences to the neo-converts. They did not attend the Christian instruction and mass, if they had to walk a good distance, for they were lazy.[207]

Lack of priests and the difficulty in learning the local language, together with the scarcity of funds to maintain the priests, slowed down the work of conversion.[208] The parish priests could not help the poor Christians because they did not have a fixed income.[209] The presence of only a few white priests was another drawback, since the Indians themselves did not accept the native clergymen.[210]

The Muslims also made attempts to convert the Hindus. These proselytizers came from Mecca, Persia and from many other parts to confuse and convert the poor Hindus.[211] The Muslim sailors and others working in the Portuguese ships, tried to make proselytes wherever they went. These new Muslim converts joined with the Muslim rulers and could pose a serious danger to the Portuguese.[212] Further, the greatest inconvenience was that Hindu or Muslim local rulers refused to accept baptism; they prevented their vassals from embracing Christianity too. It was of no use making Christians in territories ruled by Hindus and Muslims, since the former could hardly remain firm in their faith. Here the Christians soon relapsed.[213]

Despite all these 'impediments' and 'inconveniences' the kings of Portugal had two good means at their disposal to help conversions: one was of preparing religious for the missions in the college at Coimbra in Portugal; and of sending more Jesuits here, since they were the fittest for this kind of activity. The Franciscans, Dominicans and Augustinians, also virtuous religious men, despite their cloistered rules could be useful too. The other means was of helping the catechumens with baptismal dresses, bestowing many privileges on the Christians and disfavouring the Hindus by means of legislation. However, the best of all the means would be of sending pious viceroys, like D. Constantino de Bragança.[214] Unfortunately, there was a lack of almost everything necessary to sustain the work of conversion.[215]

## Conclusion

It is not enough to be simply critical of conversion policies if we want to understand impartially the affair of conversion in the Goan society that was undergoing a rapid transformation. Making conversions was neither easy nor without grave reactions and impediments. These reactions and impediments created mixed responses to the activity of conversion, which at times forced some changes in the official stand. Further, even the reception of the new religion by the locals left many missionaries unsatisfied. Continuity and change in, and resistance and impediment to, the work of conversion can be useful to re-construct a more realistic story of the reception and rejection of Christianity in Goa. Many were converted but many others were 'confused' and even 'conquered', but not at all 'convinced' when the missionaries tried to persuade or force them to accept the Christian faith.[216]

The converts were often criticized, not only for their weak Christian faith and devotion — they did not abandon their ancestral customs once for all after their conversion as demanded by Christendom — but also for not 'appearing' or not having the manners of European citizens.[217] Catholic Europe needed centuries to get rid of its syncretic practices, and in spite of serious efforts many condemned practices continued to persist among them, whereas the Goan converts were made to change their traditional customs immediately. The belief that the missionaries entertained, namely, that the second generation of local Christians would be of superior quality turned out to be illusory for the former themselves.[218] The next chapter deals with syncretic practices in the life of the neo-converts, or with 'inconsistencies' or 'relapses' as the missionaries used to call them.

## NOTES AND REFERENCES

1. Tenure of this ruler in Goa.
2. ARSI, *Miscellaneum Indiarum Orientalum*, 38 - II, fl. 281.
3. Georg Schurhammer, *Francisco Javier. Su Vida y su Tiempo*, Vol. II, p. 239.
4. Conde de Ficalho, *Garcia da Orta e o seu Tempo*, p. 172.
5. It would be interesting to know what happened to the priests, temple girls and many menial servants after the destruction of the temples, but unfortunately we have hardly any information on this.
6. Georg Schurhammer, *op. cit.*, p. 296.
7. *DI*, I, 66-68.
8. *Ibid.*, 764.
9. *Neiqebary* was a village administrator or captain of native troops. Sebastião Rodolfo Dalgado, *Glossário Luso-Asiático*, II, p. 104.
10. *Doc*, I, 154.
11. Paulo da Trindade, *op. cit.*, Part 1, p. 284.
12. António da Silva Rego, *História das Missões do Padroado Português do Oriente*, p. 251.

13. *Jogue* (*yogi*) was an ascetic or a mendicant and penitent Hindu who went about scantily dressed. He used to cover his body with ashes and kept long hair. Sebastião Rodolfo Dalgado, *op. cit.*, I, p. 515.
14. António da Silva Rego, *História das Missões do Padroado Português do Oriente*, p. 251.
15. *Doc*, I, 354.
16. *Ibid.*
17. *DI*, IV, 801-02. In 1518, "Os jogues que qua chaman pobres deve Vossa Alteza mandar que da terra firme non entrem na ilha, porque estes trazem bulas e reliquias dos seos pagodes e diabos, com que tornam a restaurar toda jentilidade destes homens." *Doc*, I, 354.
18. A report from the bishop of Dume to the king in 1522, "Acerca dos vizinhos de Goa tem em a ilha seos pagodes ordenados com as figuras do inimigo da Cruz, em estatuas e fazem suas festas cada ano honde vay muita genta cristãa, asi dos nossos como dos cristãos novos da terra, que é causa mui errada em lhe iren favorecer sua ydolatria." *Ibid.*, 425.
19. "Serviço de Deus seria nesta soo ilha de Goa destruyrem se estes pagodes e fazerem neles igrejas com santos, e quem quer que quizese viver na ilha fose cristão e teria suas terras e casas, como tem, e nam querendo, que se fose da ilha. Crea Vosa Alteza que nam ficaria nenhuma creatura que se nam tornase a fe de Cristo Noso Senhor, porque nam tem outro modo de viver tyrados da ilha, e que estes nam fosem bons cristãos, os filhos ho seriam, e tirar se ya esta ma contumancia deles e nam aviam de leixar o certo por o incerto e Deus seria servido e Vosa Alteza, por ser cousa de salvaçam de tanta gente perdida; que eles nam tem nenhuma dificuldade em se tornarem cristãos, somente por respeito dos parentes pasados e pelo custume antiguo, que eles nam crem nem adoram nada e sam doces de mover, mas creo que se nam tornam por que nos vem de mao viver, e nam fazemos o que preegamos. Se bem parecer a Vosa Alteza, podeo mandar fazer que sera grande serviço de Deus." Report from the bishop of Dume to the king. January 1522. *Ibid.*, 452-53.
20. *DI*, VI, 619.
21. *Bullarium*, Second Provincial Council, Acc. 2, dec. 5, p. 48.
22. *DI*, VIII, 341.
23. *Doc*, III, 13.
24. *DI*, XV, 656.

25. *Doc*, I, 354.
26. *Ibid.*, IV, 176.
27. *Ibid.*, 167-68.
28. *Thanadar* was a captain of a military fort, a village judge, a tax-collector of a village or custom house. Sebastião Rodolfo Dalgado, *op. cit.*, II, p. 351.
29. Fernão Mendes Pinto, *The Travels of Mendes Pinto*, p. 469.
30. *DI*, IX, 305.
31. *Ibid.*, XV, 656. Paulo da Trindade, *op. cit.*, p. 284. "Ha maes nesta ilha huma casta de jemte que se chamam bramenes synaes muyto contrairos a fee. E nam somente se nam comvertem eles mas em quamto podem, estorvam a comversam, dos outros e sostemtam este erro da gemtilidade. Sam muyto prejudiçaes a todo bom estado da repruvica, invemtores de todos os maos arbitres, dos quaes em tempo de trabalho nam avemos de esperar lealdade, porque esta tem aos Mouros e a nos atreiçam como se vio por experiemcia na guerra, que com a terra firme se teve em tempo de Nuno da Cunha. E isto nam per vertude, que se a tiverem, comnosco a devião usar, senam tudo favorecendo seu interesse." Report from Miguel Vaz to king, D. João III, on the *Estado da India*. Évora, November 1545. *Doc*, III, 202-04.
32. Sebastião Gonçalves, *Primeira Parte da História dos Religiosos da Companhia de Jesus e do que fizeram com a divina Graça na Conversão dos Infieis na nossa Sancta Fé Catholica nos Reynos e Provincias da India Oriental*, Vol. I, p. 99.
33. *DI*, XIV, 902.
34. Archilles Meersman, *The Ancient Franciscan Provinces in India 1500-1835*, p. 158, footnote no. 27.
35. "...;e como o intento a conversão dos infieis fosse o que mais obrigava a ElRey nosso senhor a conquistar estas partes da India, tendo já conquistada esta ilha de Goa, e os moradores della quietos, e seguros na sua vassalagem, querendo pôr em effeito esta sua tenção tão sancta, sendo informado que muitos destes moradores erão já christãos, e os outros estavão firmes na crença de sua gentilidade por se consentir que fizessem seus ritos e cerimonias nos pagodes que adoravão, mandou que os ditos paguodes fossem derribados, e os não ouvesse em toda a ilha de Goa e seus termos, nem se consentisse ao gentio fazer nas terras de seu senhorio nenhuma cerimonia gentilica, pera com este rigor the misericordia os obrigar

a se esquecerem do culto gentilico, e se converterem a nossa santa fé, como tinhão feito e fazião muitos que já erão convertidos, e em comprimento desta tão santa obra se desfizerão e derribarão os ditos paguodes no anno de quarenta." *APO*, 5, p. 171, footnote.

36. ARSI, *Eppistolae Goana et Malabarica*, 10 - II, fl. 320.
37. *Doc*, II, 343.
38. *Memória Histórico Eclesiastica da Archidiocese de Goa*, p. 105.
39. ARSI, *Eppistolae Goana et Malabarica*, 10 - I, fl. 3.
40. "Dareis as cartas que levais à gente dessa ilha de Goa, assym christãos como gentios, aos quaes da minha parte encommendareis que sejam bons christãos os já convertidos e os outros que se converterão; ... ; e o mesmo cuidado tereis das terras firmes, trabalhando como, mais sem escandalo poder ser, se tire toda a idolatria dellas como escrevo ao Guovernador que se faça, pondo logo cruzes nos lugares que bem parecer e onde com muitta reverencia poderem estar e quem ensine quaesquer que já forem convertidos e trabalhe por converter outros." Instructions from D. João III to the vicar-general, Miguel Vaz, regarding Christendom in India. Almeirim, 5 March 1546. *Doc*, III, 261.
41. Others even suggested that the bishop of Goa, D. João de Albuquerque poisoned Miguel Vaz. Letter of Cosme Anes to the king regarding conversions in India. Bassein, 30 November 1547. CEHU, *As Gavetas da Torre do Tombo*, IV, p. 414. *Doc*, III, 533. ARSI, *Miscellaneum Indiarum Orientalum*, 38 - I, fl. 137v.
42. *APO*, 5, Part I, doc. 111, p. 223; doc. 195, p. 319.
43. *Doc*, X, 293.
44. *Ibid.*, V, 297.
45. Letter from Manuel Nunes to the queen of Portugal, D. Catarina, in 1552. *Ibid.*, VI, 297. Simão Botelho de Andrade the sixth chief revenue superintendent (*Vedor da Fazenda*) of Portuguese India wrote to D. João III in 1552, accusing religious members stationed in Goa of spending a lot of money and giving large alms at the cost of the royal treasury. He alleged that some of these religious wanted to make Christians by force to the extent of severely threatening the Hindus. Though he added that everything those religious did was out of zeal, he also suggested that they could use means other than violent ones, which caused many Hindus to abandon Goa. J. Mendes Almeida, *Simão Botelho de Andrade*, pp. 27, 105. CEHU, *Gavetas da Torre do Tombo* V, p. 320.

46. *Doc*, V, 298.
47. *DI*, I, 780.
48. *Ibid.*, X, 742.
49. *DI*, VI, 314; IV, 327.
50. *Ibid.*, XV, 541.
51. *Doc*, IX, 250.
52. *DI*, II, 114. *Doc*, V, 356.
53. *DI*, XVII, 384.
54. *Ibid.*, III, 576.
55. *Ibid.*, 719.
56. *Ibid.*, 354.
57. Francisco de Souza, *OCJC*, pp. 133-34.
58. *Doc*, XI, 819. *DI*, III, 402-09.
59. *Doc*, XII, 819-20.
60. Francisco de Souza, *op. cit.*, p. 133. "Tres coisas que para o bem da christandade estavam proibidas pelo rei, bispo e prelados e Francisco Barreto governador as concedeu outra vez aos brahmanes que sao os mores contrarios que ca temos para a conversão dos infieis e conservação dos convertidos. A todos os religiosos se nos quebrou muyto animo... porque consentia o que ja era prohibido sendo idolatrias e muy grandes offensas a Deus.

    A prymeira he que costumavão estes bramenes depois de mortos queymarem se aas suas portas e as molheres delles se queymavão vivas com grandes cerimonias e idolatrias. Isto ha vinte anos que he prohibido e sendo jaa cousa tão esquecida lho concedeo de novo Francisco Barreto. 2ª que costumavão os bramanes quando se casavão fazer grandes idolatrias e pagodes isto sendo tambem prohibido agora lho concedeo. 3ª Ha aqui hua provisão de Sua Alteza que o cativo do gentio ou mouro que se fizer christão fique forro pollo qual recebião muytos nossa fé. Agora concedeo Francisco Barreto que fazendo se os taes cativos christãos se vendeseem em leilão e o dinheiro que nelles se fizesse dessem ao infiel cuhos cativo eram." "Os Franciscanos, Dominicanos e Jesuitas queriam escrever ao rei sobre este assunto mas os Franciscanos e Dominicanos arrependeramse." Letter from Fr. Baltazar Dias, rector of the College of St Paul. CEHU, *As Gavetas da Torre do Tombo*, V, p. 71.
61. See the decrees issued against the Gentiles by the governor, Francisco Barreto. Sebastião Gonçalves, *op. cit.*, pp. 324-26. Alessandro Valignano, *op. cit.*, p. 369.

62. Maria Benedita Araújo, "O «Pay dos Christãos». Contribuição para o estudo da Cristianização da India", p. 306.
63. *DI*, IV, 9.
64. Alessandro Valignano, *op. cit.*, p. 360.
65. *DI*, IV, 201.
66. *Ibid.*, V, 657.
67. Sebastião Gonçalves, *op. cit.*, pp. 25, 349-51, 423ff.
68. *Doc*, VIII, 52.
69. *Ibid.*, VII, 284-86.
70. *Ibid.*, VIII, 28.
71. *Ibid.*, 39.
72. *Ibid.*, 40-42. *APO*, 5, Part I, doc. 304, p. 410; doc 344, p. 457; doc 349, p. 454; doc 353, p. 458.
73. Ana Cannas da Cunha, *A Inquisição no Estado da India. Origens. (1539-1560)*, p. 249.
74. Alessandro Valignano, *op. cit.*, p. 370.
75. *APO*, 5, Part II, doc. 391, p. 488.
76. *Ibid.*, 5, Part I, doc. 285, p. 381; doc. 286, p. 383; doc. 287, p. 385; doc. 288, p. 386; doc 289, p. 387; doc. 290, p. 388; doc. 291, p. 390; doc. 292, p. 392.
77. *DI*, IV, 743.
78. *Ibid.*, 645.
79. *Ibid.*, 320.
80. *Doc*, VII, 352-53.
81. One day a religious Brother went to the house of a Brahman. After the former introduced himself and revealed his intention or the purpose of his visit, the latter said that there could not have been a more appropriate moment for Jesus Christ to enter his house and the demon to leave it. Luis de Guzman, *Historia de las Misiones de la Compania de Jesus en la India Oriental, en la China y Japon, 1540-1600*, p. 59. An old Brahman who had served in the temple for more than forty years sought permission from the priests to work for the church till the end of his life as a way of doing penance for the years wasted in serving the demons in their temples. *Ibid.*
82. *Ibid.*, p. 58.
83. *Ibid.*
84. *DI*, VI, 332.
85. *Doc*, VIII, 160.

86. ARSI, *Miscellaneum Indiarum Orientalum*, 38 - II, fl. 283. "A crystandade seja o Senhor louvado vay muyto avante. No modo della ouve algumas desordens que logo como cheguei se remedearão e se fazem christãos como devem e a Igreja manda.

    Este ano soo nesta ilha se converterão duas mil almas. Avera nesta cidade ao menos 4343 vizinhos dos quaes são portugueses 1478 e mistiços 145 os mais são da terra. No termo da cidade e suas aldeas ha 7025 vizinhos. De maneira que avera nesta ilha somente doze mil vexinhos christãos não entrando soldados e ao menos avera oitaenta mil almas christaãs. Esperamos no Senhor que mediante o fervor e cuidado de vossa Alteza que cedo não avera gentio nesta ilha. Letter from the archbishop of Goa to the king in 1561. CEHU, *As Gavetas da Torre do Tombo*, III, p. 190.
87. *DI*, IV, 318.
88. Alessandro Valignano, *op. cit.*, p. 362.
89. *Ibid.*, p. 370.
90. *Ibid.*, pp. 433-34.
91. *APO*, 5, Part I, doc. 285, p. 381; doc. 292, p. 392. *Ibid.*, 5, Part II, doc. 391, p. 488.
92. António d'Almeida Azevedo, *As Communidades de Goa. História das Instituições Antigas*, p. 154. *APO*, 5, Part II, doc. 391, p. 488.
93. *DI*, VI, 71.
94. *Ibid.*, V, 227-29.
95. Letter from Nunes Barreto to the superior-general of the Society of Jesus, Fr. Diego Lainez. Cochin, 1562. *Ibid.*, 485.
96. Alessandro Valignano, *op. cit.*, pp. 433-34. Fr. Mechior Nunes Barreto, a Jesuit rector in Cochin, wrote to his superior-general in Rome in 1562 that due to many conversions, many vested interests and illicit ambitions of the Portuguese were being frustrated. Because of this unpleasant situation some affected Portuguese began saying that conversions were made by force, and others that the money of the king was being spent on the negroes, and a few others reported that forced conversions caused the locals to migrate, which greatly harmed the crown revenue. *Ibid.*, footnote no. 59.
97. António d'Almeida Azevedo, *op. cit.*, p. 156. *APO*, 5, Part II, doc. 472, p. 543. *Ibid.*, 6, Supp. II, p. 1. Alessandro Valignano, *op. cit.*, p. 434. Cristovão Pinto, *As Gancarias de Gôa, Questões Indianas* I, p. 53.
98. *DI*, VI, 122f ; IV, 489-90, 650-51.

99. Alessandro Valignano, *op. cit.*, p. 435.
100. António d'Almeida Azevedo, *op. cit.*, p. 156. Alessandro Valignano, *op. cit.*, p. 434.
101. *APO*, 5, Part II, doc. 556, p. 602.
102. *Doc*, X, 69.
103. *Ibid.*, 20.
104. *Ibid.*, 288ff.
105. António Pinto Pereira, *História da India no Tempo em que a Governou o Visorei Dom Luís de Ataíde*, p. 27. Casimiro Cristovão de Nazareth, "Mitras Lusitanas no Oriente", pp. 186, 189, 191. See how the destruction of the temples and idols took place in Bardez and Salcete. *Doc*, X, 288-89.
106. *APO*, 5, Part II, doc. 575, p. 612.
107. António Pinto Pereira, *op. cit.*, p. 32.
108. *DI*, XIV, 922.
109. António Pinto Pereira, *op. cit.*, pp. 33-37. *DI*, IX, 277. M. J. Gabriel de Saldanha, *Historia de Goa*, Vol. I, pp. 122-23.
110. C. Alonso, "Nueva documentación inédita sobre las misiones agustinianas en la India y en Persia (1571-1609)", p. 314.
111. *Doc*, X, 73, 104.
112. *DI*, XII, 254.
113. *Ibid.*, 74-75.
114. *Doc*, XI, 294.
115. António d'Almeida Azevedo, *op. cit.*, p. 161. *APO*, 5, Part II doc. 425, p. 512; doc. 768, p. 891; doc. 773, p. 899; doc. 775, p. 901; doc. 776, p. 902; doc. 777, p. 903; doc. 781, p. 910.
116. *DI*, X, 278, 285; V, 168; VII, 99, 131.
117. *Ibid.*, 285-89.
118. *Ibid.*, 538.
119. *Ibid.*, 425f.
120. *Doc*, XII, 469.
121. *Ibid.*, 453.
122. Paulo da Trindade, *op. cit.*, p. 307.
123. In 1599, "Ouve este ano o cuidado da conservação de virtude, e aumento della e guarda das regras. Não se converteram muitos christãos inda que ouve bom numero. A causa de se não converterem tantos, como os outros anos passados foi que agora não batizamos senão os que pedem com grande vontade. O que agora fazem os

Pes. he terem grande cuidado em doutrinar e ensinar os convertidos. E agora se vêm grande fruito nos já convertidos e que até agora parece não faziam conceito das coisas de nossa fé o que agora se vem e apalpa claramente o qual fructo se ve nas confissões. Porque como dantes se ocupavão mais os padres em converter, que em ensinar, havia muito falta na cultivação dos christãos que agora himos suprindo." ARSI, *Eppistolae Goana et Malabarica*, 14, fl. 402.

124. *MR*, 3A, fl. 209.
125. *BFUP*, No. 15, , pp. 532-34. "It is a great mistake to build so many churches and monasteries and to spend so much money on the clergy and monks in the name of charity and Christian zeal." A. de S. S. Costa Lobo, (ed.), *Memórias de Um Soldado da India*, p. 192. This was not a criticism of conversions, rather he preferred this money to be used for military defence in the *Estado da India*.
126. *DI*, XV, 545-46.
127. *Ibid.*, XVI, 179.
128. António d'Almeida Azevedo, *op. cit.*, p. 161.
129. ARSI, *Eppistola Goana et Malabarica*, 15, fl. 174.
130. *Doc*, VII, 284.
131. *APO*, 1, Part II, p. 97. Pe. Nuno Roiz contratou com os gentios de Goa que lhe averia perdão geral do Visorey e Arcebispo de todas as idolatrias e cerimonias de então cometidas se dessem 1000 pardaos de renda cada ano para os catecumenos, mas não querendo elles serão também... para o futuro, concordou em que não serião castigados por se acharem nos pagodes da terra firme, tirando nas festas deles. ARSI, *Goana Historia*, 33 - I, fl. 32v.
132. BNL, *Reservados*, Cod. 866, fl. 12v.
133. *DI*, XVI, 10.
134. *Ibid.*, 178.
135. *Ibid.*, XV, 647, 737.
136. *APO*, 3, Part I, doc. 140, p. 175.
137. *Ibid.*, pp. 569-79.
138. ARSI, *Epistolae Goana*, 9 - I, fl. 8.
139. C. Alonso, "op. cit.", pp. 381-82.
140. *Ibid.*, p. 382.
141. Francisco de Souza, *op. cit.*, p. 193.
142. ARSI, *Miscellanea Indiarum Orientalium*, 38 - I, fl. 137.
143. *DI*, XI, 274-75, 322.

144. *APO*, 5, Part I, doc. 75, pp. 161ff.
145. *Ibid.*
146. Luís de Guzman, *op. cit.*, p. 59.
147. Francisco de Souza, *op. cit.*, pp. 157-58. A Brahman abandoned Goa with his family because he did not want to become a Christian. However, five years later, on knowing that his former neighbours in Goa had been converted, he returned and asked for baptism for himself and his family. ARSI, *Goana Historia*, 33 - I, fl. 75v.
148. Luis de Guzman, *op. cit.*, p. 60.
149. *Ibid.*
150. Paulo da Trindade, *op. cit.*, p. 325.
151. *Ibid.*, p. 286.
152. *Doc*, VIII, 421, 485.
153. *DI*, V, 358-59.
154. *Ibid.*, XI, 13. AN / TT, *CC* I, Maço 81, doc. 116.
155. *DI*, VI, 258-59.
156. *Doc*, XI, 790.
157. *DI*, X, 892, 964.
158. *Ibid.*, XIV, 298.
159. In Salcete in 1576 the Hindus were hiding their idols in the soil and making their offerings and ceremonies secretly in spite of a royal prohibition . *Ibid.*, VII, 62-63; X, 469. *APO*, 5, Part I, p. 171, footnote in the doc. 75.
160. *DI*, XII, 919.
161. *Ibid.*, 918.
162. António d'Almeida Azevedo, *op. cit.*, p. 149. Francisco de Souza, *op. cit.*, pp. 832-33.
163. There was a provision (August 1566) forbidding the construction or re-building of the temples. António d'Almeida Azevedo, *op. cit.*, p. 150. *APO*, 5, Part II, doc. 576, p. 612.
164. António d'Almeida Azevedo, *op. cit.*, p. 150.
165. Luis de Guzman, *op. cit.*, p. 62. *DI*, X, 942; XI, 262, 563-69, 692.
166. *Ibid.*, 562-69. Luis de Guzman, *op. cit.*, p. 63.
167. *DI*, XII, 918. Salcete was under siege in 1570-71. *Ibid.*, IX, 303.
168. *Ibid.*, XII, 617.
169. *Ibid.*, 254-57, 920; XIII, 469. Regarding paying tribute, it was decided that what belonged to the king of Portugal either by conquest or otherwise were his tributaries. This led to several friendship

treaties and alliances with other peoples, and refusal could mean destruction of their lands and cities by the Portuguese. Luis de Guzman, *op. cit.*, p. 62.

170. *Ibid.*, p. 63.
171. *Ibid.*, p. 64.
172. *Ibid.*, pp. 65-66.
173. For a report on the killing of Rudolfo Aquaviva see *DI*, XII, pp. 918, 925, 930, 976 ff. Earlier Fr. Pero Berno, one of the five killed in Cuncolim, had accompanied the Portuguese soldiers who had punished the insurgents and destroyed their temples. *Ibid.*, 903. "Ha em Salsete de Goa huãs aldeias que estão nos confins das terras do Idalção anos moradores são vassalos de S. Magestade e as aldeas são foreiras, estes sendo gentios como ainda agora o são, sobre a paga dos foros se alevantarão por muitas vezes contra o estado da India não querendo pagar e matando alguns oficiais de El' rey que la iam arrecadar os ditos forros e os que se alevantaram erão tão notorios, que por algumas vezes se formou contra eles exercito assim por terra como por mar e foram destruidos e suas aldeias assoladas e seus palmares cortados pelos nossos soldados, e todos que dos moradores das ditas aldeas se podiam aver eram logo enforcados e mortos. Mas pazes foram feitas, mas alguns dias depois da paz, foram as ditas aldeias 5 Religiosos da Companhia que residiam em Salsete e alguns oficiais de Rei da mesmas terras e alguns christãos da terra, e os gentios das ditas aldeias, vendo os sem preceder causa alguma se amotinaram huns aos outros, e todas as aldeias; de comum consentimento tomaram armas e matarão todos aqueles religiosos, officiais, de El' rey, e christãos e ate os meninos que iam em companhia dos Padres, e a um dos religiosos levaram ferido, mas ainda vivo ao seu pagode, e porque o não quis adorar o assetearão e ficarão outra vez de guerra! Pelo que o V.rei Dom Francisco de Mascarenhas pondo alvara de editos pello qual os requeria que todo o que quissesse mostrar sem culpa viesse dar razão de sy a qual citação nenhum acudio pello que os ouve por banidos e seus bens confiscados por uma provisão sua e de novo mandou contra elles exercito, e lhes tomou as terras. Estes gentios se apartaram da fidelidade e obediencia do V.rey... e tendo feito paz tornaram a guerra cometendo tantos excessos contra a fé e obrigação de vassalos e subditos." ARSI, *Foundationes Goanae*, 22 - I, fls. 93, 98. "15 Junho 1583 o martirio dos Pes. de Cunculim, aldea que confina com aldeas de Assolná, Veli e Ambeli, foram confiscados

incorporados na Coroa e seus moradores entraram na morte dos Pes. e mais desaforos que cometeram juntamente com os de Cunculim e a esse respeito se levantarão e rebellarão contra o estado. Pello que o Visorey Dom Francisco Mascarenhas os mandou castigar matando os que pode aver as mãos destruir as aldeias e confiscallas pera El-Rey." ARSI, *Quaesti. Salsetana et aliae quaesti.*, (1587-1647), fl. 55.

174. Luís de Guzman, *op. cit.*, p. 67.
175. *Ibid.*
176. In 1607, "A grande parte de Salsete esta por converter e como Salsete esta visinha dos mouros temesse retrocederem, e os Pes. da Companhia muito vigilantes. Como as terras são fronteiras esta exposta a assaltos dos inimigos e corre o risco de queimarem igrejas como ja tem sido feito." ARSI, *Eppistolae Goana et Malabarica*, 16, fl. 128.
177. *Doc*, V, 440-41. Francisco de Souza, *op. cit.*, p. 42.
178. *Doc*, V, 437-38.
179. *Ibid.*, 438.
180. *Ibid.*, XI, 280.
181. Luís de Guzman, *op. cit.*, p. 61.
182. "Soo do povo desta ilha gentio lhe fazemos lenbrança, dentro do qual ha muita soma obstynados nesta sua sympleza, ho que causão alguns bramenes, pesoas honrradas antre eles, porque se cometem alguns deste povo gentio pera que se façam christãos, dizem que não ho hão de ser ate que estes honrrados se não fação, porquanto lhes dão mui maao trato e os correm muito e eles não ouzão de falar; são estes homens possantes antre eles pera esta obra e trabalhão muito pera que se não faça nenhum christão, mas antes trabalhão pelos sostentar em seus enganosos costumes e gentilidade, os quaes bramenes, se os lançasem fora da ilha, estaa muy certo o povo gerall ser mui facillmente convertido ha fee de Noso Senhor. E não abasta a estes bramenes impidirem ha esto povo que se não faça christão, mas antes ha pubriqua voz e fama que daneffição em outras cousas de muito peso, porque são mui odiosos." The Chapter of the Cathedral of Goa (*Cabido de Goa*) wrote to the king in 1547. *Doc*, III, 521.
183. António Custódio Gonçalves, "A Acção evangelizadora e cultural de Portugal no Congo (1491-1543)", pp. 565-78. António Ambrósio, "Alguns problemas da evangelização em África no século

XVI. D. Frei Gaspar Cão, OSA, Bispo de São Tomé (1554-1574)", pp. 501-63. Julieta Maria Aires de Almeida Araújo / Ernesto Jorge Oliveira dos Santos, "Os Portugueses e o Reino do Congo. Primeiros contactos", pp. 637-60. Conversions in Sumatra and Ceylon were not easy either. A. de S. S. Costa Lobo, (ed.), *op. cit.*, p. 233.

184. AN / TT, *CC* II, Maço 104, doc. 3.
185. *APO*, 3, p. 279.
186. *Doc.*, XI, 590.
187. Luís de Guzman, *op. cit.*, pp. Introduction.
188. *Doc*, VII, 327.
189. Luís de Guzman, *op. cit.*, p. 15.
190. ARSI, *Miscellanea Indiarum Orientalium*, 38 - I, fl. 139.
191. *Ibid.*, fl. 16.
192. *Ibid.*, fl. 61.
193. *Doc*, XI, 453.
194. *Ibid.*, 590.
195. ARSI, *Miscellanea Indiarum Orientalium*, 38 - I, fl. 138.
196. Luís de Guzman, *op. cit.*, pp. 15-16.
197. ARSI, *op. cit.*, fl. 39. *DI*, XII, 254.
198. *Ibid.*, 138.
199. *Ibid.*
200. A. Valignano wrote that those Portuguese who alleged the use of force in conversions, did so not because they were a very religious people, nor because they were concerned about the increase of the faith, for they were no better than the others as far as religion was concerned. Rather the real reason behind such allegations was that conversions gave the converts protection against their exploitation, which resulted in substantial losses to these Portuguese. The obstacles to conversions were the sins of the Portuguese and those who persecuted blindly the Christians, he added. *Doc*, XI, 588. "Acá se ha levantado un rumor que puede ser que aya ydo a las orejas de V. P., porque como se izesen en la ysla de Goa muchos gentiles christianos etos años pasados con gran trabajo y gasto de los nuestros Padres y favor del Viso-Rey Don Constantino, y con esta conversión de gentilidade tirase muchos yntereses y ganancias ilícitas a muchos purtugueses, alevantaran que se fazían en San Pablo por fuerça." *DI*, V, 484-85.
201. *Ibid.*, 592.

202. ARSI, *op. cit.*, fl. 138v.
203. *Ibid.*
204. *Ibid.*, fl. 138.
205. *Doc*, XI, 593ff.
206. ARSI, *op. cit.*, fl. 138v.
207. *Ibid.*
208. *Doc*, XI, 591.
209. ARSI, *op. cit.*, fl. 139.
210. *Ibid.*, fl. 138v.
211. *Doc*, VIII, 192.
212. ARSI, *op. cit.*, fl. 139.
213. *Ibid.*
214. ARSI, *op, cit.*, fls. 139-39v. The viceroy, D. Constantino de Bragança, said, "...aos quais como principe christianissimo, respodeo que mais queria, pera honra do mesmo estado real e gloria de Sua Alteza, a conversão do mais pobre canarim desta ilha, que o recheo das rendas della, e naos carregadas de pementa, e que tudo avia de aventurar polla salvação de huma alma..." *Doc*, VII, 328.
215. ARSI, *op. cit.*, fls. 139-39v.
216. *Doc*, VII, 256.
217. "Finalmente que se não é na Fé, em que têm muitas ocasiões para às vezes tropeçarem e afocinharem, mas em o mais receberem bem a cristandade e os costumes dela." Paulo da Trindade, *op. cit.*, p. 287.
218. José Mattoso, "Raízes da missionação portuguesa", p. 74.

# 9

# SYNCRETISM IN THE LIFE OF CONVERTS

## Relapses into *Gentilismo*

This chapter discusses the survival of pre-Christian customs, habits and religious practices in the life of the new converts. The neo-converts were strongly inclined to Hindu practices.[1] Drastic measures were taken and serious efforts were made to keep the neo-converts away from Hindu practices synonymous with idolatry and superstitions. A number of decrees and privileges in favour of conversion and even the Tribunal of the Inquisition itself speak for the preventive measures against relapses. The crown and the missionaries expected all Hindus to convert sooner or later, as favours and privileges were being offered to them to join the Lusitanian citizenry. When persuasion failed, no doubt, force became the rule either to make conversions or halt relapses.

It had been argued that the first generation of the local Christians were more inclined to relapses, but facts attest that even subsequent generations of converts were not free from syncretic practices. For the missionaries, good Christians or those who lived by the law of God,[2] were rather few during the sixteenth century and after, since "inconsistency was natural to the converts".[3] But the argument that relapses or syncretism were mainly a result of forced conversions is not totally true. Relapses were the result of a highly pluralist context in which the Christians lived. The absence of a clear and defined idea of Christian orthodoxy created

'inconsistencies'. For centuries Europe was not very different in this regard too.

We do not find the term 'syncretism' in the sixteenth century documentation, instead we find the term 'relapse' which connotes a similar reality. It is better to use both these terms here without any semantic difference. Syncretism and relapse, therefore, would mean in broad terms, a reconciliation between the old and the new customs, practices and religious beliefs. Further, relapse in Goa meant going back to his/her past Hindu or Muslim religion and customs without discarding his/her newly acquired Christian customs, devotions, names, civil privileges, identity and patrons. 'Relapse' was an undesirable practice or the dark side of the story of conversions for the missionaries. This 'going back' threatened to undo years of missionary hardwork. It prevented the unity of the faith and empire. However, we could ask ourselves whether the neo-converts had ever left or wanted to leave their ancestral practices once for all. The catechumenate did not wash them clean from all the Hindu customs and influences.

There were preventive and punitive measures for the Hindus and Christians alike, so necessary to maintain the purity of the faith. Unchristian behaviour demanded correction with punishment: attending temple festivals, swearing falsely, consulting witches, making offerings to the idols, etc. At times some penitent Christians whipped themselves for mystical exaltation — a custom brought over from Hinduism — but such practices were perhaps tolerated or Christianized. We shall examine other instances of relapses below.[4]

After directing our attention to some characteristics of 'relapse', we can conclude that 'relapse' is not synonymous with 'reversion' or 'reconversion'. Reversion, if taken in the strict sense or as a formal and conscious act of rejecting the second faith in favour of the first one, was generally unknown, and the term can hardly be found in documents concerning the century under review. Relapse is not *shuddhi* (purification). However, one has to admit that some people did abandon the Christian faith then, but perhaps not in a conscious and organized manner as we see it happening at the beginning of the twentieth century in Goa. We read about some apostasies or relapses from faith in 1553, but in many cases the apostates ended up by returning repentant to the Christian fold, particularly during their illness or even before.[5] Six Christians had left the faith and went to live outside Goa, but one day they came back repentant and performed publicly their penances to the edification to all.[6] There are many narrations about the 'coming back' to the Christian community.

Relapses were not deliberate, planned and uncommon happenings. They could be spontaneous behaviour, or even unconscious local reactions against European institutional and juridical forms of religion, that sought to impose uniformity on diversity. It is undeniable that the converts did assimilate to a large extent religious, cultural and superstitious elements of European Christianity, but those who did so, a small group indeed, also retained several of their pre-conversion practices. Besides, the relatives and neighbours of the Hindu defectors pressurized them to return to their ancestral religion. These syncretic practices were bitterly criticized and attacked by the missionaries, by the Provincial Councils, and above all by the Inquisition.

Although the sixteenth century missionary discourse highlighted conversions galore as 'miracles' and downplayed relapses as the 'work of the devil', we need to separate facts from make-beliefs, and to begin analyzing our socio-religious history from 'non-edifying' discourses, from 'not-so-successful' events, and from 'non-European' moulds. We have to see the 'devil-at-work' in historiography. Syncretism or relapse or the 'devil-at-work' approach could be one of these 'non-edifying', but more realistic, discourses to understand our history. There is more than enough documentary evidence on syncretic behaviour of the neo-converts. This was something that preoccupied and discouraged the missionaries. Although not edifying in any way they wrote much about it. The more optimistic missionaries would not acknowledge the existence of this reality. It is interesting to see the twists and turns in historiography as far as relapses are concerned.

The neo-converts wavered between the two faiths, practising now one then the other, or both simultaneously.[7] This without knowing they were doing it. They did this with all spontaneity without perhaps questioning which and what could be the true faith. The two faiths could be practised simultaneously and reconciled with each other. They resisted spontaneously the rigid European orthodoxy in favour of his/her more personal religion. But the missionaries, in collaboration with the secular authority as donors of material favours and enforcers of decrees, could to a large extent control the life of their converts. The missionaries saw in any syncretic practice a threat to the purity of the faith and unity of Christendom; therefore such things could not be tolerated.

The Portuguese laymen and the missionaries themselves criticized the local Christians for their weak faith, beliefs and customs. However, Francis Xavier stated that if those who criticized only knew how little instruction these Christians had received before their baptism, and how young their faith was, they would be surprised to see how these neo-converts had not turned into worse Christians yet.[8] Despite their weak faith, many of these neo-converts showed greater devotion than the Portuguese.[9] Nevertheless, the missionaries consoled themselves with the belief that if the first Christians had not learnt about the true religion yet, their children would do better.[10] Some missionaries displayed a great admiration for the religiosity of these converts, and scoffed at the Christians in Europe for their lack of devotion.[11] An Augustinian provincial-vicar in Goa in 1587 reported that the Portuguese were Christians only in name.[12] This admiration for the faith of the neo-converts may appear irrelevant for a chapter on Christian syncretism and relapses, but that speaks volumes for the faith of the local converts.

Relapse or syncretism in the life of the local Christians, a matter of 'laughter' for the Portuguese and a great 'weakness' and 'scandal' for the missionaries, did not preoccupy the locals. Repetitive measures to control or eliminate it, did not seem to have been successful at any time during the sixteenth century. In 1518 Fr. António do Louro, a Franciscan, complained that since the neo-converts lived among, and mixed freely with, the Hindus it was difficult to inform and form them regarding their Christian duties.[13] The pastoral visitations by the bishops to the parishes in the diocese of Goa, for evangelization and reform of customs, revealed to them the many relapsing or syncretic elements among the local Christians.[14]

The Hindu converts remained Christians as long as they wore a red cap given them by the priests on their baptismal day, and as many times as they took it off they cast their Christian name out, meaning that they turned to their former Hindu practices, wrote a Portuguese soldier who served in India during last quarter of the sixteenth century.[15] In 1532 many converts relapsed to their old customs and lifestyle.[16] And others went over to the land of the Muslims and apostatized.[17] Local Christians, and even the Portuguese, took part in Hindu festivals since they felt greatly attracted to them.[18] Despite these 'weaknesses' the first converts made sincere efforts to lead a good Christian life, which was highly commendable. A man and his wife had been expelled from their village by their own convert relatives, since their conduct scandalized those who wanted to live as good Christians.[19] Francis Xavier understood very well that religious conversion or baptism alone would not suffice to make the neo-converts forget their former practices and beliefs. Cultural conversion was equally important but more difficult; hence he had requested the Inquisition for Goa and excluded the Indians from entering his religious order, the Society of Jesus.[20]

It is not only that the new convert Indians in general, and the Goans in particular, brought into the church many of their former customs and beliefs. Christianization in Europe did not consist either in spontaneously accepting the new, or rejecting the old, forms of being and living. It carried forward with it many world views, values, categories and institutions of its pagan history.[21] The pagan peasant converts were the main perpetuators of these values, unlike the minority local élite who easily identified itself with authority, and the new social and religious patterns of behaviour. Syncretic conciliation of pagan and Christian categories by the peasant converts was normal. After a long time, several centuries indeed, of religious concessions and tolerance of syncretic behaviour, Europe could boast of a more purified Catholic practice and belief. This was the beginning of a more uniform and rigorous demand on being Christian, which left him/her with little freedom for syncretic forms, or possibility of escaping clerical rebuke and condemnation in case of being found guilty of unorthodox practices.[22] Judging by these religious developments it appears that much more was expected from Christianity in Goa, and that no chance was given to syncretic practices to survive here as in Europe.

"The demons made the Hindus feel very uncomfortable after their baptism."[23] "It was usual for the demon, whom the Hindus adored, to appear to the neo-converts immediately after their baptism, and later too."[24] The demons influenced and induced the Christians to run away from Goa, to where idolatry was freely practised.[25] The ministers of the devil, with their superstitions, declared and persuaded the weak Christians of the observance of auspicious and inauspicious days, and succeeded in convincing some of them that this or that person, for having abandoned the Hindu law, now remained childless as a punishment from a certain deity disowned by them.[26] Among the Christians in Goa there was a particular caste very much attached to their superstitions and inclined to perform ceremonies to placate the devil, for fear it might destroy their fields; so that some of them even visited a temple of great fame in the land of the Adilshah. They also contributed financially for its feasts.[27] Moreover, they visited other important temples to consult their deities on matters related to their business or to complain, etc.[28] Therefore, it was not rare to hear the missionaries blaming the demon and its associates — Brahmans, priests and *jogues* — for relapses and obstruction of their work.[29]

The missionaries changed their own initial perception or 'idea of conversion' as being an easy affair when they experienced difficulties in making converts, and realized that when the neo-converts were left unaided and unwatched, they were certain to relapse.[30] The decrees of the five Provincial Councils held in Goa during the span of time being reviewed, reflected the difficulties the missionaries had to face in making converts from among the Hindus. They also confirmed the existence of syncretic practices, and the necessity to keep the converts firm in their new faith, despite Hindu pressures. The rule and power of the

Portuguese, which could reward and punish its citizens as they deserved, was the solution to this problem.[31] And only by destroying the Hindu temples and issuing harsh decrees the missionary work could bring about lasting results. Relapses did discourage many missionaries. Hinduism did cause many tears and pain among them.[32] It also created certain prejudices against the Indians which are very conspicuous in many letters and reports written about them.

Alessandro Valignano wrote in 1580 that the Japanese after their conversion did not pay any attention to their former idols, whereas the Indians despite so much missionary work and granting them several privileges, abandoned easily their Christian devotion for their ancestral idols. For this reason, Christianity in Japan was, by far, the best of all and it is for this characteristic that the Japanese converts distinguished themselves so strikingly from the Indians.[33] Further, the Christian faith seemed reasonable to the Chinese, since they had a great capacity and desire to receive it, whereas the Indians appeared to be a lukewarm people and a barbarous race.[34] The missionaries hoped that gradually the sons and daughters of the first Indian converts would behave like the Japanese and Chinese Christians.[35]

Efforts of various kinds had to be made continuously to prevent relapses. On some religious festivals rice, curry and other sorts of food were served to the new Christians as usual, so that on eating this they might be consoled and made to forget the Hindu festivals.[36] The missionaries worked hard to keep the Christians away from frequent dealings with the Hindus, a people responsible for constant relapses.[37] They lived among the Hindus and near their temples where they necessarily heard of the errors they had once left.[38] In 1560 the district of Salcete counted a thousand Christians living among about fifty thousand Hindus, and the former could not be distinguished from the latter.[39]

In the city of Goa the local Christians liked to spend a lot of money at their wedding feasts, which resembled the Hindu ceremonies. Their wedding banquets lasted for ten to fifteen days, and many of them neglected their duties on account of this.[40] The Christians obliged the Hindus in their rituals by lending them their own jewelry and other things such as musical instruments, firework material, etc.[41] The converts also participated whole-heartedly in the temple festivities and gave the Hindus the impression that Christianity did not object to such practices.[42] Hindu practices entered Christian processions too.[43] Other Christians went to the territory of the Muslims to regain their former caste.[44] Relapses were but natural and common where missionary vigilance or control was poor.[45]

The inquisitors argued that 'reversion' of the new converts could not happen, since the Hindus would not accept the converts back into their caste. It was believed that the new Lusitanian context and Christianity made it impossible for the neo-converts to return to their Hindu original forms.[46] Despite this optimistic argument, the mechanisms and measures devised by the Inquisition to prevent relapses or syncretic forms are well known. For instance, it was necessary to take the Hindu boys away from their homes and keep them in the houses for catechumens before they could be perverted by their parents and relatives. Interestingly, at times the latter came to these houses and took their children forcibly away from here, and sent them to the firm land.[47]

We come across another kind of reportings too, namely, noticeable change in the converts like the hatred they showed for their former idols and rituals. They expressed such repugnance for these things when the priests asked them if they still remembered their former religion.[48] In 1561 some orthodox Hindu converts, famed for observing their rituals with great veneration before, now defiled the Hindu sacred washing tanks with cow's blood and flesh, to prevent the Hindus from using them.[49] Some missionaries would want others to believe that Hindu superstitions and customs could not exist among the new converts, because the latter took great care to accuse each other of such practices.[50] In 1563 they wrote that superstitions and Hindu customs did not exist anymore among the local Christians.[51] However, the Christians continued to consult sorcerers when they became sick.[52] They did not shun curative incantations and invocations made by the Hindu doctors.[53] Some Hindus used to bring Hindu doctors and Brahman priests to their convert relatives' place to perform their ceremonies, but at times these Christians themselves prevented such visits for the little faith they had in the idols and their ministers.[54] In 1601 we hear of thirty-three thousand Christians in Salcete who, despite their constant dealings with the Hindu and Muslim neighbours and lack of priests among them, maintained their Christian identity.[55]

The First Provincial Council that took place in Goa (1567) approved baptism for the catechumens only after they had been instructed for a period of three months. Experience had shown that without a solid instruction many neo-converts relapsed.[56] The Constitutions of the Archdiocese of Goa (1568) decided that the Jews, the foreign Muslims in particular and the foreigners in general, and the *jogues* who wished to become Christians, had to be tried for five months, since these were the ones who relapsed more easily after their baptism.[57] No time was fixed for the local Hindus and Muslims since these were different from the others. The locals did not pose as much danger to the Christian faith as the outsiders did.[58]

The priests hesitated to baptize the *jogues* (men of undersanding) immediately, since their relapse could prevent the conversion of many other Hindus.[59] Abundant correspondence on conversion gives us the impression that the Hindu candidates had to wait patiently for their baptism, if the missionaries had doubts about the former's real motives.[60] A Brahman wishing to receive baptism immediately and without Christian instruction tried, in vain, to persuade a priest to baptize him. The priests knew too well that the conversion of even a single Brahman required a big miracle, and an even bigger one after his baptism to prevent him from apostatizing.[61] The Brahmans converted with great difficulty and a few who did, gave themselves up to all sorts of idolatry and other superstitions, since they could do nothing without religious ceremonies.[62] In 1591 Fr. F. Cabral, a Jesuit provincial, said that it would be wiser to make a few but good conversions by proper means than thousands by scandalous methods, because many of them relapsed and ran away soon afterwards.[63]

By the turn of the century Claudio Aquaviva, a superior-general of the Jesuits, preoccupied with relapses in Salcete, wrote that some Christians behaved like Hindus, giving false witness, approaching the sacraments unworthily or abandoning them altogether. The new converts in the villages of Santa Cruz, Santo Aleixo, Curtorim, S. João Baptista, Benaulim and S. Salvador had relapsed into Hinduism.[64] In 1608 the same superior-general wrote to Fr. Gaspar Fernandes regretting that the old missionary zeal was dying out among the subjects and superiors alike in Goa.[65]

Relapses were not so uncommon elsewhere. Some Portuguese noblemen crossed over to the Muslim camp and even became captains and soldiers in its army. Some of them even fought against the Portuguese crown.[66] Circumstances of famine or personal interests forced a few Portuguese to renounce their Christian status.[67] Some went to live in Bijapur and possibly adopted Islam.[68] There were many Portuguese renegades in Belgaum.[69] The soldiers who came from Portugal were often ill-treated and forced to live on alms from the monasteries. With the situation becoming unbearable, especially when they were left to fend for themselves and without any state support, many allied with the Hindu or Muslim rulers, thus adopting their masters' customs and religion to survive. More than a thousand Portuguese renegades served several Hindu and Muslim rulers.[70] The Portuguese, particularly soldiers, living outside the territories under Portuguese control, adopted more easily the customs and religion of those they served.[71] In Mombasa the new converts abandoned their faith whenever it seemed expedient to do so, and some Portuguese renounced their faith in favour of Islam, when the natives in East Africa threatened to exterminate the Portuguese there.[72] There were relapses in Congo too.[73]

Syncretism in Goa was not only one way. The devotion and superstitions of the Christians also influenced the Hindus. "Among the Hindus, at any rate, customs die very hard. All sorts of taboos and superstitions have continued, even spread to, or survived, among the Christian converts, who in return have given (us) a few superstitions of their own."[74] In the village of Carambolim a pregnant Hindu woman made a vow to Jesus that in case a son was born to her she would make him a Christian.[75] Many Hindus asked for baptism for the sick in their own household.[76] We find Hindus taking their sons to be made Christians, but they themselves preferred to remain Hindus, or vice-versa.[77]

The Hindus attended Christian religious ceremonies, not only out of mere curiosity but with devotion. They participated in Christian festivals too.[78] Their devotion to our Lady and St Anthony was praiseworthy.[79] When the Christians sought Hindu craftsmen and painters to make holy objects and to paint their holy images respectively, the latter had no inhibitions in accepting the former's requests. But the First Provincial Council forbade the Christians the use of such services, because of the hatred the Hindus entertained against the Christian religion and for their spending on idols the money they had earned by making sacred things.[80] Interestingly, some Hindus learnt the Christian doctrine foreseeing that sooner or later they would be forced to convert, and to avoid the trouble of learning it when they had to.[81] Some Hindus took Christian names — names often given them by the Portuguese for whom they worked.[82] The Hindus showed devotion to the crosses; and they asked the priests to place them in their fields and pathways. Some cultivators had also asked for Christian protection against the devil for their fields.[83]

In real life, cultures and religions could be reconciled in a most spontaneous manner. Sick Hindus, unable to be cured by their idols and doctors, came to the church or to the hospital for the locals for relief. They also brought their sick children to the church and offered them to St Paul for healing, and in return they offered oil for the lamps in the churches.[84] Others who had come to the hospital for treatment showed such faith to the extent of astonishing the missionaries, and they were immediately baptized. A few after being cured were taken to the College of St Paul to be baptized, and after their baptism some men brought their wives to become Christians too, and the latter brought in turn their sons, daughters, sisters, relatives and friends.[85] The Hindus respected the Christian practices, showed respect for the churches, and followed the counsels the priests gave them.[86]

## Causes of Relapses

We continue to deal with some other circumstances that favoured syncretic practices. The missionaries believed that several factors were responsible for relapses, but lack of support from the Portuguese to the activity of conversion was the main one. However, the Portuguese laymen had other reasons for these relapses, and did not agree wholly with the arguments of the missionaries. The common causes the laymen attributed to relapses or weak faith of the neo-converts could be summarized thus: first, the constant dealings they entertained with the Hindus which were inevitable, since both lived in the same quarters of the village; second, the insufficient Christian instruction given to them before and after their baptism; third, the wrong methods used to convert them; and fourth, the lack of missionary vigilance or control over the local Christians and Hindus alike. Moreover, the policy of mixed marriages was another factor responsible for syncretic behaviour and relapses. Some local women or wives of Portuguese settlers, their daughters and sons, declared that they were Portuguese by birth only, but not in customs.[87]

Often political and religious conversion took place without any cultural change. But for the missionaries the new religion and the local culture stood always in conflict with each other. It was necessary to create a cultural context that suited the new religion and demands. But syncretic practices had made it clear that the Goan or Hindu cultural environment could not be changed just by a few decrees in favour of conversion. Hence, some zealous persons had suggested earlier the creation of separate quarters for the Christians and Hindus, but it was an impractical project.[88] The governor, Francisco Barreto, decided on what he thought was a more practical approach to the problem of relapses. In 1557 he forbade, by a decree, the Hindus and Muslims to dress like Christians. Further, he ordered them to have some harmless sign on them, by which they could be identifed immediately as non-Christians, under the penalty of losing their belongings if they failed to comply with the order.[89]

It is interesting to note that those signs should be such that they had nothing to do with any Hindu customs or with anything that had been forbidden by the Provincial Councils, as for instance the sacred thread of the twice born.[90] The new sign had to distinguish the Hindus from the converts in order to restrict their social dealings. Separation was to protect the converts from the heathen influences, so much so that in 1559 the decree was ratified.[91] With this restriction, when the converts wanted to talk with their Hindu relatives, they had to do so only during the day and in public places; and Christians who wanted to visit their Hindu relatives required permission from their parish priest. Regardless of the consequences, they met their relatives whenever they liked during the night.[92] The efforts the Brahman Hindus made to prevent conversions and help the converts to revert or win back their caste have already been examined.[93] A certain decision of a Provincial Council testifies amply to the need for discriminating and separating the Christian and the Hindu communities.[94] Throughout the sixteenth century, separation of these communities continued to be insisted upon by the priests as a means against faith damages.[95]

I have already said that relapses cannot be merely attributed to the ignorance of orthodox doctrine. No doubt, religious ignorance prevailed among the local Christians and many had become Christians simply to receive favours. Most Christians had received baptism with little or no instruction at all, and soon left the faith.[96] But convert slaves relapsed when they were captured by the Muslims. Many Muslims and Hindus, vassals of the king of Portugal, who had asked for baptism on their own accord and learnt the Christian doctrine reasonably well, soon showed not only less interest in receiving baptism but some even left Goa to practise their own rituals. They undertook many penances and pilgrimages to their temples, performed innumerable prayers and ceremonies and consumed filthy drinks as demanded by the Hindu priests, in order to cleanse themselves from the food given to them by the Christians. But after undergoing such penances they returned and lived among the converts without fearing the missionaries who considered this to be a serious scandal and encouragement for some to abandon their faith too.[97] Delays in offering the catechumens the much-awaited baptismal dresses was sufficient for many catechumens to lose their initial enthusiasm to become Christians. Besides, this situation gave the necessary time to the relatives of these catechumens to persuade or pressurize the latter to return to Hinduism. Thus many catechumens relapsed to their old practices.[98]

The converts were left to themselves without any vigilance and care. In Salcete in 1558, the priests hardly visited and instructed the Christians, so much so that they could scarcely be recognized as such, but for their names.[99] But in the city of Goa there were about twenty thousand Hindus, who despite great vigilance by the priests, continued to perform their ceremonies, thus prompting many converts to abandon their faith. Hence, it was suggested that the king should expel these harmful people, enemies of the Christian faith, from the city.[100] The missionaries complained that Hindu religious ceremonies had increased in Goa, and that probably the Christians consulted Brahman sorcerers.[101] Another serious reason for relapses was that by the turn of century the Jesuits began permitting the Hindus to go out to the firm land and worship their idols on payment of a tax.[102]

Some missionaries, however, attributed this syncretic situation to the 'bad examples' of the Portuguese and of many clergymen.[103] Certain contradictions between preaching and practice might have confused the converts and Hindus alike. What could have been the other 'bad examples' that led the Christians to relapse? Extortion of money, public concubinage, womanizing, forced conversions, adultery, bigamy, sodomy, extravagant spending, gambling, etc.[104] Could the activities of the Inquisition too, which were far from being exemplary, not lead the Christians to relapse or the Hindus to shun conversion? Internal disagreements and controversies among the inquisitors themselves, including the attitude of some clerics who told the Hindus to remain away from the Catholic religion, together with the tyrannical acts of the civil authority and of the Brahmans over the converts, could be some of the other major factors in favour of relapses.[105]

The missionaries understood well that 'good examples' or customs although necessary, were not sufficient to stamp out ancient and lingering beliefs of the pre-Christian period. When the sick approached the Portuguese, the personal kind of attention they received from them, probably made the Hindus more receptive to the new religion as well as to the political rule of the Portuguese. However, this receptivity was not strong enough to make them abandon family traditions and cut themselves off from their Hindu kith and kin. The idea of 'good examples' and 'good customs', (or abandoning the local Hindu customs) as being one of the important conditions to make conversions and prevent relapses, was rooted in the European belief of their cultural superiority, and that Christianity alone contained and could inspire the practice of 'virtues' and 'goodness'. The Hindus, Muslims, barbarians and pagans did not possess virtues and goodness, hence they could hardly practise them as they had no knowledge of these things, alleged the Europeans. Therefore, only after their baptism they were able to show examples of virtue and courage.[106] Be that as it might, good customs and good examples failed to convince, convert or prevent relapses for certain.

The Portuguese realized that relapses were inherent to the social context, traditions and customs of the people. The local culture and religion had greater attraction on the local converts than had the 'good examples' and 'virtuous customs' proposed by the missionaries. Even the behaviour of the Portuguese men and women in the East attested to this attraction. In short, the missionaries could do very little about relapses but complain that the converts still had their hearts in their former temples and false gods.[107]

The absence of priests among the converts, which meant lack of direct control over them and the Hindus alike, was one of the chief reasons for several syncretic practices. The Christians complained to the bishop about lack of priests, but it was not easy to find clergymen willing to reside in churches among the locals. A list referring to the difficulties and situations, all related to relapses, created by the absence of priests in the villages in Margão as reported in 1603 states as follows. (i) Many poor converts were the only breadwinners and every day was important for them.

When they needed a priest for their spiritual needs, these Christians had to walk miles to get him, which meant that they remained without earning their living on that day. (ii) Many children and catechumens died without baptism, and many Christians died without confession or without the sacrament of the sick. When the priest reached the sick person it was often too late. Hence, the Hindu priests took advantage of this situation and performed the last rites for them. (iii) The priest's helpers or servants buried the dead, which turned out to be a serious scandal to the people. (iv) About two hundred Christians, from among five hundred, belonging to S. Salvador parish had reverted and left for the firm lands. (v) Churches that had about three thousand Christians generally only around five hundred came for mass. (vi) The converts rarely received Christian instruction and just a few boys came for catechism classes; whereas many more had forgotten it altogether. (vii) Catechism in schools disappeared. (viii) The Hindus performed their ceremonies almost publicly in the villages. (ix) There were vices galore and almost all cases of concubinity and other sins were known in the village. (x) When the ministers of the devil and the witches heard about a sick or dying person, they rushed from the firm land to see whether they could get alms for their temples, and they recommended to the infirm all sorts of superstitions. (xi) The priest became a stranger to the convert boys, so much so that when they saw a priest, they hid themselves from him as if they were Hindus. (xii) Sometimes the poor Christians died for lack of food or any other vital need, but if a priest resided in the village, he could perhaps have helped them with alms. (xiii) The report speaks of many litigations, hatred and false accusations in the village. The local Christians themselves were by their nature inclined to falsehood and this, the report suggested, could be remedied only if the priests resided among them. (xiv) Some villagers, including Christians, gave alms to some idols and temples. (xv) The events had reached such proportions that even the priests neglected their duties. They visited the villages like strangers and refused to learn the local language. (xvi) But when a priest was available in the village the poor approached him with their grievances, since the civil authority denied them due justice. These

Christians had to be looked after, since most had been converted by violent means.[108]

The missionaries built many churches and began residing among the Hindus, without which conversions would be rather difficult and relapses galore.[109] They realized that constructing churches in the villages and residing there could be more effective than simply going to the villages from the College of St Paul.[110] However, reports suggest that there were difficulties in finding priests who were ready to reside in some churches.[111]

## Measures Against Relapses

Relapses — errors or false practices and abuses — needed to be destroyed root and branch. To stamp out relapse or syncretic behaviour several measures had been decreed and implemented. These were also measures in favour of conversion or to increase the number of Christians. We have already dealt with some of them. These preventive measures or the 'remedies against temptations' varied from place to place and in time. Often they were in the form of threats and penalties, but they could also be material favours or civil privileges. Institutions also, like the Catechumenate, the *Pay dos Christãos*, the Tribunal of the Inquisition, Confraternities or lay associations which helped the Christians or the Hospital for the locals were other factors and incentives. But since human nature was corrupt, and kind words alone would not suffice as corrective measures, several punitive steps should be introduced, declared the Council of Trent.[112] The previous chapters attempted to show that the activity of conversion which included reform of local customs, had its agents, supporting institutions, laws, privileges and penalties that worked in tandem with each other. In the section that follows we shall discuss some other recommendations and penalties that seemed more practical and effective solutions against relapses. Since the Tribunal of the Inquisition also dealt with relapses and its prevention it will be included here, but only its preventive aspect, to avoid unnecessary repetition of known facts.

(a) *Recommendations and Solutions against Relapses*

In 1537 Pope Paul III granted the bishops and parish priests in India the faculty to absolve and to re-admit within the Catholic church, after healthy penance, the Christians who had left the faith.[113] D. João de Albuquerque, bishop of Goa, issued a pastoral letter in 1545 threatening with divine wrath all those Christians with lax customs and bad habits. With another letter issued in 1547, he warned the Christians who followed Hindu rituals with severe penalties. Moreover, he appealed for the expulsion of all idolaters from the public offices. In the same year the king, D. João III, ordered the expulsion of all harmful Hindus, and the ban on their temples and ceremonies in Goa.[114]

The erring converts who had committed the crime of heresy, could be arrested and kept apart from the rest, and only after receiving a solid Christian instruction and renouncing heresy completely, they would then be allowed to live a normal life.[115] Probably, they were kept in houses for catechumens to be 'cured' and tried.

Many local Christians, with little fear of God, performed Hindu rituals before or after baptizing their children. They gave them Hindu names instead of Christian ones.[116] Christians kept their Hindu names and this abuse had to be stopped. If they continued to keep them they could be punished with six lashes on the palm of the hand in front of the church, and if it was found that the parents called their children by Hindu names, after their baptism, they could be imprisoned for thirty days and receive thirty lashes.[117] Curiously, the Hindu name of a convert was also recorded along his baptismal name on the church's register.

The First Provincial Council (1567) ordered the Christians to have little dealings with the Hindus.[118] It may be recalled that some missionaries had suggested that after baptism the converts should not have any communication with their Hindu relatives, rather the Hindus should live separately in the islands of Divar and Chorão.[119] This separation never took place; instead practical measures were devised almost always. The converts had to remain away from any influence and occasion that hindered Christian virtues. Hence, the First Provincial Council offered solutions against some evils found among them. Henceforth, no Christian could give his son or daughter, even if he/she were a Hindu, in marriage to another Hindu. The converts could not mourn for their departed dear ones as they did before their conversion, or according to the Hindu customs. They were forbidden to attend the temple ceremonies, participate in their feasts, or make contributions to them. A Christian could not permit any Hindu, even if the latter were his/her own father, to visit him/her when sick. They could not attend Hindu weddings; they could not go out to the firm land on the days of Hindu festivals; and the Christian women at no time could go there without the permission of the parish priest. Those who flouted these orders could be punished.[120] The same Council had received some information about some Christians favouring Hindu practices, which harmed seriously the Catholic faith. These Christians could be excommunicated *ipso facto* and handed over to the Tribunal of the Inquisition to be judged.[121]

The sacrament of communion was little frequented by the converts.[122] They did not beat their chests, as it was the custom among the Portuguese, when the Blessed Sacrament was raised. This grave omission called for correction and serious vigilance on the part of the priests.[123] It was very common among the Christians, as it was among the Hindus, to swear falsely.[124]

It was decided that no woman could exercise the profession of midwifery without knowing how to baptize a child. The parish priest had to see that they knew the necessary prayers in their own language, and only after an examination and an explicit consent could they exercise their profession. If, however, they exercised this profession without the required authorization they could be punished with one month in prison and thirty lashes.[125]

The missionaries doubted the validity of the Hindu marriage rite for married converts; nevertheless, a couple's marriage was regularized immediately after their baptism.[126] But some converts had not regularized their Hindu marriage as per the demands of the church; it had to be done in the church in the presence of the people. If there were impediment, even of consanguinity or affinity, the priest could marry them after proper dispensation; however, the marriage ceremony had to be conducted hastily, perhaps to avoid scandals.[127]

The archbishop, D. Aleixo de Meneses, in one of his pastoral visitations to Salcete in 1596, discovered several syncretic practices in the life of Christians, and perhaps some of them had been converted long before. He found that the Christian parents did not call the parish priest when their newly born children were in danger of death, thus many died without baptism. If the parents failed to inform the priest of such cases, he/she could be punished with fifteen days in prison and receive thirty lashes in the presence of the people.[128]

The parish priests were recommended to have a list of names of all the Hindus living in the vicinities of his parish, to enable the clerics to visit them when they were sick and exhort them to receive baptism.[129] Sick Christians were asked to receive the sacrament of the dying without waiting for the moment of danger, and to facilitate this each church had been ordered to have a palanquin to carry the sick person to the church.[130]

Someone had to look after the idle Christians and urge them to work, since idleness caused them to relapse.[131] The Christians were forbidden to work in their fields on Sundays and holy days.[132] They were rebuked for working for the Hindus on Sundays.[133] Participating in Hindu festivals, dealing with, or looking at, the objects that invoked superstitions and idolatry could attract punishment.[134] Spies were sent to the Hindu festivals to observe and punish any Christian present there.[135] Nevertheless, many Christians attended these festivities.

The church had decided that only after completing the age of fourteen years a male convert, and twelve years for a female, could contract marriage. Besides, they needed to know a few prayers, like the Our Father, the Hail Mary, the Creed and the Commandments, without which knowledge they could not marry. It was common among the neo-converts to perform, after the church marriage ceremony, the Hindu marriage rituals too.[136]

In 1600 Christianity in Bardez had many idolatrous elements due to the laxity and negligence of the Franciscans, as indicated by the number of persons condemned by the Inquisition to the *autos-*

*de-fé.* But converts of other religious orders were not very different, either.[137] In 1605 the king, aware of the negligence on the part of these religious orders, recommended special care and vigilance in matters of Christian instruction to the catechumens, since several relapses took place soon after their baptism.[138]

In Goa, during the same year, in spite of great vigilance and care taken by the parish priests, the Hindus continued to perform their idolatrous ceremonies, thus encouraging many converts to relapse. The inhabitants from the city of Goa requested the king to expel the harmful social elements from the city; consequently a decree was issued to this effect without leaving room for appeal. Expulsion was for good. If they returned, the penalty could be loss of their lives and property. Some zealots demanded that, for the welfare of the converts, such Hindus must be made to migrate to São Tiago ou Passo Seco, a place near the territory of the Adilshah. This measure could deter the Hindus from indulging in anti-conversion activity just as it could motivate many Hindus to conversion. It is clear that the Portuguese magistrates favoured the Hindus in their idolatries and permitted them to move about in Goa without any restrictions.[139]

The archbishop, D. Aleixo de Meneses, during one of his many pastoral visitations to Salcete in 1604, found a Hindu practice among the newly married converts, namely, of them not living together. Before her pregnancy or delivery the wife stayed with her parents or relatives who often followed Hindu practices. Conversely, very often the woman's Christian parents refused to send her back to her husband, accusing him of following Hindu customs. Henceforth, the couples were ordered to live together, and in case they did not obey for whatever reason, their parents or relatives would be held responsible and punished adequately for breach of law.[140] The Third Provincial Council which met in Goa in 1585 established well-defined rules on marriage celebration for the converts, since they continued to follow Hindu rituals too.[141]

The Hindus visited sick Christians and reminded them of their former gods, informed a report in 1604. The purpose of these visits was also to see whether the sick person left any alms or donation in his will for their temples. In order to prevent such visits it was decreed that any Hindu, except doctors, found in Christian homes, could be jailed and taken to the city of Goa to be punished.[142] Schools for boys, and residences for priests and religious Brothers, were built in the villages where the Christians lived to better preserve their faith. The priests and religious Brothers continuously visited and instructed the converts.[143] There was constant preaching and reprehensions too.[144]

The priests took special care to stop any Hindu festival from being celebrated. In spite of this measure, the Hindus continued by night to celebrate openly their joyful occasions and weddings according to their custom. The wedding party used to go in procession making much noise through the city and villages. The decree in 1558 forbidding such occasions and frolic, openly or privately, did not deter the Hindus. They continued to make statues of their deities despite several prohibitions. We recall that the decrees in favour of conversion and possible raids on the houses of suspect Hindus might have forced them to have their deities painted on leaves, since it was easier to hide them during such occasions. The Christians were exhorted to be vigilant, and to denounce to the priests any Hindus suspected of practising their customs even secretly.[145]

### (b) *The Inquisition*

The tyrannical activities and instructions (*Regimento*) of the Tribunal of the Inquisition of Goa are sufficiently familiar to us. However, certain facts need to be made more obvious. Throughout the history of the church there has been some kind of inquisition or control to prevent heresies from affecting the Catholic orthodoxy and unity. It is curious to note that the Inquisition was not introduced in India when the first requests for it had been made. The Inquisition and the Provincial Councils conducted in Goa, made particular forms of European Christianity a universal norm. This was a logical follow up of the decisions taken at the Council of Trent. The Inquisition was introduced primarily to prevent relapses and plurality, as its decrees and punitive measures (*Regimento*) sought to impose purity of the faith and unity in Christendom.[146]

If the work of converting Hindus had been a success as often alleged by the missionaries, perhaps, anyone would like to know the reason for the establishment of the Tribunal of the Inquisition in India. Perhaps the activity of conversion was not so successful as most missionaries wanted it should be or that others should believe; as a matter of fact it was far from being an agreeable affair, if we go by some reports sent to Lisbon and Rome. The faith of the converts was interwoven with syncretic practices or Hindu customs, as has been amply mentioned. Syncretic practices were not simply a question of failure and weakness for the locals. They were so for the missionaries. Syncretic practices were an unavoidable social and religious reality, but they were not seen thus by all the missionaries. However, relapses had to be overlooked at times for the sake of social harmony. Nevertheless, the cosmopolitan and pluralistic context of Goa posed a constant and great danger to the purity of the Christian faith of the converts. It may be recalled that the European colonies had become a safe haven for the Jewish converts (New Christians) and that many of them had settled comfortably in those places. There were a few rich New Christians leading a scandalous life in Goa. They still practised their former religion and scandalized the local converts too.[147] Continuous emigration of these New Christians from Portugal to Goa and to other parts of the *Estado da India*, brought the Tribunal of the Inquisition to Goa.[148] The Inquisition had to intervene and change this pluralistic and unchristian context. This institution was supposed to mitigate the bad customs among Christians, since there was much *soltura e braveza na fé e religiam* (laxity and abuses within the faith).[149] Moreover, one of the aims of this tribunal consisted in offering protection to the local converts who were persecuted by the New Christians and civil authorities. The Inquisition also aimed at preventing social conflicts among the Jews, Muslims and Hindus.[150] Preventive measures alone proved to be dysfunctional as long as the original social context remained intact. Hence, the inquisitors' interference in the non-Christian context and the issuance of harsh measures to disturb it.

In 1543 Miguel Vaz, the vicar-general, asked for the establishment of the Inquisition in India to reform the unhealthy customs of the New Christians.[151] In 1546 Francis Xavier had also made a similar request. Besides, he appealed for many missionary preachers to teach the New Christians who lived just like Jews and Muslims, without any fear of God. Only preaching without the Inquisition would hardly produce the desired results, stated Francis Xavier.[152] In 1559 Fr. Belchior wrote that the Inquisition was more necessary for India than for any other place, since here the Christians mixed more freely with the Hindus, Jews and Muslims, and still worse, the variety of cultures of this land perverted the conscience of its peoples.[153] The Muslims and heretics contaminated the faith of the good Christians. These Christians lived among so many heretics that without the Inquisition no true faith was ever possible.[154]

We also find opinions against the establishment of the Inquisition in India. In 1555 Fr. Baltazar Dias argued that the Inquisition in Goa would serve no purpose, since it could not lead anyone to conversion; hence he requested the home authorities not to introduce it in Goa.[155] He alleged that the faith of the local Christians was weak by nature, because their ancestors had not been Christians.[156] Instead Fr. Baltasar Dias proposed the sending of more missionaries to India, because without them what had been achieved would be soon lost.[157] Fr. P.M. Carneiro, another Jesuit, wrote in 1555 that the Inquisition could cause the already feeble and weak faith of the Goan converts to disappear totally, hence he recommended that for at least twenty years no rigorous inquiry should be conducted on the lives of the converts. Besides, any interference in the life of the neo-converts could prove a serious impediment for further conversions. It was necessary to go slow with these people, because God could not ask more than what one's nature was capable of.[158] The governor, Francisco Barreto, had also objected to the establishment of the Inquisition in Goa.[159] Finally, after rejecting several requests for the Inquisition, the crown officially established the Tribunal for the entire *Estado da India* in 1560, with the headquarters in Goa. It is not a mere coincidence that during the government of the viceroy, D. Constantino de Bragança (1558-1561), a period of great proselytizing activity, the Inquisition came to Goa.

The original purpose of the Inquisition was more preventive than punitive. But the Reformation and the Wars of Religion in Europe altered the aim of this institution.[160] Then without losing its concern for orthodoxy of the faith and unity of Christendom, it became an institution of terror to all. It might have been more violent at times depending on the support given by the state and church to the inquisitors and on the moods of the missionaries.

The Inquisition was a secular or state tribunal with religious and social concerns: it was a great leveller and sought to minimize religious and social conflicts that weakened the state. Suspects in matters of faith and customs were held as potential enemies of the state. The Inquisition demanded that a person denounce suspects, in religious or political matters, even though they be their family members. Paradoxically, it also maintained a strict socio-religious discrimination between Christians and others, and anyone who opposed its *Regimento* (rules), or a convert who betrayed signs of relapses, could have his goods confiscated.[161]

The conversion policy of the government and of the Inquisition could differ from each other despite both having to work together. At times the government could be more tolerant than this Tribunal which was controlled by the clergy. Nevertheless, the attitude of the church seemed to be more of precaution and prevention rather than punitive. The decrees of the Provincial Councils reflect the main concern of the church, namely, preserving the purity of the faith or preventing it from weakening. The councils aimed at guarding the Christians from relapsing. The stronger the Hindus became the easier they could make the weak converts revert. Needless to say that it is imperative to understand decisions, decrees, historiography and praxis, but without delving into their contexts, intentions or arguments that justified their idea and praxis of conversion in Goa, we may run the risk of remaining with a seriously distorted point of view. Attention to intentions, contexts and practices directly related to the 'making of a citizenry' for the empire, which could lend great 'political stability to the *Estado da India*', is indispensable to realize the functioning of the Tribunal of the Inquisition and the resolutions of several Provincial Councils regarding relapses. It is a fact that the aim (rules) of the Inquisition differed substantially from its praxis (implementation). Hence, one has to consider objectively the existence of lacunae between historical intentions and practices while reviewing history.

In short, the aim of this tribunal, just as of the other institutions of conversion, was mainly the orthodoxy of the faith and a large citizenry for Christendom. And to increase the number of converts, it had necessarily to interfere with the Hindu group, and in its context. There is no doubt that the practices of the Inquisition to prevent relapses and strengthen orthodoxy deviated from its original intention, thus becoming one of the most tyrannical and criminal institutions known in history.

## Concluding Remarks

Syncretism implies a quality criterion. In the case of syncretism in Goa the criterion was that of the missionaries. Their information tells us that Christianity in Goa was more a 'graft' (an external element that merges and combines with its hosts) than a 'transplant' (an external element moved into a new area where it grows relatively independent of its new surroundings therefore, retaining the main characteristics it had before it moved in). The Goan converts made many local forms and customs an integral part of their Christianity during the sixteenth century.[162] Reconciliation between 'our' and 'their' religious forms and customs was not a taboo for the locals and even for the Portuguese laymen.

The ethos of the Goan people was unable to integrate vast Portuguese cultural areas. Indigenous converted élite could assimilate better some Portuguese religious and cultural patterns, for they had more to gain by doing so. If so, the converts from the lower groups might have relapsed more easily into syncretic practices; this being the main reason why the local clergy came, to a very large extent, from the élite groups.

Symbols, when deprived of their primary concrete meaning can die away, but the new symbols and myths by themselves could not deprive the old ones of their meaning and attractions. Substitution of the old forms and symbols for the new ones was a complex process; and the missionaries knew perfectly well that conversion called for more than merely presenting new symbols, myths and doctrines to the converts, for without first depriving the old ones of their primary significance and removing them from their sight, the task ahead would be very difficult. Hence, the constant propaganda against the 'devil worship', and the breaking of temples and idols. It is clear that monotheistic religions have condemned syncretism and religious dialogue throughout their history.

The continuous contacts and dialogue between the neo-converts and others endangered the Christian faith.[163] We have several petitions to separate the new converts from the Hindus and Muslims as a preventive measure against relapses.[164] The church fought syncretism when it threatened to become widespread. Syncretism, or relapse, weakened the church and the state, since it was synonymous with losing control over the Christians. The church after becoming dominant could be in danger of losing its proselytes.

Governments persecuted heretics when they became dangerous to the political stability of the country. The French, Spanish and Portuguese monarchs saw that no heretic arose in their colonies, whereas the English allowed all kinds of heretics.[165] A letter written by the Portuguese settlers in Goa to the king of Portugal, D. Filipe II, in 1599 asking him to destroy the heretics and enemies of the holy faith for the increase of the Catholic Church, had more political weight than religious.[166] By the turn of the century the Dutch threat and the English menace to the Lusitanian empire had increased. These enemies of the state were fought with religious arguments too: the heretics, Hindus, heathens, foreigners were faithless or unbelievers and unreliable; hence a constant potential danger to the converts. Even the foreign Christians like the Ethiopians, Armenians, Syrians with customs so contrary to those of the Roman church were held as suspect.[167] They weakened the unity of the local Christedom with their many errors and cultural pluralism.

Caste continuance, or social barriers, among the converts is one of the most striking although unfortunate, features of Indian Christianity. Social division, and status based on caste, was not considered as a harmful Hindu cultural or religious element. Hence, its survival in Goa did not constitute an incentive for relapses or an obstacle to conversions, rather it facilitated the latter at times. Approval of caste system did attract the élite to Christianity. After all, the Europeans of the sixteenth century held social division as divinely established.[168] But when the variety of customs and laws became shortcomings they had to be regulated by secular and divine law.

The Council of Trent decided, among other things, on the renewal of religious devotion, reform of customs, increase of converts, uprooting of heresies and fighting against the enemies of the Christian people. In brief, it encouraged conversion of infidels, defeat of heretics and perseverance of the faithful.[169] All the five Provincial Councils held in Goa, adapted the directives of the Council of Trent to local contexts. The Roman Catholic church thought of religion in terms of purity of faith and heresies. However, such concepts did not preoccupy the converts, but the purity and pollution of caste or the 'break down' of caste rules did. Therefore, it is not surprising to see that the converts could shed neither their caste nor their previous status and honour. They retained the old forms of living despite acquiring new ones which demanded a break with the past, and how well they could reconcile both the forms is not easy to guess.

The context of forcible conversions need not necessarily lead to syncretic behaviour or be the only reason for it. Relapse as a criterion to establish whether the converts had been instructed well or not, is insufficient either. The uncontestable fact is that the cultural context and the indispensable daily social relations imposed themselves on the converts. Even in voluntary conversions the group absorbed only the elements important to them, but retained other traditional forms of living and being.

Nowhere, could Christianity be handed over in its original form to a new recipient group. The old religious forms continued to exist side by side with it or marginally, no matter what sort of penalties or sanctions awaited syncretic behaviour.[170] Mass conversions did occur, but not mass reversions or reconversions as they did during the first half of the twentieth century in Goa. In regions outside the Portuguese control, the Christians might have found little support or they had to face greater hostility from the Hindu rulers, therefore apostasies by, and disappearance of, weak Christian communities could easily occur.[171]

In Goa in 1557, fears had increased that the Christians might revert due to the little favour and protection they received from the Portuguese. The priests began asking the governors to issue decrees in favour of conversion and of the Christians. It was necessary that all public offices, so far entrusted to the Hindus, should be given immediately to the local Christians.[172] This resulted in a number of 'laws and privileges in favour of conversion' which have been reviewed in chapters five and six. Conversions had to be made and relapse prevented not only with penalties but also with favours. Conversion, if not accompanied by protection, material favours and civil privileges, could hardly be sustained, let alone increased.[173]

It was a common complaint that the Hindus converted for convenience sake and not for the faith, and that nothing changed them except fear of punishment or hopes of reward.[174] These Hindus did not convert for the love of God but for material gains, the natural means God used to attract them to the church, alleged the missionaries. "Some asked for baptism by virtue of being unfortunate, poor and lacking in courage when they were caught for breach of law;[175] others asked for baptism for ugly and dirty things that are not worth mentioning", wrote Fr. Nicolao Lanciloto.[176] But it was hopefully expected that after their conversions, if instructed well, they could become excellent Christians.[177]

To conclude, it is unquestionable that the converts continued to practise their ancestral customs and religion: 'superstitions', 'idolatry' and 'bad customs'. Relapses or syncretism persisted among the Goan Christians and even more among the peasantry, despite several decrees, preventive and punitive measures to establish orthodox norms for Christian conduct so that the converts might resemble the Portuguese Christians. Equally true is the fact that after the locals had adopted Christianity they did not abandon it, even when they could, or when the secular power and the church did not help them, or when they found themselves in the most hostile environments.[178] It is obvious that in spite of their relapses or syncretic tendencies the converts were recognized as such for more than their Christian 'names' or 'red cap' (a baptismal gift) they wore, or for the absence of *xenddi* (hair-tuft). And despite finding it difficult to abandon the local customs, the common folk showed deep Christian devotion which stood out as an example to the religiously slack Portuguese.[179]

## NOTES AND REFDRENCES

1. ARSI, *Eppistolae Goana et Malabarica*, 14, fls. 232v-33v. "Estava na terra firme um pagode, que dantes fôra de uma destas aldeias de Salsete; veio-se a entender que alguns destes cristãos fracos na fé, por mêdo de lhes facer mal, o iam lá adorar e fazer-lhe suas ceremónias, mas levados outros seo zêlo da fé, se determinaram ir à terra firme a o abrasar, o que fizeram em uma noite muito a seu salvo." Fernão Guerreiro, *Relação Anual das coisas que fizeram os Padres da Companhia de Jesus nas suas Missões*, Vol. I, p. 5.
2. ARSI, *Eppistolae Goana et Malabarica*, 10 - I, fl. 314v.
3. ARSI, *Goana Historia*, 34 - I, fl. 222.
4. AN / TT, *Conselho Geral Geral do Santo Officio*, Maço 32.
5. *Doc*, II, 100.
6. *DI*, XVIII, 664.
7. C. R. Boxer, *The Church Militant and Iberian Expansion 1440-1770*, p. 88.
8. Instruction written by Francis Xavier to the missionaries working in Travancore and Fishery Coast (Pescaria), in 1548. *Doc*, IV, 42.
9. *Ibid.*, VIII, 416.
10. Report by the bishop of Dume to the king of Portugal. January 1522. *Ibid.*, I, 452-53.
11. ARSI, *Goana Historia*, 33 - II, fl. 211.
12. C. Alonso, "Nueva documentación inédita sobre las misiones agustinianas en la India y en Persia (1571-1609)", p. 324.
13. *Doc*, I, 353.

14. BNL, *Reservados*, Cod. 176, fl. 117v.
15. A. de S. S. Costa Lobo, (ed.), *op. cit.*, p. 198.
16. *DI*, II, 230.
17. *Ibid.* XVI, 326.
18. "Acerca dos vezinhos de Goa, tem em a ilha seos pagodes ordenados com as figuras do imiguo da Cruz, em statuas, e fazem suas festas cada ano, honde vay muyta gente cristãa, asi dos nosos como dos cristãos novos da terra, que he cousa mui errada em lhe hirem favorecer sua ydolatria." Report by the bishop of Dume to the king of Portugal. January 1522. *Doc*, I, 452.
19. Luís Guzman, *op. cit.*, p. 60.
20. *Doc*, III, 351.
21. The word pagan probably derives from the Latin 'pagus' which means village. It refers to those rustic peasants who practised traditional polytheism. The pagan cults resisted longer in the 'pagi' (villages). The Christian urban élite considered barbarian or pagan any cult different from theirs.
22. José Matoso, "Raízes da missionação portuguesa", pp. 66-67.
23. *DI*, XVIII, 896.
24. Luís de Guzman, *op. cit.*, p. 58.
25. *DI*, VI, 118. *Doc*, IX, 224.
26. *DI*, XVIII, 891.
27. Letter written in 1606. ARSI, *Goana Historia*, 33 - II, fl. 211v.
28. António d'Almeida Azevedo, *op. cit.*, p. 29.
29. *DI*, VI, 332; XII, 609.
30. "Todos estes favores e outros muitos são necesarios nestas terras de Vosa Alteza, porque a jemte dela hee muito mal inclinada a comverterem-se muito de vagar com gramde trabalho, de maneira que, como quer que comummente se comvertem mais facilmente gemtios que os mouros, são estes gemtios tão afeisuados a seus costumes, que tamto se comvertem dos mouros como dos gemtios e todos muito de vagar e com trabalho." Letter from D. Frei João de Albuquerque to the viceroy, D. João de Castro. November 1547. *Doc*, III, 532.
31. Alessandro Valignano, *op. cit.*, p. 69.
32. *Doc*, IV, 35. Letter written by the archbishop of Goa, D. Aleixo de

Meneses. AHU, *Caixa da India,* No. 1, doc. 43.

33. *Doc*, XI, 539. *DI*, I, 50-51.
34. *Ibid.*, VII, 612-13. *Doc*, IV, 141, 143.
35. A. B. de Bragança Pereira, "História Religiosa de Goa", p. 212.
36. *DI*, I, 781.
37. *Doc*, IX, 247.
38. *DI*, IV, 214-15.
39. *Doc*, VIII, 160.
40. *APO*, 3, p. 659.
41. *Bullarium*, First Provincial Council, Acc, 2, dec. 10, p. 8, decs. 32, 24, 25, 37, p. 32-33.
42. *Ibid.*, First Provincial Council, Acc. 2, dec. 10, p. 8.
43. *Ibid.*, Third Provincial Council, Acc. 4, dec. 17, p. 81.
44. *DI*, XVI, 321.
45. In 1576 in Malabar, Bassein and Thana the converts looked like Hindus rather than Christians, especially where there were no priests. Many converts turned back to their previous Hindu practices. It was hard for the missionaries to see the work of many years go to waste and many souls being lost. *Ibid.*, X, 740, 742.
46. *MR*, 173, fls. 414v-16.
47. Fernão Guerreiro, *Relação Anual das coisas que fizeram os Padres da Companhia de Jesus nas suas Missões*, Vol. I, p. 348.
48. *Doc*, X, 109.
49. *Ibid.*, VIII, 422.
50. *DI*, VI, 118.
51. *Doc*, IX, 245.
52. *DI*, XVIII, 657.
53. *Ibid.*, 665.
54. *Ibid.*, 891. Often the sick persons treated by the Portuguese doctors did not survive whereas those treated by the Hindu physicians did much better. However, this might not have been the reason why the people preferred the latter. Fátima Gracias, *Health and Hygiene in Colonial Goa 1510-1961*, p. 88. On local doctors in Goa see Filinto Cristo Dias, *Esboço da História da Literatura Indo-Portuguesa*.

55. Fernão Guerreiro, *op. cit.* p. 4. Note that in Salcete serious work of conversion started in 1560, but more intensely and aggressively after 1585.

56. *Bullarium*, First Provincial Council, Acc. 2, dec. 37, p. 14. Josef Wicki, (ed.), *LPC*, p. 20.

57. *Jogue* was a kind of learned pilgrim who renounced the world and lived in lonely places doing penance. João de Barros, *Decada da Asia* II, Part I, (1777), p. 464. In 1568 some *jogues* came to the city of Goa with letters from their temples. This was a great obstacle for the conversion of Hindus, hence these *jogues* were forbidden to enter the city. *APO*, 3, p. 20.

58. *Doc*, X, 498. *Bullarium*, First Provincial Council, Acc. 2, dec. 37, p. 14.

59. *DI*, IV, 807.

60. *Bullarium*, First Provincial Council, Acc. 2, dec. 36, p. 14.

61. Francisco de Souza, *OCJC*, p. 180.

62. *DI*, IV, 307.

63. Fr. F. Cabral wrote in 1591, "Escrevem que se fizeram tantos mil Christãos, se elles se fazem de maneira que depois de feitos tornão muitos a retroceder e fugir, e milhor hé escrever, que 200 pola porta e como se devem fazer, que 2000 polla janela e por meios que escandalizão." *Ibid.*, XV, 583.

64. ARSI, *Extracto das cousas*, 1a, fl. 29v. In 1607 it was reported, "Pouca segurança de fé que há na maior parte dos christãos de Salsete por muitos deles serem pouco convertidos o que é perigo de suas almas retrocederem e de unirem com os infieis." ARSI, *Eppistolae Goana et Malabarica*, 16, fl. 128v.

65. ARSI, *Extracto das cousas*, 1a, fl. 85.

66. *Doc*, VI, 273.

67. CEHU, *Documentação Ultramarina Portuguesa* I, p. 568.

68. A. Lopes Mendes, *A India Portuguesa*, Vol. I, p. 152.

69. Georg Schurhammer, *Francisco Javier. Su Vida y su tiempo*, II, p. 245.

70. *DI*, X, 399.

71. Rodrigo José de Lima Felner, *op. cit.*, p. ii, 83. Even in 1510 some Portuguese had turned Muslims and they became very rich. Afonso

Brás de Albuquerque, *op. cit.*, Vol. I, Part II, p. 218.

72. In Zanzibar, Mafia and Pemba. Justus Strander, *The Portuguese Period in East Africa*, pp. 254-55.
73. João de Barros, *Decada da Asia*, I, (1945), p. 114.
74. D. D. Kosambi, *Myth and Reality*, p. 158.
75. *DI*, IV, 795.
76. *Ibid.*, 799.
77. Alessandro Valignano, *op. cit.*, pp. 352-53. *DI*, V, 553.
78. ARSI, *Eppistolae Goana et Malabarica*, 14, fl. 381.
79. *DI*, XVI, 726. In 1647 the people, not only from Goa but also from other parts of India, who came to venerate the body of Francis Xavier made vows to him and gave alms for the graces received. ARSI, *Goana Historia*, 34 - I, fl. 215v.
80. *Bullarium*, First Provincial Council, Acc. 2, dec. 28, p. 12. *DI*, I, 86; XV, 89. *Doc*, III, 223. This request was also made by the *Pay dos Christãos* to the viceroy, D. Duarte de Meneses. *BFUP*, No. 1, p. 40. Decree by the same viceroy granting this request in 1588. *Ibid.*, pp. 40, 51.
81. *DI*, XVI, 720.
82. *Ibid.*, III, 728.
83. *Ibid.*, XVI, 320. In Manapar, in South India or Fishery Coast, the Christians and Hindus showed devotion to a cross. *Ibid.*, 42. In Punicale the Hindus showed respect for the church and whenever they had some differences of opinion among themselves they swore by the church while settling their disputes. *Doc*, IV, 312. In Cochin in 1573 the Hindus offered oil to the churches for their lamps. *DI*, IX, 353. For more cases about syncretism see *Christianisation of the Goa Islands, 1510-1567* by Anthony d'Costa, pp. 155, 159, 165.
84. *DI*, III, 728
85. Letter written by Br. Pero Afonso to his companions in 1560. *Doc*, VIII, 170.
86. *DI*, XVIII, 665.
87. *Doc*, III, 351.
88. In 1559 Fr. Pedro Fernandes Sardinha wrote that the separation between the Hindu and Christian communities was necessary to

reform local customs. "Depois que se forem christãos não conversem mais nem rirão com os parentes gentios, e por que os não tornem ao que herão, e mal podera o filho prevalecer na fee de Christo, conversando com o pay gentio e idolatra, pelo que devião os gentios de Goa viver apartados na ilha de Divar ou na de Chorão." *Doc*, IV, 558.

89. *Doc*, VII, 216. *LFC*, fls. 5v, 40.
90. *Bullarium*, Second Provincial Council, Acc. 2, dec. 9, p. 49.
91. *BFUP*, No. 1, p. 33.
92. Josef Wicki, (ed.), *LPC*, p. 137.
93. *DI*, XVI, 324. *Bullarium*, Third Provincial Council, Acc. 2, dec. 7, p. 66.
94. *Ibid.*, Third Provincial Council, Acc. 2, dec 14.
95. *MR*, 2A, fl. 274.
96. *DI*, I, 13-14, 31-32, 182-83.
97. *Bullarium*, Third Provincial Council, Acc. 59, dec. 2, p. 87.
98. ARSI, *Eppistolae Goana et Malabarica*, 14, fls. 298v-99v.
99. *DI*, IV, 214.
100. Letter written by some Portuguese residing in the city of Goa to the king in 1600. *APO*, 1, Part II, p. 83.
101. AHU, *Registo de cartas*, Cod. 281, fl. 203v.
102. *APO*, 1, Part II, pp. 97-98.
103. *Doc*, II, 19, 230. António da Silva Rego, *História das Missões do Padroado Português do Oriente*, pp. 512-15.
104. *Doc*, II, 235-37, 364-69; III, 229-31.
105. *APO*, 1, Part II, pp. 20, 36, 53. *DI*, III, 408.
106. Luís de Guzman, *op. cit.*, p. 59.
107. *Doc*, V, 440.
108. ARSI, *Eppistolae Goana et Malabarica*, 15, fls. 147-48.
109. *Doc*, X, 229.
110. *DI*, VI, 615.
111. The priest could employ a sacristan, cook, dispensary manager and a boy to accompany him to the village, besides an apparitor, interpreter and two foot soldiers. ARSI, *Eppistolae Goana et Malabarica*, 15, fl. 148.

112. *Bullarium*, First Provincial Council, Acc, 4, dec. 30, p. 29.
113. A. B. de Bragança Pereira, "História Religiosa de Goa", p. 63.
114. *Memória Histórico Eclesiastica da Arquidiocese de Goa*, p. 105. The king, D. Sebastião, wrote to a viceroy, "Primeiramente terão cuidado que os gentios não refarão as casas de ydolatrias nem as farão de novo e a farão castigar os bramanes que injuriãc ou vituperão os christãos como os novamente convertidos farão trabalhar de maneira que não vivão mall por ociozidade e castigando e amoestando se não emendarem..." ARSI, *Fundationes Goana*, 22 - I, fl. 12.
115. Ana Cannas da Cunha, *op. cit.*, p. 299.
116. *Doc*, X, 500. Constitutions of the Archdiocese of Goa, 1568.
117. BNL, *Reservados*, Cod. 176, fl. 118 v.
118. *DI*, VIII, 65. *Bullarium*, First Provincial Council, Acc. 2, dec. 10, p. 8.
119. *Doc*, IV, 558.
120. *Bullarium*, First Provincial Council, Acc. 2, dec, 42, p. 15.
121. *Ibid.*, Acc. 2, dec. 47, p. 16.
122. BNL, *Reservados*, Cod. 176, fl. 117.
123. *Ibid.*, fl. 116.
124. *Ibid.*, fl. 119.
125. *Ibid.*, fl. 117v.
126. Josef Wicki, "S. Francisco Xavier", p. 11, note 41.
127. Memoria para a História Eclesiastica do Arcebispado de Goa e Seus Suffraganeos. BNL, *Reservados*, Cod. 176, fl. 118.
128. *Ibid.*, fl. 117v.
129. *Ibid.*, fl. 117.
130. *Ibid.*, fl. 116.
131. *Bullarium*, First Provincial Council, Acc. 4, dec. 9, p. 25.
132. BNL, *op. cit.*, fl. 118v.
133. *DI*, VIII, 57.
134. BNL, *Reservados*, Cod. 866, fl. 11.
135. *Ibid.*, Cod. 176, fl. 121.
136. *Ibid.*, fl. 118.

137. J. H. da Cunha Rivara, *Ensaio Histórico da Lingua Concani*, p. 27.

138. *Documentos Remetidos da India* ou *Livros das Monções*, I, p. 20.

139. *APO*, 1, Part II, p. 83. The governors hardly favoured the work of conversion. *DI*, III, 357. There were several complaints against the Portuguese civil authority for not favouring conversions. *Doc*, VIII, 301.

140. BNL, *Reservados*, Cod. 176, fl. 120.

141. *Bullarium*, Third Provincial Council, Acc. 2, dec. 24, p. 71.

142. BNL, *Reservados*, Cod. 176, fl. 121.

143. "Eu escrevo ao Guovernador que pellas ilhas de Goa nas aldeas della onde ouver christãos, se façam escollas em que se ensine a douctrina cristãa e que algumas veses no anno vam alguns pregadores pellas aldeas da ditta ilha a fazer suas pregações e constrajam vir a ellas os gentios que não sam christãos. Tereis cuidado de lhe fazer disto lembrança para que se faça assy como lho escrevo." Instructions from D. João III to Miguel Vaz regarding Christendom in India. Almeirim, 5 March 1546. *Doc*, III, 265.

144. *Ibid.*, IV, 132.

145. *Ibid.*, VI, 469.

146. "Sabe-se porem que no seculo XVII foi a christandade de Bardez mais que as outras perseguida da inquisição como relapsa na idolatria, e ritos gentilicos, ou porque de feito era assim, ou porque o santo officio se não atrevia a entrar nas terras administradas espiritualmente pelos Jesuitas com a mesma facilidade, com que entrava nas que estavam a cargo dos Franciscanos." J. H. da Cunha Rivara, *Brados a Favor das Communidades das Aldeias do Estado da India*, p. 83.

147. ARSI, *Miscellaneum Indiarum Orientalum*, 38 - I, fl. 137.

148. "Dos outros cristãos novos que vierão e vem do reyno esta toda a India chea e todo o trato em suas mãos ẽ dizem que com suas dadivas jaa começão a governar e mandar a terra." Letter from Fr. Baltazar Dias, rector of the College of St Paul in 1555. CEHU, *As Gavetas da Torre do Tombo*, V, pp. 71-72.

149. *DI*, IV, 2-4.

150. António Baião, *A Inquisição de Goa*, Vol. I, pp. 27-35. A. K. Priolkar, *The Goa Inquisition*.

151. *Doc*, II, 338-39.

152. Ana Cannas da Cunha, *op. cit.*, p. 128.

153. *Doc*, VII, 238.

154. *Ibid.*, 239. There were some Lutherans in the prison of the Inquisition in Goa. *Ibid.*, VI, 117.

155. *Ibid.*, XI, 821.

156. *DI*, III, 408.

157. *Ibid.*, 354.

158. *Ibid.*, 357.

159. Ana Cannas da Cunha, *op. cit.*, p. 126.

160. Joaquim Veríssimo Serrão, *História de Portugal*, p. 260.

161. *DI*, XVI, 495. "Parece que pera serviço de Ds e aumento da nossa fe catholica avia por bem que os christãos da terra que forem presos pelo crime de heresia e apostasias não percam de suas fazendas mais que o que parecer a mesa do Santo officio da Inquisição por ser muito novos na fé e sera escandalo aos outros convertidos e impedimento à conversão se em todos se executar igualmente; e tambem se deve pela mesma razão aver um breve de sua santidade pera que sedo relapsos não serem entregues à justiça secular quanto a mesa parecer." Letter from the archbishop of Goa, D. Jorge Temudo, to the king of Portugal. ARSI, *Miscellaneum Indiarum Orientalum*, 38 - II, fl. 255v.

162. "Quanto alla cristianità dell'India, per quello che veggo con gli occhi proprii et nelle lettere ch'al Provinciale et Visitatore passati si scrivevano et ne tengo informatione, è in tutte queste parti universalmente la christianità molto fiacca... La causa di questa fiacchezza nasce (oltre la mala inclinatione et qualità delle genti, che sono habituate in una sorte di vita vitiosa et licentiosa, come sole essere sempre dove non ci è cognitione di nostro Segnor et regna l'abominabile idolatria) particolarmente da due cause principali et universali, l'una è, perché ordinariamente non sono intrati per la vera porta, et gli nostri, se bene con santa intentione et zelo, non so quanto accertatamente, hanno sempre cercato di questi mezzi humani dell'interessi et favori per moverli ad accettare la fede, et non hanno lasciato con suavità per se stesso operare alla parola dell'Evangelio et alla virtù dello Spirito Santo, il quale, quando egli vuole, attingit a fine usque ad finem fortiter et operatur omnia suaviter." Letter from Fr. A. Valignano to the superior-general of the Society of Jesus. December 1574. *DI*, IX, 526-27.

163. *Doc*, III, 351-52.
164. *Bullarium*, First Provincial Council, Acc. 2, dec. 10, p. 33.
165. D. Furman, *Religion and Social Conflict in the USA*, p. 35.
166. *APO*, 1, Part II, pp. 65, 75.
167. *Bullarium*, Third Provincial Council, Acc. 2, dec. 28, p. 72.
168. António da Silva Rego, "A liberdade religiosa e o 1° Concilio Provincial de Goa", pp. 41-55. *DI*, VII, 660.
169. Miguel Ferreira D'Almeida, (trans.), *Canones e Decretos do Concilio Tridentino*, pp. 35, 42.
170. *DI*, V, 655. *Ibid.*, VIII, 45-46. *Bullarium*, Fourth Provincial Council (1592), Acc. 2, dec 5. *APO*, 3, p. 99.
171. The collapse of the church that had been established by the missionaries, for instance by Joseph Beschi and Robert de Nobili, with its hundreds of thousands of converts many of them of high caste, in Madurai in South India, was not strange. The persecution of Christians in Japan is another example of the collapse of a community of converts.
172. *DI*, III, 718-19. There were other important decrees.
173. *Doc*, X, 19. *Ibid.*, IV, 74. In 1580, A. Valignano wrote about India, "Esta gente como não se convertem ni se pode conservar sino es con darles muchas ayudas y favores temporaes y son muy tiraniçados de seus senhores tienen leys y costubres perversos..." *Ibid.*, XI, 480.
174. *DI*, XIII, 422.
175. *Doc*, VIII, 299-300.
176. Letter from Fr. Nicolao Lanciloto to Fr. Ignatius of Loyola. Coulão, 1550. *Doc*, VII, 32-33.
177. *DI*, IV, 9. *Bullarium*, Third Provincial Council, Acc. 2, dec. 23, p. 70.
178. C.R. Boxer, *The Church Militant and Iberian Expansion 1440-1770*, pp. 102-04.
179. *Doc*, VIII, 192.

# 10

# MISSIONARIES AND LOCAL CLERGY: CHRISTIAN WOMEN

## Missionaries

"The life of missionaries in the East cannot be compared with that of the merchants, whose chief concern was to acquire spices and precious stones, but with that of true soldiers of Christ ever ready to conquer souls, convert infidels, destroy idols and expel idolatry from India, in order to plant a new Christendom here", wrote Paulo da Trindade in the first half of the seventeenth century.[1] 'Spiritual heroism or achievement', an expression to be understood from the sixteenth century missionary mentality or historiography, became so exclusive to the missionaries that they did not wish to share it with the local Christians. According to the missionaries, the local converts were by nature incapable of performing spiritual feats. Domingos, Afonso and Francisco, the Goan converts, who were killed along with Fr. Rudolfo Aquaviva and his Jesuit companions during the Cuncolim riots in Salcete in 1583, were excluded from the list of martyrs of the faith when the church beatified the Jesuit missionaries. Paulo da Costa, a local secular priest, was not beatified as a martyr either.[2] Not that anyone is trying to make such a claim today. The converts did not share the same worldview and lifestyle of the missionaries and Portuguese laymen in the East; rather the former's constant dealings with their Hindu neighbours — demanded by their daily and concrete life and this was the real world of the converts — frustrated the missionary endeavour to integrate them into Christendom.[3] Some reportings about Hindus turning against the converts could be exaggerations or wrong perception of the reality originating from biased missionaries. The continuous co-existence with the Hindu cultivators and labourers was an economic and social necessity. These spontaneous and necessary contacts made the converts only half-Christians, weak in European customs, which finally debarred them from entering the religious orders.

The missionary zeal to make conversions did not match their cultural formation and numerical strength. Besides being new in the field, they did not have general norms to deal with the complex local situations in daily life. These were the new problems and difficulties they had to confront, and solutions were not found in their manuals.[4] This missionary frustration and their own incapacity to adjust to the 'other', led them to press the government to introduce laws and a code of behaviour — which came to affect individuals, family life, and the local social customs drastically — to check unacceptable or unchristian practices. But obviouly, many decrees and stipulations were often flouted not only by the locals but also by the Portuguese authorities themselves, to the missionaries' face. The laws left no loopholes for Hindu practices or syncretic religion, but actual practices escaped missionary vigilance. The missionaries were determined to make of Goa, the capital of the overseas eastern empire, a city with Portuguese and Catholic customs, laws and religion.

The partition of a territory among the religious orders was a common practice then. This official territorial division functioned as a prevention of many conflicts arising among the religious orders working near one another in the same field. The methods of conversion used by one religious order could differ from the methods used by another, and often quarrels between religious orders arose over these methods. It need not be over-stressed that conversions, or lack of them, depended to a large extent on the collaboration, or rivalry, or even unhealthy competition, between the religious orders.[5] Since conversions also depended on the number of missionaries available in the field, we have the recurring idea in missionary historiography, that with more priests working for conversions a lot more people would find salvation.[6] A missionary wrote in 1555 that in this land of plenty — especially for priests, who could walk on gold if they accepted everything the people wanted to give them — there was unfortunately a great lack of missionaries.[7] But there was no lack of priests in Goa, it being the centre of Christendom; rather there was a great need for learned missionaries and competent administrators in Goa, as elsewhere in Europe.[8] There were eighty churches and monasteries in Goa by the turn of the sixteenth century when Goa was in its rapid decline; and unbelievably, there were thirty thousand priests and monks in India. There were more clergymen and monks in India than there were soldiers, wrote a viceroy in 1633.[9]

The locals who entered the seminaries in India had neither the skills, nor virtues, nor the zeal to convert the Hindus. They needed many years of mortification and experience, hence Francis Xavier did not mind having here European priests though they were of few talents or poor skills. He felt these men would certainly do better than the locals.[10] Fr. Jeronimo Nadal requested Fr. Diego Lainez, the second superior-general of the Society of Jesus, to send to the missions robust but not so bright recruits — especially those who served no purpose in Germany — for they could be very helpful to convert the heathens in the East.[11] The policy of Alessandro Valignano was to send to, or keep in, India the Jesuits with less virtue or with not so edifying behaviour, and take the best men for the mission in Japan.[12]

Many candidates for the priesthood and religious life in India came from among the former Portuguese soldiers, who had incurred numerous canonical impediments to ordination on account of their incessant involvement in wars; nevertheless, the vicar-general dispensed them from these impediments.[13] Besides, the missionaries and the soldiers usually worked closely together, but a very small group of missionaries argued that this conspicuous and contemptuous alliance could erode the confidence of the already hostile natives.[14] Many candidates who came from Portugal and entered the Society of Jesus to become Brothers, were illiterate.[15] Therefore, the use of force in conversions was but natural to some of these religious persons.

Fortunately, some did not take long to understand that the 'good-for-nothing' missionaries from Europe, harmed the work of conversion more than facilitated it. There had been several requests from missionaries here to their religious superiors in Europe not to send more useless missionaries to India, because a few like them already stationed here did not help conversions at all.[16] These missionaries were imperfect, ignorant, without experience and knowledge, with wrong opinions, and held a view that knowledge was not necessary to work in the missions. Some of them could hardly read the mass prayers.[17] Some local missionaries expressed the view that the presence of learned missionaries would be highly appreciated in order to refute the false religions of the Hindus and Muslims.[18] Missionaries who were able to discuss and write treatises that could show by rational arguments the falsity of these religions and the truth of Christianity were welcome.[19] The more intelligent and shrewder missionaries, besides working for the conversion of the élite and rulers, also played a crucial role as agents of diplomacy for the Portuguese. Some missionaries might have excelled in sciences and arts, education and pioneering work, but their main purpose was conversions.[20]

Although strange as it might appear to us, some religious orders had prisons in their monasteries in Goa, for the religious rules demanded it for their more rebellious members. These prisons were for religious and local converts alike. In 1594 the king wrote to the viceroy condemning the continuous use of guards to 'hunt' Hindus, the punishment meted out to Christians, and private prisons in the monasteries. The religious orders had overstepped their proper jurisdiction. The king called for a stop to all these abuses. He suggested that the offences committed by the local Christians could be dealt with by ordinary means. The existence of prisons in the monasteries had been forbidden in 1579, but the religious authorities paid no heed to that warning.[21]

In 1581 Fr. L. de Abreu complained that one of the reasons for lack of priests to hear confessions in India was, that most wanted to be preachers, even those who had no talent for it. He added that so much preaching was hardly necessary here, for even in Portugal it was not a normal practice to preach outside the lenten season.[22] However, without knowing the local language they preached, which is rather surprising; but they preached through interpreters. To hear confessions they required the knowledge of the local language; so perhaps, the missionaries who did not know it well avoided it, thus engaging themselves in much preaching. Nevertheless, they insisted on the study of the local languages in their seminaries and colleges.[23]

It is often stated that the seventeenth century is characterized by a decrease in missionary zeal. If we go by the number of conversions made or by historical biases of the time it might be true. However, this should not be the criterion to judge missionary zeal. The number of local priests went on increasing. The local conflicts between the *Padroado* and the *Propaganda Fide* created an impression that the religious zeal had given way to greed and lax morality among the clergymen of the *Padroado*. But religious intolerance continued unabated; the policy of exclusion of local secular clergy from ecclesiastical offices that mattered did not change, the doors of religious orders remained firmly closed to the Goan candidates, and many 'decrees and privileges in favour of conversion' were issued. The political and economic context was changing significantly, but not the religious one; the missionary zeal and proselytizing attitude did not match the changing times.

## Local Clergy

### (a) *Local Collaboration in Conversions*

The Hindu partnership — especially tradesman and Brahman — with the Portuguese is unquestionable. We have only to recall that the Muslims were expelled from Goa in 1510, and several times thereafter, with the Hindu help. The Portuguese-Hindu joint business and trade, and the tendency to allocate government jobs that mattered to the Hindus, is well known; but often and deliberately this collaboration has been overlooked in contemporary historical debate on conversions.[24] Without the Hindu support the *Estado da India* could not have been sustained. However, the help given by the Hindu converts to the work of conversion is less obvious, or rather less emphasized. It is beyond doubt that the conversion of some led others to convert themselves; however, this is not the point being discussed here. Converts were also actively involved in the work of conversion, especially when favours and indulgences were granted to those who converted a Hindu or Muslim to the Christian faith.[25] A convert asked a Hindu to receive baptism.[26] The converts worked to win Hindus to Christianity to the extent of forcing the priests to baptize them, but fearing that such baptisms might not be valid, the priests refused to oblige.[27] The convert Santu Sinay (Salvador Pinto) helped to spread the Christian religion in the village of Candolim.[28] After baptism the neo-converts promised to bring all to the church.[29] There are a few reportings on the active association of the neo-converts with missionary activity.[30] However, this kind of collaboration in the activity of conversion, by and large, was not reported, since 'spiritual feats' or conversions belonged to the missionaries alone. Besides, the missionary hardly gave any opportunity or responsibility to the more ambitious and enterprising local clergy.

The spiritual conquest of Goa was not maintained by the missionary undertaking alone. The founding of a seminary was a clever and successful strategy to win local collaborators for missionary work.[31] Francis Xavier made use of two local deacons from Goa, in Tuticorim.[32] Indian seminarians helped the missionaries as interpreters.[33] Unfortunately, the local clergy was mistrusted, relegated and denied minimum equality with the Portuguese missionaries — regular and secular clergy. They not only received insufficent attention that mattered, but they were also frequently criticized.

In the beginning the Portuguese did not mind the presence of foreign missionaries in their overseas territories, but when the Spanish missionaries plotted the conquest of Portuguese lands, Portugal became alarmed. The presence of foreigners preoccupied frequently the Portuguese Jesuit missionaries and the royal officials, who complained about this menace.[34] Another serious problem the missionaries had to confront — besides this foreign menace — was their own numerical weakness and ignorance of local languages, and that the Goan converts could not be ordained as priests yet. They were still too young in the faith.[35] But under no circumstances could the faith prosper and Christendom expand without the aid of the native clergy. The foreigner, layman and missionary alike, was looked upon as potential threat to the commercial interests of the Portuguese crown. Added to this, the Portuguese Jesuits complained that their non-Portuguese superiors in Europe placed more trust in the foreign missionaries than in themselves. With this political and religious situation prevailing, the Portuguese missionaries preferred a subservient and weak local clergy as helpers in their work of conversion, which necessarily led to the founding of the first seminaries for Indians.[36]

When intense work of conversion began in Goa from 1540, the insufficient number of missionaries could hardly be in a position to sustain the new Christendom.[37] The climate in Goa was not such that it killed the missionaries or kept them away, as in other tropical regions. But on the other hand, Goa did not offer any great incentive to the more ambitious *reinóis* nor presented many opportunities to make quick fortunes. Therefore, the lack of clergy and their own ignorance of the local languages could have been some of the reasons that forced them to educate some natives to become priests. They were to serve the missionaries merely as assistants and interpreters.[38]

From 1510 till 1540 only a few Franciscans and a few Portuguese secular clergy lived in Goa. They continued to serve their countrymen on land, after serving them spiritually on the Portuguese ships that sailed to the East, but many of them soon returned to Portugal. This task of serving the Portuguese might have occupied most of their time, since conversion of the locals was not their main concern yet. (We need to recall that the idea of mass conversions came about only after this period.) Besides, the secular clergy and the religious did not cooperate with each other in the work of conversion.[39] Curiously, at the beginning of the seventeenth century (1604) the king had to forbid the missionaries to board the ships leaving Lisbon with destination to India and other places, without the permission of the viceroy. There were more clergymen in Goa than it could contain or needed, and less opportunities to make conversions.[40]

(b) *The Seminary*

In 1541, Miguel Vaz, vicar-general of the diocese of Goa, and Fr. Diogo Borba came up with a practical idea of founding an association for the purpose of propagating the faith in Goa, an association that came to be known as the *Confraria de Santa Fé* or Confraternity of the Holy Faith. This confraternity had the highest government officials and some rich converts as its patrons and associates. In the same year, this lay association or confraternity decided to found a seminary exclusively for the local converts to study for the priesthood.[41] However, the Portuguese and *mestiço* students were subsequently admitted to this seminary.[42] The purpose of establishing this seminary was the education of young boys who would join one day the cadre. Priests, catechists, interpreters, personnel for any other service directly related to the work of conversion and instruction to the neo-converts, and government employees would be formed in the seminary.[43] The aim of this seminary was conversion and nothing else.[44]

This seminary known as *Seminário da Conversão da Fé*, (Seminary of Conversion to Faith) and also as *Seminário de Santa Fé de Goa* (Seminary of Holy Faith of Goa) taught the most talented and virtuous young converts, first the faith and good customs, and then those found suitable for the priesthood learnt philosophy, theology, ethics and how to conduct liturgical services. The less talented ones would help the missionaries as interpreters and catechists in the vast diocese of Goa erected in 1533.[45] This seminary instructed also convert boys from other places and nations, who would be sent back one day to their native places, to propagate the faith either as priests or catechists.[46] We recall that the priestly formation given to the local seminarians before the Council of Trent (1563) was rather short and elementary.

This seminary, a quasi-pioneer project in the East in 1541,[47] counted among its benefactors chiefs of the villages and noblemen.[48] However, its main source of income came by a decree passed by D. João III. This king, zealous in the conversion of Hindus, donated generously to the seminary the rents that once belonged to temples .[49] By another decree in 1548, the king granted annually an amount of 800 000 *reis* in addition to the rent of 600 000 *reis* it already received.[50] Moreover, the Royal Treasury gave another 200 000 *reis*. The seminary could have still another 1000 *cruzados* every year if the local soldiers (*lascarins*) cared to give it, and all the gifts the Hindu and the Muslim rulers sent to the queen of Portugal. Many Portuguese donated money to the Jesuits for the work of conversion.[51]

The seminary did not appear to have had financial problems, but it had to face other difficulties which were not uncommon then. There was a wrong choice of candidates, and a few candidates had been forced to enter the seminary.[52] Fr. Diogo de Borba caught some boys, *pagãos* (pagans) and *mouros* (Moors), and kept them in the seminary after baptizing them. He also forced some Christian boys to join it.[53] At the seminary there were some boys who not long before had served and worshipped the demon and their idols, but as converts they showed a great contempt for them.[54] We are told that the students who frequented the seminary were talented, but with very little religious fervour.[55] Nevertheless, all were boys of the missionaries, since many of these students helped the missionaries. I shall discuss later more about what, and how, these young converts, some of them candidates for priesthood, learnt at the seminary for the locals and about those who managed it.

In 1542 the Society of Jesus (the Jesuits) came to Goa.[56] With the arrival of the Jesuits here conversions entered a new phase. This phase was intensely marked by their militant methods. Their well organized conversion drive, supported by the state, sought first the conversion of the high castes. "The Jesuits brought to Goa its illustrious, though restless and domineering, tendencies."[57]

Francis Xavier, the first Jesuit to come to Goa, was fully aware of his status as papal nuncio as well as that of a very high envoy of the king of Portugal, D. João III.[58] The other Jesuits who followed him, although less influential than Xavier, made it their policy to write to the kings of Portugal requesting them for their full support. They also tried to convince the governors and other officials to favour their work of conversion.[59] The Jesuits gained so much power that even some governors had to follow their dictates and "grant them whatever they wanted".[60] Francisco de Souza, another Jesuit, writing at the beginning of the seventeenth century, summarized the Jesuit behaviour and attitude thus: "...the great apostle of the East and his companions, like courageous soldiers of Christ and faithful ministers of the gospel, performed heroic deeds, undertook difficult tasks, opened new missions, erected a great number of crosses, built innumerable churches, destroyed idols, pulled down Hindu temples, founded seminaries, residential houses and colleges, taught Gentiles, eliminated Jews and converted Moors, defeated schismatics, reformed Catholics, baptized kings, suffered fatigues, crossed tumultuous seas, suffered many shipwrecks, crossed barbarian and uncivilized countries, learnt difficult languages, worked marvelous deeds, sanctified prisons, died for the faith, and expanded the empire of Jesus Christ with such zeal . . . ."[61]

In 1544 the seminary was offered to the Jesuits who accepted it, after the Franciscans turned the offer down.[62] It came to be known as College of St Paul. The recruitment and formation of candidates for the priesthood was done with that same militant attitude, suitable to the new phase of conversions, that had begun in 1540. In 1549 the Jesuits took up the management of this college, but only in 1551 the king ratified it and granted them the ownership of the seminary building, its properties and the rights over it.

The College of St Paul became the centre of conversion activity. From this college the Jesuits would launch out "to conquer the peoples of India attacking the forces of evil with impetuous spirit and examples of virtues".[63] Everyday in 1554 three or four Muslims or Hindus, richly dressed, wearing gold chains and many rings on their fingers came to the college to ask to be instructed for baptism.[64] The newly converted poor boys from the city stayed in a house at St Paul and learnt how to read and write. When they grew up a job was given to each one of them for a decent standard of living.[65] The college had a section for the converted orphan boys, where some of them prepared themselves for religious or clerical life.[66]

As seen earlier, the college was founded only for the converted boys, the Portuguese and *mestiços* being forbidden to enter it. But the Portuguese students and candidates for the Society also attended this college. These Portuguese boys demanded more attention, resulting in the neglect of the local boys. Besides, the former could at times turn dangerous and unruly *(son muy peligrossos y tabajossos de governar)*, and having them here was hardly profitable, since much money was spent on them to the detriment of the more deserving local students. The administrators of the college decided that the existing local boys only could sing in the church's choir, but the college never became exclusively for the converted boys.[67] Hindus and Muslims also studied here.[68] At times this college showed in its roll about four hundred boys from different nationalities or groups: Brahmans, Persians, Arabs, Malabaris, etc. The age and number of students allowed from each country had been laid down by the college statutes.[69]

At the College of St Paul the students continued to learn arts (philosophy, Latin, rhetoric and music) and virtues to help the priests in their works.[70] The school of virtues taught them how to practise mortification, obedience, penances and works of charity. It focused on teaching the ignorant, visiting the poor in prisons and hospitals, accompanying the priests to the sick and doing other similar works.[71] Perhaps, theology was not taught to the local canditates for priesthood in the same way as it was to the Portuguese seminarians. Interestingly, some argued that the local candidates were incapable of learning it, others said that they could become arrogant after mastering it, but a few missionaries held that the lack of theological studies was a drawback in their formation, for the newly ordained local priests would not be able to instruct the Christians well and clarify their doubts.[72]

Be that as it may, the locals were excluded from entering the Society of Jesus, and the other religious orders followed the same policy.[73] Lack of pioneering proselytizing spirit among the locals was a liability; besides many of them did not pass the test of religious fervour and virtues, hence no local was ever admitted to the Society of Jesus. Those who had been admitted (or might have been admitted) in the early years of the Society had to be "tried more than the others", since they were weak in faith.[74] The locals had neither the virtue nor the ability to meet all demands of the Society of Jesus.[75] Religious life must have been very hard then; in any case the locals stood no chance of surviving the test in the Society. The Jesuits had too many prejudices against the locals.[76]

In 1595 the college had a separate section only for the locals, and from here many joined the priesthood or other religious orders or administrative services.[77] The Jesuit conversion strategy consisted in winning over the high castes for the priesthood. The Franciscans did the same.[78]

Till 1598 the College of St Paul was preoccupied with the conversion of Hindus. Thereafter, the professed house of the Society of Jesus took charge of conversion activity, since such work caused much distraction from studies to those in the college.[79] Later in 1610, due to unhealthy conditions of the place, the Jesuits built another college, the New College of St Paul (to distinguish it from the old one) commonly known as the College of St Rock, not very far from the first college. Henceforth, the Old St Paul remained only for catechumens.[80] Earlier in 1574, the Jesuits founded another college in Margão, Salcete, but being exposed to constant attacks by the troops of the Adilshah, they transferred it to Rachol, also in Salcete, in 1610, as the city was then better protected by a wall. Here local priests were also formed by the same methods.

Interestingly, the sons of Europeans born in India, the *castiços*, could not be received into the Society, except very rarely, wrote the superior-general of the Jesuits, Fr. Everardo Mercuriano, in 1575. Likewise, five years later Alessandro Valignano,. another Jesuit who knew very well the situation in the East, advised that the *mestiços* (half-caste) and *castiços* (Portuguese born in India of white parents) should not as a rule be admitted to the Society of Jesus, except seldom.[81] Discrimination in the Society between the 'sons of Europe' (*reinóis*) and the 'sons of India' (*castiços*) was no secret affair. In 1594 Fr. Claudio Acquaviva, superior-general of the Society of Jesus, intervened and requested the Jesuits in India to avoid such offensive language and attitudes;[82] that even the whites, born in India of Portuguese parents, could not easily be admitted to the Society of Jesus may appear rather strange.[83]

The Franciscans were the first to organize the work of conversion in Goa. They had a monastery in the city of Goa whose purpose was to gather convert men and women to be instructed in the faith. During the first years when the Franciscan order was the only missionary group in Goa, its religious members had been accused of only burying the dead, chanting the requiem masses, and of neglecting the work of conversion.[84] This may not be entirely true, but they did not display that Jesuit militant and proselytizing attitude from the beginning. The Franciscans did not accept the Seminary of the Holy Faith when it was offered them; instead they built another college at Verem, in Bardez in 1555, known as the College or Seminary of Reis Magos.[85] It may be recalled that the district of Bardez was given to the Franciscans for the work of conversion during the government of D. Afonso de Noronha (1550-1554). The first church built in Bardez was that of Reis Magos, and it became the centre of Christianization in Bardez. They had also a house or school for catechumens in the same church, and a college and seminary for orphans in 1595.[86]

Some local converts had been accepted by the Franciscan order in Goa despite the disapproval of their superiors in Europe. The Franciscan superiors in Portugal had forbidden their local commissary in Goa to accept novices in India, even aspirants born of Portuguese settlers. Contrary to this prohibition, some Portuguese and Eurasians (*mestiços*) were admitted. Goans remained excluded. The Franciscans in Goa had a hard time to convince their superiors in Europe that the *mestiços* were almost as good as the European-born Portuguese.[87] The locals, they argued, could also make good religious. Moreover, this move would facilitate the conversion of their maternal relatives, so believed the Franciscans who worked in Goa.[88] If a few locals were admitted to the Franciscan order, most of them *mestiços*, it was simply for lack of personnel from Portugal. They needed men to maintain the huge monastery they had built in Goa. But they did not take long to follow in the footsteps of the Jesuits namely, of excluding the locals from membership of their religious order.[89] Neither the *Canarins* nor the *mestiços* were wanted as parish priests by the Franciscans throughout the sixteenth century. When the royal letter in 1603 demanded the substitution of secular priests (not local but Portuguese) for the Franciscans in the parishes in Bardez held by them, they refused to step down.[90]

When the question regarding formation of local candidates for the priestly life arose in India, there was no discussion on whether the seminary should be here or elsewhere. In 1540 Goa had already the fame of being the centre of Christendom in the East. However, when at the beginning of the seventeenth century the need was felt to form an African clergy in West Africa, the idea that the African candidates for the priesthood should be formed in Portugal, and not in Africa, gained the majority of votes. They argued that in Portugal these candidates could be instructed in good habits and political duties (*doctrinados em milhores costumes e mais politicos)* better than in Africa. They also held that a seminary in Portugal would be of superior quality, and the exemplary or saintly life of the religious men and laity in Portugal could help in their formation. Candidates for the African clergy were expected to emerge from among the sons and relatives of the local chiefs. They were urgently needed to control the dangers posed by the political, religious and commercial activities of the heretical Dutch in Africa. The clergy for Africa, just as the seminaries in Goa and in India, formed part of a larger scheme namely, of checking the potential menace created by foreign missionaries (non-Portuguese), to the Portuguese empire.[91]

Apologetic historians of today find the discrimination or exclusion of the locals from the religious life then, as something just and natural. They argue that the first generation of converts still had pagan elements in their lives. However, even in the following centuries when these pagan traits had perhaps disappeared long back, this sort of discrimination and prejudices against them continued as before. What could be the other reason for closing the doors of the religious orders to the local candidates? The inflated self-image of the missionary had to be maintained intact at all costs, and this would be possible only by preventing close contacts with the locals. The missionaries believed that if the locals entered the religious orders, they would certainly lower the missionary prestige in the eyes of the local population. This was a serious obstacle to their work of conversion.

The commonest missionary argument for excluding the locals from the membership of the religious orders was their innate low motivation and morals, which traits were also attributed to the existing local secular clergy; the Indians were lazy and could hardly keep the vow of celibacy, and there was no solution to this shortcoming.[92] They had some unpleasant manners and habits which they were not willing or were incapable of changing, since they were by nature inclined to them. They failed the test of the Portuguese refined and cultured tastes due to their slipshod lifestyle, said the missionaries. However, the Brahmans — in spite of the missionaries' prejudices against them — had better chances of success. The recruitment of candidates for the seminary was commonly done from among the high castes.[93] André Vaz, a *Canarim* or Goan, was the first to be ordained as a secular priest in 1558. Many more followed him.[94]

The missionaries doubted the possibility of any real conversion of the locals. By their very nature they could neither be trained nor changed. The Latin language, the rules and discipline in the Roman seminaries, the long formation, etc, constituted serious obstacles to the candidates belonging to a non-Christian cultural context. The hierarchy of the *Padroado*, being rigid and exclusive, did not permit the local clergy to fulfil their ambitions. Locals had been kept out of the religious orders for fear of backslidings or relapses. In Jesuit terminology 'vocation for India' from among the 'sons of Europe', meant persons with a lot of virtue and exemplary life to convert the Hindus and others. 'Vocations from India' were excluded from the religious orders, since they did not display long-standing virtue or any thirst for the conversion of Hindus.[95] If the *castiços* and *mestiços* were excluded from entering the religious orders, one could not expect a better treatment for the sons of the soil.

The locals had many other shortcomings as for instance

colour and caste.[96] As mentioned earlier, the Brahmans made it to the clerical life with more spontaneity and with greater ease due to their "intelligence and refined manners".[97] Native clergy in Goa, recruited from among the social élite, became the associates of the Portuguese or loyal citizens of the empire. Unfortunately, most remained in subordinate places. During the second half of the sixteenth century the Goan clergy formed a fairly large group. Although left powerless, they did not become totally submissive nor without social ambitions.[98]

We know that a section of Jesuits had suggested against forming a local clergy, for they strongly upheld that this type of clergy would fail to inspire confidence in the Portuguese. Missionary writings tell us that the locals did not come up to the expectations of the Europeans. And after much mudslinging on the local clergy, some of it stuck and created lasting stereotypes. There was a strong belief, for instance, that the Portuguese laymen would not like to confess to, or confide in, the local or *mestiço* clergymen.[99] It appears that the seminary training and the missionaries themselves could not, or were unwilling to, prepare the local canditates in 'virtue' and 'knowledge'. Perhaps the seminaries and the missionaries themselves contributed new prejudices against the locals and reinforced old ones. There is no information about the number of students and priests formed in the seminaries and colleges during the sixteenth century.[100] It is certain that the sons of benefactors of the colleges, mostly Brahmans and nobles, studied here.

The local candidates for the priesthood came from the high castes, frequently from the Brahman and sometimes from the Chaddo castes, as a result of the very religious nature of these communities or of their persistent need for upward mobility. The Goan church had more than sufficient number of regular and secular local clergy — although almost always discredited by the missionaries — much before 1961 when Goa became politically free. Churches in many other countries had to depend on foreign missionaries after their independence. Despite religious and social prejudices held against the Goans, it became clear that Christianity in Goa could not be sustained only by foreign missionaries.[101]

The first serious attempt at forming a local clergy dates from 1541, with Fr. Diogo Borba, Miguel Vaz and a few others who had suggested the foundation of the Seminary of *Santa Fé* (Holy Faith) for religious education and training of only Asian and East African youths. This seminary became the famous College of St Paul and the main centre for conversion activity when the Jesuits took over in 1544. Those who graduated in Latin and theology and showed good behaviour and virtues demanded from them, could be eligible for ordination as secular priests. This college, and other seminaries, trained Asian catechists and candidates for priesthood destined to sustain and expand Christendom in the vast lands of the *Padroado*.

## Christian Women

Most facts, interpretations, approaches and historiography related to the 'affair of conversions' we are familiar with, speak from the male point of view. The sixteenth century historiography of conversions has hardly any place for women. History itself has not been kind to women. However, we should not forget that the local women were the first Lusitanian citizens of the empire. They were 'used' to create and sustain this empire and Christendom. In 1512 Afonso de Albuquerque wrote that many women became Christians because they could have a comfortable life, and could earn a lot of money among the Portuguese.[102]

The role played by women in the activity of conversion deserves some attention. The presence and the life of the women did not go unrecorded. However, it is necessary to sift carefully historical evidence to re-create history with the least sexist bias. Perhaps this attempt will help us to re-think our historical and social context in different categories, rather than restricting ourselves to the dominant and edifying, but terribly biased historical reportings, left by the missionaries.

Although the Indo-Portuguese historiography of expansionism did highlight the feats and behaviour of the Portuguese — viceroys and governors, noblemen, settlers, missionaries, soldiers, factores, businessmen, renegades, or certain qualities of the converts, or those of the Hindus and Muslims — the Portuguese pioneers and administrators in Goa realized that by themselves they could not sustain and hold this territory without a settled way of life. Family life alone could provide this.[103] The presence of *casados* or Portuguese settlers was very essential for carrying on the political and economic duties of the state. But in the beginning the Portuguese married men came to India without their wives, which meant that they would return home one day. Besides, there were no Portuguese women overseas for the eligible Portuguese bachelors. If a Portuguese bachelor wanted to marry, he had no choice but to take a local convert woman for his wife. Therefore, a visible and stable Portuguese society and polity or authority could not be maintained in Goa without the conversion of some local women. From the outset we can state with certainty that the local women and children were the first to be converted: the Muslim women who were taken prisoners, between the two conquests of Goa, became the first converts and the first to marry the Portuguese. Some other local Christian women became wives of the Portuguese who wanted to settle down in Goa.[104] In 1548 the city of Goa had about five thousand Christians, most of them married women, their children, and also single women.[105]

Albuquerque conquered and defended Goa with the help of Hindus, but he knew that neither their support nor their confidence in the Portuguese would last long. Female conversions became absolutely necessary to begin his miscegenation programme between the Portuguese and local convert women, in order to create a new social order loyal to the Portuguese, to fill military outposts and fleets, and for political and administrative purposes. However, miscegenation was just a temporary arrangement until the arrival of Portuguese women.[106] Even later, conversions of local women to marry the Portuguese would continue, since it was certain that a sufficient number of women would not be forthcoming from Portugal. While upholding mixed marriages, Albuquerque had expressed simultaneously his dissatisfaction with the king, D. Manuel, for not permitting the Portuguese women to travel to India.[107] The institution of miscegenation within an endogamic society was nothing new, and was perhaps prevalent in Goa, too, during the Muslim rule. The Arab conquerors also Islamized non-Muslim girls and married them.[108] However, miscegenation was not the ideal to sustain Albuquerque's programme of conquest.

The programme of creating a group of loyal people to sustain the Portuguese network could be executed very well in Goa, according to Albuquerque. This city was sufficiently rich and belonged to the king of Portugal, unlike Cochin and Cananor which were only borrowed lands.[109] But on the whole the Portuguese were not certain whether it was worth retaining, and investing in, Goa, or whether the city would be profitable to the crown and mercantile schemes, or whether this land would not be reconquered by the Muslims. As a result of these doubts, Albuquerque did not have much support for his programme of miscegenation. Despite all the odds against Albuquerque's dreams of founding an empire, he was firm in retaining Goa as Portugal's possession; hence his optimism about the project of mixed marriages.

Expansion and conquests, to use the conventional historiographical terminology of the sixteenth century, opened a new possibility for greater geographical mobility. However, at the beginning of the sixteenth century, Portuguese women hardly ventured into these new areas. They were forbidden to board the ships. There had been cases of women hiding on board with the conivance of the crew, but when caught, the ship captains ordered them to be whipped and imprisoned, and then they put these women off wherever possible in the Atlantic islands. In 1523, three women had boarded clandestinely a ship of the fleet of Vasco da Gama, and after being caught the latter gave orders to whip them publicly on arriving in India, to serve as a deterrent. Official and public requests and protests of sympathy in favour of these women by the Franciscans and members of the 'Casa da Misericordia' only infuriated Vasco da Gama. He not only did not pay any heed to their requests and protests, but he also warned them severely that such requests and transporting of women clandestinely on board was not to be repeated.[110] Only the governors, captains and high ranking officials were allowed to take their wives and daughters along with them.[111] The demographic gender ratio in Portugal during the sixteenth century was one man to two women. We know that despite four or five Portuguese ships sailing to India every year, hardly any woman could be found on board during the first half of this century.[112]

The reasons for not permitting women to embark to the East were not explicitly mentioned in the historiography of the time, and I am not aware of any royal decree on such matter, but the punishment for disobeying this prohibition is already known to us. Under no pretext could women board the ships bound for India. Probably, women were not allowed to sail because the Portuguese ships, a constant target for the Muslims and corsairs, had to have its crew and soldiers on constant alert against the enemy. The presence of women on board of the ships could distract them from their duties, first, by making them effeminate and weak, namely, making them neglect their offensive and defensive obligations; and second, the sailors would give themselves up to sensual pleasures, diminishing thus the high risk-taking quality so indispensable at the time of war.[113] Besides making the ships' crew negligent and vulnerable, women on board the ships weakened the Christian virtues as well, which could attract God's punishment and defeat. Moreover, during the sieges by the enemy, the presence of women could impose a heavy burden on the already scarce food in the fortresses.[114] The dangers that the sailors faced, in case women came with them in the ships, was the main reason to exclude them, but the hard living condition on board was also another important factor. Perhaps, women were also considered as 'useless people' from the point of view of war and commerce, occupying mighty precious space in the ships.[115] Portuguese conservatism was another obstacle that prevented women from embarking overseas.

It may be recalled once more the order given by the governor, Afonso de Albuquerque, to hang Rui Dias, a soldier of his fleet, when he was found guilty of spending many nights in pleasure with Muslim women, whom Albuquerque had forcibly taken on board when the Portuguese were forced to withdraw from Goa after its first abortive conquest. He did so, not because he wanted to convert and marry these women to the Portuguese, nor because he respected these women, nor because sin could bring defeat to them.[116] Brás de Albuquerque, Afonso de Albuquerque's son, who had never been a soldier, commenting on the behaviour of Rui Dias said that his act could bring a big punishment from God, more so because they were Muslim women. The Portuguese believed that sin could bring defeat.[117] I think that in such circumstances Albuquerque demanded examples of military discipline before a difficult mission. Besides, he also needed to assert his command and authority amidst his hostile and reluctant captains. Women on board could erode military discipline.[118] When they travelled they had to be kept locked in separate quarters. These could be some of the reasons why women were forbidden to embark to India until 1545.

Mortality rate among the Portuguese women in India was rather high, even in the seventeenth century.[119] It was very rare for a woman to survive after the delivery, but if she did survive her child did not.[120] However, Germano da Silva Correia, through his *História da Colonização Portugueza na India* in six volumes, peopled the sixteenth century India with many Portuguese and Luso-descent heroines, mostly of the nobility. They appear to be so virile and a warlike people.[121] This kind of historiography and statements find no support in documentation and facts.

### (a) *Portuguese Orphan Girls*

From 1545 more women, including orphans and young invalid girls, came from Portugal to Goa for the purpose of marrying the Portuguese, but they were rather few. Some of the orphans sent overseas were undesirable even here, therefore Goa could dispense with them.[122] The viceroy, D. Antão de Noronha, wrote to the queen not to send such girls to Goa and other Portuguese-controlled territories, due to the high expenditure incurred on them and the difficulties in finding suitable husbands for them in Goa. Besides, there were many girls, daughters of noblemen and of other important persons, who had died for the cause of the king, and it would be unreasonable to favour the orphans of the king to the neglect of those women.[123] The archbishop of Goa supported the opinion of the viceroy.[124]

The orphans of the king continued to be sent to India.[125]

The question was not so much about the availability of Portuguese women, nor even about their physical looks, as about attractive dowries. For the hard-up Portuguese good looks did not matter. In 1595 the king demanded the same treatment to the orphans of the noble Portuguese, who had served the crown, as was given to the orphans of the king. Perhaps the former were neglected for lack of dowry, unlike the latter who came overseas with substantial dowries.[126]

(b) *Goan Women*

It is beyond doubt that the Goan women were the first to be converted, but their families and relatives remained Hindu. At times only the women became Christians but not their husbands, who then preferred to live outside Goa. They made several attempts to take their adamant wives along with them. However, we are made to believe that on account of a very good Christian instruction these women had received, they not only refused to live with their Hindu husbands, but they also informed the Portuguese authorities about their husbands' unlawful intentions.[127] It is pretentious to think that this behaviour became a norm. The convert women knew very little about the Portuguese customs, and much less about the Christian faith. They would rather follow their former superstitions and idolatrous practices — errors in which they brought their children up too.[128] The convert women married to the Portuguese men did not share in the social life of their husbands. Rather, they had a great influence on their Portuguese husbands. We recall that some Portuguese *casados* carried away by their convert Muslim wives planned to surrender Goa to the Adilshah in 1512.[129]

In Goa, every *casado* or resident Portuguese was bound to teach his wife and slaves the Christian doctrine.[130] Frequent attendance at church was compulsory in order to prevent relapses and stamp out all vestiges of their ancestral faith. It is an acceptable fact that the women did not have more religious instruction than the men, but they were definitely more devout. The role the women played in handing on the tradition and transmitting character was well known during the sixteenth century.

Soon after the conquest of Goa, the Portuguese soldiers captured some Hindu women, but Afonso de Albuquerque did not permit his men to retain them. He expected that the good treatment and favours granted to these women, and the liberal attitude of the Portuguese, would lead the relatives of these women to ask for baptism.[131] Later in 1514, despite his countrymen's criticisms against his policy of mixed marriages, Albuquerque wrote to the king, D. Manuel, asking him to support this project in Goa and other places, stressing at the same time the fine qualities of some Indian women.

Brahman women of Divar and Chorão (the entire islands had been converted by 1560) were held in high esteem and looked upon as being very reserved and honest. They were naturally modest and greatly submissive to their husbands. These women served their husbands with a slave-like attitude. When their husbands died, they shaved their heads and did not wear coloured clothes after the prohibition of *sati*.[132] Some local women from the island of Goa, on the occasion of their baptism, wore so much gold to the extent of astonishing the missionaries. They belonged to a caste called *Chararos* or Chaddos, which was a caste of warriors. They were even better, in character and manners, than the Brahmans.[133] But by-and-large the foreign travellers had a very negative opinion about the Indian woman, and pictured her as someone who succumbed easily to pleasures.[134]

Albuquerque wanted the Portuguese to marry the local women, but only with the 'best' women, to force the Portuguese to settle in the *Estado da India*.[135] The marriages of which he approved he claimed to be a success, but admitted that material incentive was present in them. However, some *casados* began caring less for the defence of the fortresses. This might have been the reason why the king discouraged the Portuguese from marrying and disapproved the policy of miscegenation althogether.[136]

Most Portuguese officials did not agree with the idea of mixed marriages, for the local women were considered by the Portuguese as the meanest and lowest people in India, hence their offsprings would fare no better.[137] In 1585 there were not even ten Goans in the Portuguese fleet because they cared for no job, except for sexual pleasures in which they were brought up, wrote a Portuguese. Hence more women were invited from Portugal, since the *Canarim* (Goan) women belonged to a small-minded race.[138] The ecclesiastical and civil authorities favoured, rather tolerated (but not always) mixed marriages with Christian women. Not all the viceroys and governors appreciated the idea of mixed marriages even with the convert women.[139]

The coming of married men without their wives to Goa led to their divorce, bigamy and concubinage. A royal letter in 1584, ordered the viceroy, D. Duarte de Meneses, to send immediately back to Portugal one Jerónimo Correia who, while in India for many years, had neglected his wife in Portugal.[140] Legal marriages of the Portuguese were easily annuled and new ones blessed overseas. Practically every *casado* and *fidalgo* made of their slave women their concubines, living an absolutely dissolute existence, so much so that they looked like anything but Christians.[141] Adultery had increased and it created scandals in Goa, according to a complaint in 1588.[142] The greatest of all evils in Goa was the carelessness of men in living with five or six women as if they were their own wives.[143] Some Hindu women of this island, after committing adultery, came to the College of St Paul to become Christians, for their own personal security.[144]

Some poor Portuguese men married local women to improve their luck.[145] If one of the viceroy's servants, room or bell boys decided to settle in Goa, the viceroy would use all his artifices and power to compel a rich widow or a noble orphan girl to marry his protégé who in his own country performed a very lowly job.[146] We do not know whether the first converts married their daughters before they reached the age of puberty, according to their former Hindu custom, just to prevent the Portuguese from marrying them. But if these marriages were performed, it is certain that they had no validity before the Canon Law and civil authority. Whether there is any documentary evidence that the local women readily accepted alliances with Portuguese men, we have to investigate. Our common sense might suggest that by marrying the Portuguese, these women acquired better opportunities to settle in life with more luxurious ease. Goan women accepted the Portuguese without religious scruples, unlike the Malabar nair women.[147] If a woman desired to receive baptism in spite of her family opposition, the government came to her rescue with a pension.[148]

Local Christian heiresses always remained in great demand by the young Portuguese bachelors.[149] Some convert noble girls lived with respectable Portuguese families and were given in marriage to the Portuguese.[150] There was never any lack of Portuguese men willing to marry convert women. But during his time Afonso de Albuquerque did not permit any or every Portuguese to marry and to settle down; only the noblemen for the services they rendered to the crown. He married them to the daughters of the newly converted chiefs of the land. Albuquerque believed that on seeing what was being done for their daughters, grand-daughters and sisters conversions would increase.[151]

It is probable that the *solteiras* — unwedded mothers and independent women or prostitutes — converted more easily. In 1530 Fr. Vincent de Laguna reported to the king that many *solteiras* (read prostitutes) after their baptism went back to their former practices of worshipping their gods and taking back their old Hindu customers.[152] Many *solteiras* might have found that conversion would facilitate their profession and dealings with the Portuguese, who sought their services.[153] We know that the Portuguese soldiers were encouraged to use convert prostitutes, but Hindu prostitutes continued to be sought after. Christian and Hindu prostitutes were kept in different quarters to avoid greater evils.[154] Contacts between Hindu dancing girls and the Portuguese were common affairs. *Bailadeiras* (dancing girls) caused many men to go astray, especially Portuguese soldiers, who spent all their money on them and ruined their own health too. The presence of such women was not only an offence to God, but also a danger to the safety of the state. They could be spies for the Adilshahs and distract the soldiers from their military duty. *Fidalgos* had them as their paramours too.[155] Singing and dancing girls and also those who played musical instruments were forbidden to participate in processions in 1606, because of their sensualism.[156] After the destruction of the temples the *bailadeiras*, who lost their jobs, might have become Christians. Probably these were also the women who were regarded as *solteiras*. Some were given in marriage and others were kept at the houses of respected persons.[157]

The Eurasian class tended to approximate the lifestyle of the Portuguese in certain manners and customs. However, the local convert women or wives of the Portuguese and their daughters made a display in their way of dressing and behaviour, to the extent of being compared to the Hindu idols. They offended God and distracted men with carnal desires. The priests reprehended and condemned this feminine pride and forced them to conform to Christian modesty. Pyrard de Laval, a traveller in Goa, gives a vivid description of the local women going about the city and to the church in palanquins accompanied by a number of slaves.[158] Yet despite all these elaborate rituals of church-going, these women tended to show great signs of relapses. Their ignorance in things of religion was so noticeable among the convert women that a Provincial Council recommended that they should attend some preaching once a month.[159]

Some Portuguese women who came to Goa brought their ancestral practices, such as witchcraft, and used them to solve problems of health and love. Lack of Christian instruction was responsible for this situation. Crime of abortion and witchcraft, if unchecked, could grow out of proportion.[160] Portuguese men were so jealous of their wives that the latter were kept confined to their homes most of their time, surrounded by their convert slaves, who influenced them by their semi-Hindu morality. Each Portuguese and local woman, if married to a Portuguese, could have several slave girls. It is certain that almost all these slaves were Christians. Even every bachelor *fidalgo* could have five or six slaves. There were many illegitimate unions and from these relations many illegitimate children were born, and perhaps many of them were kept in the houses for orphans. In 1516 the Judge of the Orphans reported that seventy orphans, sons and daughters of Portuguese, had been born out of wedlock from slaves, prostitutes and other women in Goa.[161]

### (c) *Local Widows*

When a Christian woman became a widow at an early age, she did not think about a second marriage, as per the Hindu custom. Widowhood was considered bad luck. Her parents held with contempt the second nuptials and abhored the Portuguese who re-married. This caused many men to live with mistresses and ruin many women. Some women aborted and killed their newborn children. Since women aborted and killed their newly born children, the priests had to take note of all the pregnant women, either widows or unmarried, to be kept with decent men till delivery. In the last quarter of the sixteenth century an order was issued compelling a widow of less than forty years of age to remarry — but not before one year of her husband's death. The women who preferred to keep continence were sent to the houses of honest Portuguese and Goan families in the city of Goa to live without scandal.[162]

Some widows remained for years without going to church, when they were obliged to attend the mass two months after the death of their husbands.[163] Perhaps, to alleviate the plight of the widows and to facilitate their re-marriage, they received some favours from the government. But in 1605 it was suggested to the king that no rights over the inheritance share of their children should be granted to these widows, even if they re-married.[164] The inheritance share of the children of the first marriage was often used up by these women and stepfathers, leaving nothing for the children when they reached adulthood.[165] The Judge of the Orphans looked after the interests of the widows and orphans.

### (d) *Convent for Nuns*

The kings and the missionaries were greatly concerned about seminaries and creation of a local clergy in their overseas possessions. But the fact that the Portuguese crown never allowed the foundation of a convent for nuns in Goa and in its entire eastern empire during the sixteenth century, might appear rather strange.[166]
Travellers noticed the absence of convents in Goa, while elsewhere

in the Spanish possessions there were many convents for nuns. Jan Huyghens van Linschoten who was in Goa in 1585, attributed the lack of convents to the moral character of Indian women. Indian women were looked upon by some foreigners as slaves for sensual pleasures, and whose faith was to serve Venus. Pyrard de Laval was reflecting only the European mentality of his time when he spoke of local women as people seeking pleasures at the earliest opportunity.[167] But even in some passages in the Laws of Manu or the *Manusmrti* it is hard to see 'reverence, love and trust' towards women.[168]

We have to understand that at this time a rigid cloistered rule had been imposed on the nuns' convent in Europe, particularly after the Council of Trent (1545-1563). Besides, the convents for nuns in Europe did not have the same function as the seminaries. But when finally one convent was founded in Goa after much debate on the need for an institution of this kind, it is difficult to imagine how the local women could have been admitted to this convent or religious life (Eurasians stood better chances), when local men were excluded from the religious orders. However, it is more interesting to know whether this convent was founded for the purpose of accommodating local women. It is obvious that this convent was meant essentially for white women: girls, divorcees, abandoned women and widows, those without dowry, or those unwilling to marry, or women of unhappy marriages.[169]

The great need of the hour for the Portuguese was to have all the women outside in the world to sustain the *Estado da India*. This prevented the emergence of convents for nuns in the East. The Portuguese authority feared that the convents would attract many women to them, thus reducing the already-thin Portuguese community overseas. They thought that if such an institution also attracted to itself Eurasian and Portuguese girls and widows who could be eligible for marriage, and worse still women with good dowries, the convent itself would defeat its very purpose. This fear led the crown to reject several requests made by the Council of Goa for convents throughout the sixteenth century, the most prosperous period for the *Estado da India*.[170] The king refused permission to found a convent for nuns in Goa in 1594;[171] rather he suggested in 1597 that instead of a convent, they should think in terms of a house to shelter girls and married women, when their fathers and husbands, respectively, were away from home.[172]

The first convent for nuns was founded in the city of Goa in 1607 by D. Aleixo the Meneses, the Augustinian archbishop of Goa, amidst much uproar and opposition.[173] It came to be known as the 'Monastery of Santa Mónica'. The foundation stone of Santa Mónica was laid in 1607, but the building was completed only in 1627.[174] It was not easy for girls and widows to enter its portals and join it, due to several external pressures.[175] The *fidalgos* who came from Portugal and wanted to marry chose Eurasians, female descendents of mixed marriages. The parents of these girls were ever anxious to marry them to European-born Portuguese, whenever possible, even if these men were of lowly birth.[176]

Besides the Monastery of Santa Mónica there were two other houses, one a charitable institution and another to shelter recluse women: the 'Nossa Senhora da Serra' for girls and the other 'S. Maria Magdalena' for fallen women, who wanted to correct their way of life.[177] The retreat house of Nossa Senhora da Serra was founded in 1605, also by D. Aleixo de Meneses, for girls or daughters of poor noble Portuguese, until they could find their vocation and discover their talents.[178] The nobles who went on official duty to Portugal or elsewhere, or those who could afford to pay, kept their wives here to guard themselves against any unpleasant surprises on their return. Scandals of adultery were rather common in Goa.[179] This house had nearly sixty young women and orphan girls in 1609, chiefly daughters of noblemen, some of whom became nuns, while others got married. Here they were kept out of danger of the blacks and soldiers who spoiled many young women. Before the founding of this house many orphans went astray.[180] The house of 'S. Maria Magdalena' was founded in 1610 for repentant convert women.[181] From here some women married, others joined the convent and lived the rest of their lives doing penance for their past.[182]

The Monastery had a house for the aspirant young women. They lived under the guidance of a nun mistress, who taught them virtues and good habits. Later many of these girls joined the convent.[183] Santa Mónica was founded for the Portuguese and Eurasians, and as per its rules it excluded Indian women although there were among its candidates/novices some Brahman girls. Many *fidalgos* could not afford to provide dowry for more than one of their daughters, and this might have been the main reason for founding a nunnery, which could accommodate unmarried girls who would take the veil.[184] In 1627 wealthy and unmarried women joined the convent, leaving the *fidalgos* with the difficult task of finding young women with good dowries when they wanted to marry. To conclude, the activity of conversion and the expansion of the empire needed the help of local Christians, especially convert women — the ideal and loyal Lusitanian citizens — without whom the Portuguese could neither hold on to their territorial conquests nor fulfil their ambitions and duties.

## NOTES AND REFERENCES

1. Paulo da Trindade, *CEO*, Part I, pp. 72, 125, 274.
2. *DI*, XII, 925-29.
3. *Ibid.*, VI, 120. "...como se convertem os da terra, perdem todo o socorro e bem fazer dos seus naturaes, e ficam-lhe por imigos. Se nam acharem emparo naqueles que os comvertem, em casos de gramdes necesydades que forçadamente requerem favor, perder-se-a;..." *Doc*, III, 219.
4. José Correia Souto, *Dicionário da História de Portugal*, Vol. III, p. 72.
5. Leopoldo da Rocha, *op. cit.*, p. 2.
6. *DI*, I, 410-11; IV, 344.
7. *Ibid.*, II, 210.
8. *Ibid.*, XIII, 455.
9. Justus Strandes, *op. cit.*, p. 269.
10. *Doc*, IV, 238.
11. Dauril Alden, *The Making of an Elite Enterprise: The Jesuits in the Portuguese Assistancy, 16th to 18th Centuries*, p. 16. Serafim Leite, *História da Companhia de Jesus no Brasil*, Vol. 2, p. 437.
12. *DI*, XVI, 207, 521.

13. Georg Schurhammer, *Francis Xavier. His Life and Times* Vol. II, p. 160.
14. Jesuit Brothers in Bassein went about with guns at their waist, a scandal indeed despite a clear order issued by their religious superiors forbidding them to keep fire arms at their houses.
15. *Doc*, IV, 338.
16. *Ibid.*, VI, 74-75; X, 272.
17. *Ibid.*, XV, 223, 226; XIII, 424.
18. *Ibid.*, X, 245. ARSI, *Epistolae Goana et Malabarica*, 10 - I, fl. 14.
19. *DI*, X, 268.
20. Fernão Guerreiro, *op. cit.*, Vol. I, p. 3. *DI*, XIV, 881.
21. *MR*, 2A, fls. 261, 103v.
22. *DI*, XII, 391.
23. Even the king ordered the religious to study the local language in 1598. *MR*, 2B, fl. 470. ARSI, *Eppistolae Goana et Malabarica*, 15, fl. 174v.
24. Panduranga Pissurlencar, "Colaboradores Hindus de Afonso de Albuquerque", pp. 22-42. G. V. Scammell, "The Pillars of Empire: Indigenous Assistance and the Survival of the 'Estado da India' c. 1600-1700", pp. 473-89.
25. *DI*, VI, 402.
26. *Doc*, V, 391.
27. *DI*, VIII, 67.
28. Archilles Meersman, *The Ancient Franciscan Provinces in India 1500-1835*, pp. 105-06.
29. *DI*, IV, 222.
30. "Hé cousa pera muito se louvar o Senhor, ver que os que eram gentios e ministros do demonio e que aviam de ser sacerdotes dos idolos agora os incitem louvar a Deus. Dous estam en casa que todollos domingos à tarde successivamente pregam en sua lingua natural, não porque sejam já de muitas letras pera pregar; entendem latim bem, . . . ." *Doc*, III, 378.
31. *DI*, IX, 276.
32. Georg Schurhammer and Josef Wicki,(eds.), *Epistolae S. Francisci Xaverii*, Vol. I, p. 147.
33. Georg Schurhammer, *Gesammelte Studien. Xavierana*, Vol. III, p. 118.
34. Dauril Alden, *op. cit.*, pp. 16-17.

35. *DI*, XIII, 386.
36. *Exponi nobis*, a papal brief by Leo X, dated 12 June 1518, gave permission to the royal chaplain at Lisbon to ordain "Ethiopians, Indians and Africans" who might have reached the moral and educational standards required for the priesthood. C. R. Boxer, "The Problems of the Native Clergy in the Portuguese and Spanish Empires from the Sixteenth to the Eighteenth Centuries", p. 86.
37. *DI*, I, 410-11.
38. *MR*, 2A, fls. 99, 103v.
39. "Señor, ay em estas partes alguns padres clerigos los quales no tan solamente dan mal exemplo a los Portugueses, pero, tambien a los nuevos cristianos de la tierra." Letter written by Frei Vincent de Laguna to the king of Portugal in 1530. *Doc*, I, 192.
40. AHU, *Caixa da India*, No. 1, doc. 43. A distinction needs to be made between the missionary clergy (priests): the regular (religious) and secular (diocesan) clergy. The regular clergy worked to convert peoples to Christendom whereas the secular clergy administered the already constituted Christian communities. This distinction is important because the locals were allowed to become only secular priests or assistants to the white priests. The religious clergy rated themselves higher than the secular clergy.
41. *DI*, I, 784. *APO*, 3, p. 4. "...o seminario de St[a] Fé de Goa fundado em 1541 *para perseguir a idolatria e favorecer os novos cristãos.*" Ricardo Micael Teles, *Os Franciscanos no Oriente e seus Conventos*, p. 5, footnote no. 3.
42. *DI*, I, 127-28. This college (colegio) or seminary came to be known by several names: some called it 'Colegio da Conversão da Fé', but the locals preferred to call it 'Colegio de São Paulo'; and others called it 'Seminário da Sancta Fé'. *DI*, III, 242. At times it is mentioned as the 'Colegio da Conversão de São Paulo'. *Ibid.*, 277. Georg Schurhammer and Josef Wicki, (eds.) *Epistolae S. Francisci Xaverii*, Vol. I, p. 134. ARSI, *Eppistolae Goana et Malabarica*, 10 - I, fl. 12. The College of Goa was founded or sanctioned by a royal order and its purpose was the education of the male converts. *DI*, VII, 580.
43. *Ibid.*, X, 240-41.
44. *Ibid.*, I, 65.
45. *Doc*, III, 277. *DI*, XVIII, 812, 814. It consisted of all the territories from the Cape of Good Hope passing through India upto China,

and this remained so till 1557, when the diocese of Cochin was established. Despite the vastness of the archdiocese of Goa, it did not have enough churches and offices to accommodate even the Portuguese clergymen. The diocese of Goa was made into an archdiocese in 1555.

46. Georg Schurhammer and Josef Wicki, (eds.), *op. cit.*, p. 134. Luis de Guzman, *op. cit.*, p. 55.
47. Fr. Vicente de Lagos founded a seminary for the local convert boys in Cranganore in 1540. The Council of Trent (1563) had stated that each diocese had the duty to establish its own seminary and the responsibility to prepare canditades for the priesthood. It seems that the diocese of Goa had anticipated the Tridentine decision regarding the formation of the local clergy by several years.
48. Georg Schurhammer and Josef Wicki, (eds.) *Epistolae S. Francisci Xaverii*, Vol. I, (1535-1548), p. 134.
49. For more information on the income of the College of St Paul see *Doc*, IV, 332.
50. *Ibid.*, 76; III, 361.
51. *Ibid.*, 185. *DI*, XV, 22.
52. Gaspar Correia, *Lendas da India*, Vol. IV, pp. 290-91.
53. *Ibid.*
54. *Doc*, IV, 229.
55. "Antre elles há engenhos bons e boas yncrinações, mas nam há spiritu (devotion), nem consideraçam." *DI*, I, 411.
56. During the sixteenth century the Jesuits residing in Goa were known as *Paulistas* because of the College of St Paul they owned in the same city.
57. Conde de Ficalho, *Garcia da Orta e o seu Tempo*, p. 159.
58. Francis Xavier said that, "... nunca homem veyo à India com tantas honrras... como eu". Georg Schurhammer, *Gesammelte Studien. Xavierana*, Vol. III, p. 117. Georg Schurhammer and Josef Wicki, (eds.), *Epistolae S. Francisci Xaverii*, Vol. II, pp. 118-19.
59. AHU, *Registo de cartas*, Cod. 281, fl. 58v.
60. C. Alonso, "Nueva documentación inédita sobre las misiones agustinianas en la India y en Persia (1571-1609)", p. 350.
61. Francisco de Souza, *OCJC*, p. 11.
62. Luis de Guzman, *op. cit.*, Introduction.
63. ARSI, *Eppistolae Goana et Malabarica*, 10 - I, fl. 12.
64. ARSI, *Ibid.*, 10 - II, fl. 314v.

65. Sebastião Gonçalves, *op. cit.*, p. 93.
66. ARSI, *Goana Historia*, 31 - I, fl. 27' *DI*, II, 466-67.
67. *Ibid.*, X, 240f.
68. Georg Schurhammer and Josef Wicki, (eds.), *Epistolae S. Francisci Xaverii*, Vol. I, p. 169.
69. *DI*, I, 185, 120.
70. *Ibid.*, XVII, 382.
71. *Ibid.*, VI, 110; XI, 662.
72. ARSI, *Extracto das cousas*, 1A, fl. 6.
73. *DI*, VII, 575. Indians of whatever caste were forbidden to enter the Society of Jesus, but the Japanese were admitted to it without difficulties. *Ibid.*, XIV, 834.
74. *Ibid.*, I, 411; II, 169. Carlos M. de Melo, *The Recruitment and Formation of the Native Clergy in India. (16th-19th Centuries). An Historico-Canonical Study*, p. 116.
75. *DI*, X, 284.
76. *Ibid.*, XIV, 834.
77. *DI*, XVII, 384.
78. "Os da terra (que estudam no collegio) são bramanes honrados, de limpa geração e de grandes abilidades dos quais muitos são sacerdotes com cuja doutrina e exemplo se convertem muitos à fé." Paulo da Trindade, *op. cit.*, p. 289.
79. *DI*, XVIII, 880, footnote no. 39; XVI, 813.
80. BNL, *Reservados*, Cod. 176, fls. 99-99v.
81. ARSI, *Summarium eorum quae pertinent ad Indiam Orientalem*, 6, fl. 62v.
82. ARSI, *Extracto das cousas*, 1A, fls. 5, 16. *DI*, XV, 820.
83. *Ibid.*, XI, 749-50. "A gente que não serve pera a Companhia (de Jesus) são filhos da India, ainda nascidos de pais e maes europeos, porque o clima da terra e criação e costumes destes moços em que se crião logo de crianças são taes que os fazem inutilissimos pera a religião... eles não tratão das paixões." They lacked virtue and good Portuguese customs. This was the opinion and experience of the missionaries. ARSI, *Fundationes Goana*, 22 - I, fls. 138, 139v. It was believed that man transmitted character in general, and the mother transmitted moral character to the child. The state could not continue with marriages between Portuguese and local women, since the Eurasians were not an ideal group from whom one could expect high moral standards. The fusion of races could give rise

only to syncretic religious behaviour. Virtues were intransmissible through miscegenation, hence the sending of the 'orphan girls of the king' from Portugal. Therefore, the retrictions in admitting the *castiços* and *mestiços* into the religious orders and the total exclusion of the Indians from them.

84. Paulo da Trindade, *op. cit.*, p. x.
85. *Ibid.*, p. 270.
86. *Ibid.*, p. 288. Note that when the viceroys and governors arrived from Portugal they disembarked at Reis Magos in Bardez. Here they took charge of the *Estado da India,* amidst a pompous ceremony. They were also buried here. Leopoldo da Rocha, *op. cit.*, pp. 89-90. The Franciscans founded another college of St Bonaventure in the city of Goa in 1602.
87. C. R. Boxer, "The Problems of the Native Clergy in the Portuguese and Spanish Empires from the Sixteenth to the Eighteenth Centuries", p. 87.
88. Letter from the commissary, Fr. Rodrigo de Serpa, to the king in 1532. *Doc*, II, 213-14.
89. Between 1510 and 1661 only half a dozen Indians seemed to have been admitted to the Franciscan order. C. R. Boxer, *op. cit.*, p. 86.
90. Paulo da Trindade, *op. cit.*, p. 286. Ricardo Micael Teles, *Os Franciscanos no Oriente e seus Conventos*, p. 8.
91. Nuno da Silva Gonçalves, *Os Jesuitas e a Missão de Cabo Verde (1604-1642)*, pp. 80, 82-83.
92. Niceno de Figueiredo, *Pelo Clero de Goa. Duas Lendas: O Cisma de Goa e A Ignorância do Clero Goês*, pp. 28, 30. In 1589 Fr. Castro said, "Na India são poco acasionados para a virtude e forças da alma e muito para as delicias do corpo e fraqueza do espirito de modo que o clima está manifestamente inclinado ao corpo e à preguiça e delicias... e não há remedio para isso." *DI*, XV, 420.
93. Niceno de Figueiredo, *op. cit.*, p. 17.
94. *DI*, I, 411, 478; IV, 214. ARSI, *Fundationes Goana*, 22 - I, fl. 13v.
95. Luis de Guzman, *op. cit.*, p. 22.
96. *DI*, VI, 74-75.
97. "Os filhos (de bramenes) são abilissimos alvos, gentis homens e de boa filosofia; depois de Christãos, folgão de nos conversar e de aprender as cousas da fee." *Doc*, IX, 249.
98. Fr. Pedro Rodrigues wrote from Goa in 1600, when he needed some

money for the college in Bassein, "Quem duvida que quatro mil Pardaos que este Collegio de S. Paulo gasta cada ano com uns poucos de corvos, que depois nos tiram os olhos, quero dizer com um golpe de Canarins que estão neste Seminario de Goa." ARSI, *Epistolae Goana et Malabarica*, 15, fl. 16.

99. *Doc*, IV, 183.
100. In 1556 there were twenty-one students from Goa. C. R. Boxer, *op. cit.*, pp. 87-88.
101. Panduranga Pissurlenca, *Goa Pré-Portuguesa através dos Escritores Lusitanos dos Séculos XVI e XVII*, pp. 38-40. About the origin of the word 'Chaddo' see in Panduranga Pissurlencar, "O Elemento Hindu da Casta Chardó".
102. "A mais gente que se torna cristaã sam molheres, porque estas tem mais certa sua vida, porque ganham muito dinheiro aquy antre nos;. . . ." Raymundo Antonio de Bulhão Pato, (ed.), *Cartas de Affonso de Albuquerque*, III, p. 41.
103. Fernão Lopes de Castanheda, *História dos Descobrimentos e Conquista da India Pelos Portugueses,* Book III, p. 599.
104. The Portuguese who married native women and settled down definitively in India received from the state a small dowry and a piece of cultivable land that had been confiscated from the Muslim aristocracy. Luís Filipe F. R. Thomaz, *De Ceuta a Timor*, p. 250.
105. Spanish women began to go to the Spanish-controlled territories in Latin America already in the second expedition, and in the third one in 1497 thirty women had boarded the ship for the New World. Maria del Carmen Pareja Ortiz, *Presencia de la Mujer Sevillana en Indias: Vida Cotidiana.*
106. Afonso Brás de Albuquerque, *op. cit.*, Vol. I, Part II, pp. 168, 178-79, 181.
107. Gaspar Correia, *Lendas da India*, Vol. II, Part I, p. 375.
108. S. A. A. Rizvi, "Islamic Proselytisation: Seventh to Sixteenth Centuries", p. 21.
109. Luis de Guzman, *op. cit.*, p. 16. Fernão Lopes de Castanheda, *op. cit.,* p. 600.
110. António da Silva Rego, *História das Missões do Padroado Português do Oriente*, pp. 265-66. Georg Schurhammer, *Francisco Javier. Su vida y su tiempo*, Vol. II, p. 271.
111. Joaquim Verrísmo Serrão, *História de Portugal*, Vol. III, pp. 162-63.

112. A. de S. S. Costa Lobo, (ed.), *op. cit.*, p. 244.
113. "...los capitanes pilotos, maestros y marinheros todos traen mugeres en las naos y navios de Vosa Alteza, por lo qual se levantan grandes continedas, y echanse a dormir. Ay mala vigia. Pierdense las naos y tanbien ay gran negligencia en la lunbre, digo, en las candeas, que todos quieren tener candea debajo de la ponte, e tanbien en las camaras, e olvidanse y ansi queimanse las naos. Digo, Señor, esto, porque lo vi, que en una nao que yo vine, se aprendio fogo dos veces, y por milagro se a morto." Letter written by Friar Vicente de Laguna from Goa in 1530 to the king. *Doc*, II, 193. "E asy ho servyra en defender que os omens purtugueses nom traguam em seus gualeões e navios molheres solteiras, como trazem, pois ho auto da guera e luguar em que andam e mais pera confisões e obras vertuosas, que pera se com elas enfrascarem, ho que he causa de se alguns navios perderem, como se perdem." News sent from Cranganore and Hormuz probably between 1543-47. *Ibid.*, III, 21.
114. Zinadim, *Historia dos Portugueses no Malabar*, (Arab Manuscript of the XVI Century), p. 81. ARSI, *Foundationes Goanae*, 22 - I, fl. 30.
115. *BFUP*, No. 46, p. 327. In 1575, it was pointed out to the king that the personal trunks the Portuguese transported to and from India were much too big, causing serious harm to navigation and royal commercial interests. Hence, the king issued a decree forbidding them to carry trunks exceeding 5 x 2.5 x 2.5 spans. AHU, *Relação das Caixas da India*, Caixa 1, doc. 3.
116. Fernão Lopes de Castanheda, *op. cit.*, p. 528.
117. Afonso Brás de Albuquerque, *op. cit.*, pp. 224-29. Fernão Lopes de Castanheda, *op. cit.*, p. 563.
118. According to the Ordenações Manuelinas a Christian who slept with a consenting Muslim woman did not deserve any punishment. *Ordenações Manuelinas*, Book V, Tit. xxi, p. 70. Ordenações Manuelinas was a modified version of Ordenações Afonsinas. It was a combination of the New and the Old Legislations of the kingdom of Portugal from the time of D. Manuel.
119. The ships arrived in Goa with many dead and sick people. AN / TT, *CC* I, Maço 75, Doc. 116.
120. C. R. Boxer, "Fidalgos Portuguêzes e Bailadeiras Indianas, (séculos XVII-XVIII)", p. 84.
121. Alberto Carlos Germano da Silva Correia, *História da Colonização Portugueza na India*, Vol. II.

122. Georg Schurhammer, *Francisco Javier. Su vida y su tiempo*, Vol. II, p. 271.
123. AHU, *Registo das cartas*, Cod. 281, p. 301. CEHU, *As Gavetas da Torre do Tombo*, II, p. 711.
124. "Cad'anno envia Vossa Alteza a estas partes muitas orfãas e pella obrigação que tenho lhe lembro que ha qua muitas honrradas e mui desemparadas cujos paes morrerão na guerra ou gastarão boa parte da vida em seu serviço. Parece que primeiro devem ser estas emparadas e mandar ao viso rey que caze cad'anno certo numero . . . ." Letter from the archbishop of Goa in 1561. *Ibid.*, III, p. 191.
125. Eight orphan girls came from Portugal in 1588. *MR*, 3A, fl. 302. *BFUP*, No. 2, p. 190. *MR*, 2A, fl. 53.
126. *BFUP*, No. 1, p. 159. *MR*, 1, fl. 48.
127. *Doc*, IX, 245. *DI*, VI, 118. "As molheres tão bem doutrinadas na casa das catecumenas, que indo depois algumas a casas de alguns portugueses, ellas são as ue incitão e exortão as outras molheres a rezar o rozario . . . e algumas ficam tão instruidas e devotas . . . ." *Ibid.*, IX, 249.
128. Alessandro Valignano, *op. cit.*, p. 49.
129. *Doc*, I, 171. Raymundo António de Bulhão Pato, (ed.), *op. cit.*, III, pp. 337-55. Gaspar Correia, *Lendas da India*, Vol. II, Part I, pp. 292-319.
130. *Doc*, I, 178.
131. Afonso Brás de Albuquerque, *op. cit.*, Vol. II, Part III, p. 50.
132. *Ibid.*, VIII, 50.
133. *Doc*, VIII, 95, footnote no. 16
134. Filipe Sasseti was in India (1583-1588) and died in Goa. Fidelino de Figueiredo, "Viagens de um Florentino a Portugal e à India, (século XVI)", p. 120.
135. "... porque eu nunqua tive devaçam de casar homens com estas molheres malavares, porque sam negras currutas em seu viver e custumes; e as molheres que foram mouras sam alvas e castas e Retraydas em suas casas e no modo de seu viver, como hoş mouros desta terra tem por costume, e as molheres de bramanes e filhas delles tambem sam castas molheres e de bom viver e sam alvas e de boa presemça." Raymundo Antonio de Bulhão Pato, (ed.), *op. cit.*, I, pp. 337-38. *Doc*, I, 220.
136. Raymundo Antonio de Bulhão Pato, (ed.), *op. cit.*, pp. 337-38. See about conversions through gifts. *Ibid.*, III, pp. 41-42. *Doc*, I, 219-

20.

137. A. de S. S. Costa Lobo, (ed.), *op. cit.*, p. 236.
138. *Ibid.*
139. C. R. Boxer, "op. cit.", pp. 83-84.
140. *BFUP*, No. 2, p. 184. *MR*, 2A, fl. 7.
141. *Doc*, II, 196.
142. *APO*, 3, p. 143.
143. Francisco de Souza, *op. cit.*, p. 44.
144. *Doc*, V, 300. A Hindu woman who could not get along with her husband left Goa to become a religious prostitute. *DI*, XII, 614.
145. *APO*, 1, Part II, p. 145.
146. A. de S. S. Costa Lobo, (ed.), *op. cit.*, pp. 144-45.
147. João de Barros, *Decada da Asia*, II, Part I, (1777), p. 559.
148. Maria Benedita Araújo, "O «Pay dos Christãos». Contribuição para o estudo da Cristianização da Índia", p. 308.
149. C. R. Boxer, *A India Portuguesa em Meados do Sécuio XVII*, p. 30.
150. *DI*, I, 781.
151. Afonso Brás de Albuquerque, *op. cit.*, p. 49.
152. *Doc*, II, 193.
153. António da Silva Rego, *História das Missões do Padroado Português do Oriente*, p. 124.
154. *Bullarium*, First Provincial Council, Acc. 4, dec. 7, p. 25.
155. C. R. Boxer, "Fidalgos Portuguêzes e Bailadeiras Indianas, (séculos XVII-XVIII)", p. 86.
156. *Bullarium*, Fifth Provincial Council, Acc. 4, dec. 12, p. 130.
157. Sebastião Gonçalves, *op. cit.*, p. 95. *DI*, XI, 666.
158. Francisco Pyrard de Laval, *Viagem de Francisco Pyrard de Laval*, pp. 79-81.
159. *Bullarium*, Third Provincial Council, Acc. 4, dec. 7, p. 79.
160. *Doc*, X, 777-78.
161. *Ibid.*, I, 287. "Na cidade de Goa e suas ilhas ha muitos canarys gentios que morrem sem herdeiros, e suas heranças que sam palmares, arozaes, hortas e outras propriedades ficam a vossa Alteza. Faça dellas merçe a Misericordia da dita cidade pera casamento de horfãs, filhas de portugueses proves, que a muitas na dita cidade e em outras fortellezas." Information written by Fr. Álvaro Penteado in favour of the Portuguese orphan girls residing in India in 1543.

*Ibid.*, II, 371.

162. BNL, *Reservados*, Cod. 176, fl. 120v.
163. *Ibid.*
164. *APO*, 1, Part II, p. 185.
165. *Ibid.*, p. 152.
166. The monastery of 'Santa Clara', another house for nuns, was founded in Macau in 1633. Ricardo Micael Teles, *Os Franciscanos no Oriente e seus Conventos*, p. 4. Paulo da Trindade, *op. cit.*, Part III, pp. 523-28.
167. Francisco Pyrard de Laval, *op. cit.*, pp. 86-88.
168. "Good looks do not matter to them, nor do they care about youth; A man! they say, and enjoy sex with him, whether he is good-looking or ugly. By running after men like whores, by their fickle minds, and by their natural lack of affection these women are unfaithful to their husbands even when they are zealously guarded here. Knowing that their very own nature is like this, as it was born at the creation by the Lord of Creatures, a man should make the utmost effort to guard them. The bed and the seat, jewelry, lust, anger, crookedness, a malicious nature, and bad conduct are what Manu assigned to women. Wendy Doniger, (Trans.), *The Laws of Manu*, p. 198, (9. 14-17).
169. *APO*, 1, Part II, pp. 17-18. C. Alonso, "Nueva documentación inédita sobre las misiones agustinianas en la India y en Persia (1571-1609)", p. 384.
170. In 1593 the king did not allow the founding of any convent for nuns in Goa due to the inconveniences it could create for the state. There were some requests by the Portuguese settlers for a convent for nuns. AHU, *Registo de cartas*, Cod. 281, fl. 301v. The governor, Manuel de Souza, suggested the possibility of using the new professed house of the Jesuits, situated in the heart of the city, as a monastery for nuns in 1588. *BFUP*, No. 15, pp. 549-51.
171. *Ibid.*, No. 2, pp. 206-10. *MR*, 2A, fls. 245-57. A royal letter disapproving the founding of a monastery for nuns in Goa in 1595. *BFUP*, p. 327. *MR*, 3B, fls. 545-47.
172. *BFUP*, No. 2, p. 225. *MR*, 2-B, fl. 365.
173. BNL, *Reservados*, Cod. 176, fl. 114.
174. The king wrote to the Senate of Goa in 1595, "E no que toca ao mosteiro que vos parece que se deve fazer nessa Cidade para recolhimento das filhas dos fidalgos e pessoas que me servem nesse

Estado, pera que me pedis licença, me pareceo vola não dever conceder por algumas rezõis que se me offerecem de serviço de Deos e meu, . . . ." *APO*, 1, Part I, pp. 108-09, 119.

175. Ana Maria Ramalho Proserpio Leitão, "As Freiras de Santa Mónica e de Santa Clara: Duas Excepções na India Portuguesa", pp. 39-40.
176. C. R. Boxer, *Portuguese Society in the Tropics: The Councils of Goa, Macao, Bahia and Luanda*, pp. 28-29.
177. Paulo da Trindade, *op. cit.*, p. 100.
178. BNL, *Reservados*, Cod. 177, fl. 263v.
179. C. Alonso, "op. cit.", p. 384.
180. *Ibid.*
181. BNL, *Reservados*, Cod. 176, fl. 114. *Ibid.*, Cod. 580, fl. 26v.
182. C. Alonso, "op. cit.", p. 383.
183. Leopoldo da Rocha, *op. cit.*, p. 133.
184. C. R. Boxer, *op. cit.*, p. 37.

# 11

# CONTINUITY AND CHANGE IN GOA: EUROPEAN STEREOTYPES

## Contrastive Demands

How did the Hindu look at the converts? Did conversions create social and family conflicts? Did the caste system hinder or help conversions? Could the motives leading to conversions be of any importance to the Hindus? We read sometimes that the Hindus held the Christians in contempt.[1] But this type of general statement does not tell us the whole truth about social relationships between the Hindus and converts.

Some of the most interesting socio-historical questions connected with the affair of conversions in Goa are definitely the survival of the caste system among the converts, and the personal/social conflicts created for the Christians and Hindus alike, by contrastive demands — conflicts between tradition and change. The previous chapters have highlighted the argument that since more information regarding the conversion and reactions of the Brahman caste has reached us, we tend to think, therefore, that it was the most affected and active caste rather than the other ones. Obviously, the former being the 'preys' (targets) par excellence of the missionaries might have reacted and responded differently. But conversions brought lasting tensions to all in the village community which gave rise to strong reactions, often, no doubt, spearheaded and encouraged by the Hindu élite, but not necessarily by them alone. This was more so when the rapid increase in conversions appeared to threaten, and throw out of equilibrium, their traditional social prestige and economic power, or more concretely, when the converts refused to perform their divinely-attributed traditional services in society, particularly the most degrading ones, and to obey their former chiefs. Paradoxically, the conversion drive, which intended to effect some radical social changes and conquer the local élite (and others), simulteneously did promise those who converted, to minimize the loss of their traditional power and honour through many favours, thus easing some of their tension and conflict resulting from the two contrastive demands.

Community life and its demands (or the traditional social organization) based on kinship and kindred (or on caste and joint family considerations) had precedence over citizenship and polity in any rural setup. The Portuguese brought, or tried to establish, a social order based on citizenship to inspire political allegiance to the state and fidelity to its religion. The society that the Portuguese intended to create could emerge only with the acceptance of citizenship. But in Goa the traditional bond or 'kinship' which held the community together conflicted with the political bond or 'citizenship' so necessary for the emergence of that new society or state. For the Goans in the sixteenth century living in self-sufficient villages, kinship and kindred were more exigent than the proposed idea of citizenship or political allegiance to the state. Hence, in the village community, caste (kinship) and the joint family (kindred) strengthened by a common religion, were ties that mattered most. If so, joint family stood in the way of individual conversion, and caste allegiance stood against the conversion of any families, as any religious defection could erode family or caste equilibrium, but paradoxically, joint family and caste did facilitate group conversions or even conversion of entire villages at times.

The greatest impediment to individual/group conversions was the caste system that forbade free communication and dealings between people professing different religions when the question of pollution was at stake. For this reason the Portuguese who ate beef were kept at a safe distance.[2] But on the other hand, caste system or the pollution principle did facilitate individual/group baptisms particularly when the Hindus found themselves without any means of regaining caste. Likewise joint family could also facilitate conversions of entire caste groups. When eighty Brahman boys were baptized — after their parents brought them back from the kingdom of Bijapur where they had gone to escape baptism — their parents also 'willingly' asked for baptism. The love for their sons and daughters who had been converted earlier forced some to become Christians.[3] Family links proved stronger than caste considerations, or even the religion they followed.

Conversion broke down family relationships and confused caste affiliations.[4] Boys ran away from their parents, and slaves from their masters, to become Christians.[5] Many married Hindu couples converted, but at times only one spouse did. But if both, husband and wife, converted they had to live together thereafter, even if they did not before. If a man before his conversion had many wives, he had to retain the first one and send the rest away. In case only one spouse converted and wanted to re-marry, he/she could do so but only two months after his/her conversion, in order to give sufficient time to the other person to convert.[6] There were cases when the woman became a Christian but her husband did not.[7] Some women ran away from their husbands to receive baptism.[8] A Hindu boy became a Christian against his father's wishes, but on the following day his parents asked for baptism too.[9] Often the conversion of one member of the family compelled others to ask for baptism.[10] But those who willingly wanted to become Christians, fearing family objections to their plans, or accusations that their conversion was not genuine, succumbed to such pressures. The Hindus who showed some inclination to receive baptism, and those who converted braving family and caste opposition were 'good', 'honest' and 'respectable' in the eyes of the missionaries; whereas those who refused to yield, and prevented others from becoming Christians were considered as the worst of their kind.[11]

The caste Hindus found it difficult to perceive and identify the low caste converts, the latter now with non-traditional names and perhaps with different occupations, confused greatly the purity-pollution principles. On the other hand, when the chiefs of the villages were converted, the masses might have found themselves in a confused state of mind on seeing that those who claimed to be the defenders and patrons of their religion and social customs, now abandoned them. In spite of the imposition of the new social order on the Goans, the converts did not become socially identical, since previous caste differences persisted among themselves and continued to decide to a large extent their daily activities, dealings and lifestyle. But undoubtedly more 'ritual neutralization', or levelling of social distinctions, prevailed among them, due to less identifiable external caste signs, new names and several civil and religious decrees that forbade Christians to behave like Hindus. Obviously, the majority of the converts did not see their economic fortunes changing immediately. However, they stood better chances of receiving some material favours, and more so those who developed closer social ties with the Portuguese. Besides, the brand of Christianity brought by the church hardly preached or practised egalitarian benefits and opportunities. The caste and skilled converts were likely to benefit the most from the decrees and privileges in favour of conversion.

One of the serious accusations levelled against Christianity in India is that it did not try to abolish the caste system; rather it respected and upheld the existing social order. However, it is not totally correct to state that caste rigidity did not suffer some change or weaken among the converts. Conversion placed all the convert Brahmans, who formerly belonged to different 'Brahman' sub-castes, within the unqualified term Brahman; in the same way the Christianized 'Chaddo' caste began including the converts from the Maratha caste and the Vaishiyas or merchants. Today, there is not among the Christians of Goa a caste corresponding to Vaishiya.[12] If this argument is correct, we can conclude that conversions levelled down several distinct social groups or sub-castes into just a few castes among the converts. Caste endogamy continued to be maintained among the converts. However, this process of levelling down sub-caste differences, offered them greater choice to find marriage partners even within a small group of converts. Restrictions on inter-dining and untouchability might not have disappeared completely within the Christian community. Porbably, the converts continued to adhere to their previous taboos, but now differently, as a result of their Christian attitude. The converts, according to the traditional social sanctions, lost caste or joined a new one. But they continued to retain the same caste and the same social differences among themselves, at least, perhaps in a little less conspicuous manner. However, any deviant behaviour can be attributed to the new foreign elements, namely, citizenship or political allegiance or vassalage to the state, so much in demand from the locals and so indispensible for those who wanted to enjoy privileges of Lusitanian citizenship, and of course to Christianity.[13]

Further, permitting the survival of caste among converts became an incentive for conversions as has already been mentioned, but caste was not allowed to take precedence over citizenship, and this the Portuguese decrees forbidding the converts to bring any sign of Hinduism can attest. The same political allegiance was demanded from the Hindus too, since they were first vassals of the crown, despite professing a different religion. Hence, more 'ritual neutralization' among Hindus too.[14]

Some changes brought by the Lusitanian citizenship could be noticed among the converts in the island of Chorão: first, these converts did not allow any Hindus, even their own relatives, living in the land of the Muslims, to enter that island without becoming Christians; second, they refused to entertain any Hindus living outside Goa; and third, they did not want to marry their daughters to Christians living in Bardez, just to avoid staying among many Hindus.[15]

We cannot deny that some of the first converts (individuals and families) were from among the most prosperous and independent inhabitants in Goa, expecting rewards in the form of share in wealth, power and prestige, which would eventually make them important citizens or collaborators of the Portuguese; and at the same time rivals of the ruling class when the promised favours were not forthcoming. The convert élite also stood as rivals to the local Hindu élite. Even if after their conversion the élite were cut off from their traditional communities, they were certainly in a better position to survive than the common folk, since the former received more protection and respect from the Portuguese to confront their rivals. However, the majority of the first converts were weak, and belonged neither to the orthodox Hindu group nor identified themselves with the Portuguese community. Thus, they formed a 'third social group'.

In the beginning, the converts came from that social group that had direct dealings with the Portuguese, namely, the women who spent their time with sailors and soldiers, and were their protégées, as also the work force in the forts and factories. The majority of those who converted were poor and neglected by their relatives.[16] Traditional society did not care to protect these people, which gradually forced them to turn to the Portuguese and to conversion when in terrible plight. Conversion brought to the surface some injustices and weaknesses of the Goan society and local religion. The missionaries used these injustices very conveniently, together with the local 'superstitions', beliefs in pollution and matters of ritualism, to further their own interests.[17]

Religious leaders and the upper castes might have nurtured thoughts of purity and freedom from pollution, but the common people, whether Christian or Hindu, had perhaps less prejudices and taboos. Despite the merciless decrees against the Hindus, we find them continuously celebrating their festivals with the local authority letting them off. Many privileges to the Christians remained merely on paper. Similarly many provisions and instructions against the Hindus were not executed, hence on the whole there might have been greater social harmony than the decrees show.

Social relations between the Portuguese and the local Christians in particular, and the Hindus in general, were cordial, but abuses on the part of the local authorities were frequent. The missionaries stood by the converts when the captains oppressed them and paid little or no heed to their grievances.[18] But many injustices and grievances would escape the vigilance of the Pay dos Christãos. The Hindus were favoured by the Portuguese officials more often than it is usually believed, as has been shown in chapter five.

Therefore, citizenship or the new social and political

demands, probably the major change brought by conversions into the traditional Goan community, merged with the old kinship and kindred elements. Citizenship weakened caste considerations, without being able to eliminate them totally. Since the Hindus were also vassals of the state and were obliged to behave like converts, their social perceptions might have also changed or been influenced by the citizenship mentality and duty.

## European Perception of *Gentilidade* (Gentilism)

We know more about how the foreigners perceived the Indians than how the Indians perceived the foreigners, simply because there are very few records that permit us to assess the stereotypes of the natives concerning the newcomers. Certain stereotypes appear conspicuously and repeatedly in the writings of these foreigners. The Europeans often founded and formed their judgement about the local population under the influence of these stereotypes, and they behaved and dealt with the locals accordingly. It should be sufficiently clear from the outset that the following prejudices and stereotypes are entirely based on historiographical information of the sixteenth century. Moreover, we need to keep in mind that these stereotypes refer to the 'Gentiles' (or the non-Christians, Jews and Muslims). Therefore, where we find Hindu(s) here, (we recall that this term does not appear at all in the sixteenth century historiography) we should also read Gentile(s) as in the original documents.

For the sixteenth century foreigners and Indians, religion served as the first source of, and feeder for, several prejudices, followed by one's lifestyle, thinking patterns and social customs. However, the European and Portuguese missionaries in particular had usually no keen interest in local social and religious customs *per se*, except when these things could contribute to increase conversions or could justify their lack, or when they could help to explain the 'weaknesses' and 'superstitions' that abounded in India.[19] Nevertheless, some travellers and chroniclers did report on several religious practices and social customs in a more impartial or unbiased manner. Frequently, the missionaries blamed these social and religious 'weaknesses' and 'superstitions' for lack of conversions: they made conversion extremely difficult and relapse perfectly normal. These few stereotypes or observations might appear to be merely individual perceptions and biases, but they undoubtedly reflected the dominant and contemporary mentality. Be that as it might, if we can bring forward some of those recurring or usual perceptual elements and stereotypes and insert them in our analytical framework, it might also enrich our historical insights, keep under check our own prejudices and cultural ethnocentrism.

Goa, predominantly Hindu during the Adilshah's rule just preceding the Portuguese conquest, accounted for several temple-oriented and self-sufficient village communities, and their inhabitants had very little to do with the Muslim central polity. The Muslim rulers had assured the Hindus the continuance of the practice of their traditional religion as well as of their own 'superstitions' — and the Muslims used them well for their own benefit — unlike the Portuguese when they began their proselytizing campaign. Those who controlled the temples certainly dominated much of the people's life and the affairs of the village community; and during the Adilshah's rule over Goa, it was not the Muslims who controlled the temples and their lands, but the local Hindu élite. It is probable that, due to intra and inter-community power conflicts and to the self-sufficient character of the village communities, a handful of Muslims could rule over and exploit the Goan population, obviously, in collaboration with the local élite, who exploited the villagers through the control they had over the affairs of the temples. No wonder the Portuguese found it necessary to pull down the temples to curb the power of the local élite. The Portuguese also exploited the existing conflicting situations, viz oppression and poverty of the people, complacency of the locals, their religious 'superstitions', caste and racial prejudices to control Goa. Interestingly, these same 'superstitions', social prejudices of the villagers and their power conflicts helped the missionaries to overcome the obstacles created by the same society in the path of conversions. But these 'superstitions' and 'weakenesses' also reminded the neo-converts about their former religion and customs, resulting in constant relapses or syncretic behaviour.

The encounter between the two different cultures created new perceptions, stereotypes and reactions which can be detected even by a casual reader of the Indo-Portuguese historical documents. The locals received the Portuguese with hostility and distrust in the very first place they landed in India, i.e. at Calicut (Kozhikode). In other parts the natives showed the same kind of hostility, not because the Portuguese practised a different sort of religion, laws and customs, but because they opposed the local customs and religion,[20] and particularly for the force the Portuguese used against the population when they could not achieve what they intended by peaceful and competitive means. Continuous wars with the Samorim, the ruler of Calicut, is just one example. Hence, the local rulers tried to make alliances among themselves to destroy the Portuguese power, making several sieges of the Portuguese fortresses and wars by sea and land.[21] The creation of local collaborators and formation of a local clergy, despite prejudices against them in Portuguese-controlled territories, were important strategies to win the confidence of the locals, and to break the initial local resistance to European presence.

Zinadim, an Arab who lived in the Malabar coast of India during the last quarter of the sixteenth century, generally very harsh to, and critical of, the Portuguese attitude towards Islam and Muslim commercial interests, nevertheless, presented the Portuguese as being friendly with the local population wherever they settled down, and as those who did not impose a heavy taxation on their territories or tributaries. His harsh criticism of the Portuguese went to their policy of restricting religious freedom to others. If a non-Christian traveller crossed any territory under the Portuguese control no one ever stopped him. However, it was almost impossible for him to offer prayers here. But the worst act of injustice was the state policy about the Hindu orphans: when a vassal of the Portuguese crown died and left minor children the state took up their custody, even if they were noble Muslims or Brahman Hindus. After instructing these children in the Christian faith the priests baptized them, wrote Zinadim.[22]

The missionaries perceived that most Hindus had no

knowledge of God, and others worshipped so many things with every kind of superstition that it was rather common for each household to have its own deity.[23] It was usual for the Hindus to represent their deities in the form of snakes, birds and other unclean animals, a worship of the devil indeed, to whom they sacrificed their lives.[24] The Hindus, the most idolatrous and sinful people ever seen in this part of the world, found it normal to adore stones and sticks with all sorts of lasciviousness and abomination, which proved how far and low these people without reason and understanding had stooped![25] The Hindus did not know anything but to offend God.[26] Therefore, they were uncivilized and rooted in customs and practices incompatible with Christianity; but after their conversion they fulfilled their religious duties with more devotion than the Europeans and *mestiços*.[27] Unfortunately, some of them sometimes wavered in the faith after their baptism.[28]

Goans, though good natured, were a very credulous people.[29] They worshipped idols like the sun, moon and animals. When the husband died his wife willingly threw herself onto the funeral pyre of her husband, and their relatives chanted that they were going to celebrate their nuptials in the other world.[30] It was mostly the custom in this kingdom of Goa for every heathen wife to burn herself alive on the funeral pyre of her husband . . . . Those who did not commit this act, on any consideration, became public prostitutes and earned money for the upkeep and construction of the temples in their district, and they died in this way. Each of these heathens could have only one wife by law. Many Brahmans made a vow of chastity and kept it forever.[31]

Great virtues were absent in India, and the people showed themselves very stubborn and arrogant.[32] They did not have any interior humility.[33] The dishonesty of the people in this land was incomparable with any known thing.[34] They could practise their penances to extremes, but no divine grace ever came through them.[35] Nevertheless, the people in this land betrayed neither less shrewedness nor less capacity in sciences and philosophy than the Europeans.[36]

Alessandro Valignano, a Jesuit priest, had plain and harsh words for the Indians, holding them in low esteem.[37] The caste system, with a number of divisions, its own ceremonies, its hierarchical differences and positions of rank among them to the extent of forbidding them to marry outside their own caste group, seemed to this Jesuit the strangest thing in the world. The Indians could not touch other people or eat together when the caste rules so prescribed, or remain together or enter someone else's house, especially when the difference between those castes was considerable. They had devised a way of avoiding physical contacts and social communication, the strangest thing that one could imagine, remarked Valignano.[38]

The Hindus believed in, and performed, innumerable ceremonies and superstitions so scrupulously that even little boys knew how to observe them, which could astonish anyone. Those who did not keep these ceremonies could be punished severely. And those who broke the established social order could lose their caste, become contaminated and severed from their wives, brothers or relatives. Besides the division of society into castes, they also had the division of labour in such a way that to each caste certain jobs and services had been attributed, and they could not change them. The women occupied themselves with domestic affairs.[39]

Further, Valignano remarked that the Indians cared much for their honour, but not for that of their women. However, they were usually vicious, bad and liars. Their consciences did not seem enlightened by the natural law hence, they had no sense of guilt.[40] The Indians were meant to serve only, although there were no bounds to their greed.[41] The *Canarins* (Goans) a people noted for their falsity and lies could not stand as witnesses, for their information was always unreliable.[42]

The Hindu was normally proud and even the lowly people acted likewise. Even the Hindu officers of low rank ran away at the sight of a Christian to avoid any sort of contact with him/her.[43] Poor as they were, the Hindus generally longed for honours, and while receiving favours they demanded them with dignity. They lived to get favours and feared being disfavoured.[44] These people's jealousy knew no bounds, and while trying to imitate the rich in order to keep up their pretentious honour and pride, they could go as far as to sell their lands and incur debts to the point of being imprisoned for not being able to pay.[45] Referring to Goa, Tomé Pires wrote : "There were a great many heathens in this kingdom of Goa, more than in the kingdom of the Deccan. Some of them were very honourable men with large fortunes, and almost the whole kingdom lay in their hands. Since they were locals, they owned the land and paid taxes . . . ."[46]

The Hindus were a people with very little understanding, hence they were incapable of answering questions and doubts regarding their law. They could not understand their errors and when challenged on this count, they could only reply that they lived according to their ancestral customs.[47] The Hindus had little knowledge, especially about the things of the other life. There were some among them who knew about many things, but only those things that interested them. Generally, their thoughts were on eating and earthly matters. Despite all this, they were rational beings who knew to govern well according to their laws. These people, if after becoming Christians were instructed well, might be able to teach others the Christian faith.[48] In 1546 Fr. Nicolao Lancilotto portrayed the Indians thus: "The people of this land are very bad and they hardly use their reason. Those who converted did so out of pure material interests. Some want baptism to become free, like the slaves of the Muslims and Hindus; some become Christians to obtain protection against the ill-treatment inflicted by their masters; and a few others became Christians only to receive a cap or a shirt or any other small gift, and others just to have relations with Christian women, to the extent of hardly anyone becoming Christian by virtue."[49]

India had many missionaries but produced very few or none, said Valignano.[50] The locals were rather weak and without the Portuguese missionaries nothing could be done here, since the Portuguese did not want to confess to Indian or Eurasian priests.[51] Fr. M. Pinheiro observed in 1593, that the Hindus and the Christians showed little respect for the priests in general and less still for the local ones, except for those belonging to the Society of Jesus. Most priests were greedy. They cared little for their chastity too.[52]

Francisco Rodrigues Silveira, a Portuguese soldier in India from 1585 till 1598, wrote that in Goa there were more than three thousand Portuguese, many of them residing here for a long time, but there were not even ten men, sons of Goa in the Portuguese fleet, when there could have been ten thousand. The reason for this was that having no other work, these Goans sacrificed themselves to Venus and Bacchus, the only thing they knew how to do well, since they were brought up only for this.[53] The Goans, a misfit lot for war, possessed so little fighting skills and strength that even a handful of Portuguese would be sufficient to defeat a great multitude of them.[54]

At times the Goans were mentioned as negroes.[55] Francis Xavier used to address the boys as my black and my Portuguese (*meo negro e meo portugues*) while teaching them the Christian doctrine.[56]

*The Brahmans*

The lifestyle and behaviour of the Brahmans fascinated as well as annoyed the missionaries. Perhaps more has been written about them than about all the other castes put together.[57] It is for this reason that several reports make a clear distinction between the 'Brahmans' (*bramanes*) and 'Gentiles' (*gentios*), or all those who were not Brahmans. The conversion of the former seemed to be always more valuable and appreciated than that of anyone else; not only because it was believed that their conversion would be followed by those of others but also because their collaboration mattered in economic and political affairs of the state. Not surprisingly the Brahmans, the keepers of the traditional law and usually standing against conversions, became a constant target in the writings and activities of the missionaries.

The Brahmans took care of their religion and of the cult of its idols, but they deceived the blind and simple Hindu people with their ceremonial falsities.[58] Francis Xavier in a severe criticism of the Brahman priests, presented them as defenders of superstitions and idolatry. They lived in their temples and looked after these idols. There could not be a worse people nor more perverse than them, and their deceitful and insincere ways were rather conspicuous. They lost no opportunity to deceive the common and poor people. If the people did not obey the Brahmans or placate their gods, they were threatened with sickness, death and persecutions by the demons; and unfortunately the credulous people, left with no other alternative, followed the orders of the Brahmans out of terror of these gods.[59]

It is interesting to observe the number of European stereotypes concerning the Brahmans. The local kings helped financially the Brahman priests and the latter were highly respected. They possessed the knowledge of their religion and they alone could learn it and teach others what its main books contained. At the beginning of the conversion drive the Brahmans raised many obstacles, and on a few occasions they even ill-treated and stoned some local converts.[60] The rich and the powerful Brahmans opposed actively the conversion of the Gentiles and the new faith.[61] In those places where the Portuguese had no political control the Brahmans did not allow conversions; and whenever they managed to gain the support of the Portuguese authorities, as they did at times even in Goa, the missionaries could not work freely.[62] In Goa the Brahmans oppressed the Christians till 1557.[63] The Hindu chiefs also supplied the Hindu people with alms to resist conversions.[64] When some Brahmans showed some inclination to become Christians they soon back-tracked, alleging that all their relatives and acquaintances would laugh at them, since they would lose their honour.[65] A few Brahmans sided with the Muslims, as during the war between Goa and Bijapur, when the governor, Nuno da Cunha (1529-38), ruled Goa.[66]

The Brahmans, particularly the Sinai Brahmans, responsible for the lack of conversions and for obstructing the work of the missionaries, were constantly threatened with expulsion from the island of Goa.[67] The missionaries believed that with their expulsion conversions would increase.[68] As a result a royal provision in 1563 ordered all the obstructionist Hindus to sell their property and to leave Goa. Only the farmers who tilled the land with their own hands — doctors, carpenters, ironsmiths, shopkeepers and supervisors could remain if proved harmless.[69] However, if the expelled Hindus returned to Goa they could be imprisoned and sent to the galleys.[70]

The devil had persuaded these Hindus that the honour of men came from their religion hence, they kept it so scrupulously. There was a caste of people called *farazes*, who were anathema among other castes for not keeping the law. Nobody spoke to them or touched them. Thus, the more they observed the law the more honourable they considered themselves, so much so that among them there was no respect but for those who followed their superstitions strictly. Hence, the Brahmans who taught the law and kept it impeccably were taken for holy people among the Hindus, and so great was the latter's respect for them. Perhaps the following story tells us how the Brahmans stood united in adversities. In 1560 a man from Goa on his hunting trip in the Bijapur kingdom, met there in the thick woods a group of about 250 Brahmans, men, women and children in a shelterless and desperate state. The hunter was astonished to find them in such a state, and on recognizing some of them he asked what had brought them here. The Brahmans told him that they were hiding from the Adilshah, who wanted to take their children away. They had been here for a few days, and the lions had already eaten about twenty persons of this group. These people had earlier left Goa for fear of conversion. They wanted to suffer this fate and persevere in their law rather than to return to Goa and become Christians.[71]

## Concluding Remarks

The Hindus displayed customs and lifestyles very different and strange from those of the Europeans. In India, they never wanted to acknowledge and love God, they rather preferred to follow their immoral practices, idolatries and monstruous customs, without ever desiring to adhere to Christendom and to the charity of Jesus Christ, wrote several missionaries without mincing their words and arguments. Nevertheless, expectations of their conversions never died. When in 1545 some rulers and chiefs had converted to the Catholic faith, the missionaries expected that many others would soon follow suit.[72]

The analysis of the Indian context by the Portuguese themselves made them aware that it was extremely difficult to convince the Muslims and Hindus to follow the Portuguese customs and laws as something profitable and good for them. The Hindus and Muslims were so greedy that they would rather be tormented than let go of a coin of little value from their hand, said Francisco Rodrigues Silveira, a Portuguese soldier in India. He asked, "When the Portuguese themselves did not live by them (their customs and laws), or gave little importance to what they taught others to do, how could they expect the locals to take them seriously?"[73] He suggested to his countrymen that those who despised what the Hindus and Muslims prized most should go and preach to them, or else it would be next to impossible to persuade them to leave their rituals and customs in which they were brought up.[74]

In spite of the Portuguese self-evaluation which showed that they themselves needed to be reformed and the poor chances of changing the Indians, the former hardly stopped from interfering in the local customs and religion. The Portuguese wanted to replace the native 'weaknesses' and 'superstitions' with new predictable forms of thinking, living and worshipping — and above all, with the Lusitanian citizenship. The missionaries had a keen interest to bring the nations of infidels and barbarians to the light of civilization. This could become a reality only through conversion, which demanded reform of local customs and many social changes.

The missionaries converted some people, but the new religion could not wipe out the old customs. In conclusion, men in India held on to the "laws and customs of their ancestors as the best part of their heritage, keeping them with deligence and rigour, and only with untold difficulties could the missionaries stop these idolaters from professing their false religion".[75] Nevertheless, changes in the Goan society did occur as a result of conversions. For the converts and Hindus alike the Goan society became a blend of the old and the new, a synthesis of contrastive demands, despite initial resistance to social changes.

## NOTES AND REFERENCES

1. *Bullarium*, First Provincial Council, Acc. 2, dec. 2, p. 6.
2. CEHU, *Documentação Ultramarina Portuguesa* I, p. 260.
3. Francisco de Souza, *OCJC*, pp. 158-59.
4. *DI*, XVII, 387.
5. *Doc*, VI, 348.
6. *Ibid.*, X, 567. See Constituitions of the Archdiocese of Goa - 1568.
7. *DI*, XVIII, 883.
8. *Doc*, VI, 348.
9. *DI*, XVIII, 884.
10. P. D. Xavier, *Goa, A Social History*, p. 117.
11. *DI*, III, 576.
12. Panduranga Pissurlencar, "O Elemento Hindu da Casta Chardo", pp. 9-10.
13. The Muslim converts from Hinduism also retained their previous caste differences among themselves.
14. Among the Catholics of Goa there is a caste called Chaddo. The term Chaddo was not a creation of the Portuguese. There were also Hindu Chaddos outside Goa, but today this word has become obsolete among the Hindus of Goa. The word was used for the first time in 1599. Panduranga Pissurlencar, "op. cit.".
15. *Doc*, XI, 786.
16. António da Silva Rego, *História das Missões do Padroado Português do Oriente,* p. 219.
17. "Entre a gentilidade a hy um costume que quando as molheres parem vão perguntar seus maridos aos caneanes, que são feiticeiros, que sua molher avia parido, que lhe dicesse se a criança avia de ser boa ou se nascera em boa hora, e pera que ho feiticeiro lhes diga isto, ão-de ser primeiro peitados; responde então o caneane o que quer, dizendo: "teu filho nasceo em boa hora, crio (sic), porque a-de ser bom homen". E se lhe dis, "tal filho qual te agora a-de nascer a-de ser muito amo, nasceu em ruim hora, em nenhuma maneira o cries, porque a-de ser muito pessimo" vendo o pay e a may isto não o matarão os filhos, mas os trazem aos christaos que os criem e fação christãos; e desta maneira achava muitos meninos em poder dos

nossos christãos os quais. . . ." *Doc*, V, 54.

18. *DI,* III, 357. *Doc*, VIII, 301.
19. ARSI, *Eppistolae Goana*, 8 - I, fl. 3.
20. Jaime Cortesão, *Os Descobrimentos Portugueses*, Vol. II, p. 179.
21. Alessandro Valignano, *op. cit.*, p. 40.
22. Zinadim, *op. cit.*, pp. 107-08.
23. Sebastião Gonçalves, *op. cit.*, p. 90.
24. *Ibid.*, p. 89.
25. Paulo da Trindade, *CEO*, Part I, p. 277. "Todos os deoses dos gentios som demonios." *Doc*, II, 347.
26. ARSI, *Eppistolae Goana et Malabarica*, 10 - II, fl. 320.
27. *Doc*, VIII, 416.
28. *DI*, II, 481.
29. ARSI, *Goana Historia*, 34 - I, fl. 222.
30. Martim Fernandez de Figueroa, *A Spaniard in the Portuguese Indies* (1512), pp. 103, 127.
31. Armando Cortesão, (ed.), *The Suma Oriental of Tome Pires*, Vol. I, p. 59. The pretty women of Goa dress well and those who dance do likewise, rather better than those in any part of the world. *Ibid.*
32. *DI*, II, 243, 597.
33. ARSI, *Eppistolae Goana et Malabarica*, 10 - I, fl. 246.
34. *DI*, II, 405-06.
35. *Ibid.*, 600.
36. *Ibid.*, 380.
37. Alessandro Valignano, *op. cit.*, pp. 24-28.
38. *Ibid.*, pp. 28-29.
39. *Ibid.*, pp. 29-30.
40. *Ibid.*, p. 28.
41. *Ibid.*, pp. 24-25.
42. "Canarins pessoas notadas de falsidade e mentiras e como a taes esta ordenado que não sejam admitidos a testemunhar a cousa alguma, nem se receberão informações e testemunhos desta ma gente." ARSI, *Eppistolae Goana et Malabarica*, 14, fl. 68. *Canarins* were indigenous Goans. *DI*, VIII, 549, 341; X, 717. Goans were

known as *Canarins.* Alessandro Valignano, *op. cit.*, p. 69. *DI*, XVI, 722.

43. Sebastião Gonçalves, *op. cit.*, p. 90.
44. *DI*, IV, 207.
45. *APO*, 3, p. 659.
46. Armando Cortesão, (ed.), *op. cit.*, p. 58.
47. *Doc*, VIII, 59.
48. Alessandro Valignano, *op. cit.*, p. 30.
49. *DI*, I, 182. A. Valignano wrote about the Indians in 1580, "Y conforme a esto aunque unos son de mas o menos... sao gente de pouco primor . . . ." *Doc*, XI, 475.
50. *Ibid.*, XI, 549.
51. *DI*, I, 416.
52. *Ibid.*, XVI, 498.
53. A. de S. S. Costa Lobo, (ed.), *op. cit.*, p. 236.
54. *DI*, XIV, 902.
55. "Negros da terra de Salsete." ARSI, *Eppistolae Goana et Malabarica*, 14, fl. 68. *DI*, XVI, 285, 290.
56. *Ibid.*, III, 336. *Doc*, VI, 34. Slaves of dark skin, Africans and Asians, were generally referred to as *negros*; The term *cafre negro* was used particularly for an African. João de Barros, *Decada da Asia*, II, (1628), pp. 3v-4, 6v.
57. "Los bramenes en essas partes son tan estimados de los naturales." *DI*, XV, 824.
58. Alessandro Valignano, *op. cit.*, p. 33.
59. Francisco de Sousa, *op. cit.*, pp. 70-71. "Ay en estas partes entre los gentiles una generación, que se llaman bragmanes: estos sustentan toda la gentilidad. Tienem cargo de las casas donde están los ídolos: es mla gente más perversa del mundo . . . . Es gente que nunca dize verdade, y siempre piensan cómo an de sutilmente mintir y engañar los pobres símplices y ignorantes, dizendo que los ídolos demandan que les llevem a offrecer ciertas cosas, y éstas no son otras sino las que los bragmanes fingen y quieren para mantener sus mugeres, hijos y casas. Hazem creer a los símplices que comen los ídolos, y ay muchos que antes que coman ni cenen offrecen cierta moneda para el ídolo. Dos vezes al día con grande fiesta de

atabales comen, dando a entender a los pobres que comen los ídolos. Antes que les falte lo necessario a los bragmanes dizen al pueblo que los ídolos están muy enojados contra ellos, porque no les mandan las cosas que por ellos le mandan pedir, e que si no proveen, que se guarden ellos, que los an de matar, o darles enfermedades, o que an de mandar los demonios a sus casas: y los tristes símplices, creyendo que será así, de miedo que los ídolos no les hagan mal, hazen lo que los bragmanes quieren . . . . Y se no uviesse bragmanes, todos los gentiles se converterían a nuestra fee." Georg Schurhammer and Josef Wicki, (eds.), *Epistolae S. Francisci Xaverii*, Vol. I, pp. 170-71.

60. Paulo da Trindade, *op. cit.*, p. 285.

61. *DI*, III, 407.

62. Alessandro Valignano, *op. cit.*, p. 434.

63. *DI*, III, 718.

64. *Doc*, IV, 132.

65. *Ibid.*, VIII, 56.

66. *DI*, I, 68. "O bramene mais prejudicial e contrario ha christandade de Goa he Dadagi, filho de Crisnaa, que veio a este reino, e recebeu muitas merces e onrras de el-rey Dom Manoel, vosso padre, que santa gloria haja, e lhe prometeo de ser christão, tanto que tornasse ha India, com toda sua familia, por cujo respeito lhe foi feito merce do officio de tanador-moor e lingoa do governador, em sua vida, e elle nunca se fez christão, antes elle e o filho são os mores adversarios da nossa santa fee, que ha em Goa, pello que se devia comprir inteiramente o que Vossa Alteza mandou na carta que escreveu per Miguel Vaz." A report from Fr. Pedro Fernandes Sardinha of the Society of Jesus to the king D. João III. *Doc*, IV, 560.

67. *Ibid.*, III, 205. *DI*, I, 69.

68. *Doc*, III, 521.

69. *APO*, 5, Supl. II, doc. 472, p. 543-45.

70. *LFC*, fl 42. *Doc*, VIII, 174, 176. In 1559, "Quanto de la conversión a la fee determinan aora y trabaja el Pe. Antonio que se hechen desta isla de Goa los bramines, que es muy prejudicial generación pera los gentíos se convertieren. Siempre aquy se hazen christianos quasi cada dia, y ansy con la aiuda del Señor se va haziedo obra para que sea toda esta isla christiana." *Ibid.*, IV, 334. "Onde há poucos brahmenes se fazem muitos Cristãos." *Ibid.*, IX, 243, 250.

Miguel Vaz wrote, "Porquanto os bramenes são aquelles que mais contradizem esta santa obra da christandade, seria muito serviço de Deos que fossem lansados fora, mayormente da ilha de Goa . . . ." *Ibid.*, IV, 560.

71. *Ibid.*, VIII, 56.
72. ARSI, *Eppistolae Goana et Malabarica*, 10 - I, fl. 11.
73. A. de S. S. Costa Lobo, (ed.), *op. cit.*, pp. 195-96.
74. *Ibid.*, p. 197.
75. Sebastião Gonçalves, *op. cit.*, p. 87.

12

# *CANARIM* — PORTUGUESE CITIZENRY

## Christian (and Hindu) Population in Goa

### City of Goa, Salcete and Bardez; Divar and Chorão

From the outset I must say that it is not easy to give accurate statistics on conversions in Goa. The number of conversions effected in Goa was directly related to the methods or means, which include state policies for making converts. But the rapid increase of converts in Goa — a fact that the Hindus and even some Portuguese criticized and condemned for suspecting involvement of force — was mainly a result of the Portuguese political and economic control over the Hindus, the vassals of the crown. Conversions would never increase if there was no vassalage to the Portuguese authorities, since the Hindus were naturally against conversions, agreed the Portuguese.[1] A few zealous proselytizers believed that vassalage was a *sine qua non* condition for conversions. Hence, it is not difficult to understand why the religious orders constantly meddled in politics, particularly when the law enforcers were careless in demanding the vassalage of the people, to the extent of attracting at times a royal warning as in 1598, for abusing their authority or interfering in matters outside their jurisdiction.[2] Where the Portuguese had only factories and fortresses conversions were not as easy to make as in the Portuguese-controlled territories. There permission had to be obtained from the local Hindu kings and rulers to convert and build churches, whereas in Goa the Hindus had to ask permission to build or rebuild their own temples and perform their rituals, forbidden by royal and ecclesiastical decrees. The Hindus almost never got any official permission to their requests concerning religious matters. The people under political pressure and economic disfavours, and with no choice, opted in large numbers for the new religion. But kinship, kindred and local customs — rather than citizenship, the royal and ecclesiastical stipulations and penalties repeated *ab inicio* — continued to direct and decide much of the life of the converts and Hindus.

As mentioned earlier a detailed quantification on conversions during the sixteenth century is impossible; nevertheless, I must state that Goa stands a better chance of assessing its conversion growth rate, vis-à-vis any other territory under the Portuguese control. The baptized had to be registered in order to ascertain the number of conversions, but often they were not registered due to negligence on the part of the parish priests.[3] The *Pay dos Christãos*, although responsible for taking the census of the Christians, did not see this task with much concern. The Franciscan humility and simplicity did not permit them to speak or boast about the number of converts they made. It was sufficient that God knew about it, they argued, but by the end of the sixteenth century, when their enemies or rivals accused them of lack of zeal in missionary activity, then they began 'boasting' about the number of baptisms they made. Hence, from Bardez we have hardly any numerical information.[4] On the other hand, the Jesuits did not spare efforts to publicize and turn their conversion activity into statistics, as one of the most powerful and convincing strategies to influence the king and their own superiors in Europe. The purpose was first, to prepare more candidates with 'vocation for India' and second, to attract royal funds for their work. The other religious orders came to Goa late, and worked chiefly in the city of Goa and its islands, where most of the population in these parts had already been converted. They added very little to the already-vast numbers of converts. Since Goa had been divided among the missionary orders, the island or the city of Goa and the two districts of Bardez and Salcete being the three units, we are often given the number of conversions effected in each place separately. Obviously, each religious order would speak only about their own conversion activity. But there is still a great deal of confusion regarding the number of converts in each district or division.

When the missionaries sent reports and letters to the kings or their superiors in Europe on statistics of conversions, these were frequently done without indicating important details like the village, caste and gender of the converts. Often this quantified information was presented in a simplified form: 'many' or 'few' conversions, or 'entire' village converted, or 'great increase of Christendom'.[5] We must not forget that the missionaries particularly the Jesuits, wrote for edifying and publicity purposes; hence, the village, caste and gender were details of no consequence for them. These details became of even less importance when these letters or numbers were written to be read in the churches in Europe. We know that the kings of Portugal ordered these statistics to be read in the churches in Portugal.[6] The 'publicity' and 'edifying' aspects of these reports could perhaps be illustrated by what was said in a sermon delivered in Europe: the preacher attributed 600 000 conversions to Francis Xavier.[7] The Europeans, ignorant and misinformed of what happened in India, easily believed that the pagans were just waiting to be baptized; in turn the European ignorance of things Indian and their prejudiced imagination encouraged the missionaries to inflate numbers. Besides, as each religious order reported only on its own conversions, one could ask whether there was not any sort of competition among the orders, hence exaggerations or a tendency among them to 'make up conversions' cannot be excluded. They wrote only things that would encourage and edify others in Europe.[8] Keeping in mind the missionary mentality we have to make allowances for inflation and interpolation of numerical data.

As has been said before, the reports on numbers tell us very little about which caste was converted, but the converts were generally classified either as *Bramenes* (noblemen) or *Gentios* (commoners). At times the conversion of noble and Hindu chiefs appear deliberately emphasized and described at length for some dramatic effect. There is a general historical consensus that some

Brahmans were expelled either for refusing to embrace Christianity, or for harmful activities in the state. Others chose to leave the land rather than convert. But it is equally acknowledged that there were more conversions in Goa from among the upper castes than elsewhere in India. A categorical statement that the lower castes surrendered easily or with little resistance to the missionaries, after the conversion of their chiefs, is not totally correct. But it seems true that having to choose between conversion and migration, generally the lower castes preferred conversion to remain in possession of the land they cultivated.[9]

Could the number of churches and chapels tell us anything about the number of converts? We can only say with greater certitude that wherever there was a church or chapel, and there were many all over Goa, Christian communities had emerged here. The optimism and ignorance of some missionaries led them to believe that conversion of the Hindus was only a question of more churches and a strong missionary presence among them. Soon after the conquest of Goa by Afonso de Albuquerque the Hindus did not feel attracted to Christianity as expected. Some missionaries doubted the intentions and the quality of many conversions, and spoke of a great number of relapsed and weak Christians. In that large number of conversions, there were crypto-Hindus galore.

The present Old Goa, then the city of Goa, certainly reflects the history of Christianity in the sixteenth century and later. The size and number of churches and chapels everywhere in Goa do not *ipso facto* imply a great number of Christians, much less the facility and rapidity with which conversions were effected, just as the absence of Hindu temples and mosques (after their destruction) do not tell us anything about the number of the 'non-converts' and of their religious practices.

Temples and mosques in plenty in India (and Goa) astonished the Portuguese. It was natural that the Portuguese would like to show their superiority in religious matters too. The religion of the ruler had to match its superior military and naval power. Moreover, the construction of some huge churches was the result of a competitive mentality among the religious orders, whose aim was to outdo the other in all aspects. Each religious order had one main church and many other small ones.

During the sixteenth century, some government officials had argued that the missionary activity was responsible for the political and economic decadence of the Portuguese eastern empire. This is not a criticism or condemnation of the number of conversions effected in Goa, but of the methods used to convert people, which antagonized the Hindus and Muslims and gradually caused erosion of their confidence in the Portuguese. The high state expenditures with the missionaries, churches and religious cult constituted another cause of the decadence of the empire. It is difficult to calculate the number of clergymen in Goa, but by the turn of the sixteenth century there were more priests here than it needed.[10] Goa accounted for eighty churches then.[11] But this criticism did not deter the crown from continuing to favour the construction of new churches in Goa in 1591.[12] Likewise, the crown continued to remind the local authorities to favour and help the missionaries in their work of conversion.

We know that at the initial stage of conversion activity (1510-1540), the missionaries expected the locals to convert in the most natural way as a result of their daily contacts with the Portuguese. Nevertheless, the Franciscans were able to convert only eight hundred Hindus by 1518. They alleged that many more could have received the Christian faith, but for the secular clergy who obstructed their work of conversion.[13] At this stage the people of Goa had a good opinion about the Franciscans.[14] Then in 1526 an 'entire' village in Goa had turned Christian;[15] and 'many' Hindus converted continually.[16] The city of Goa could boast of three to four thousand Portuguese and ten thousand local Christians in 1540. The Franciscans alone christianized Goa till 1542.

During the last years of the decade of thirties, the city of Goa and its adjacent islands became entirely Christian.[17] It was often reported that Goa (city of Goa) had become almost entirely Catholic or rather that no Hindus lived here. In 1541 the Inspector of the Treasury, Fernão Rodrigues Castelo-Branco, acting governor in the absence of the governor, D. Estêvão da Gama, from Goa, wrote that there had been so 'many' conversions in the islands of Goa, Divar and Chorão, and that almost all the temples there had been destroyed. In the same year other Hindus and Muslims from the same islands became Christians. Many more would have converted, but for some persons (like Krishna, Loquu and Anu Synai and some of their relatives) who persuaded them against embracing the new faith.[18] Further, in the same year 'many' poor people, leaving their Hindu families, received baptism.[19] It is obvious that the Christian appearance of the city of Goa was not only a result of conversions — voluntary, coercive or convenient — but also of the self-exile of many Hindus to the neighbouring lands.

When the Jesuits arrived in Goa in 1542, they found 'many' Christians here.[20] In 1542 Francis Xavier, in his first letter written from Goa to Rome, reported that the city of Goa looked like a Christian place, which feature astonished him. The city accounted for many Franciscans residing in their monastery and the majestic cathedral which accommodated several canon priests. Churches could be seen in plenty. It was something worth praising God for, since his name was acknowledged in the most remote areas among the infidels, said Xavier.[21] Goa had fifteen to twenty thousand Christian inhabitants in 1542. This number includes the Portuguese and local Christians living in the city of Goa, Divar and Chorão, perhaps in the entire territory.[22] But only the city of Goa was considered a 'Christian place'.[23] Alessandro Valignano who was not a contemporary of Francis Xavier contradicted the latter's observation, saying that Goa had 'very few' local Christians in 1542.[24] But a little later in 1545 we are informed that bishop, João de Albuquerque, felt the need to create four parishes, (Cathedral of Santa Catarina, churches of Nossa Senhora do Rosário, Nossa Senhora da Luz, and Santa Luzía in the city of Goa), since the number of Christians here was already quite 'sizeable'.[25]

Other reports stated that five thousand Christians took part in a procession in 1546; one thousand pagans received baptism in the churches of Goa in 1548.[26] In the island of Goa there were more than forty thousand Hindus and over five to seven thousand Christians in 1548.[27] In the following year the number must have increased, since every day there were conversions, especially after the conversion of Loquu, baptized Lucas de Saa, who began working for the faith.[28] 'Many' Hindus had converted in 1549.[29]

In 1551 the 'great number' of Christians around the city of Goa mixed freely with the Hindus, and the viceroy, D. Pedro de Mascarenhas, wishing to preserve the former and convert the latter, ordered several churches to be built.[30] In 1552 twelve thousand persons visited the relics of one of the eleven thousand virgins, exposed for veneration in the city of Goa.[31] In 1554 a 'great' part of the population in Goa was still Hindu.[32] In 1556 'many' Hindus became Christians at the College of St Paul.[33] 'Many thousand' were converted, Hindus and Muslims, in 1557; and the priests of the Society of Jesus alone converted 1800 souls.[34] In 1558 nearly 1900 persons received baptism, some Brahmans, and others Naiks who were like the soldiers among the Hindus. 'Many' jewellers of a noble caste, merchants, cultivators, shepherds, officers, men, women and boys were converted too.[35] About 3300 persons were baptized in the College of St Paul in 1559.[36] These numbers belong to the Jesuit reports about their own conversions. In 1560, 12 700 souls from the island of Goa and from the other neighbouring ones received baptism at the College.[37] The island of Goa, Bardez and Salcete boasted of about fifty thousand Christians around this time. It is rather interesting to observe that most of this harvest had been reaped between 1550 and 1559, when only a relatively small number of missionaries were active in the field.[38]

During the tenure of D. Constantino de Bragança (1558-1560), the most zealous or fanatic viceroy Goa had ever seen, conversions went up as never before. Probably, more conversions were effected during the rule of D. Constantino de Bragança than during all the previous years since the conquest of Goa. Total number of Christians in the islands of Goa, Divar, Chorão, in the districts of Bardez and Salcete had reached over twenty thousand.[39]

We hear of a group baptism with more than a hundred persons in Batim, Bardez, in 1560 and the people themselves had asked for it. The women were dressed up well and wore plenty of gold. In fact all had dressed well at their own cost, and they were warriors.[40] In 1560, Salcete had about a thousand Christians and fifty thousand Hindus, but the former behaved just like the latter.[41] In the same year, in the islands of Goa and Divar, the Jesuits baptized 13 092 Hindus;[42] again in the same year and concerning the same islands the missionaries reported 12 700 Christian souls.[43] We also hear that in 1560 the island of Goa could count twenty-five thousand Christians.[44]

In 1560 'very few' Hindus could be seen in the island of Goa, since most of them had abandoned the land earlier. The optimistic Fr. Luís Frois wrote that most Goan Hindus would be converted even before the arrival of next fleet from Portugal.[45] The nobles and Hindu chiefs of this land asked themselves how the conversion of so many of their countrymen could be possible in such a short period of fifty or sixty years. They concluded that it could not be possible to convert so many without the use of force,[46] and accused the missionaries of using forcible methods.[47] Then in 1561 we have a report with an astronomical figure of eighty thousand Christians in Goa.[48] It may be recalled here that from the sixties the missionary attention shifted to Bardez and Salcete. A few years earlier these districts had been handed over for the work of conversion to the Franciscans and to the Jesuits respectively.

The Jesuits baptized 685 souls in 1562. More than seven hundred persons joined the Christian fold through the College of St Paul in 1563. The missionaries succeeded in convincing the Hindus about the superiority of Christianity and other advantages they could obtain on becoming Christians; thus 'many' converted freely.[49] In 1563 in the city of Goa and its islands the number of Christians reached the figure of seventy thousand, mostly converted during the previous six years.[50] However, Fr. Gabriel Oliver said in 1565 that Gentilism (Hinduism) prevailed among millions of infidels in Goa.[51]

In Rachol, Salcete, the Christians added up to only 1800 in 1566.[52] Salcete counted a population of 250 000 inhabitants, but only four thousand were Christians in 1567.[53] In 1569, Goa was almost as populated as Rome, and Salcete alone had 120 000 inhabitants.[54] (There seems to be a discrepancy in reporting numbers of inhabitants in Goa and of Christians too.) The king reminded the civil authorities to help and favour the missionary activity in 1568.[55] Conversions depended to a very large extent on the religious zeal of the viceroys and civil authority, but these people, ever ambitious and on the look out for maximum personal profit, cared least for conversions.[56]

Almost half of Salcete remained Hindu till 1575,[57] but the city of Goa was nearly Christian around this time.[58] A. Valignano mentioned, without differentiating, about the existence of more than twelve to fifteen thousand Hindu and Christian households in the city of Goa in 1576.[59] Several hundred of catechumens awaited baptism in 1576.[60] In 1579 'very few' conversions took place in the city of Goa and its islands, since the Hindu merchants refused to embrace the Christian faith, for fear of losing their business.[61] In the same year the work of conversion came to a halt as result of the war with the Adilshah and other serious impediments. Many Christians living in Salcete fled their lands and settled in the city of Goa. The previous war with the Adilshah in Salcete in 1572, had already forced many Christians to the city, due to increasing poverty. Despite suffering several privations, they showed themselves firm in their faith.[62] Poverty and other difficulties caused by the war might have contributed to further conversions.[63] In 1578 the city of Goa accounted for around ninety thousand Christians. Christians and Hindus together numbered 150 000.[64]

Two hundred persons received baptism in 1581.[65] In 1582 we hear that Salcete had eighty thousand inhabitants, nearly all Hindus, of whom seven to eight thousand were Christians, mostly converted during the previous twelve years. These Christians lived together with the Hindus, an unavoidable situation but very harmful to their new faith.[66] By 1586 its Christian population increased to fourteen thousand;[67] twenty thousand faithful in 1588;[68] twenty-three thousand Christians in 1590;[69] twenty-five thousand in 1591;[70] two years later in 1593 the number of converts in Salcete went up to 27 123; in 1594 we read about 28 473 Christians;[71] and in the following year 30 502 faithful.[72] Conversions went on increasing in Salcete.[73]

Candolim was the first village in Bardez to be converted. In 1585 the Franciscans had already seven rectories with churches in Bardez: Reis Magos, Nagoa, Sirula, Candolim, Siolim, Nerul and Aldona. By 1595 four more were erected: Mapusa, Colvale, Calangute and Pomburpa. This points to the existence of Christian communities in these places. Strange as it might be, there was a time when the number of Christians exceeded that of Hindus in Bardez.[74]

In 1596 the king of Portugal stated that the missionaries continued to make many conversions. This was certainly a statement based on the reports sent by the missionaries themselves. It was customary for the Portuguese crown to make such statements to justify the Portuguese conquests, to remind the agents of conversion of their duties and to assert the patronage rights. We should suspect this kind of royal statements.[75] During the last years of the sixteenth century few people were converted; whereas some Christians abandoned their faith.[76] Salcete counted thirty-five thousand local Christians in 1597.[77] Favours continued to be granted to the Hindus to win them over. It was said again that Salcete reached the figure of thirty-five thousand converts in 1598.[78] At the end of the century the Jesuits reported that a thousand baptisms took place annually (I suppose that this calculation refers only to the conversions in Salcete).[79]

In 1599 there were few conversions as compared with the previous years and the reason for this was that the Jesuits had stopped baptizing the Hindus, except for those who asked for it persistently. Instead, the missionaries took time to instruct the converts who showed great ignorance about things Christian. Earlier the priests had given precedence to conversions rather than instruction, but by the turn of the century preserving the faithful seemed equally important.[80] In 1600 the Cathedral of St Catarina in the city of Goa had more than eighty thousand Christians.[81] In the same year only two thousand Hindus and Muslims resided in the city of Goa. [82]

Christianity continued to grow in Salcete.[83] The Jesuits made five thousand converts in the city of Goa and Salcete in 1601-02.[84] In 1602 Salcete boasted of thirty-five thousand Christians, just as in 1597-1598 as we have seen.[85] These converts, although a people of some understanding, shared the Jewish nature and mixed freely with the Hindus (Brahmans constituted one fifth of the population), a serious impediment for good Christian behaviour.[86] In 1603 there were forty thousand Christians in Salcete,[87] and in 1606 over forty thousand.[88] In 1607-1608 that number did not change.[89]

In 1607-1608, 1300 persons became Christians in Goa. Claudio Aquaviva, the superior- general of the Society of Jesus, based on reports he had received from here, wrote to a Jesuit provincial in India in 1608, regretting that the old religious zeal was dying out among the subjects and the superiors alike.[90] The town of Margão, in Salcete, totalled 3900 Christians in 1609.[91] The city of Goa in 1623 reached the figure of sixty thousand Christians who lived among 100 000 non-Christians.[92] In 1629 Bardez had 32 000 Christians.[93]

In 1635 we hear again that there were sixty thousand Christians in Goa and over 100 000 Hindus.[94] In 1667 the number came down to 53 450 faithful, but every year at the group baptisms more than five hundred souls joined Christendom. By this time there were very few catechumens, since the entire island of Goa, Salcete and Bardez had already been Christianized.[95] By 1666 Christendom in Goa had gone through three generations of converts. Bardez had been the centre of Hinduism, but by this time there was hardly much evidence of it here. Perhaps in 1667, there were only two or three Hindu households in the parish of Mapusa.

We have also important information about the islands of Divar and Chorão. Divar was the holy land — Rome for the Hindus and the backbone of their temples.[96] The temple of Saptanatha, in Divar, attracted more than thirty thousand Hindu pilgrims from Goa itself during its annual festival. This temple had been destroyed by the Muslims before the arrival of the Portuguese.[97]

Till 1560 Divar saw as many as 1455 converts, and eighty more persons awaited baptism. Among those awaiting baptism there were sixty boys, who had been taken away by their parents to the Muslim land, but later their own parents brought them back to be baptized.[98] In 1560 it was reported that Divar and Chorão had more than twenty thousand (read two thousand only) Christian souls.[99] Some noble Hindus and *fidalgos,* who suspected that force was being exerted on the people, used to comment on the huge number of converts.[100] In the same year almost all the inhabitants in Chorão were already baptized, and the figure reached 1207

Christians.[101] In 1566 Divar counted 2120 Christians and just a few Hindus.[102] In the same year in Chorão there were about 2470 Christians and the few Hindus living here had promised to become Christians.[103] By 1567 all the inhabitants of the islands of Divar and Chorão had already been converted.[104]

In 1572 there were no Hindus in Chorão.[105] Four year later Chorão had become entirely Christian, and the Hindus and Muslims who came from outside to reside here were also converted.[106] But they adhered secretly to some idols in their native land.[107] In 1578 only Christians resided in the island of Chorão[108] which boasted of having fifteen thousand Christians.[109] Chorão numbered three thousand Christians in 1580.[110]

In 1582 there were three thousand converts in Chorão. All its inhabitants were Christians and many came from outside to receive baptism.[111] These Christians did not allow any Hindus, even if they were their own relatives, to enter the island. Thus anyone wanting to come here converted. Despite Chorão's proximity to the Muslim territory, these converts had no dealings with their Hindu neighbours living there.[112] We can easily notice some confusion or contradictory information regarding the number of Christians in the two islands of Divar and Chorão. Nevertheless, we can conclude that there were not more than six thousand Christians by the end of the century in these two islands.

## NOTES AND REFERENCES

1. H. A. Viotti, *Nóbrega e a conversão do gentio*, p. 85.
2. *BFUP*, No. 3, pp. 413-14. *MR*, 4, fls. 592-94.
3. *Doc*, VII, 333. BNL, *Reservados*, Cod. 176, fl. 117.
4. J. H. da Cunha Rivara, *Brados a Favor das Communidades das Aldeias do Estado da India*, p. 83.
5. J. H. da Cunha Rivara, *Ensaio Historico da Lingua Concani*, p. 21.
6. Francisco Rodrigues, *op. cit.*, p. 521.
7. *Sermons em varias Celebridades que pregou o Padre Simam da Gama da Companhia de Jesus,* Part VI, p. 175.

8. ARSI, *Extracto das cousas,* la, fl. 21v.
9. Rui Gomes Pereira, *Goa. Hindu Temples and Deities*, p. 18.
10. *BFUP*, No. 2, p. 259. *MR,* 3A, fl. 110.
11. For a description given in 1606 about the Christian faith, churches (so majestic as to envy the whole world...) and conversions see, *APO*, 1, Part II, p. 147.
12. A royal letter to the viceroy, Matias de Albuquerque, in 1591.*BFUP*, No. 2, pp. 196-97. *MR*, 2A, fls. 98-100.
13. Georg Schurhammer, *Francis Javier. Su vida y su tiempo*, Vol. II, p. 209.
14. Georg Schurhammer, *Francis Xavier. His Life, His Times*; Vol. II, p. 162.
15. *Doc*, II, 143.
16. *Ibid.*, 188.
17. António da Silva Rego, *História das Missões do Padroado Português do Oriente*, p. 226.
18. *DI*, I, 792.
19. *Doc*, II, 294.
20. Luis de Guzman, *op. cit.*, p. 18.
21. Georg Schurhammer and Josef Wicki, (eds.),*Epistolae S. Francisci Xaverii*, Vol. I, pp. 121-22.
22. Georg Schurhammer, *Francisco Javier. Su vida y su tiempo*, Vol. II, p. 347.
23. *Doc*, IV, 35.
24. Alessandro Valignano, *op. cit.*, p. 45.
25. CEHU, *Documentação Ultramarina Portuguesa*, p. 560.
26. Georg Schurhammer, *op. cit.* Vol. II, p. 347.
27. *DI*, I, 253, 408. Georg Schurhammer, *op. cit.* p. 230.
28. *DI*, I, 408.
29. *Doc*, IV, 453.
30. CEHU, *op. cit.*, p. 626.
31. Sebastião Gonçalves, *op. cit.*, p. 98.
32. ARSI, *Eppistolae Goana et Malabarica*, 10 - II, fl. 314v.
33. *DI*, III, 576.
34. Luis de Guzman, *op.cit.*, p. 56.
35. *DI*, IV, 213. Alessandro Valignano, *op. cit.*, p. 360. Luis de Guzman, *op. cit.*, p. 56.
36. *DI*, IV, 334, 369. Luis de Guzman, *op. cit.*, p. 56.

37. *DI*, V, 63-64.
38. Note that these conversions took place before the establishment of the Tribunal of the Inquisition in Goa in 1560. C. R. Boxer, *The Portuguese Seaborne Empire 1415-1825*, (1973), p. 81.
39. ARSI, *Indiarum Orientalum Miscellanum*, 38 - II, fl. 283.
40. *Boletim Eclesiastico da Arquidiocese de Goa*, Ano IV, No. 7, p. 275. *Doc*, VIII, 95, see note.
41. *Ibid.*, 160. *DI*, VI, 742.
42. *Memória Histórico Eclesiastica da Arquidiocese de Goa*, p. 105.
43. Luis de Guzman, *op. cit.*, p. 56.
44. *Doc*, VIII, 175.
45. A letter written by Fr. Luis Frois from Goa to the colleges of the Society of Jesus in Europe in 1560. *Ibid.*, p. 53.
46. A letter written by Luis Frois from Goa in 1560. *Ibid.*, 211-12.
47. *Ibid.*, 298. See the decree issued in 1567 by the viceroy to the Council on forced conversions. *Ibid.*, X, 412.
48. *DI*, V, 229. "A crystandade seja o Senhor louvado vay muyto avante. No modo della ouve algumas desordens que logo como cheguei se remedearão e se fazem christãos como devem e a Igreja manda.

    Este ano soo nesta ilha se converterão duas mil almas. Avera nesta cidade ao menos 4343 vizinhos dos quaes são portugueses 1478 e mistiços 145 os mais são da terra. No termo da cidade e suas aldeas ha 7025 vizinhos. De maneira que avera nesta ilha somente doze mil vexinhos christãos não entrando soldados e ao menos avera oitaenta mil almas christaãs. Esperamos no Senhor que mediante o fervor e cuidado de vossa Alteza que cedo não avera gentio nesta ilha." Letter from the archbishop of Goa, to the king, in 1561. CEHU, *As Gavetas da Torre do Tombo*, III, p. 190.
49. Alessandro Valignano, *op. cit.*, p. 434, see footnotes nos. 5 and 6.
50. *DI*, VI, 741-42.
51. *Ibid.*, VI, 485.
52. *Ibid.*, 59. *Doc*, X, 100.
53. *DI*, VII, 397f. *Doc*, X, 100.
54. *DI*, VIII, 122.
55. *APO*, 3, p. 9.
56. A. de S. S. Costa Lobo, (ed.), *op. cit.*, p. 146.
57. *DI*, X, 243.
58. *Ibid.*, 465.

59. "Terná más de doze o quinze mil fuegos o casas entre los portugueses y canarines." *Ibid.*, XI, 363, see note no. 135. *Ibid.*, X, 628.
60. *Ibid.*, X, 735.
61. *Ibid.*, XI, 677.
62. *Ibid.*, 259, 262, 658.
63. ARSI, *Goana Historia*, 31 - I, fl. 247.
64. *DI*, XI, 363-64.
65. *Doc*, XII, 738.
66. *Ibid.*, XI, 488, 789.
67. *DI*, XIV, 33*.
68. *Ibid.*, XV, 95.
69. *Ibid.*, XIII, 266; XV, 543.
70. *Ibid.*, 653.
71. *Ibid.*, XVI, 719, 1010.
72. *Ibid.*, XVII, 9*, 295, 389.
73. *MR*, 3B, fl. 515.
74. Paulo da Trindade, *CEO*, Part I, p. 286.
75. AHU, *Registo de cartas*, Cod. 281, fl. 315, 343v, 351.
76. *Ibid.*, fl. 351v.
77. *DI*, XVII, 9*.
78. *Ibid.*, XVIII, 870, 889.
79. ARSI, *Extractos das cousas*, 1a, fl. 17.
80. ARSI, *Eppistolae Goana et Malabarica*, 14, fl. 402.
81. Boies Penrose, *Goa - Rainha do Oriente / Goa - Queen of the East*, p. 69.
82. AHU, *Registo de cartas*, Cod. 282, fl. 97.
83. ARSI, *Eppistolae Goana*, 9 - I, fl. 9v.
84. Fernão Guerreiro, *op. cit.*, Vol. I, p. 348.
85. ARSI, *Goana Historia*, 33 - I, fl. 75.
86. ARSI, *Eppistolae Goana et Malabarica*, 15, fl. 119.
87. *Ibid.*, fl. 174. Fernão Guerreiro, *op. cit.*, Vol. II, p. 355.
88. ARSI, *Goana Historia*, 33 - II, fl. 210. It was said in 1606 that, " A conversão dos infieis sempre foi negocio de grande vagar e molestias em todas a nações do mundo. E muito mais vagarosa deve ser nesta gente pela sua grande rudeza e pouca aplicação às cousas de Deus e pouca lembrança das coisas futuras." ARSI, *Eppistolae Goana et Malabarica*, 16, fl. 180.
89. Fernão Guerreiro, *op. cit.*, Vol. III, p. 1.

90. ARSI, *Extractos das cousas*, 1a, fl. 85
91. ARSI, *Goana Historia*, 33 - I, fl. 184v.
92. P. D. Xavier, *op. cit.*, p. 146.
93. Ricardo Micael Teles, *Os Franciscanos no Oriente e seus Conventos*, p. 6, footnote no. 2.
94. M. N. Pearson, *op. cit.*, p. 102.
95. *Doc*, V, 405.
96. *Ibid.*, VIII, 230.
97. Georg Schurhammer, *Francisco Javier. Su vida y su tiempo*, Vol. II, pp. 294-95, 301. *DI*, IV, 205-06.
98. *Doc*, VIII, 94.
99. *Ibid.*, IV, 780.
100. *Ibid.*, 794.
101. *Doc*, VIII, 94.
102. *Ibid.*, X, 99.
103. *Ibid.*, 98.
104. *DI*, VII, 398.
105. ARSI, *Goana Historia*, 31 - I, fl. 273.
106. Luis de Guzman, *op. cit.*, p. 60. *DI*, XI, 275.
107. *Ibid.*, X, 466.
108. *Ibid.*, XI, 275.
109. *Ibid.*, 323.
110. *Doc*, XII, 487.
111. *DI*, XII, 613.
112. *Ibid.*

# CONCLUSION

More than the methods of conversion *per se*, it was the sizeable number of people that had been converted in a short span of time that made the whole affair of conversion a delicate one during the sixteenth century. For the same reasons and others even today a discussion on conversions in Goa becomes very interesting and polemic. During the first half of the sixteenth century, when conversions were few and constituted no real threat to the local élite, or caused no major social and economic disequilibrium, proselytizing methods, even when not persuasive, were probably not contested or commented upon by the locals, as when the conversion drive intensified.

The number of converts was astronomical indeed in Goa during the sixteenth century, but this factor alone did not suffice to earn for that period the title of 'Christian Century'. I am recalling the history of Christianity in Japan. Japan did not have a Christendom so flourishing as Goa during the sixteenth century, nevertheless this period in Japanese history came to be known as the 'Christian Century'. However, Goa of this period has been acclaimed as the 'Golden Goa' or *Goa Dourada* and 'Rome of the East', due to its prosperity, glittering buildings and imposing churches. I think that if that period was never considered as a 'Christian Century', it is because Goa had neither local Christian martyrs nor an orthodox form of Christianity. The Goan Christians relapsed, and did not easily give up their ancestral customs as their Japanese and Chinese counterparts did, so believed the missionaries.

It is difficult to estimate the number of conversions that took place during the sixteenth century, not only because of lack of statistics but also because of exaggerations in reporting numbers. Nevertheless, as mentioned earlier, Goa has more numerical records regarding conversions than any other territory christianized by the Portuguese. Goa being the capital of the *Estado da India* needed a more efficient machinery for governance, and conversions could satisfy that need. These facts enable us to state with certainty about the fast growth rate in conversions, even going by conservative estimates, during the sixteenth century.

In the context of forced conversions and huge number of converts, the pertinent question to be asked would be whether the converts improved their social and economic conditions, on account of their post-conversion status and Portuguese citizenship, which claimed to give them new rights and privileges. Regarding motives leading to conversions it is not possible for a historian to penetrate the intentions of the converts. But a historian can study the context and the social structures that motivated or prevented conversions, and the opinions in this regard. Conversion rarely occured in a social or existential vacuum. *Conversions and Citizenry* made attempts to present the different motives at play in the reception of Christianity.

Regarding the authenticity of conversions, even the missionaries doubted and suspected the real intention that brought so many Hindus to the doors of the church. Hence, the missionaries needed to test the requests for conversion or Portuguese citizenship. One has only to go through the decrees of the five Provincial Councils that took place in Goa during the sixteenth century and a little after, to appreciate the persistence of old 'superstitions' and 'idolatry' among the converts. Those Ecclesiastical Councils never stopped condemning relapses which were caused by superstitions and idolatry.

The clerics tried to impress upon the catechumens that any 'suspect behaviour' in their lives would not be tolerated. This serious warning was directed against the very 'superstitious' and 'idolatrous' elements — synonymous with less allegiance to the empire and Christendom — which the missionaries noticed in the lives of the local converts. These elements, however, were so deeply rooted in the Goan culture that they were almost incapable of being abandoned. Nevertheless, the cleansing of such unchristian elements from Goa, or the total conversion of the converts, was an urgent demand. Only then could the converts become 'total citizens' for, and collaborators of, the empire. But ironically, many who did not convert or even those who consistently refused to convert and opposed Christendom overtly, continued to receive from the Portuguese more honours, favours and jobs than the converts themselves or the 'total citizens' did. This was done with the view of gaining their collaboration too.

Although I can claim that we have come a long way to understand a little more the affair of conversion in Goa during the sixteenth century, a perennial debate that never loses its fascination, this work is not yet the last word on that affair; rather no work will ever be.

# APPENDICES

Nine documents or original letters or reports with their summary translation follow. They may offer us some insights into the terminology and mentality of the time. They speak about the importance of spreading the Christian faith, the activity of conversion, the royal duty, the methods of conversion, Hindu reactions to conversion, some characteristics of Hinduism, etc.

## *APPENDIX – 1*

A letter from the first bishop of Goa, D. João de Albuquerque, written in 1550.

"... a ydolatria hé tamanha ofenssa de Deos, que não devo eu consentir que a aja nas terras dessas partes... defendais que não haja na dita ilha de Goa alguns dos ditos pagodes publicos nem secretos, e que nenhum oficial possa facer nem faça de pedra, nen de apo, nen de cobre nem de outro algum metal. E assy mesmo que em toda a ilha se não fação algumas festas gentilicas publicas, nem os moradores della recolhão em suas cazas pregadores bramenes da terra; ordenareis que se busquem as cazas de todos os bramenes e gentios, em quem se tiver presunção por sospeita que estão idolos.... onde quer que acharem pagodes feitos ou começados a fazer ou a reparar, os destruão e derribem, para o qual lhe dou poder e autoridade."

(Josef Wicki, (ed.), *O Livro do "Pai dos Cristãos"*, Lisboa, Centro de Estudos Historicos Ultramarinos, 1970, p. 162; J. H. da Cunha Rivara, (ed.), *Archivo Portugues-Oriental*, Fasc. 5, Part I, New Delhi, Asian Educational Services, 1992, doc. 111.

**Summary translation of document**

.... idolatry is such an offence to God that it should not be permitted in my land. Take care that no idols exist in the island of Goa and that no craftsman make them either of stone,or wood, or copper, or any other metal. Moreover, no Gentile festival should be permitted here, and its inhabitants should not shelter any Brahman preacher. The Brahmans and other Hindus suspected of possessing idols should have their houses searched ... and wherever they are found they should be destroyed. I empower you with this authority.

***APPENDIX – 2***

Law forbidding idols, temples and any other Gentile practice in the island of Goa and other parts of India under the Portuguese control.

Dom Sebastião per graça de Deos Rei de Portugal e dos Algarves daquem e dalem mar em Africa, senhor de Guiné, e da conquista, navegação, comercio de Ethiopia, Arabia, Persia, e da India. Faço saber aos que esta minha lei virem que eu são enformado que na Ilha de Goa nas partes da India, e nas outras Ilhas a ella annexas se fazem muitas offensas e deserviços a noso senhor pelos infieis e gentios dellas, adorando e festejando publicamente os hidolos e pagodes, e usando de seus ritos diabolicos, sendo de meus senhorios, em em presença de christãos; e querendo a isso prover, ei por bem e mando que daqui em diante na dita ilha de Goa, e nas outras suas annexas, não aja mais pagodes nem idolos em casa alguma nem fora dela, e se queimem e desfação todos os que ahi ouver, e que nenhum official nem outra alguma pessoa os faça, nem possa fazer, de páo, nem de pedra, nem de nenhum metal, nem doutra alguma cousa e que se não fação, nem consintão fazer nenhumas festas gentilicas publicas nas casas nem fora dellas, nem aja bramenes, prégadores de sua gentilidade, nemse festeje a festa da arequeira que costumavão fazer, nem lavatorios de gentios, nem se consintão queimar, e tendose sospeita que em alguma casa ou casas dos ditos gentios ha os ditos pagodes e idolos, as pessoas a cuja noticia vier o denunciarão logo ao ouvidor geral das ditas partes, o qual com parecer do Arcebispo da dita cidade de Goa, ou de seu Provisor, sendo o Arcebispo ausente, procederão nos taes casos como for justiça, e por seu mandado e autoridade farão os meirinhos as diligencias nas taes casas para saber dos ditos idolos e pagoges, e não em outra maneira, salvo achando as partes em fragante delicto, e em escandalo publico contra forma desta Lei, porque neste caso poderão prender logo os culpados, e os levarão perante o dito Arcebispo, ou perante o dito ouvidor geral, ou Provisor; e qualquer pessoa que for contra o conteudo nesta Lei, e lhe for provado, perderá toda sua fazenda, ametade para quem o acusar, e a outra metade se aplicará para as obras da Igreja em cujo limite e juridição se cometer o delicto, e alem disso os delinquentes e culpados ficarão captivos pera as galés sem remissão; e mando ao meu capitão mór e governador das ditas partes, e a todas as justiças, e oficiaes, e pessoas a que o conhecimento pertencer que em todo cumprão e guardem, e façam inteiramente comprir esta Lei, e ao Chanceler das ditas partes que a publique na chancelaria, e faça publicar na dita ilha de Goa e suas anexas, e transladar na dita chanceleria, e na camara da dita cidade de Goa. Lisboa, 25 Março 1559.

A Rainha

(J. H. da Cunha Rivara, *Archivo Portuguez Oriental*, Fasc. 5, Part I, New Delhi, Asian Educational Services, 1992, doc. 291, pp.388-90. Also in Josef Wicki, *Documenta Indica* IV, Rome Institutum Historicum S. I., p. 328, note No. 30 and in António da Silva Rego, *Documentação para a História do Padroado Português do Oriente* VII, Agência Geral das Colónias, pp. 284-85.)

**Summary translation of document**

(Letter from the queen-regent, D. Catarina, on behalf of the king, D. Sebastião.)

D. Sebastião, by the grace of God, king of Portugal and Algarves, of the seas in Africa, master of Guiné, of conquered lands, of navigation and of commerce in Ethiopia, Arabia, Persia and

India. I am informed that in the island of Goa and its adjacent islands, as well as in other territories that belong to us, many offences are committed against God. The Hindus and Muslims worship their gods and celebrate their festivals with diabolic rituals in the presence of Christians. Wishing to take precautions, I order that henceforth in the island of Goa and its adjacent lands, there should not be any temples or idols in any house or outside. The existing ones should be burnt and destroyed. No craftsman or any other person should ever make them either of wood, or stone, or any other metal or material. No public Hindu festival should be allowed in any house or outside. No Brahman nor Hindu preacher should be allowed in my territories. The feast of *arrequeira* should not be permitted nor their washing ceremonies. The person who has any knowledge about Hindus possessing idols should report it to the authorities, and after ascertaining the truth they can be imprisoned. Anyone who transgresses this law and is found guilty will lose his property, half of it being for the accuser, and the other half for the church. The guilty will be made captives for the galleys. I order my captain-major and governor in those parts and all the officials to uphold and execute faithfully this law. This should be noted down in the Chancery and made known in the island of Goa. Lisbon, 25 March 1559.

The Queen

## *APPENDIX – 3*

Annual letter from Luys Flores. Goa, 1 January 1561.

El orden que se tiene en esta isla de Goa en la ensenãnça desta nueva Christandad es la que ya por las cartas passadas escrevimos, sino en quanto ser las necessidades mas urgentes en partes donde no avia doctrina fue necessario acrecentar mas gente, el Domingo de madrugada despues de aver oydo Missa se reparten los padres y hermanos dos en dos por la isla a suas aldeas ordinarias y assi van a Nossa Senora de Guadalupe y a otro lugar que se llama Gazayn a Santiago a S. Joan, a la Madre de Dios, al poso seco, a Santa Luzia donde primero por la manãna declaran el evangello del Domingo a los Christianos y les platican un poco de los articulos de la Feé por miños interpretes hilos de los mesmos christianos que aqui se crian en el collegio despues los ensenãn un poco la doctrina la qual tambien despues se les recita por su proprio ydioma por unas cartillas que aqui se imprimieron en casa en la tarde tornã los mesmos hermanos por las aldeas tanendo sus campanillas donde acude gran numero de niños y vanse con ellos cantando la doctrina hasta llegar a los iglesias y lugares honde los han de enseñar y para melor acudir tine los hermanos entre ellos sus alguaziles que los andon allegando y despues de seles enseñar la doctrina por espacio de una hora y media todos se les toma quenta de lo que saben y van preguntando se por las aldeas ay algunos gentiles que se quieran hacer christianos y para se cathequizar y comummente por lo miã de Nosso Señor se hallan algunos que quieran ser hace esta doctrina que los padres y hermanos enseñan notable provecho en esta nueva Christandad y anda las crianças y niños de muy poca edad continuamente por las aldeas de noche y de dia cantandola por las calles y ensenãndo la a los padres y madres; pocos tempos ha que yendo un hombre honrrado de priesa por estos rios a riba aun negocio que le importava vio unos ninõs de pocos meses hechos christianos que de una parte y de otra andavan apacentando ganado de sus padres los quales asentados unos a la custa de os otros estavan en dos choros entonando la doctrina unos que decian dos palabras de una parte y otros por el mesmo tono les respondia de la otra quedo el hobre tan captivo desta musica que con lagrimas.... Son estes christianos bien inclinados y devotos por la mayor parte inclindos a cosas de Nosso Señor segun su capacidad e para gente tan nueva en la fe son sus obras confusion para muchos portugueses a la doctrina ordinarioa de laos dias de la semana van solamente en Coran 150 niños y niños los domingos es cosa pra mucho loaar a dios ver las turbas de los niños en una aldea 200, en otra 200 en otra 300 y the ay para ariba y las madres dellos con las criaturas en los pechos y otros por las manos que vienen tambien con ellos a parender la doctrina donde acuden las casadas viudas y de toda suerte y viela de 80 y de 90 años que a poco tempo que se baptizaron... y lo que mucho sienten es aver pocos sacerdotes que sepan la lengua canerin por les confessar...

(Archivum Romanum Societatis Iesu, *Goana Historia*, 31 - I, (1539-1572), Rome, fl. 126-26v.)

**Summary translation of document**

The Christian doctrine is taught to the converts in the following manner: the priests and Brothers go in pairs to the villages soon after they finish their dawn Sunday mass. They explain the Sunday gospel to the converts, followed by an instruction on the articles of the faith. The boys brought up in the College of St Paul serve as interpreters to the missionaries. Then a little doctrine is taught in the local language with the help of a booklet printed in the same college. In the afternoon the priests and Brothers go through the villages ringing bells, and many children gather together. Singing the Christian doctrine they proceed to the church where they are instructed for one-and-a-half hours. Then the Brothers ask them whether there is any Hindu willing to receive baptism. If there is, the Christian doctrine is taught to him. The children go about singing the Christian doctrine and they teach it to their parents. The local Christians are very devout, each one according to his/her own capacity. The converts, in spite of being very young in the faith, put to shame the Portuguese. The number of women and children who attend the teachings is something to praise God for, but unfortunately there are very few priests who know the local language to hear their confessions.

## *APPENDIX – 4*

A report about the caste system, ceremonies and superstitions in India. (Diversas castas de Indios. Item cerimonias e superstições).

Ai entre los Canarines otra casta que se llaman chararos que son como hombres de guierra que (cor)responden a los Naires entre los Malabares, solo tienen esta differençia que los Naires no puden andar sin armas y los espingarderos con sus espingardas, los lançeros con sus lanças y los de espada con su espada y los flecheros con sus arcos e flechas lo qual an de traer continuo en todas las partes que estuvieren a lo que no son obligados ni es costumbre entre los chararos; y esto parece que nasce porque como esta naçion Canarin nunca tuvo rey proprio y fue siempre suhieta alas otras gentes por esso no usan tanto delas armas puesto que las tuvieron para martyrizar estos santos ao Pe. Rudolfo, porque la poblacion y gente principal que cometio este sacrificio fue la que se llama dela casta de los chararos, la qual habita en aquellos limites como fronteros dela tierra firme.

Ai otras muchas castas diversas entre las qualles nopuede aver mestura ni aun aprender el officio uno de otro de modo que los xastres no pueden ser çapateros ni pedreros, ni pescadores etc ni los otros puedn ser xastres y lo mismo se entiende de los mas officios; ni lo que es de una casta por mas rico y poderoso que sea no puede tener mas grado ni honra, y assi cada uno ha de hazeer lo que sus padres hizieron.

Hai otra gente de diversas castas y naciones que son como peregrinos cuia vida es peregrinar por esse mundo, observan gran pobresa y tienen grandes praivilegios porque pueden comunicar con todas las castas ỳ entrar en todos los pagodes y son mui venerdos y estimados por santos, son grandes echizeros y tienen infinidad de supersticiones con que enganan a todas las otras gentes, estos son los que se llaman Jogues.

Ai en toda esta costa grandes e sumtuosos pagodes y tanto que muitos exceden a los maiores y suntuosos templos de toda Europa, y en ellos se gasta infinidad de dinereos en limosnas parte delas gruessas rentas que tienen, parte delas grandes y continuas linosnas que los pelegrinos les hazen; toda esta costa es poblada de gentiles mui dados a peregrinaçiones a sus pagodes. Tienen cada año muchas fiestas; en algunas hazen processiones llevando sus idolos sobre grandes carros triumphantes mui grandes de dos y tres sobrados labrados de maçanaria mui linda y puestos sobre seis y ocho ruedas como de carros salvo que son mui maiores y todas chapadas de laminas de hierro, costumbran llevar estos carros gran numero de hombres, y algunos con fervor de la devocion se enchan en las estradas por donde han de passar las ruedas las quales los hazen en pedaços y son tenidos por martires. E nel carro va el idolo en lo mas alto y otros idolos no tan principales van por los sobrados mas baxos. Delante van muchas danças y bailos y sus sacerdotes todos untados de oleo, y con mucho genero de invenciones. De ordinario de la renta del pagode se da de comer a todo peregrino en que se gasta mucho. Ai tambien muchos hombres que hazen versos e canciones en su lengoa y las van cantando y comummente de las fabulas que tienen fingido de sus antepassados.

Tienen comummente delante la puerta de sus pagodes una mui alta coluna de metal toda dorada que puede ser como la mas alta que ay en Roma, y en la punta della se penduran algunos hombres en unos canchos que estan enel sumo della por los lombos y muchos mueren; otros se cuertan con cuchillos, por la carne tirando mucha de su cuerpo. Los idolos principales estan siempre puestos en una capilla mui escura de modo que no tienen otra luz que la que dan muchas alampadas que de continuo arden. Contodo pareçe una cueva de inferno; a la puerta que es mui pequeña, siempre han de estar bailando hombres y mugeres quasi desnudos, untados de oleo, y quasi todo se unta deste oleo; tienen otras muchas cerimonias y fiestas.

(Archivum Romanum Societatis Iesu, *Indiarum Orientalum Miscellanum*, 38 - II, (1544-1583), Rome, fl. 245.)

## *APPENDIX – 5*

The deep attachment that the converts have to their ancestral religion, superstitions and traditions, which was a serious danger to the Christian faith.

"Os novamente convertidos são eles tão naturalmente inclinados aos pagodes que, ainda daqueles que se convertem e baptizam, com pouca força e ocasião tornam à adoração deles; e muitos assim recebem a Fé, que guardam no coração um escaninho para as suas superstições. Para o que os excita, nesta ilha de Bardez, a continua comunicação que seus moradores têm com a terra firme, aonde por todo o tempo de verão vão em cáfilas buscar mantimento que compram a troco de sal que de cá levam, onde acham seus parents que não deixam de lhes trazer à memória a lei de seus antepassados e a obrigação que tinham de a guardar e se conservar na nobreza de sua casta que eles fundaram sobre o alicerce da idolatria e superstição, encadeando uma coisa com outra, e os levam aos seus pagodes a lhes mostrarem suas festas; o que tudo causa nos que não são tão firmes na Fé, em uma terrível tentação de a deixarem.

E cá mesmo na ilha têm muitos parentes e amigos gentios que vivem entre eles, os quais não cessam de martelar neles lembrando-lhes os seus deuses e cantando-lhes muitas cantigas em que contam as suas histórias a que, como dissemos, são por extremo afeiçoados."

(Paulo da Trindade, *Conquista Espiritual do Oriente*, Part I, Lisboa, Centro de Estudos Historicos Ultramarinos, 1962, p. 349. He wrote this in 1633.)

**Summary translation of document**

The converts are so naturally inclined to their idols that a little encouragement is sufficient to make them turn back to their former idols. Thus many receive the faith, but keep their hearts attached to their superstitions. The Christian people in Bardez are compelled to buy food in the Muslim land throughout the summer, and constant dealings with the latter is unavoidable. Besides, their relatives living here continually remind them of their ancestral law and obligation to keep the purity of their caste. Every sort of idolatry and superstition or joining in the Hindu festivals here, are temptations for many to abandon their faith.

Even in the island of Goa the converts have many Hindu relatives and friends who never cease reminding them of their former gods. The converts hear many Hindu songs and stories, and they are very fond of them.

## *APPENDIX – 6*

Letter from Fr. Duarte Leitão. Goa, 17 November 1571.

No colegio dos meninos orfãos de que tem cuidado dous Irmãos da cõpanhia avera perto de cen meninos entre portugeses e da terra o modo que se ten en seu ensino e o mesmo que se tem scrito os años pasados alguns deles studão e cõ preposito de servir a Deus e outros aprendem a ler e escrever e aos outros se procuran outros modos de vida como aprenderem alguns officios e daremos a homens que os posan aproveitar o que pricipalmente se pretende e que os que desta casa saen vão ben instruidos assim na doutrina Christa como nas virtudes e bons costumes e que onde quer que forem dem mostras de bons Christaos.

(Archivum Romanum Societatis Iesu, *Goana Historia*, 31 - I, (1539-1572), Rome, ff. 246v-247)

**Translation of document**

At this college (St Paul) there are about a hundred Portuguese and local boys. Some of them study with the aim of serving God, and others learn how to read and write. After they complete their studies jobs are given to them or they are kept with persons who can employ them. Our purpose is to see that the boys on leaving this house practise good customs and virtues, so that wherever they go they might show themselves as good Christians.

## *APPENDIX – 7*

Law of viceroy Dom Francisco da Gama on behalf of the king Dom Filipe of Portugal against Bailadores e Bailadeiras (dancing-men/women). Goa 27.10. 1598.

"Dom Phelippe per graça de Deos Rey de Portugal e dos Algarves daquem e dalem mar em Africa, Senhor de Guiné, e da conquista, navegação, e comercio d'Ethiopia, Arabia, Persia, e da India, e dos Reinos de Maluco etc. Aos que esta minha carta de ley virem faço saber que eu sou informado que na ilha da cidade de Goa e adjacentes a ella vão muitos bailadores das terras firmes gentios e mouros a fazer seu officio, e tornão para ellas com o que ganhão, que sempre he muito em seu respeito, e nos ditos bailos e ensaios delles metem muitas cousas torpes, e cantigos ruins, e outras cousas que só por arte diabolica as podem fazer, nas cantigas metem seus pagodes e idolatrias, o que tudo he contra o bem commum da republica christã, e contra a boa criação, que tanto trabalhão e desejão os cultivadores do evangelho de arrancar e tirar dos novamente convertidos a nossa santa fé catoliqua, por aver já nas partes da India muitos christãos, e homens e mulheres que com limpeza, e bom exemplo fazem o mesmo officio, e querendo evitar este abuso tão perjudicial ao serviço de Deos e meu, e bem da christandade, ey por bem, e me praz, e por esta mando e defendo que da pubricação desta minha ley em diante, que o bailador, homen ou molher, que vier da terra firme á cidade de Goa, ou ás ilhas adjacentes a ella, pague vinte pardáos pela primeira vez, e pela segunda corenta, ametade pera os cativos, e outra pera o acusador, e pela terceira serem desgredados dos homens dous annos pera as galés dos estado, e as molheres serão cativas pera a minha fazenda, e vendidas em pubriquo leilão a quem por ellas mais der; e isto se entenderá nos bailadores mouros ou gentios que vierem da terra firme, e não nos meus vassallos moradores na ilha da dita cidade de Goa, e nas suas adjacentes, posto que sejam gentios,..."

(J. H. da Cunha Rivara, (ed.), *Archivo Portuguez-Oriental*, Fasc. 6, Asian Educational Services, New Delhi, 1992, doc. 896, pp. 725-26.)

**Summary translation of document**

D. Philip, by the grace of God king of Portugal and Algarves, of the seas in Africa, master of Guiné, of the conquered lands, of navigation and of commerce in Ethiopia, Arabia, Persia, India, and in the kingdoms of the Moluccas, etc. To whomsoever it may concern. I am informed that in the city of Goa and adjacent islands there are many dancing men and women from the firm land. They perform many obscene dances, sing dirty songs and do all sorts of things that only reflect a diabolic state. All this is against the welfare of the Christian state and good customs which the missionaries seek to cultivate in those who have been converted to the Christian faith. To avoid these abuses, so harmful to the service of God and mine and for the good of Christendom, I order any dancing man or woman who comes to the city of Goa and adjacent islands to pay twenty pardaus as fine. The second time they come forty pardaus, and the third time the men will be sent to the galleys for two years, and the women will be imprisoned and sold in an auction. This law is applicable to Hindu and Muslim dancing persons who come from outside or firm land, but not to my vassals or Hindus from Goa and its adjacent islands.

## *APPENDIX – 8*

Letter written by the king of Portugal, D. Philip I. He forbade the foundation of a convent for nuns in Goa in 1593.

"E no que toca ao que dizeis que ha muitas molheres nesse estado que de sua ymclinada incllinação sam onestas é que folgarião dese recolher em Rellegião é que podiam seçar muitos e grandes inconvenientes se em Goa se fizesse um mosteiro de freiras por ser materia que se tem tratado muitas vezes. E em que se oferecem rezoes pera se não dever, ordenar, vos mandey escrever nas vias do ano passado como não havia por serviço de Deus nem meu fazerse este mosteiro pello que de novo não há nesta materia que vos escrever".

(Arquivo Historico Ultramarino, *Registo de cartas de 1589-1597*, Lisboa, Cod. 281, fl. 301v.)

**Translation of document**

Regarding the foundation of a convent in Goa for many honest women living here, and the concern that many and serious problems could be avoided if there was one convent, has been dealt with several times before. The reasons why a convent for women should not be founded have been given in writing last year, namely, that it is not a service to God and myself to found a convent. Hence, there is nothing new to write about on this matter.

## *APPENDIX – 9*

A description of how the temples were made and of their architectural beauty.

"A honrra de sus dioses hazem en muchas partes templos de piedra muy sumptuossos y ricos, entre los quales hazen algunos muy grandes, que llevan mucho artificio, todos de piedra de sillarería labrada y juntada de tal manera, que hazen con ellas sus arcos y sus bóvedas, y finalmente sus templos todos, sin nenguna manera de cal, tan limpios y tan fuertes, que en nenguna manera se puede ymaginar la hechura de su obra; porque están las piedras tan justas y encaxadas unas con otras, que parecen pegadas con cal; mas son sueltas y desatadas, sin nenguna manera de betumen, que cierto es cosa para ver, y gusté yo mucho de los ver muchas vezes. Mas aunque sean sus templos grandes y hermosos por de fuera, están todos hechos por dentro de tal manera, que muestran bien el amo cuyos son, porque todos son escuros, melancólicos y feos, y sus ydolos y figuras mal hechas y monstruosas, llenas de mal olor por el azeite con que los untan. Y tienen los templos al derredor de sí diversas casas de malas mugeres, que son bayladoras consagradas a sus ydolos, con las quales solennizan sus nefandas y sacrílegas fiestas bailando y cantanto y dándose a toda a deshonestidad con los romeros y peregrinos, que visitan los dichos ídolos."

(Alessandro Valignano, *Historia del Principio y Progresso de la Compañía de Jesus en las Indias Orientales (1542-64),* Roma, Institutum Historicum, S. I., 1944, p. 34-35.)

**Translation of document**

The Hindus make many majestic and richly decorated temples in honour of their gods, among which there are some huge ones. These temples are made of stone. Some of them are fine pieces of architecture and contain remarkable carvings. The stones are put together — no lime is used — in such a way that it is difficult to notice the joints. These temples have many beautiful arches and domes. Their solidity is noteworthy. Although these temples appear to be marvelous and imposing, they are dark, uninspiring and ugly inside. Their idols and statues lack finesse. They are covered with oil, which the devotees pour constantly on them. Around these temples there are brothels where the dancing women (consecrated to the idols) live. These women solemnize the religious festivals by dancing, singing and giving themselves up to all kinds of sins with the pilgrims who visit these temples.

# BIBLIOGRAPHY

## PRIMARY SOURCES

**Directorate of Archives, Archaeology and Museum, Government of Goa. Goa.**

*Monções do Reino* (*MR*)
*MR*, 1, Vol. I, (1585-1599)
*MR*, 2A, Vol. I, (1583-1595)
*MR*, 2B, (1595-1601)
*MR*, 3A, (1585-1589)
*MR*, 3B, (1589-1593)
*MR*, 4, (1595-1598)
*MR*, 5, (1595-1690)
*MR*, 6B, (1605)
*MR*, 8, (1601-1602)
*MR*, 9, 10, 11, (1604-1609)
*MR*, 54, (1689-1690)
*MR*, 58, (1693-1694)
*MR*, 63, (1692-1699)

*Leis a Favour da Cristandade*, 7693, Vol, 1, Panaji.

**Arquivos Nacionais / Torre do Tombo. Lisbon.**

*Corpo Cronologico*, (CC) I, Maços, 16, 75.
*CC*, II, Maço 104, doc. 3.
*Conselho Geral do Santo Officio*, Maço 32.

**Arquivo Historico Ultramarino. Lisbon.**

*Registo de cartas, provisões etc. para a India para os viso reis e mais autoridades. Livro onde se registam vias que Sua Magestade envia a India pelas naos que este ano de 1589 vão para as ditas partes (1588-1597)*, Cod. 281, Lisbon.

*Registo de cartas, provisões, etc., para a India para os viso reis e mais authoridades. Livros das cartas da India de sua Magestade dos anos 1600 até 1604*, Cod. 282, Lisbon.

*Caixas da India*, No, 1. Lisbon.

**Biblioteca Nacional de Lisboa. Lisbon.**

*Reservados*, Cods. 59, 175, 176, 177, 580, 866.

**Archivum Romanum Societatis Iesu. Rome.**

Provincia Goana et Malabarica

*Extracto das cousas*, 1a, (1552—1613).
*Summarium eorum quae pertinent ad Indiam Orientalem*, 6, (1580-1588).
*Eppistolae Goana*, 8 - I-III, (1549-1572).
*Eppistolae Goana*, 9 - I, (1569-1742).
*Eppistolae Goana et Malabarica*, 10 - I, (1545-1588)
*Eppistolae Goana et Malabarica*, 14, (1590-1599).
*Eppistolae Goana et Malabarica*, 15, (1600-1606).
*Eppistolae Goana et Malabarica*, 16, (1606-1609).
*Fundationes Goanae*, 22 - I, (1541-1702).
*Goana Historia*, 31 - I-II, (1539-1580).
*Goana Historia*, 33 - I-II, (1600-1624).
*Goana Historia*, 34 - I-II, (1626-1659).
*Goana Historia*, 35, (1600-1699).
*Indiarum Orientalum Miscellanum*, 38 - I-II, (1544-1583).
*Questiorum Salsetana et aliae questiorum Goanae*, 67, (1587-1647).

Academia Real das Sciencias de Lisboa, *Documentos Remetidos da India ou Livros das Monções*, Tomo I, Lisboa, Typographia da Academia

Real das Sciencias, 1880.

Albuquerque, Afonso Brás de, *Comentarios de Afonso de Albuquerque*, Tomos I-II, Lisboa, Imprensa Nacional - Casa da Moeda, 1973.

Alonso, C., "Nueva documentación inédita sobre las misiones agustinianas en la India y en Persia (1571-1609)", *Analecta Augustiniana*, Vol. XXXIII, Rome, 1970.

———, "Documentación inédita para una biografía de Fr. Alejo de Meneses, O.S.A., Arzobispo de Goa (1595-1612)", *Analecta Augustiniana*, Vol. XXVII, Rome, 1964.

Barros, João de, *Decada da Asia* I, Hernani Cidade and Manuel Múria, (eds.), Divisão de Publicação e Biblioteca Agência Geral das Colonias, Lisboa 1945.

———, *Decada da Ásia* II, part I, Lisboa, Regia Officina Typografica, 1777.

———, *Decada da Asia* I , Coimbra, Imprensa Nacional - Casa da Moeda, Imprensa da Universidade, 1932.

Bulhão Pato, Raymundo Antonio de, (ed.), *Cartas de Affonso de Albuquerque*, I & III, Lisboa, Tip. da Academia Real das Sciencias de Lisboa, 1884, 1903.

Castanheda, Fernão Lopes, *História do Descobrimento e Conquista da India Pelos Portugueses*, Books I - IX, Porto, Lello & Irmãos, 1979.

Centro de Estudos Históricos Ultramarinos, *As Gavetas da Torre do Tombo*, 12 Vols., Lisboa, 1960-1977. ( II, (Gav. III - XII); III, (Gav. XIII - XIV), Lisboa, 1963; IV, 1964; V, (Gav. XV, Maços 16-24), 1965; IX, (Gav. XX, Maços 8-15).

———, *Documentação Ultramarina Portuguesa* I, Museu Britanico - Add. 28461, Eg. 1646, Lisboa, 1960.

Correia, Gaspar, *Lendas da India*, Vol. II, Part I, Coimbra, Imprensa da Universidade, 1923.

———, *Lendas da India*, Vol. IV, Lisboa, Academia da Ciencias de Lisboa, 1969.

Couto, Diogo do, *Decada da Asia*, VIII, Lisboa, 1786.

Cunha Rivara, Joaquim Heliodoro da, *Archivo Portuguez-Oriental*, Vols. 1 - 6, New Delhi, Asian Educational Services, 1992.

Figueroa, Martim Fernandez de, *A Spaniard in the Portuguese Indies* (1512), James B. McKenna, (trans., ed.), Harvard University Press, Cambridge, 1967.

Gonçalves, Sebastião, *Primeira Parte da História dos Religiosos da Companhia de Jesus e do que fizeram com a Divina Graça na Conversão dos Infiéis na nossa Sancta Fé Catholica nos Reynos e Provincias da India Oriental*, Vol. I, ed. Josef Wicki, Coimbra Atlantida, 1957.

Guerreiro, Fernão, *Relação Annual das Cousas que fizeram os Padres da Companhia de Jesus nas partes da India Oriental e em algumas outras qua conquista deste reyno nos annos de 607. & 608 e do processo da conversão & Christandade daquellas partes, com mais hua addiçam a relação de Ethiopia*, Lisboa, Pedro Crasbeeck, 1611.

———, *Relação Anual das coisas que fizeram os Padres da Companhia de Jesus nas suas Missões*, Vol I, (1600-1603), Vol. II, (1604-1606), Vol. III, (1607-1609), Coimbra, Imprensa da Universidade, 1930, 1931, 1942.

Guzman, Luis de, *Historia de las Misiones de la Compania de Jesus en la India Oriental, en la China y Japon — 1540 - 1600*, Bilbao, Administracion de «El Mensajero del Corazon de Jesus», 1891.

Lobo, A. de S. S. Costa, (ed.), *Memórias de Um Soldado da Índia*, (Compiladas de um manuscrito português do Museu Britânico), Lisboa, Imprensa Nacional - Casa da Moeda, 1987.

Manso, Paiva, (ed.), *Bullarium Patronatus Portugalliae Regum in Ecclesiis Africae, Asiae atque Oceaniae*, Lisboa, Typ. Nationali, 1872.

Sá, Artur Basílio de, *Documentação para a História das Missões do Padroado Português do Oriente*, Lisboa, Agencia Geral do Ultramar, 1955.

Schurhammer, Georg and Josef Wicki, (eds.), *Epistolae S. Francisci Xaverii*, Vol. I (1535-1548), Vol. II (1549 - 1552), Rome, Monumenta Historica Societatis Iesu, 1945.

Silva Rego, António da, *Documentação para a História das Missões do Padroado Português do Oriente*, Vols. I-XII, Lisboa, Divisão de Publicações e Biblioteca, Agência Geral das Colónias, 1947-1958.

Sousa, Francisco de, *Oriente Conquistado a Jesus Cristo pelos Padres da Companhia de Jesus da Provincia de Goa*, Porto, Lello & Irmão-Editores, 1978.

Trindade, Paulo da, *Conquista Espiritual do Oriente*, Part I & III, Lisboa, Centro de Estudos Historicos Ultramarinos, 1962, 1967.

Valignano, Alessandro, *Historia del principio y progresso de la Compañía de Jesús em las Indias Orientales (1542-64)*, Vol. II, Josef Wicki, (ed.), Roma, Institutum Historicum S. I., 1944.

Wicki, Josef, (ed.), *Documenta Indica*, Vols. I-XVIII, Roma, Monumenta Historica Societatis Iesu, 1948- 88.

———, (ed.), *O Livro do "Pai dos Cristãos"*, Lisboa, Centro de Estudos Historicos Ultramarinos, 1969.

Zinadim, *Historia dos Portugueses no Malabar*, (Arab Manuscript of the XVI century), David Lopes, (ed.), Lisboa, Imprensa Nacional, 1898.

## SECONDARY SOURCES

Albuquerque, Viriato A. C., "Casa de Catechumenos em Goa" *O Oriente Portuguez*, Vol. I, Nova Goa, Imprensa Nacional, 1904, pp. 362-369.

Albuquerque, Luís (ed.), *Portugal no Mundo*, séculos XV-XVIII, Vol. II, Lisboa, Publicações Alfa, 1989.

Albuquerque, Martim de, *Estudos de Cultura Portuguesa*, Vol. I, Lisboa, Imprensa Nacional - Casa da Moeda, 1983.

Alden, Dauril, *The Making of an Elite Enterprise: The Jesuits in the Portuguese Assistancy, 16th to 18th Centuries*, The Associates of the James Ford Bell Library, University of Minnesota, 1992.

Almeida Araújo, Maria Julieta Aires de, and Ernesto Jorge Oliveira dos Santos, "Os Portugueses e o Reino do Congo. Primeiros contactos", *Missionação Portuguesa e Encontro de Culturas*, Vol. I, Braga, Barbosa & Xavier, Ltd., Artes Gráficas, 1993.

Alvares, Claude and Norma Alvares, "The Christian and the Wild", T. R. de Souza, (ed.), *Discoveries, Missionary Expansion and Asian Cultures*, New Delhi, Concept Publishing Company, 1994, pp. 19-31.

Ambedkar, B. R., *Christianizing the Untouchables*, Madras, Dalit Liberation Education Trust, 1994.

Ambrósio, António, "Alguns problemas de evangelização em África no século XVI. D. frei Gaspar Cão, OSA, Bispo de São Tomé (1554-1574)", *Missionação Portuguesa e Encontro de Culturas*, Vol. I, Braga, Barbosa & Xavier, Ltd., Artes Gráficas, 1993.

Américo Cortez Pinto, *"Talant de bien Faire" - A Divisa Infante e a Criação do Estado da India*, Lisboa, Agencia Geral do Ultramar, 1955.

Araújo, Maria Benedita, "O 'Pay dos Christãos'. Contribuição para o estudo da Cristianização da Índia", *Missionação Portuguesa e Encontro de Culturas*, Vol. II, Braga, Barbosa & Xavier, Ltd., Artes Gráficas, 1993.

Ayalla, Furtado, "A Misericordia de Goa", Revista da Commisão Archeologica da India Portugueza, *O Oriente Portuguez*, Nova Goa, Imprensa Nacional, 1904, pp, 192-201.

Azevedo, António d'Almeida, *As Communidades de Goa: História das Instituições Antigas*, Lisboa, Viuva Bertrand & C.ª Successores Carvalho & C.ª, 1890.

Baião, António, *A Inquisição de Goa*, Vols. I-II, Lisboa, Academia das Ciencias, 1945.

Balsemão, Eduardo Augusto de Sá Nogueira Pinto de, *Os Portuguezes no Oriente: Feitos Gloriosos Praticados pelos Portugueses no Oriente*, (1510-1600), Part I, Nova Goa, Imprensa Nacional, 1881.

Barbuda, Claudio Lagrange Monteiro, *Instrucções com que El-Rei D. José I mandou passar ao Estado da India o Governador, e Capitão General, e o Arcebispo Primaz do Oriente no anno de 1774*, 2nd ed., Nova Goa, Imprensa Nacional, 1903.

Barreto, Luís Filipe, *Descobrimentos e Renascimento*, Lisboa, Imprensa Nacional-Casa da Moeda, 1983.

Beozzo, José Oscar, "O Diálogo da Conversão do Gentio. A evangelização entre a persuasão e a força", *Missionação Portuguesa e Encontro de Culturas*, Vol. II, Braga, Barbosa & Xavier, Ltd., Artes Gráficas, 1993.

Block, Marc, *Introdução à História*, Portugal, Publicações Europa - América, 1974.

*Boletim Eclesiastico da Arquidiocese de Goa*, Série II, Ano I, N° 1, Bastorá, Tipografia Rangel, Julho 1942.

Bouchon, Geneviève, "Portuguese Documents on Sixteenth Century India", *Indo-Portuguese History: Sources and Problems*, Bombay, Oxford University Press, 1981, pp. 85-98.

Boxer, C. R., *Portuguese Society in the Tropics: The Councils of Goa, Macao, Bahia and Luanda*, USA, North Central Publishing Co., 1965.

———, "The Problem of the Native Clergy in the Portuguese and Spanish Empires from the Sixteenth to the Eighteenth Centuries", offprint of *The Mission of the Church and Propagation of the Faith*, Studies in the Church History, Vol. 6, Canon Cuning, (ed.), Cambridge University Press, 1970. pp. 85 - 105.

———, *The Portuguese Seaborne Empire, 1415-1825*, London, Hutchinson & Co., Great Britain, 1973.

———, "Fidalgos Portuguêzes e Bailadeiras Indianas (séculos XVII-XVIII)", offprint of *Revista de Historia*, No. 45, São Paulo, 1961.

———, "A Note on Portuguese Missionary Methods in the East: 16th-18th Centuries", *Ceylon Historical Journal*, X, Nos. 1-4, (July 1960 - April 1961), pp. 77-90.

———, *The Church Militant and Iberian Expansion - 1440 –1770*, Baltimore, The Johns Hopkins University Press, 1978.

———, *Portuguese India in the Mid-Seventeenth Century*, Delhi, Oxford University Press, 1980.

———, *The Christian Century in Japan*, 1549-1650, London, Cambridge University Press, 1951.

———, *A India Portuguesa em Meados do Século XVII*, Lisboa, Edições 70, 1982.

Brettell, Caroline B., "Introduction: The Individual and the State in Portuguese Society", *International G.G.P., Portuguese Study Review*, 1993.

*Breve Notícia dos Cinco Martyres de Salsete ou Conculim e do P. Antonio Baldinucci Missionario todos da Companhia de Jesus recem-Beatificados*, Lisboa, Administração do Novo Memsageiro do Coração de Jesus, 1893.

Brito, Raquel Soeiro de, *Goa e as praças do norte*, Lisboa, Orbis-Edições Ilustradas, Ltd., 1966.

Brochado, I. da Costa, "Joaquim Bensaúde e o Plano das Indias", Academia Portuguesa da Historia, *Dois Centenarios*, Lisboa, Editora Gráfica Portuguesa, Lda., 1962, pp. 45-51.

Callahan, William J. and David Higgs, *Church and Society in Catholic Europe of the Eighteenth Century*, England, Cambridge University Press, 1979.

Camões, Luís de, *Os Lusíadas*, Lisboa, Editorial Verbo, Gris Impressores, 1972.

Camoens, Luis Vas de, *The Lusiads*, William C. Atkinson (trans.), Great Britain, Penguin Book, 1952.

Centro de Estudos Históricos Ultramarinos, *Boletim da Filmoteca Ultramarina Portuguesa*, Nos. 1 - 50, Lisboa, Imprensa Portuguesa, 1956-1993.

Charles, Pierre, "Missiologie Antiféministe", *Le Rôle de la Femme dans les Missiones*, 20 Semaine de Missiologie de Louvain 1950, Paris, Desclée de Brouwer, 1951, pp. 20-35.

Chatterjee, Partha, "Claims on the Past: The Genealogy of Modern Historiography in Bengal", *Subaltern Studies VIII . Essays in Honour of Ranaji Guha*, David Arnold and David Hardiman, (eds), Delhi, Oxford University Press, 1994.

Clark, Francis X., *An Introduction to the Catholic Church in Asia*, Manila, Ateneo University Publications, 1987.

Clough, John E., *Social Christianity in the Orient*, New York, Macmillan, 1914.

Collingwood, R. G., *The Idea of History*, Great Britain, Oxford University Press, 1966.

Congresso Internacional de História, *Missionação Portuguesa e Encontro de Culturas*, Vols. I-IV, Braga, Barbosa & Xavier, Lda., 1993.

Correia, Alberto Carlos Germano da Silva, *Historia da Colonização Portugueza na India*, Vols. V - VI, Lisboa, Agencia Geral do Ultramar, Divisão de Publicações e Biblioteca, 1954.

Correia-Afonso, John, *Jesuit Letters and Indian History: A Study and Development of Jesuit Letters from India and their Value for the Indian Historiography*, Bombay, 1969.

________, (ed.), *Indo-Portuguese History. Sources & Problems*, Bombay, Oxford University Press, 1981.

________, "Indian History in the Cartorio dos Jesuitas", *Indo-Portuguese History: Sources and Problems*, Bombay, Oxford University Press, 1981, pp. 72-85.

Cortesão, Armando, (ed.), *The Suma of Tome Pires*, Vol. I, New Delhi, Asian Educational Services, 1990.

Cortesão, Jaime, *Os Descobrimentos Portugueses*, Vol., II, Lisboa, Editora Arcádia.

Costa, João Paulo, "A Colonização portuguesa na Asia", *Portugal no Mundo*, séculos XV - XVIII, Vol. II, Luís de Albuquerque, (ed.), Lisboa, Publicações Alfa, 1989, pp. 158 -179.

Cunha, Ana Cannas da, *A Inquisição no Estado da India - Origens (1539*

- *1560)*, Lisboa, Estudos e Documentos, Arquivos Nacionais / Torre do Tombo, 1995.

Cunha Rivara, Joaquim Heliodoro da, *Additamento as Reflexões sobre o Padroado Portuguez no Oriente*, Nova Goa, Imprensa Nacional, 1858.

———, *Ensaio Histórico da Lingua Concani*, Nova Goa, Imprensa Nacional, 1857, 1858.

———, *O Manisfesto Preventivo dos Propagandistas da India Contra a Concordata Apostillado Pelo Auctor das Reflexões sobre o Padroado Portuguez no Oriente*, Nova Goa, Imprensa Nacional, 1860.

———, *Brados a Favor das Communidades das Aldeias do Estado da India*, Nova Goa, Imprensa Nacional, 1870.

———, *Gramatica da Lingua Concani*, Nova Goa, Imprensa Nacional, 1857.

Cunha, T. B., *Denationalisation of Goans*, Goa, Gazetter Department, 1995.

D'Almeida, Miguel Ferreira, (trans.), *Canones e Decretos do Concílio Tridentino*, Vizeu, Typ. da "Revista Catholica", 1900.

D'Costa, Anthony, *Christianisation of the Goa Islands: 1510 - 1567*, Bombay, India Printing Works, 1964.

———, " The Demolition of the Temples in the Islands of Goa in 1540 and the Disposal of the Temple Lands", offprint of *Neue Zeitschrift für Missionswissenschaft*, Switzerland, 1962, pp. 161-176.

D'Souza, B. G., *Goan Society in Transition - A Study in Social Change*, Bombay, Bombay Popular Prakashan, 1975.

D'Souza, Jerome, *Sardar Panikkar and Christian Missions*, Trichinopoly, St. Joseph's Industrial School Press, 1957.

Dalgado, Sebastião Rodolfo, *Glossário Luso-Asiático*, Vols. I-II, New Delhi, Asian Educational Services, 1988.

Danvers, Frederick Charles, *The Portuguese in India*, Vol. I, New Delhi, Asian Educational Services, 1988.

David, M. D., (ed.), *Asia and Christianity*, Bombay, Himalaya Publishing House, 1985.

———, *Western Colonialism in Asia and Christianity*, Bombay, Himalaya Publishing House, 1988.

Dias Farinha, Maria do Carmo Jasmins, *Os Arquivos da Inquisição*,

Lisboa, Serviço de Publicações e Divulgação, ANTT, 1990.

Dias, Filinto Cristo, Esboço da História da Literatura Indo-Portuguesa, Goa, Tip. Rangel, 1962.

Dias, Luís Fernando de Carvalho, "O ultramar português e a expansão na Africa e no Oriente", offprint of *"Garcia de Orta", Revista da Junta das Missões Geográficas e de Investigações do Ultramar*, 1956.

———, "As Ordenações da India", offprint of *"Garcia de Orta", Revista da Junta das Missões Geográficas e de Investigações do Ultramar*, 1956.

Disney, Anthony, "Contrasting Models of "Empire": The Estado da Índia in South Asia and East Asia in the Sixteenth and Early Seventeenth Centuries", pp. 26-37. in Francis A. Dutra and João Camilo dos Santos, (eds.), *The Portuguese and the Pacific*, International Colloquium at Santa Barbara, Centre for Portuguese Studies, Santa Barbara, University of California, 1995.

———, "The Portuguese Empire in India c. 1550-1560", John Correia-Afonso, (ed.), *Indo-Portuguese History: Sources and Problems*, Bombay, Oxford University Press, 1981, pp. 148-162.

Doniger, Wendy, (trans.), *The Laws of Manu*, New Delhi, Penguin Books, 1991.

Dutra, Francis A., and João Camilo dos Santos, (eds.), *The Portuguese and the Pacific*, International Colloquium at Santa Barbara, Centre for Portuguese Studies, Santa Barbara, University of California, 1995.

*Encounter of Cultures: Eight Centuries of Portuguese Mission Work*, Lisbon, Printer Portuguese, 1996.

Estevão, Tomás, *Doutrina Cristã em Língua Concani*, Mariano Saldanha, (ed.), Lisboa, Centro de Estudos Historicos Ultramarinos, 1945.

Faria e Souza, Manuel de, *Ásia Portuguesa*, Vol. I, Porto, Livraria Civilização, 1945.

Feio, Mariano, *As Castas Hindus de Goa*, Lisboa, Estudos de Antropologia Cultural, No. 11, 1979.

Felner, Rodrigo José de Lima, *Subsídios para a História da India Portugueza*, Vol. V, Lisboa, Typ. da Academia Real das Sciencias, 1868.

Ficalho, Conde de, *Garcia da Orta e o seu Tempo*, Lisboa, Imprensa Nacional - Casa da Moeda, 1983.

Figueiredo, Junior J. M., "Goa Pré-Portuguesa", offprint of *STVDIA*, Lisboa, Centro de Estudos Historicos Ultramarinos, 1963-64.

Figueiredo, Niceno de, *Pelo Clero de Goa, Duas Lendas: O Cisma de Goa e A Ignorancia do Clero Goês*, Bastora, Tip. Rangel, 1939.

Figueiredo, Fidelino, "Viagens de um Florentino a Portugal e à India" (século XVI), *Revista de Historia*, Vol. 12, No. 49-52, Emprêsa Literária Fluminense, Lda., Lisboa, 1924, pp. 107-125.

Fonseca, José Nicolau, *An Historical and Archaeological Sketch of the City of Goa*, Bombay, Thacker & Co. Ltd., 1878.

Freitas, Frei Serafim, *Do Justo Império Asiático dos Portugueses*, Vol. I, Lisboa, Instituto Nacional de Investigação Científica, 1983.

Freitas, Jordão de, "A Inquisição em Goa. Subsídios para a sua História", *Archivo Histórico Portuguez*, Vol. V, Lisboa, Officina Typ. Calçada do Cabra, 1907, pp. 216-227.

Frykenberg, R. E., "On the Study of Conversion Movements: A Review Article and a Theoretical Note", *The Indian Economic and Social History Review*, Vol. XVII, No. 1, New Delhi, Vikas Publishing House Pvt. Ltd., Jan-March 1980, pp. 121-138.

Furman, D., *Religion and Social Conflict in the USA*, USSR, Progress Publishers, 1981.

Gandhi, M. K., *Christian Missions: Their Place in India*, Ahmedabad, Navajivan Press, 1941.

Gomes, Cunha Cipriano, "A Cristianização de Bardêz", offprint of *Boletim do Instituto Vasco da Gama*, Bastorá, Tip. Rangel, 1975.

Gonçalves, Nuno da Silva, *Os Jesuítas e a missão de Cabo Verde, (1604–1642)*, Lisboa, Brotéria, 1996.

Gonçalves, António Custódio, "A Acção evangelizadora e cultural de Portugal no Congo (1491-1543)", *Missionação Portuguesa e Encontro de Culturas*, Vol. I, Braga, Barbosa & Xavier, Ltd., Artes Gráficas, 1993.

Gracias, J. A. Ismael, "A India em 1623-1624: Excerptos das Memórias do viajante italiano Pietro della Valle", *O Oriente Portuguez*, Nova Goa, Imprensa Nacional, Jan-Feb. 1905, pp. 1-8 and 17-28.

———, "Albuquerque e as Mulheres Indianas" *O Oriente Português*, Vol. XIII, Revista da Comissão Arqueologica da India Portuguesa, Nova Goa, Imprensa Nacional, 1916, pp. 1-10.

Gracias, J. B. Amancio, "Casa dos Cathecumenos em Betim", *O Oriente*

*Portuguez*, Nova Goa, Imprensa Nacional, Jan-Fev. 1905, pp. 40-55.

Gracias, Fátima, *Health and Hygiene in Colonial Goa - 1510-1961*, New Delhi, Concept Publishing Company, 1994.

Grey, Edward, (ed.), *The Travels of Pietro Della Valle in India*, Vol. II, New Delhi, Asian Educational Services, 1991.

Guha, Ranajit, (ed.), *Subaltern Studies III. Writings on South Asian History and Society*, Delhi, Oxford University Press, 1984.

———, (ed.), *Subaltern Studies I, III - Writings on South Asian History and Society*, Delhi, Oxford University Press, 1982, 1994.

Gupta, Ashin Das, "Some Problems of Reconstructing the History of India's West Coast from European Sources", John Correia-Afonso, (ed.), *Indo-Portuguese History: Sources and Problems*, Bombay, Oxford Univesity Press, 1981, pp. 174 - 182.

Harrison, J. B., "Five Portuguese Historians", C. H. Philips, (ed.), *Historians of Indian Pakistan and Ceylon*, London, Oxford University Press, 1961.

Hebblethwaite, Peter, *In the Vatican*, Great Britain, Oxford University Press, 1986.

Hennessy, H. E., *A History of India - With Notes on Administration (1526-1925)*, Bombay, The Examiner Press, 1925.

Heras, H. "The Decay of the Portuguese Power in India", *Journal of the Bombay Historical Society*, Vol. I, 1928.

———, *The Conversion Policy of the Jesuits in India*, Bombay, Indian Historical Research Institute, 1933.

Instituto de Investigação Científica Tropical, *Colecção de São Lourenço* III, Colecção Ultramarina Portuguesa VIII. Lisboa, 1983.

Kakodkar, Archana, "Shuddhi: Reconversion to Hinduism Movement in Goa", P. P. Shirodkar, (ed.), *Goa: Cultural Trends*, Panaji, Directorate of Archives, Archaeology and Museum, Government of Goa, 1988, pp. 242-263.

Kosambi, Damodar Dharmanand, *Myth and Reality*, Bombay, Popular Prakashan, 1962.

Kulkarni, A. R. "Social Relations in the Maratha Country", (Medieval Period), Presidential Address, Medieval India Section, 32nd Session of the Indian History Congress, Jabalpur, December, 1970.

———, "The Proselytisation and Purification Movement in Goa and Konkan", Teotonio R. de Souza, (ed.), *Discoveries, Missionary Expansion and Asian Cultures*, New Delhi, Concept Publishing Company, 1994.

László, Polgár, *Bibliographie sur L'Histoire de la Compagnie de Jésus II, (1901-1980), Les Pays, Amérique, Asie, Afrique, Océanie*, Roma, Institutum Historicum Societatis Iesu, 1986.

Laval, Franciso Pyrard de, *Viagem de Francisco Pyrard de Laval*, Joaquim Heliodoro da Cunha Rivara, (ed.), Porto, Livraria Civilização. 1862.

Leitão, Ana Maria Ramalho Proserpio, "As Freiras de Santa Mónica e de Santa Clara: Duas Excepções na India Portuguesa", *Os Rostos Femeninos da Expansão Portuguesa* II, Congresso Internacional, São Paulo, 1995.

Leite, Serafim, "As raças do Brasil perante a ordem teológica, moral e juridica portuguesa nos séculos XVI a XVIII", offprint of *Scientia Ivridica*, Tomo XIII, No. 70, Nov. - Dez. 1964, Braga, pp. 1-23.

Lopes, Felix, "Os Franciscanos no Oriente Português de 1504 a 1590" in *STUDIA*, No. 9, Lisboa, Centro de Estudos Historicos Ultramarinos, Jan. 1962, pp. 29-142.

Machado, José Pedro e Viriato Campos, *Vasco da Gama e a Sua Viagem de Descobrimento*, Lisboa, Camara Municipal de Lisboa, 1969.

Mancedo, Jorge Borges de, "Para o Estudo da Mentalidade Portuguesa do Século XVI", *ICALP*, No. 7, 1987, pp. 73-106.

Manuel Lobato, "The Moluccan Archipelago and Eastern Indonesia in the Second Half of the 16th Century in the Light of Portuguese and Spanish Accounts", Francis A. Dutra and João Camilo dos Santos, (eds.), *The Portuguese and the Pacific*, International Colloquium at Santa Barbara, Centre for Portuguese Studies, Santa Barbara, University of California, 1995, pp. 38-63.

Marques, João Francisco, "A Evangelização da India no Epistolário de Afonso de Albuquerque e S. Francisco Xavier", *Missionação Portuguesa e Encontro de Culturas*, Vol. II, Braga, Barbosa & Xavier Ltd., Artes Gráficas, 1993.

Marshall, T. W. M., *Christian Missions. Their Agents and their Results*, Vol. I, London, H. Tuck, Longman, 1863.

Martins, Mario, "Teatro Sagrado nas Cristandades da Índia Portuguesa, séc XVI", offprint of *Didaskalia*, Vol. V, 1975.

Martires Lopes, Maria de Jesus dos, *Goa na Segunda Metade de Setecentos: Esboço de um Ensaio Sócio-Cultural,* Dissertação de Doutoramento em História apresentada à Faculdade de Ciências Sociais e Humanas da Universidade Nova Lisboa, Lisboa, 1993.

Mathew, K. S., "The Portuguese and the Malabar Society during the Sixteenth Century: a study of mutual interaction", *STUDIA*, Lisboa, 1989, pp. 39-68.

———,"Church Economics in the 16th Century Goa", P. P. Shirodkar, (ed.), *Goa Cultural Trends*, Goa, Directorate of Archives, 1988, pp. 123-130.

Matoso, José, "Raízes da missionação portuguesa", *Missionação Portuguesa e Encontro de Culturas*, Vol. I, Braga, Barbosa & Xavier, Ltd., Artes Gráficas, 1993.

Meersman, Archilles, *The Ancient Franciscan Provinces in India, 1500-1835*, Bangalore, Christian Literature Society Press, 1971.

Meirelles, José Rui, "Contacto de Culturas Perspectivas de Estudo" (1936 - 1971), *Economia e Sociologia*, No. 17, Évora, Instituto Superior Económico e Social, 1974, pp. 5-84

Melo, Carlos M. de, *The Recruitment and Formation of the Native Clergy in India, (16th -19th Century), An Historico-Canonical Study*, Lisboa, Agência Geral do Ultramar, 1955.

*Memória Histórico Eclesiastica da Arquidiocese de Goa (1533 - 1933)*, Nova Goa, Tip. "A Voz de S. Francisco Xavier", 1933.

Mendes, A. Lopes, *A India Portugueza*, Vol. 1, New Delhi, Asian Educational Services, 1886 (1989).

Mendonça, Délio de, *The Suppression of Konkani Language in 1684*, pp. 1-14, a paper presented at the IX Local History Seminar (Goa), Goa University, February 1995.

Merêa, Paulo, "Os jurisconsultos portugueses e a doutrina do «mare clausum», *Revista de Historia*, Vol. 13, No. 49-52, Lisboa, Emprêsa Literária Fluminense, Lda., 1924, pp. 6-23.

Milward, Peter, (ed.), *Portuguese Voyages to Asia and Japan in the Renaissance Period*, Japan, The Renaissance Institute, Sophia University, 1994.

Miranda, Jacintho Caetano Barreto, *Quadros Historicos de Goa: Tentativa Historica*, Caderneta I, Margão, Typographia do Ultramar, 1863.

Moraes, George Mark, *A History of Christianity in India*, Bombay, P. C.

Manaktala ans Sons Pvt. Ltd., 1964.

Mundandan, A. Mathias, "Church and Missionary Works on Indo-Portuguese History", John Correia-Afonso, (ed.), *Indo-Portuguese History: Sources and Problems*, Bombay, Oxford University Press, pp. 2-18.

Nazareth, Casimiro Cristovão de, "Mitras Lusitanas no Oriente", *Boletim da Sociedade de Geografia de Lisboa*, Serie 12, Nos 3-4, Lisboa, 1895.

Oddie, G. A. (ed.), *Religion in South Asia: Religious Conversion and Revival Movements in South Asia in Medieval and Modern Times,* New Delhi, Ajay Jain Manohar Publications, 1991.

Oliveira e Costa, João Paulo A. de ,*A Missão de João de Brito*, Biblioteca Evangelização e Culturas, Cucujães, Escola Tipográfica das Missões, 1992.

*Ordenações Manuelinas*, Book V, Lisboa, Fundação Calouste Gulbenkian, 1984.

Ortiz, Maria del Carmen Pareja, *Presencia de la Mujer Sevillana en Indias: Vida Cotidiana*, Sevilla, Excma. Disputación Provincial de Sevilla, 1994.

Pearson, M. N., *Coastal Western India*, New Delhi, Concept Publishing Company, 1981.

Penrose, Boies, *Goa - Rainha do Oriente / Goa - Queen of the East*, Lisboa, 1960.

Pereira, Rui Gomes, *Goa: Hindu Temples and Deities*, Panaji, Printwell, 1978.

Pereira, A. B. de Bragança, *Arquivo Portuguez-Oriental*, Bastorá, Tip. Rangel, 1937.

———, *Goa Portuguesa*, Goa, Imprensa Nacional, 1952.

———, "História Religiosa de Goa", offprint of *O Oriente Português*, Vol. 1, Bastora, Tip. Rangel.

Pereira, Isaías da Rosa, "O ensino da doutrina cristã nos séculos XIII a XVI", *Missionação Portuguesa e Encontro de Culturas*, Vol. I, Braga, Barbosa & Xavier, Ltd., Artes Gráficas, 1993.

Pereira, António Pinto, *História da India no Tempo em que a Governou o Visorei Dom Luís de Ataíde*, Lisboa, Imprensa Nacional-Casa da Moeda, 1987.

Perera, S. G., *Portuguese Missionary Methods or The Myth of "Forced*

*Conversions"*, Colombo, The Caxton Printing Works, 1936.

Pierce, Frank, (ed.), *Os Lusíadas*, Oxford, Clarendon press, 1973.

Pinto, Cristovão, *As Gauncarias de Gôa*, Questões Indianas I, Nova Goa, Imprensa Nacional, 1880.

Pinto, Fernão Mendes, *The Travels of Mendes Pinto*, Rebecca D. Catz, (ed. trans.), Chicago, The University of Chicago Press, 1989.

Pissurlencar, Panduranga S., *Roteiro dos Arquivos da India*, Arquivo Historico do Estado da India, Bastorá, Tip. Rangel, 1955.

———, *Goa Pré-Portuguesa através dos Escritores Lusitanos dos Séculos XVI e XVII*, Bastorá, Tipografia Rangel, 1962.

———, *Agentes da Diplomacia Portuguesa na India: Hindus Muçulmanos, Judeus e Parsees*, Bastorá, Tip. Rangel, 1952.

———, "O Elemento Hindu da Casta Chardó", (Estudo Etnológico), offprint of *O Oriente Português*, Nova Serie no. 12, Bastorá, Tipografia Rangel, 1936.

———, "Um Passo do Cronista Barros Elucidado à Luz Duma Inscrição Sânscrita", offprint of *O Oriente Português*, No. 18, Bastorá, Tipografia Rangel, 1937.

———, "Colaboradores Hindus de Afonso de Albuquerque", Boletim do Instituto Vasco da Gama, No. 49.

Priolkar, A. K., *The Goa Inquisition*, Bombay, University Press, 1961.

Rêgo, Raul, *O Último Regimento e o Regimento da Economia da Inquisição de Goa*, Lisboa, Biblioteca Nacional, 1983.

Remedios, J. Mendes dos, *Os Judeus em Portugal*, Coimbra, F. França Amado, 1895.

Rizvi, S. A. A., "Islamic Proselytisation: Seventh to Sixteenth Centuries", G. A. Oddie, (ed.), *Religion in South Asia: Religious Conversions and Revival Movements in South Asia in Medieval Times*, New Delhi, Ajay Jain Manohar Publications, 1991.

Rocha, Leopoldo da, *As Confrarias de Goa - Séculos XVI–XX; Conspecto Histórico-Jurídico*, Lisboa, Centro de Estudos Históricos Ultramarinos, 1973.

Rodrigues, Francisco, *Historia da Companhia de Jesus na Assitencia de Portugal.* A Fundação da Provincia Portuguesa 1540-1560, Tomo I, Vol. II, Porto, Apostolado da Imprensa, Emprêsa Editora, 1931.

Saldanha, M. J. Gabriel de, *História de Goa*, Vol. I-II, Bastora, Tipografia Rangel, 1925-26.

———, *História de Goa, Political e Arqueológica*, Vols. 2, New Delhi, Asian Educational Services, 1990.

Sardar, Ziauddin, and Ashis Nandy, Merryl Wyn Davis, Claude Alvares, *The Blinded Eye - 500 Years of Christopher Columbus*, Goa, The Other India Press, 1993.

Scammell, G. V., "The Pillars of Empire: Indigenous Assitance and the Survival of the 'Estado da India' c. 1600-1700", offprint of *Modern Asian Studies*, Great Britain, Cambridge University Press, 1988, pp. 473-489.

———, "Indigenous Assistance in the Establishment of Portuguese Power in the Indian Ocean", John Correia-Afonso, (ed.), *Indo-Portuguese History: Sources and Problems*, Bombay, Oxford University Press, 1981, pp. 163-173.

———, *The World Emcompassed: The First European Maritime Empires C. 800 - 1650*, London, Methuen, 1981.

Scholberg, Henry, *Bibliography of Goa and the Portuguese India*, New Delhi, 1982

Schurhammer, Georg, *Francis Xavier. His Life, His Times*, Vol. II, India, (1541-1545), Rome, The Jesuit Historical Institute, 1977.

———, *Francisco Javier, Su Vida y su Tiempo*, Tomo II, India - Indonesia 1541-1547, Bilbao, Gráficas Lizarra, S. L., Estella, 1992.

———, *Gesammelte Studien*, Xavierana, Vol. III, Rome, Institutum Historicum Societatis Iesu, 1964.

Sebastião Rodolfo Dalgado, *Glossário Luso-Asiático*, Vols. I-II, New Delhi, Asian Educational Services, 1988.

Sen, Surendra Nath, "A preliminary report on the historical records at Goa", *Calcutta Review*, May-Oct. 1925, Calcutta, University Press.

———, *Studies in Indian History: Historical records at Goa*, New Delhi, Asian Educational Services, 1993.

Sen, S. P., *Sources of the History of India*, Calcutta, Institute of Historical Studies, 1978.

*Sermons em varias Celebridades que pregou o Padre Siman da Gama da Companhia de Jesus*, Part VI, Lisboa, Officina de Antonio Pedrozo Galrão, 1713.

Serrão, Joaquim Veríssimo, *A Historiografia Portuguesa: Doutrina e Crítica - Séculos* XII - XVI, Vol. III, Lisboa, Editorial Verbo, 1972.

———, *História de Portugal (1495 -1580)*, Vol. III, Lisboa, Editorial

Verbo, 1980.

Shirodkar, P. P.,(ed.), *Goa Cultural Trends*, Panaji, Directorate of Archives, Archaeology and Museum, Government of Goa, 1988.

Shourie, Arun, *Missionaries in India. Continuities, Changes, Dilemas*, New Delhi, ASA Publications, 1994.

Silva Rego, António da, *História das Missões do Padroado Português do Oriente, India*, (1500-1542), Vol. I, Lisboa, Agência Geral das Colónias, 1949.

———, "A liberdade religiosa e o I Concilio Provincial de Goa", Memorias da Academia das Ciencias, Classe de Letras, t. X, Lisboa, 1967.

Singh, K. S., (ed.), *People of India — Goa*, Vol. XXI, Bombay, Anthropological Survey of India, Popular Prakashan Pvt. Ltd., 1993.

Souto, José Correia, *Dicionário de História de Portugal*, Vol. III, Lisboa, Zairol, Lda., 1985.

Souza, Teotónio R. de, "Christianisation and Cultural Conflict in Goa, 16th - 19th Centuries", *Missionação Portuguesa e Encontro de Culturas*, Vol. IV, Braga, 1993, pp. 383-393.

———, "The Voiceless in Goan Historiography. A Case for the source value of Church Records in Goa", *Indo-Portuguese History. Sources & Problems*, John Correia-Afonso, (ed.), Bombay, Oxford University Press, 1981, pp. 114-131.

———, *Goa To Me*, New Delhi, Concept Publishing Company, 1994.

———, and Charles Borges, (ed.), *Jesuits in India: In Historical Perspective*, Jesuit Documentation Series, No. 1, Macau, Instituto Cultural de Macau, 1992.

Strandes, Justus, *The Portuguese Period in East Africa*, East Africa Literature Bureau, Nairobi, 1971.

Tapan Raychaudhuri and Irfan Habid (eds.) *The Cambridge·Economic History of India*, Vol. I, (1200–1750), Cambridge, Cambridge University Press, 1987.

Teles, Ricardo Micael, *Os Franciscanos no Oriente e seus Conventos*, Nova Goa, Tip. Rau & Irmãos, 1922.

Thomas, P., *Christians and Christianity in India and Pakistan*, London, George Allen & Unwin Ltd., 1954.

Thomaz, Luís Filipe F. R. , " Descobrimentos e Evangelização. Da Cruzada à missão pacífica", *Missionação Portuguesa e Encontro de Culturas*,

Vol. I, Braga, Barbosa & Xavier, Ltd., Artes Gráficas, 1993.

———, *De Ceuta a Timor*, Viseu, Difel Difusão Editorial, S. A., Tipografia Guerra, 1994.

——— and João P. Oliveira e Costa, "A Bíblia e a Expansão Portuguesa" offprint of *Didaskalia*, Vol. XX, Gráfica Coimbra Ltd., 1990.

Vergé-Franceschi, Michel, *Henri de Navigateur - Un Découvreur au XV siècle*, Paris, Editions du Félin, 1994.

Viotti, Hélio Abranches, *Nóbrega e a conversão do gentio*, Conferência do ciclo Comemorativo do IV Centenário da Morte do Pe. Manoel da Nóbrega, São Paulo, 1970.

Whiteway, R. S., *Rise of Portuguese Power in India (1497-1550)*, Westminster, Archibald Constable & Co., 1899.

Wicki, Josef, "Mais Documentos de Miguel Vaz Coutinho Primeiro Vigário-Geral de Goa - (Princípios de 1545), offprint of *STUDIA*, Lisboa, Centro de Estudos Históricos Ultramarinos, 1970.

———, "Problemas Morais no Oriente Português do Século XVI", offprint of *Centro de Estudos Históricos Ultramarinos e as Comemorações Henriquinas*, Lisboa, Tip. Silvas, 1961.

———,Wicki, Josef, "Missionskirche im Orient", *Neue Zeitsscrift für Missionswissenschaft*, Supplementa, Vol. XXIV, Switzerland, 1976.

———, "S. Francisco Xavier", *Brotéria*, July 1958.

———, "Ainda o IV Centenário da Primeira Imprensa de Goa", *Brotéria*, Vol. LXIII, No. 6, Dezembro 1956.

Wiebe, Paul D., *Christians in Andhra Pradesh*, Madras, The Christian Literature Society, 1988.

Winius G. D., *The Black Legend of Portuguese India*, Delhi, Concept Publishing Company, 1984.

Witte, Ch.-M., "Aux origines de la 'Congrégation' indienne de l'Ordre des Fréres Prêcheures (1546-1580)", offprint of *Archivum fratrum Praedicatorum*, XXXVI, 1966.

Xavier, Felippe Nery, *Defensa dos Direitos das Gão-carias, Gão-cares, e dos seus Privilegios*, Nova Goa, Imprensa Nacional, 1856.

Xavier, P. D., *Goa: A Social History*, Panaji, Rajhauns Vitaran, 1993.

Zelliot, Eleanor, "Psychological Dimensions of the Buddhist Movement", in G. A. Oddie, (ed.), *Religion in South Asia*, New D[illegible] Electric Press,1991, pp. 191-214.

# INDEX